Multimedia Database Management Systems

For a complete listing of the *Artech House Computing Library*, turn to the back of this book.

Multimedia Database Management Systems

Guojun Lu

Artech House
Boston • London

Library of Congress Cataloging-in-Publication Data
Lu, Guojun, 1963-
    Multimedia database management systems / Guojun Lu.
        P.   cm. — (Artech House computing library)
    Includes bibliographical references and index.
    ISBN 1-89006-342-7 (alk. paper)
        1. Mulitimedia systems. 2. Database managment.   I. Title.
    QA76.575.L84   1999   99-41773
    006.7—dc21   CIP

British Library Cataloguing in Publication Data
Lu, Guojun, 1963-
    Multimedia database management systems. — (Artech House
    computing library)
    1.Multimedia systems 2. Database management
    I. Title
    005.7'4

    ISBN 0-89006-342-7

Cover design by Elaine K. Donnelly

© 1999 ARTECH HOUSE, INC.
685 Canton Street
Norwood, MA 02062

International Standard Book Number: 0-89006-342-7
Library in Congress Catalog Card Number: 99-41773

10 9 8 7 6 5 4 3 2 1

To Fengxia, James, and Colin

Contents

Preface

A few years ago, the main focus in multimedia research and development was on multimedia communications and multimedia authoring and presentation. Since more and more digital multimedia data in the forms of image, video, and audio are being captured and stored, the focus has shifted in last few years to efficient and effective storage and retrieval of multimedia information. A similar situation happened about thirty years ago when more and more alphanumeric data were stored in computer-readable form. This led to the development of database management systems (DBMSs), which are now one of the most popular computer applications and are used in almost every organization. Due to the differences between the characteristics and requirements of alphanumeric data and multimedia data, a traditional DBMS is not capable of effectively handling multimedia data. Thus new multimedia indexing and retrieval techniques are required.

This book provides comprehensive coverage on issues and current technologies in multimedia database management. It starts with a discussion on the main characteristics and requirements of multimedia data. It then describes general design issues of multimedia database management systems to meet these characteristics and requirements. We discuss techniques for the indexing and retrieval of text documents, audio, images, and video. The commonality among these techniques is that they all try to extract main features from raw media data, and then try to retrieve items relevant to the user's query based on the similarity or the distance between the extracted feature vectors of the stored items and the query. As multiple media types usually appear together in multimedia objects or documents and different techniques capture different features or contents of them, we discuss how to integrate various indexing and retrieval techniques for effective retrieval of multimedia documents. Since the features extracted from raw media data are usually represented by multidimensional vectors, it would be very time-consuming to calculate the similarity between the query feature vector and the feature vector of each of the stored items. We discuss various techniques and data structures so that the search and retrieval can be carried out efficiently.

Multimedia databases are usually accessed remotely over a network. Multimedia objects identified as relevant to the query must be retrieved from the server and transmitted to the client for presentation. A set of requirements involving factors including delay and delay jitter, called quality of service, must be met to achieve multimedia presentation in a smooth and timely fashion. We describe computer architecture, multimedia storage, operating system, and networking support to meet these requirements.

In traditional DBMSs, the main performance concern is efficiency (how long it takes to answer a query). In multimedia database management systems (MMDBMSs), efficiency is important too. In addition, retrieval effectiveness (ability to retrieve relevant items and ability to reject irrelevant items) becomes important. This is because MMDBMSs retrieve items based on similarity measured using a similarity metric instead of exact match. Since it is difficult to extract all features of multimedia items and design a similarity metric that exactly conforms to human judgment, it is likely that some items determined as relevant by the system are actually judged irrelevant by the user and some relevant items are not retrieved. Thus we also discuss performance measurement issues in MMDBMSs. Finally, we briefly describe current products, application development, and other issues such as security and standardization.

This book is intended for the following groups of readers:

- University students at senior levels and postgraduate students. Many universities around the world have started or will start to offer subjects related to multimedia technology and MMDBMSs. This book serves as a text for such subjects.
- System designers and developers who want to learn various issues and techniques in developing multimedia database management systems.
- Researchers who want to learn the current developments and new research directions in MMDBMSs.
- Other professionals who want to know technical issues and the current status of MMDBMSs.

I would like to thank Associate Professor Bob Bignall for his constant encouragement and support, and for proofreading all chapters for me. I thank Templar Hankinson for preparing the three graphs in Chapter 5, and Dengsheng Zhang and Shyh Wei Teng for correcting some errors in the original manuscript. I would also like to thank my colleagues and friends at Gippsland School of Computing and Information Technology of Monash University for their support during the last three years.

Dr. Ilias Petrounias of UMIST in Machester, United Kingdom, reviewed the book and provided many helpful comments and suggestions, for which I am most grateful.

I dedicate this book to my wife Fengxia, sons James and Colin, without whose support and understanding the writing of this book would not have been possible.

Chapter 1

Introduction

The initial focus in multimedia research and development was on multimedia communications and multimedia authoring and presentation [1-4]. In the past few years, more and more digital multimedia data in the forms of image, video, and audio has been captured and stored. There is now a strong research interest in efficient and effective storage and retrieval of multimedia information. A similar situation happened about thirty years ago when more and more alphanumeric data was stored in computer readable form. This led to the development of database management systems (DBMSs), which are now one of the most popular computer applications and are used in almost every organization. However, DBMSs cannot handle multimedia data effectively because of the differences between the characteristics of alphanumeric data and multimedia data. Therefore, new multimedia indexing and retrieval techniques are required.

The main purpose of this book is to describe issues and current technologies in multimedia indexing and retrieval. The area of multimedia indexing and retrieval is still in its early development stage. But it is expected that multimedia database management systems (MMDBMSs) will be as popular as current DBMSs in the near future [5-7].

This chapter first defines some important terms and concepts used throughout the book, and explains why traditional DBMS cannot handle multimedia information and why new technologies are required to support efficient and effective multimedia information retrieval. It then gives an overview of multimedia indexing and retrieval systems (MIRSs). Some expected capabilities and common applications of MIRSs are presented. The chapter concludes with an outline of the organization of the following chapters.

1.1 SOME IMPORTANT DEFINITIONS

To avoid any confusion or misunderstanding, this section provides definitions for some important terms and concepts used in this book.

1.1.1 Media Types and Multimedia

Media refer to the types of information or types of information representation, such as alphanumeric data, images, audio, and video. There are many ways to classify media. Common classifications are based on physical formats and media relationships with time. In this book, we classify media based on whether or not there are time dimensions to them. This convention leads to two classes of media: *static* and *dynamic (*or *time continuous)*.

Static media do not have a time dimension, and their contents and meanings do not depend on the presentation time. Static media include alphanumeric data, graphics, and still images.

Dynamic media have time dimensions, and their meanings and correctness depend on the rate at which they are presented. Dynamic media include animation, audio, and video. These media have their intrinsic unit intervals or rates. For example, to convey a perceptually smooth movement, video must be played back at 25 frames per second (or 30 frames, depending on the video system used). Similarly, when we play back a recorded voice message or music, only one playback rate is natural or sensible. Playback at a slower or faster rate distorts the meaning or the quality of the sound. Because these media must be played back continuously at a fixed rate, they are often called *continuous media*. They are also called *isochronous media* because of the fixed relationship between each media unit and time.

Multimedia refers to a collection of media types used together. It is implied that at least one media type is not alphanumeric data (i.e., at least one media type is image, audio, or video). In this book, "multimedia" is used as an adjective—so we will specifically say multimedia information, multimedia data, multimedia system, multimedia communications, multimedia applications, and so forth. Multimedia data refers to the computer-readable representation of multiple media types. Multimedia information refers to the information conveyed by multiple media types. Sometimes, multimedia information and multimedia data are used interchangeably.

We sometimes use multimedia or media item and object to refer to any autonomous entity in an MIRS that can be queried, retrieved, and presented. The term "object" may not be properly defined in the technical object-oriented (OO) sense. The context should make it clear whether it is used in a general sense or refers to a properly defined object in an OO approach.

1.1.2 Databases and DBMSs

In the literature, databases and DBMSs are sometimes used interchangeably. In this book, database refers to a collection or repository of data or media items. We use DBMS to refer to the entire system that manages the database.

1.1.3 Text Document Information Retrieval

Automated information retrieval (IR) systems were developed to help manage the huge amount of scientific literature that has been created since the 1940s [8, 9]. The main function of an IR system is to store and manage a large number of text documents in a way so that documents relevant to user queries can be retrieved quickly. Note that the acronym IR specifically refers to *text document retrieval*, although the full term *information retrieval* can refer to retrieval of any type of information. We will discuss IR techniques in Chapter 4.

1.1.4 Multimedia Indexing and Retrieval

DBMSs retrieve items based on structured data using exact matching. IR is also called text-based retrieval. Content-based retrieval refers to retrieval based on actual media features such as color and shape, instead of text annotation of the media item. Content-based retrieval is normally based on similarity instead of an exact match between a query and a set of database items.

MIRS refers to a basic system providing multimedia information retrieval using a combination of DBMS, IR, and content-based retrieval techniques. In an MIRS, some issues such as versioning and security control may not be fully implemented. A fully fledged MIRS is called a multimedia DBMS (MMDBMS).

1.1.5 Feature Extraction, Content Representation, and Indexing

In MIRSs, one of the most important issues is feature extraction or content representation (what are the main features or contents in a multimedia item). Feature extraction may be an automatic or semiautomatic process. In some of the content-based retrieval literature, feature extraction is also called indexing. We follow this convention in this book. When the term "index" is used as a noun, it refers to a data structure or to the organization of extracted features for efficient search and retrieval.

1.2 NEED FOR MIRS

The need for MIRS can be explained by the following three facts. First, more and more multimedia data is being captured and stored. In order to use the information contained in this data, an efficient and effective indexing and retrieval system is required. Second, multimedia data has special characteristics and requirements that are significantly different from alphanumeric data. The traditional DBMS, therefore, is not suitable for handling multimedia data. Third, although IR techniques can help in multimedia retrieval, they alone are not adequate to handle multimedia data effectively.

1.2.1 Proliferation of Multimedia Data and Its Characteristics

We are currently faced with an explosion of multimedia information. For example, a large amount of images and video are being created and stored on the Internet. Many paintings and pictures in printed form are being converted to digital form for easy processing, distribution, and preservation. Pictures from TV news and newspapers are also being converted into digital form for easy maintenance and preservation. A large number of medical images are being captured every day and satellites are producing many more. This trend is going to continue with the advancement of storage and digital technologies. Creating a mere repository for this ever-increasing amount of multimedia information is of little use, however. It will be impossible to fully use this multimedia information unless it is organized for rapid retrieval on demand.

Not only is an increasing amount of data being stored, but also the types of data and its characteristics are different from alphanumeric data. We discuss different media types and their characteristics in Chapter 2. We list the main characteristics of multimedia data below:

- Multimedia data, especially audio and video, is very data intensive. For example, a 10-minute video sequence of reasonable quality requires about 1.5 GB of storage without compression.

- Audio and video have a temporal dimension and they must be played out at a fixed rate to achieve the desired effect.

- Digital audio, image, and video are represented in a series individual sample values and lack obvious semantic structure for computers to automatically recognize the contents.

- Many multimedia applications require simultaneous presentation of multiple media types in a spatially and temporally coordinated way.

- The meaning of multimedia data is sometimes fuzzy and subjective. For example, different people may interpret the same picture in entirely different ways.

- Multimedia data is information rich. Many parameters are required to represent its content adequately.

1.2.2 DBMSs and Their Role in Handling Multimedia Data

DBMSs are now well developed and used widely for structured data. The dominant DBMSs are relational database management systems (RDBMSs). In RDBMSs, information is organized in tables or relations. The rows of the table correspond to information item or records, while the columns correspond to attributes. The structured query language (SQL) is used to create such tables and to insert and retrieve information from them.

We use a simple example to show how to use SQL to create a table and insert and retrieve information from it. Suppose we want to create a table containing student records consisting of the student number, name, and address. The following statement is used:

    create table STUDENT (
        stu# integer,
        name char(20),
        address char(100));

The above statement creates an empty table as shown in Table 1.1. When we want to insert student records into the table, we use the SQL *insert* command as follows:

    insert into STUDENT values (10, "Lew, Tom", "2 Main St., Churchill, Australia");

The above statement will insert a row in the STUDENT table as shown in Table 1.2. More student records can be inserted into the table using similar statements.

Table 1.1
The Initial STUDENT Table

stu#	name	address

Table 1.2
The STUDENT Table After One Record Inserted

stu#	name	address
10	Lew, Tom	2 Main St., Churchill, Australia

Information in the table is retrieved using the SQL *select* command. For example, if we want to retrieve the name of a student with student number 32, we use the following query statement:

select name
from STUDENT
where stu#=32

Attributes in a RDBMS have fixed types with fixed widths. In the above example, the attribute stu# is an integer type of fixed length of 32 bits. Thus RDBMSs are well suited for handling numeric data and short alphanumeric strings.

To support large variable fields in a RDBMS, a concept called binary large objects (BLOBs) was introduced. A BLOB is a large bit string of variable length. For example, if we want to store students' pictures in the above student record example, we can create a table using the following statement:

create table STUDENT (
*   stu# integer,*
*   name char(20),*
*   address char(100)*
*   picture BLOB);*

BLOBs are normally just bit strings and operations such as comparison can not be carried out on them. That is, a RDBMS does not know the contents or semantics of a BLOB. All it knows is a block of data.

Another type of DBMSs is object-oriented database management systems (OOD-BMSs). Note that a detailed coverage of object-oriented techniques is beyond the scope of this book. The reader is referred to [10, 12, 13] for a complete coverage. OODBMSs combine database capabilities (such as store and search) and object-oriented features (encapsulation, inheritance, and object identity). One common approach is to combine object-oriented features with a relational database. The combined system is called an object relational database system. In such a system, objects are properly defined in the object-oriented sense. That is, each object contains properties or attributes and methods or functions used to manipulate the properties. For example, we can define a class of type called IMAGE as follows:

```
create type IMAGE (
private
        size integer,
        resolution integer,
        content float[],
public
        ...
);
```

We then declare picture as a type of IMAGE that can be used in a table as follows:

```
create table STUDENT (
        stu# integer,
        name char(20),
        address char(100)
        picture IMAGE);
```

The main difference between the BLOB and the object is that the object is properly defined, including its properties and allowed operations on the properties, while the BLOB is not.

The concepts of BLOBs and objects are a step toward handling multimedia data [5, 10-12]. But BLOBs are used just to store large data. While objects contain some simple attributes, mANY more capabilities should be developed to handle content-based multimedia retrieval. Some of the required capabilities are as follows:

- Tools, to automatically, or semiautomatically extract contents and features contained in multimedia data;
- Multidimensional indexing structures, to handle multimedia feature vectors;
- Similarity metrics, for multimedia retrieval instead of exact match;
- Storage subsystems, redesigned to cope with the requirements of large size and high bandwidth and meet realtime requirements;
- The user interface, designed to allow flexible queries in different media types and provide multimedia presentations.

The above capabilities and related issues are the focus of this book.

1.2.3 IR Systems and Their Role in Multimedia Retrieval

In addition to DBMSs, there is another type of information management system that focuses on text document retrieval. This type of system is called an information retrieval (IR) system [8, 9]. IR techniques are important in multimedia information management systems for two main reasons. First, there exist a large number of text documents in many organizations such as libraries. Text is a very important information source of an organization. To use information stored in these documents, an efficient and effective IR system is needed. Second, text can be used to annotate other media such as audio, images, and video. Conventional IR techniques can be used for multimedia information retrieval. However, the use of IR for handling multimedia data has the following limitations:

- The annotation is commonly a manual process and time consuming;
- Text annotation is incomplete and subjective;
- IR techniques cannot handle queries in forms other than text (such as audio and images);
- Some multimedia features such as image texture and object shapes are difficult, if not impossible, to describe using text.

1.2.4 Integrated Approach to Multimedia Information Indexing and Retrieval

From the above discussion we see that DBMSs and IR cannot fully meet the requirements of multimedia indexing and retrieval, so new techniques to handle special characteristics of multimedia data are required. Nevertheless, we recognize that DBMSs and IR can play important roles in MMDBMSs. Parts of multimedia data, such as the creation date and author of a multimedia document, are structured. This structured data can be handled with DBMS techniques. Text annotation is still a powerful method for capturing the contents of multimedia data, so IR techniques have an important role to play.

To summarize, an integrated approach combining DBMSs, IR, and specific techniques for handling multimedia data is required to develop an efficient and effective MIRS.

1.3 AN OVERVIEW OF THE MIRS

Figure 1.1 provides an overview of MIRS operation. Information items in the database are preprocessed to extract features and semantic contents and are indexed based on these features and semantics. During information retrieval, a user's query is processed and its main features are extracted. These features are then compared with the features or index of each information item in the database. Information items whose features are most similar to those of the query are retrieved and presented to the user.

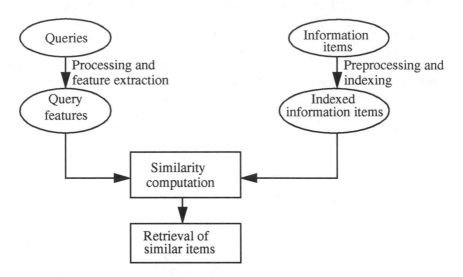

Figure 1.1 A general information retrieval model.

There are many issues to be addressed in the above model. For example, information items can be in any combination of media types. How can we extract features from these media items? How can these features be stored and structured for efficient retrieval? How do we measure the "similarity" between two media items? What do we need to do to enable the user interface to be able to accept complicated, fuzzy, and flexible queries? How do we compare the retrieval performance of different MIRSs? How can we meet the temporal requirements during multimedia data transmission and presentation? We discuss these and other issues in the rest of the book.

1.4 EXPECTED CAPABILITIES AND COMMON APPLICATIONS OF MIRS

MIRSs are expected to be powerful and flexible. Their capabilities are illustrated by the types of queries that they can support. Expected query types are as follows.

Metadata-based queries
Metadata refers to the formal attributes of database items such as author names and creation date. An example query in a video on demand (VOD) application can be "List movies directed by *NAME* in 1997." This type of query can be handled by DBMS capabilities.

Annotation-based queries
Annotation refers to the text description of the contents of database items. Queries are in keywords or free-text form and retrieval is based on similarity between the query and annotation. An example query can be "Show me the video segment in which *ACTOR* is

riding a bicycle." This type of query assumes that items are properly annotated and can be handled by IR techniques.

Queries based on data patterns or features
Data patterns refer to statistic information about multimedia data, such as loudness, color distribution, and texture description. An example query might be "Show me a video frame with color distribution like *THIS.*" To answer this type of query, statistical information about database items should be precollected and stored.

Query by example
Queries are in multimedia objects such as images, a sketches, and sound pieces. An example query can be "Show me a movie in which there are similar scenes like *THIS PICTURE.*" This type of query can be complicated by including spatial and temporal relationships between objects.

Application-specific queries
There are many types of application-specific queries. For example, queries can be based on very specific and detailed information such as the size of of an object and the aging process of a person.

We see that MIRSs are expected to support diverse types of queries, and thus will have wide applications, including:

- *Medicine.* A doctor takes a new ultrasound image and wants to retrieve images with a comparable degree of left ventricular hypertrophy from an ultrasound image base.
- *Security.* A policeman presents the system with a picture of a human face and wants to retrieve all other images and associated records of persons resembling this picture from a security information base.
- *Education.* A student scans in an animal picture and wants to retrieve all facts (including sound, images, and text description) about this type of animal from an education database. Alternatively, a student emulates the sound of an animal and wants to retrieve pictures and descriptive information of this type of animal.
- *The press.* A reporter writing an article on a person wants to retrieve that person's pictures and associated information that has appeared in newspapers and television in the last 20 years.
- *Entertainment.* A viewer wants to retrieve video clips similar to what he or she is viewing from a large video database.
- *Trademark registration.* An officer processing a trademark application wants to determine whether a similar trademark has been previously registered. To do this, he or she needs a trademark database with which to compare the most similar existing trademarks to the new trademark.

Ultimately, MIRSs will focus on information itself instead of media types and information representation can be mapped or translated from one media type to another. This means, for example, that video material may be queried using video, text, music, speech, and the like. It is up to the search engine to match the query data and the database items.

1.5 ORGANIZATION OF SUBSEQUENT CHAPTERS

This book consists of 13 chapters, including this one. This section outlines the subsequent 12 chapters.

MIRS is required to handle data in types of text, graphics, images, audio, and video. It is therefore essential to understand these media types and their main characteristics which are described in Chapter 2. Multimedia data is commonly stored in compressed form, so common multimedia compression techniques and standards are also included in the chapter.

Chapter 3 presents MIRS requirements and design issues. Overall architecture, feature extraction, data modeling, indexing structure, user interface, storage architecture, performance measurement, and operating system and network support are discussed. These issues and related techniques are discussed in detail in Chapters 4 to 12.

Chapters 4 to 7 are devoted to text, audio, image, and video, respectively. For each of these media types, we discuss how to extract features or how to represent their contents. The media items are then represented in a set of extracted features, called feature vectors. We describe how to measure similarities between feature vectors for retrieval.

Different media types need different indexing and retrieval techniques. Different techniques can be used for a single media type. Users may be interested in relevant information, regardless of media types. The problem is how to integrate different techniques to retrieve relevant information in response to the user's query. There are many issues to be addressed to solve this problem, such as query specification and processing, similarity weighting, and composite object presentation. Chapter 8 discusses these issues and describes an integrated approach to multimedia indexing and retrieval.

For efficient retrieval, appropriate indexing structures are needed. As feature vectors are multidimensional and MIRSs retrieve items based on similarity instead of exact match, indexing structures used in DBMSs are not suitable for MIRSs. Chapter 9 describes a number of indexing structures proposed for MIRSs.

A set of requirements involving factors including delay and delay jitter, called quality of service, must be met for multimedia data transmission and presentation. Chapter 10 describes operating system and networking support to meet these requirements. Storage servers are also discussed in this chapter.

In DBMSs, the main performance concern is efficiency (how long it takes to answer a query). In MIRSs, efficiency is even more important due to the large size of multimedia data. In addition, retrieval effectiveness (ability to retrieve relevant items and ability to reject irrelevant items) becomes important. This is because MIRSs retrieve items based on similarity measured using a similarity metric instead of exact match. Since it is difficult to design a similarity metric that exactly conforms to human judgment, it is likely that some items determined as relevant by the system are actually judged irrelevant by the user and some relevant items are not retrieved. Chapter 11 discusses performance measurement issues in MIRSs.

Chapter 12 briefly describes current products, application development, and other issues such as security and standardization. These give us an idea of what to expect in the future.

PROBLEMS

Problem 1.1

Describe media types handled by MIRSs.

Problem 1.2

What are the main characteristics of multimedia data and applications?

Problem 1.3

Why can DBMSs not handle multimedia data effectively?

Problem 1.4

What are IR systems? Are they suitable for handling multimedia data? Why?

Problem 1.5

Describe the basic operation of an MIRS.

Problem 1.6

Describe the types of queries that are expected to be supported by MIRSs.

REFERENCES

[1] Minoli, D. and R. Keinath, *Distributed Multimedia Through Broadband Communications*, Norwood, MA: Artech House, 1994.

[2] Szuprowicz, B. O., *Multimedia Networking*, McGraw-Hill, Inc., 1995.

[3] Jeffcoate, J., *Multimedia in Practice —Technology and Applications*, Prentice Hall, 1995.

[4] Fluckiger, F., *Understanding Networked Multimedia: Applications and Technology*, Prentice Hall, 1995.

[5] Narasimhalu, A. D., "Multimedia Databases," *Multimedia Systems*, No.4, 1996, pp.226-249.

[6] Nwosu, K. C., B. Thuraisingham, and P. B. Berra, "Multimedia Database Systems - A New Frontier," *IEEE Multimedia*, July - September 1997, pp. 21-23.

[7] ISO/IEC JTC1/SC29/WG11 N2207, "MPEG-7 Context and Objectives," March 1998, available at http://drogo.cselt.stet.it/mpeg/public/w2207.html.

[8] Frakes, W. B., and R. Baeza-Yates (ed.), *Information Retrieval: Data Structures and Algorithms*, Prentice Hall, 1992.

[9] Salton, G., and M. J. McGill, *Introduction to Modern Information Retrieval*, McGraw-Hill Book Company, 1983.

[10] Khoshafian, S., and A. B. Baker, *Multimedia and Image Databases*, Morgan Kaufmann Publishers, Inc., 1996.

[11] Donald, A., and Kinsley C. Nwosu, "Multimedia Database Management - Requirements and Issues," *IEEE Multimedia*, July-September 1997, Vol. 4 No.3, pp.24-33

[12] Pazandak, P., and Jaideep Srivastava, "Evaluating Object DBMSs for Multimedia," *IEEE Multimedia*, July-September 1997, Vol. 4 No.3, pp.34-49

[13] Simon, J. Gibbs, and Dionysios C. Tsichritzis, *Multimedia Programming - Objects, Environments and Frameworks*, Addison-Wesley, 1995.

Chapter 2

Multimedia Data Types and Formats

2.1 INTRODUCTION

MIRSs are required to process, index, store, retrieve, transmit, and present multimedia data including text, graphics, image, audio, video, and their combinations. The differences between an MIRS and a conventional DBMS stem from the different characteristics and requirements of multimedia data in comparison to traditional alphanumeric data. Thus an understanding of these characteristics and requirements is essential to understanding the issues in MIRS design and to implementing the required functions of an MIRS.

The objective of this chapter is to discuss the basic characteristics and requirements of text, graphics, digital audio, image, and video. For each media type, we introduce its basic or raw format and its common compressed formats. Understanding of common compression techniques is important as most multimedia data is stored in compressed formats. (Note that this chapter does not deal with the formal modeling of multimedia data, which is covered in Chapter 3.) For each media type, the reader should understand

- How computers "see" and store data;

- The common compression techniques;

- How easily feature extraction and indexing is carried out;

- Storage requirements;

- Communication requirements;

- Presentation requirements.

In Section 2.2, we discuss the medium of text and its common compression techniques. Text not only is one of the most common media but it also can be used to annotate other media such as audio, image, and video. Thus text indexing and retrieval are important.

There are two types of graphics and animation: vector and bitmapped. Bitmapped graphics are the same as digital images and bitmapped animation is the same as digital video. Section 2.3 briefly describes vector graphics and animation.

Section 2.4 is devoted to audio. We study the properties of analog audio signals, the process of converting analog signals to digital signals, digital representations of common audio applications, and common audio compression techniques. The analog-to-digital conversion (ADC) principle is important and will be used when we discuss digital representation of images and video.

Section 2.5 deals with digital images and common image compression techniques. Details include basic representation of digital images, storage requirement calculation, why image data can be compressed, spatial subsampling, predictive coding, transform coding, vector quantization, fractal image coding, and the compression standards Joint Photographic Expert Group (JPEG) and JPEG 2000.

Section 2.6 discusses video representation and compression techniques and standards. Digital video is represented as a sequence of images (frames) played out at a fixed frame rate. Most image compression techniques can be used for video compression. In addition, techniques can be used to exploit the similarity between neighbouring frames. We also cover one set of the most important multimedia standards, namely Motion Picture Expert Group (MPEG) including MPEG-1, MPEG-2, MPEG-4, and MPEG-7.

Section 2.7 briefly describes standards or formats for composite multimedia documents, including the standard generalized markup language, office document architecture, Acrobat Portable Document Format, HyTime, and Multimedia and Hypermedia Information-Encoding Expert Group (MHEG).

Section 2.8 summarizes major characteristics and requirements of multimedia data and applications. These characteristics and requirements have a major impact on MIRS design. Section 2.9 concludes the chapter.

2.2 TEXT

2.2.1 Plain Text

In its most basic form, text consists of plain alphanumeric characters. The most common representation of characters is the American Standard Code for Information Interchange (ASCII). Seven bits are used for each ASCII code, but 8 bits are normally used to store each character with the extra bit being a 0, a parity bit, or used for other purposes. There are other character representations that can represent non-English text.

As each character is uniquely represented, text items such as individual characters and words are easily identified. The storage space requirement in bytes for a text document is moderate, being equal to the number of characters (including spaces) in the document. For example, a typical book with 300 pages, each of which has 3,000 characters, requires 900 KB storage.

The barriers to high performance text document retrieval (IR) are that text documents do not have fixed attributes like records in traditional databases and words or terms have multiple meanings. We discuss text retrieval techniques in Chapter 4.

2.2.2 Structured Text

Most text documents are structured, consisting of titles, sections, paragraphs, and so on. Different parts of a structured document may have a different appearance when displayed or printed. There are many standards and formats for encoding this structural information. Examples of these formats are common word processor formats, Standard General Markup Language (SGML), Office Document Architecture (ODA), LaTex and Portable Document Format (PDF). Since they allow incorporation of graphics and images in addition to text, we discuss these formats in Section 2.7.

Normally, a file header is used to indicate the format of the document. When the file format is known, the structure information can be extracted and used to help text retrieval. For example, words or terms that appear in title or section headings are more important than words in text and should have greater weight during the indexing and retrieval process. The document relevance can also be determined based on its relation (via links) to other documents if the document is part of a hypertext collection.

2.2.3 Text Compression

Although the storage requirement for text is moderate compared with other media types such as audio and video, it is still desirable to compress text when a large number of files need to be stored. The major feature of text compression is that the compression is lossless, meaning that the exact text can be recovered after decompression.

Text can be compressed due to the fact that some characters appear more often than others and some characters normally appear together. In the following we briefly describe the compression principles of Huffman coding, run length coding, and Lempel-Ziv-Welch (LZW) coding.

Huffman Coding

The most commonly used lossless coding is Huffman coding. It assigns fewer bits to symbols that appear more often and more bits to symbols that appear less often. It is efficient when the probabilities of symbol occurrences vary widely. It is usually used in combination with other coding schemes (e.g., to compress the quantized transformed coefficients) as described later.

We use an example to show how Huffman coding works. Suppose we have a file containing a total of 1,000 characters, with four distinct characters e, t, x, and z. The occurring probability for e, t, x, and z are 0.8, 0.16, 0.02, and 0.02, respectively. In a normal uniform coding method, we need 2 bits to represent each of the four characters. So we need 2,000 bits to represent the entire file. However, using Huffman coding, we can use a different number of bits to represent these characters. We assign bit 1 to represent e, 01 to t, 001 to x, and 000 to z. In this case the total number of bits required to represent the entire file is $1,000(1*0.8 +2*0.16+3*0.02+3*0.02) = 1,240$ bits. So although we used more bits to represent x and z, since they appear very rarely the total number of bits required for the entire file is still less than that for the uniform coding scheme. The rules of assigning bits (codes) to symbols are called *codebooks*. Codebooks are normally expressed in tables, as shown in Table 2.1.

The key issue of Huffman coding is how to obtain the codebook. Readers interested in this issue are referred to [1-3].

Table 2.1

An Example Codebook

Symbol	Probability	Code
e	0.8	1
t	0.16	01
x	0.02	001
z	0.02	000

Run-Length Coding

Run-length coding is a data compression method that physically reduces any type of repeating character sequence once the sequence of characters reaches a predefined number of occurrences. The repeated occurrence of the same character is called a *run*, and the number of repetitions is called the *length* of the run. Run-length coding replaces a run with the repeated character and the length of the run. In practice, an additional special character is needed to indicate the use of run-length coding. Thus a run of any length is represented by three characters, as shown in Figure 2.1.

Sc	X	C

Figure 2.1 A run is represented by three characters: *Sc* is a special character indicating that run-length coding is used; *X* is the repeated character in the run; and *C* is the character count, or run length.

We use an example to illustrate how run-length coding is used. Assume that we are going to encode a text sequence that has many long runs, such as "eeeeeeetnnnnnnnn." If we use the character @ as the special character indicating that the following character is run-length coded, then these 16 characters will be encoded as: @e7t@n8. In this case, we encoded 16 characters into 7 characters. During the decoding, the decoder reads the encoded message sequentially. When it encounters the character @, it knows that the next character should be repeated the number of times equal to the number following the character. If there is no @ preceding a character, it will be output as is.

We see that when the run length is greater than 3, run-length coding should be used to achieve data compression. The longer the run, the higher the compression ratio.

LZW Coding

LZW coding works by building a dictionary of phrases (groups of one or more characters) from the input stream. When a phrase is encountered, the compression engine checks to see if that phrase has been recorded in the dictionary. If not, the phrase is added to the dictionary and a token that identifies the phrase's position in the dictionary is output. If the phrase has already been recorded, then the compressor simply outputs the token for the existing phrase. While run-length coding lends itself well to a sequence of data with repeating single characters, LZW works very well on data with repeating groups of characters. The English language uses many repeating character patterns, such as "the," so LZW is usually a good choice for compressing text files.

The following example shows the effectiveness of LZW coding. Suppose we have a file of 10,000 characters. If we represent this file directly using 8 bits per character, a total of 80,000 bits are required. Alternatively, we can encode it using an LZW algorithm. Assuming the file has 2,000 words or phrases out of which 500 are distinct, then we need 9 bits as the token to identify each distinct word or phrase. Hence we need a total of 18,000 bits to encode the entire file, compared with the original 80,000 bits. We achieve a compression ratio of about 4.4. Most text compression programs use this principle. In practice, a dictionary storing all unique phrases must be stored as well, lowering the actual achievable compression ratio.

2.3 VECTOR GRAPHICS AND ANIMATION

There are two basic types of graphics: vector-based and pixel-based. In the latter, the graphic is divided into small picture elements called pixels. Each pixel corresponds to a dot on the screen. The intensity or color of pixels are sequentially stored in a pixel-based graphics file. In this format, graphics has the same characteristics of images, which we discuss in Section 2.5.

In vector graphics, graphics elements are represented in predefined models or mathematical formulas. For example, for a rectangle element, an identifier of rectangles plus the coordinates of two opposite corners are stored. Graphics elements can be changed easily by modifying these parameters. Storage requirements are very low, because only the essential instructions for reproducing the graphics are stored.

It is relatively easy to extract the contents of vector graphics. The properties of each element, such as its shape and size, can be extracted from the graphics file and used for indexing and retrieval.

Animation is produced by sequential rendering a number of frames of graphics. When the graphics are pixel-based, the animation is the same as video, which we discuss in Section 2.6. For vector-based animation, indexing and retrieval can be carried out in a similar way to that used for vector graphics, except that we have an extra temporal dimension that indicates the frame or time the graphics element appears.

2.4 AUDIO

2.4.1 Basic Characteristics of Audio Signal

Audio is caused by a disturbance in air pressure that reaches the human eardrum. When the frequency of the air disturbance is in the range of 20 to 20,000 Hz, the human ear hears sound (i.e., the frequency of audible sound ranges from 20 to 20,000 Hz).

Another parameter used to measure sound is amplitude, variations in which cause sound to be soft or loud. The dynamic range of human hearing is very large: the lower limit is the threshold of audibility, and the upper limit is the threshold of pain. The audibility threshold for a 1-kHz sinusoidal waveform is generally set at 0.000283 dyne per square centimeter. The amplitude of the sinusoidal waveform can be increased from the threshold of audibility by a factor of between 100,000 and 1,000,000 before pain is reached. It is difficult to work with such a large amplitude range. Thus the audio amplitude is often expressed in *decibels* (dB). Given two waveforms with peak amplitudes X and Y, the decibel measure of the difference between these two amplitudes is defined by

$$dB = 20\log_{10}(X/Y)$$

If the above audibility threshold of 0.000283 dyne per square centimeter for a 1-kHz signal is used as the reference for 0 dB, then the threshold of pain for most people is reached at a sound pressure level of around 100 to 120 dB [4, 5].

A sound wave is continuous in both time and amplitude: it changes all the time and the amplitude can take any value within the audible range. Figure 2.2 shows an example sound wave.

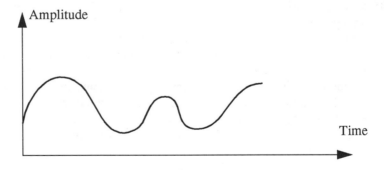

Figure 2.2 Example sound wave.

2.4.2 Digital Representation of Audio

The continuous audio waveform is converted into a continuous electrical signal by a microphone. For example, the audio waveform in Figure 2.2 will be converted to an electrical signal of the same shape, although the amplitude may be multiplied by a positive number. This electrical signal is normally measured in volts. We call this type of signal

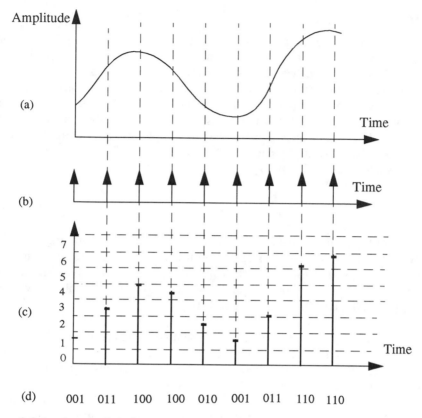

(d) 001 011 100 100 010 001 011 110 110

Figure 2.3 Analog-to-digital conversion process: (a) original analog signal; (b) sampling pulses; (c) sampled values and quantization intervals; and (d) digitized sequence.

with continuous amplitude and time an *analog signal.*

For computers to process and communicate an audio signal, the continuous electrical signal must be converted into a digital signal. Three stages are involved in ADC: sampling, quantization, and coding (Figure 2.3).

Sampling

The process of converting continuous time into discrete values is called *sampling*. Figure 2.3(b) and (c) show the sampling process. The time axis is divided into fixed intervals. The reading of the instantaneous value of the analog signal is taken at the beginning of each time interval. This interval is determined by a clock pulse. The frequency of the clock is called the *sampling rate* or *sampling frequency*. The sampled value is held constant for the next time interval. The circuit for doing this is called a *sampling and hold circuit*. Each of the samples is still analog in amplitude: it may have any value in a continuous range. But it is discrete in time: within each interval, the sample has only one value.

Quantization

The process of converting continuous sample values into discrete values is called *quantization*. In this process we divide the signal range into a fixed number of intervals. Each interval is of the same size (we discuss nonfixed size intervals later) and is assigned a number. In Figure 2.3(c), these intervals are numbered from 0 to 7. Each sample falls in one of the intervals and is assigned that interval's number. In doing this, each sample has a limited choice of values. In our example, a sample value can only be an integer number between 0 and 7. Before quantization, the last two samples in Figure 2.3(c) have different values. But they have the same value of 6 after quantization. The size of the quantization interval is called the *quantization step*.

Coding

The process of representing quantized values digitally is called *coding* (Figure 2.3(d)). In the above example, eight quantizing levels are used. These levels can be coded using 3 bits if the binary system is used, so each sample is represented by 3 bits. The analog signal in Figure 2.3(a) is represented digitally by the following series of binary numbers: 001, 011, 100, 100, 010, 001, 011, 110, and 110.

From the above process, we see that if the sampling rate and the number of quantizing levels are high enough, the digitized signal will be a close representation of the original analog signal. When we need to reconstruct the original analog signal from the digital data, a digital-to-analog converter (DAC) is used. Figure 2.4 shows the DAC process. Quantized values are determined based on the digital representation and the quantization step. Each of these values is held for a time period equal to the sampling interval, resulting in a series of step signals as shown in Figure 2.4(b). These step signals are then passed through a low-pass filter to reconstruct an approximation of the original signal (Figure 2.4(c)). We say that an approximation of the original signal is reconstructed because the reconstructed signal will not be exactly the same as the original due to the introduction of quantization error in the ADC process (more will be said about this). The principles of ADC and DAC described here also apply to video and other signals.

In the ADC process, the most important issues are how to choose the sampling rate and the number of quantization levels for different analog signals and different applications. We discuss these two issues in the following subsections.

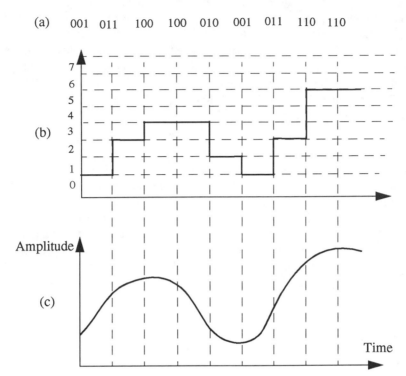

(a)   001 011   100   100   010   001   011   110   110

(b)

(c)   Amplitude

Time

Figure 2.4 Digital-to-analog conversion process: (a) digital sequence; (b) step signals; (c) signal removed after passing through a low-pass filter.

Determination of Sampling Rate

The sampling rate depends on the maximum frequency of the analog signal to be converted. According to the Nyquist theorem, if an analog signal contains frequency components up to f Hz, then the sampling rate should be at least $2f$ Hz. If the sampling rate is exactly $2f$ Hz, we call it *critical sampling*. In practice, the sampling rate used is slightly higher than $2f$ Hz. For example, the sampling rate of CD-audio is 44.1 kHz, and the sampling rate of digital audio tape (DAT) is 48 kHz to cover the audible frequency range of 20 kHz. The main frequency components of the human voice are within 3.1 kHz. Thus the analog telephone system limits the signal to be passed to 3.1 kHz. To convert this voice signal to a digital signal, a sampling rate of 8 kHz is commonly used.

If the bandwidth (frequency range) of an analog signal is greater than half of the sampling frequency, the signal bandwidth must be reduced by using a low-pass filter so that it is less than or equal to half the sampling rate. Otherwise, an effect called *aliasing* is caused (Figure 2.5). Figure 2.5(a) shows a sampling clock of 8 kHz. One frequency component of the signal to be sampled is 6 kHz (Figure 2.5(b)). Figure 2.5(c) shows the sample values taken from the 6-kHz component. If these samples are stored and converted back to analog format using DAC, the signal reconstructed will be as shown in Figure 2.5(d) with a frequency of 2 kHz. This 2-kHz signal replaces the original 6-kHz signal. Thus the 2-kHz signal is an *alias* of the 6-kHz signal. Since 2 kHz is in the audible range, it appears as noise on top of the original audio. Aliasing is a serious problem with all systems using a sampling mechanism when the signal to be sampled has frequency components higher than half of the sampling rate.

Determining the Number of Quantization Levels

The number of quantization levels used determines the amplitude fidelity of the digital signal relative to the original analog signal. The maximum difference between the quantized sample values and the corresponding analog signal values is the quantization step. This difference is called *quantization error* or *quantization noise*. The larger the number of quantization levels, the smaller the quantization step, and the smaller the quantization noise. The number of quantization levels determines how many bits are required to represent each sample. Their relationship is determined by

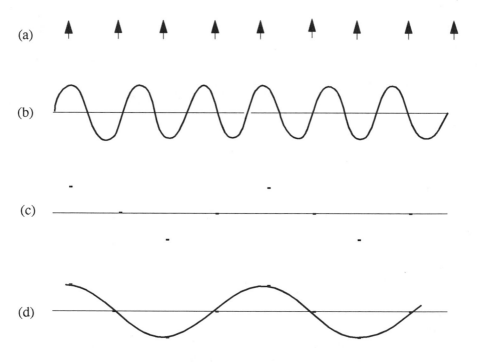

Figure 2.5 An input signal with frequency greater than the half-sampling frequency generates an alias signal at a lower, different frequency: (a) sampling clock of 8 kHz; (b) a 6-kHz analog signal; (c) a series of sample values; and (d) reconstructed signal.

$$b = \log_2 Q \tag{2.1}$$

where b is the number of bits needed to represent each sample and Q is the number of quantization levels. In practice, we want to work out the number of quantization levels Q, given the number of bits used for each sample. Transforming (2.1), we have

$$Q = 2^b \tag{2.2}$$

The digital signal quality relative to the original analog signal is measured by the signal-to-noise ratio (SNR) in decibels. It is defined as

$$SNR = 20\log_{10}(S/N) \tag{2.3}$$

where S is the maximum signal amplitude and N is the quantization noise. Assuming the quantization step is q, then $N=q$ and $S=2^b q$. Substituting into (2.3), we have

$$SNR = 20b\log_{10}2 = 6b \tag{2.4}$$

This equation indicates that using one extra bit to represent samples increases the SNR by 6 dB.

If we consider the audibility threshold and threshold of pain in this context, the quantization noise should be smaller than the audibility threshold. If it is larger than the audibility threshold, we hear the noise. The threshold of pain, around 100 to 120 dB, is the maximum signal range. Therefore the SNR of a digitized audio signal should be at least around 100 dB for us not to hear the quantization noise. CD-audio uses 16 bits per sample, so we have SNR=96 dB. It is marginally lower than the desired 100 to 120-dB threshold, but since 16 is an integer power of 2, it is easier to handle and process in digital systems. Thus 16 bits are used per sample instead of 17 bits per sample.

To summarize, digital audio needs to be sampled continuously at a fixed rate. Each sample is represented by a fixed number of bits. Table 2.2 shows the sampling rate and the number of bits used for each sample for a number of common audio applications. Note that for stereo-audio, like CD-audio, two channels are used.

What we have presented so far is linear quantization. *Nonlinear quantization* can reduce the amount of data required to represent the same quality digital audio, or to use the same amount of data to represent higher quality audio. Nonlinear quantization is really a data compression technique that we discuss in Section 2.4.4.

Table 2.2

Common Digital Audio Characteristics

Applications	No. of channels	Sampling rate	Bits per sample
CD-audio	2	44,100	16
DAT	2	48,000	16
Digital telephone	1	8,000	8
Digital radio, long-play DAT	2	32,000	16

2.4.3 Musical Instrument Digital Interface (MIDI)

Instead of representing music in a sequence of samples, MIDI defines a set of messages or commands to represent music [6]. A music device with MIDI capability (called a synthesizer) will synthesize or produce music based on MIDI messages.

MIDI music files are more compact than sample-based music files. In addition, MIDI files are structural with a set of defined commands consisting of a number of defined fields. Therefore, we can make use of this structural information for MIDI music indexing and retrieval.

The limitations of MIDI are that (1) it is difficult to represent and produce complex music pieces using many instruments, and (2) different synthesizers may produce different sound from the same MIDI data due to the use of different audio palettes (patches).

2.4.4 Audio Compression

Nonlinear Quantization

In the uniform quantization of audio signals, the same quantization step size is used in the ADC process regardless of the signal amplitude. The uniform ADC process is often referred to as *pulse-coded modulation* (PCM). It is simple, but is not efficient in terms of data bit usage because the linear quantization will result in a higher SNR at a region of higher signal amplitude than a region of lower signal amplitude. This increased SNR at higher signal amplitudes does not increase the perceived audio quality because we are most sensitive to lower amplitude components.

To exploit this factor, a quantization step size that increases logarithmically with the signal amplitude is widely used for quantizing speech signals. In this quantization scheme, the quantization steps are smaller when the signal amplitude is lower and the quantization step is larger when the signal amplitude is higher [7].

In practice, a uniform quantization is applied to a transformed nonlinear signal, instead of applying a nonuniform quantization to a linear signal. The results of these two approaches are the same. The process of transforming the linear signal into a nonlinear signal is called *companding*. Uniform digitization of a companded signal is called *companded PCM*. The common transform functions used are *A-law* and μ-*law*. The A-law transform function is:

$$y = Ax/(1+\ln A) \qquad \text{when} \quad 0 \le x \le \frac{1}{A}$$

$$y = (1+\ln(Ax))/(1+\ln A) \qquad \text{when} \quad \frac{1}{A} \le x \le 1$$

where x is the original input signal amplitude, y is the transformed signal amplitude, and A is a constant. For standard telephone work, A is set to 87.6.

The following is the μ-law transform function:

$$y = \ln(1+\mu x)/\ln(1+\mu)$$

where x and y have the same meaning as in the A-law transform function, and μ is a constant. For standard telephone work, μ is set to 255.

Companding is actually an analog compression technique, because the analog signal is "compressed" before ADC and "expanded" after DAC, as shown in Figure 2.6.

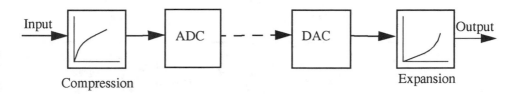

Figure 2.6 A system with a companding technique.

Using the companding technique, the 8-bit signal can produce a signal quality equivalent to that of 12-bit PCM-coded signal. Companded PCM is sometimes called *log-PCM* because the logarithms are used in the transform functions.

Predictive Coding

Rather than coding the value of a sample being transmitted, *predictive coding* codes the difference between a prediction for that sample value and the actual sample value [7]. If this difference or prediction error is quantized and coded, the predictive coding scheme is called *differential pulse-coded modulation (DPCM)*. Normally, fixed-length code words are used to encode the quantized prediction errors. Since the prediction value for each sample is calculated only from the past history of the encoded picture signal, the prediction value is available to both the coder and the decoder. To reconstruct a sample at the decoder, the corresponding transmitted prediction error is added to the prediction value of that sample. The efficiency of DPCM is obtained by exploiting the fact that the neighboring sample values are correlated and the prediction error will normally be smaller than the original sample value. Since the prediction error has a small amplitude range, fewer bits can be used to encode it.

For example, if we are compressing an audio stream of 16 bits per sample, and we use 4 bits to represent the prediction error, the audio quality can be maintained at the same level as the original 16 bits per sample if the prediction error is always less than the 16 original quantization steps. If the prediction error is larger than the 16 quantization steps, the original audio quality will not be maintained. The reconstructed signal at the decoder will approach the original signal when the signal amplitude change becomes smaller.

To improve the performance of DPCM, an adaptive DPCM, or ADPCM, is used. To handle both signals that change quickly and signals that change slowly, the quantization step size between adjacent samples varies according to the signal itself; that is, if the waveform is changing rapidly, large quantization steps are used, and vice versa.

The International Telecommunication Union–Telecommunications Sector (ITU-TS) recommends a series of schemes for compressing speech. These recommendations are summarized in Table 2.3. Note that the target applications of these recommendations are speech transmission. Thus the audio bandwidth is limited to 3.4 or 7 kHz. Except in G.722, 8 bits are used for each sample in the ADC process. Most of these recommendations are based on ADPCM techniques, except that G.722 uses a subband ADPCM and G.728 uses a vector quantization technique.

Table 2.3
Summary of ITU-TS Recommendations on Speech Coding

Recommendation	Compression technique	Speech bandwidth (kHz)	Sampling rate (kHz)	Compressed bit rate (kbps)
G.711	PCM (no compression)	3.4	8	64
G.721	ADPCM	3.4	8	32
G.722	Subband ADPCM	7	16 (14 bits per sample)	48, 56, 64
G.723	ADPCM	3.4	8	24
G.728	Vector quantization	3.4	8	16

In the subband ADPCM, the speech signal is divided into two subbands (low and high-frequency bands), each of which is coded using ADPCM. The purpose of dividing the signal into two subbands is that the low-frequency subband is more important, so it needs to be coded more accurately. The coarsely coded high-frequency subband provides additional information to improve the speech quality over the low-frequency subband.

The vector quantization technique used in G.728 is similar to the LZW compression technique in principle. A number of speech samples are grouped into a vector. Each vector is represented by an index (token) of the entry in the dictionary. The only difference is that the match between a vector and a pattern in the dictionary (called codebook) does not have to be exact; that is, vector quantization is lossy. We describe vector quantization in more detail in the next section when we discuss its application in image compression.

Compression Technique Using Masking Property: MPEG-Audio

We have so far discussed audio coding techniques specifically designed for speech, with an assumption that the audio bandwidth is within 3.4 kHz or maximum 7 kHz. We now introduce a generic audio compression technique that can be used to compress sound within the entire audible range of 20 kHz.

It has been shown that one sound can make it impossible to hear another, or one sound may shift the apparent loudness of another. This is called *masking*. The masking of one sound may be total or partial. Parts of one sound can mask parts of another sound. We all have experienced this masking effect: when loud music is played, we cannot hear other lower level sounds around us.

Since masked sounds are not audible, we can safely discard them without affecting the audio quality. This is the strategy used by the international standard MPEG-Audio [8, 9] (details of MPEG are discussed later).

MPEG-Audio is a generic audio compression standard. Unlike many other encoders specially tuned for speech signals, the MPEG-Audio coder gets its compression without making assumptions about the nature of the audio source. Instead, the coder exploits the perceptual limitations of the human auditory system. Much of the compression results from the removal of perceptually irrelevant parts of the audio signal. Since removal of such parts does not cause audible distortions, MPEG-Audio can compress any signal meant to be heard by the human ear.

MPEG-Audio allows three sampling rates: 32, 44.1, or 48 kHz. The compressed bitstream can support one or two audio channels. The compressed stream can have one of several predefined fixed bit rates ranging from 32 to 244 kbps per channel. Depending on the audio sampling rate, this translates to compression ratios ranging from 2.7 to 24.

Because MPEG-Audio only removes inaudible parts of the sound, perceptually it is lossless compression, although original audio data cannot be reconstructed bit to bit after compression. The MPEG-Audio committee conducted extensive subjective listening tests during the development of the standard. The tests showed that even with a 6:1 compression ratio and under optimal listening conditions, expert listeners could not distinguish between coded and original audio clips with statistical significance. The audio clips used in the tests were chosen as difficult to compress.

MPEG-Audio is not a single compression algorithm but a family of three audio compression schemes. They are called MPEG-Audio layer 1, layer 2, and layer 3. The complexity of the algorithm increases with the layer number. Thus layer 3 is the most complex. In general, increased complexity produces a higher compression ratio. These three layers are hierarchically compatible; that is, a layer 2 decoder can decode bitstreams encoded with a layer 1 encoder, and a layer 3 decoder can decode bitstreams encoded with layer 2 and layer 1 encoders. Detailed information on MPEG-Audio can be found in [8, 9].

2.5 DIGITAL IMAGES

Digital images are commonly obtained by the following methods. The first method is to digitize photographs and printed pictures using a scanner. The digitization principle is similar to that of digitizing audio as described in the previous section. In digital cameras, ADCs are built in. The second source of digital images is from individual frames of digitized video. In the third method, images are generated by some sort of graphics (painting) package. In raw (bitmap) format, all digital images are represented in the same way regardless of the different original sources. In this section we describe how digital images are represented, the main parameters used to describe digital images, and common image compression techniques and standards.

2.5.1 Digital Image Representation

Images can be in grayscale or in color. It is easier to understand the representation of grayscale images. Thus we first describe their representation and then extend it to color image representation.

Representation of Grayscale Images

An image displayed on a computer monitor consists of many small dots. These small dots are called picture elements or pixels. There are a fixed number of pixels on a horizontal line and a fixed number lines in the vertical dimension (i.e., a digital image consists of a rectangular array of pixels). Different pixels may have different brightness or intensity. The intensity range from black to white depends on the required image quality or number of bits used for each pixel. For example, when 8 bits are used to represent a pixel, a total of 256 different intensity levels can be represented, black being 0 and white being 255. From this description, it is clear that a grayscale image can be represented as a two-dimensional array. Each array element corresponds to a pixel.

The arrangement of these pixel values in a contiguous region of memory is called a *bitmap*. This name comes from the idea that we map the physical image composed of pixels into adjacent addresses of memory. In a bitmap, there is a memory location uniquely corresponding to each pixel in the display. A bitmap is the common arrangement used in display devices. The memory used to store bitmapped image data is commonly called a *framestore*, or frame *buffer*.

Representation of Color Images

A color image also consists of a rectangular array of pixels. The only difference from grayscale images is that we need three values to represent each pixel. Each value represents one primary color. This representation is based on the tristimulus theory of color production, which states that any color can be reproduced by an appropriate mixing of three primary colors. The primary colors used in television systems and computer monitors are red, green, and blue.

Therefore, a color image can be represented by three two-dimensional arrays, corresponding to the red, green, and blue components of the image, respectively.

2.5.2 Main Parameters of Digital Images

Image quality is measured by a number of parameters. The first parameter is image size, which is specified by the number of pixels on each horizontal line and the number of lines in the vertical dimension. Thus we normally say the size of an image is x pixels by y lines. To maintain original (photo, picture, and video frame) image quality, the pixel number per line and the number of lines should be at least be equal to the minimum values as determined by the Nyquist theorem. For example, if an original picture resolution is 300 dpi (dots per inch), then number of pixels (samples) per inch required should be at least 300. Otherwise, the digital image will be distorted from the original image.

Another important parameter is pixel depth, which specifies the number of bits used to represent each pixel. For a reasonable quality grayscale image, 8 bits per pixel are required. For a color image, 24 bits are required for each pixel (8 bits for each color component). These are typical numbers for average quality images, derived from the discrimination capacity of human vision.

The discussion here is very brief. Interested readers are referred to Chapter 2 of [1] for details on how these parameters are determined.

When the image size and pixel depth are known, the amount of data D required for the image can be calculated using the following formula:

$$D = xyb$$

where x is the number of pixels per horizontal line, y is the number of horizontal line, and b is the number of bits per pixel. For example, for an image of 512 pixels by 512 lines with pixel depth 24 bits, the required amount of data $D = 512 * 512 * 24$ bits = 768 KB.

2.5.3 Image Compression

From the previous subsection we see that raw digital images require a large amount of data. Thus, image compression becomes essential in multimedia applications. Before discussing common image compression techniques and standards, we explain why images can be compressed.

Image compression is achieved by exploiting redundancies in images and human perception properties. In a digital image, neighboring samples on a scanning line are normally similar. Neighboring samples on adjacent lines are also similar. These similarities are called *spatial redundancy*. Spatial redundancies can be removed using predictive coding techniques and other techniques such as transform coding.

The end users of digital images are normally human beings. Human beings can tolerate some information error or loss without affecting the effectiveness of communication. This means that the compressed version does not need to represent the original information samples exactly. This is in contrast to alphanumeric data where any data loss or error is normally not allowed, especially for computer programs.

There is another feature we can use to achieve a high compression ratio: perception sensitivities are different for different signal patterns. Some information is more important to human perception than others. Thus, a compression technique should try to keep the important information and remove the unnecessary information.

In the following we describe some common image compression techniques and standards.

Spatial Subsampling

As image data contains redundancy, we don't have to retain every original pixel to keep the contents of the image. The technique exploiting this is called spatial subsampling. At the encoder, one pixel every few pixels is selected and transmitted (or stored). At the decoder, the missing pixels are interpolated based on the received pixels to regenerate the original video sequence at a lower resolution. Alternatively, the decoder may just decode and display the smaller spatially subsampled images.

If pixels are represented with luminance and chrominance components, the chrominance components can be subsampled at a higher ratio and quantized more coarsely, using the fact that the human eye is less sensitive to chrominance components.

This technique is very simple but quite efficient. For example, when one pixel every four pixels is transmitted, a 4:1 compression ratio is achieved. It is often used as preprocessing before using other compression techniques; that is, spatially subsampled image data can be further compressed using other techniques.

Predictive Coding

The principle of image predictive coding is the same as that of audio predictive coding. In general, the sample values of spatially neighboring picture elements are correlated. Correlation or linear statistical dependency indicates that a linear prediction of the sample values based on sample values of neighboring picture elements results in prediction errors that have a smaller variance than the original sample values. One-dimensional prediction algorithms use correlation of adjacent picture elements within the scan line. Other more complex schemes also exploit line-to-line and frame-to-frame correlation and are denoted as two-dimensional and three-dimensional prediction, respectively. The smaller variance of the signal to be quantized, coded, and transmitted, can, in a predictive coding system, diminish the amplitude range of the quantizer, reduce the number of quantizing levels, and lessen the required bits per pixel (than that in a PCM system) without decreasing the signal-to-quantizing-noise ratio.

Transform Coding

The main idea behind transform coding is to decorrelate the image pixels (i.e., convert statistically dependent image elements into independent coefficients) and concentrate the energy of an image onto only a few coefficients, so that the redundancy in the image can be removed [10, 11].

In transform coding, an original image is usually divided into a number of rectangular blocks or subimages. A unitary mathematical transform is then applied to each subimage that transforms the subimage from the spatial domain into a frequency domain. As a result, most of the energy is concentrated into relatively few samples in the low-frequency area. Note that applying a transform to image data does not reduce any data. It only converts the image data from the spatial domain to a frequency domain. If the data in the spatial domain is highly correlated, the resulting data in the frequency domain will be in a suitable form for data reduction with techniques such as Huffman coding and run-length coding.

Transform coding takes advantage of the statistical dependencies of image elements for redundancy reduction. Many kinds of unitary transforms can be used for this purpose [10]. Commonly used transforms are the Karhunen-Loeve transform (KLT), the discrete cosine transform (DCT), the Walsh-Hadamard transform (WHT) and the discrete Fourier transform (DFT). Among them, the KLT is the most efficient for decorrelation performance. Because of the existence of computationally fast algorithms for the DCT and its relatively high efficiency, however, the DCT is most widely used for image coding.

In implementing a practical transform coding system, there are four main steps. The first one is to select the transform type. The best transform represents a satisfactory compromise between efficient decorrelation and energy-packing ability on the one hand and practicality of implementation on the other. In most cases, the DCT represents the best compromise and thus is the most widely used.

The second step is to select block size and apply the selected transform on it. If the block size is too small, the correlation between neighboring pixels cannot be fully exploited. But on the other hand, too big a block size increases the complexity of hardware implementation and causes block boundaries to be visibly objectionable. A good compromise of block size is 8 by 8.

The third step is to select and efficiently quantize those transformed coefficients to be retained for transmission or storage. The fourth step is bit allocation for those quantized coefficients. Huffman coding and/or run-length coding can be used.

Vector Quantization

In the coding schemes discussed above, the actual quantization or coding is done on scalars (e.g., on individual real-value samples of waveforms or pixels of images). Transform coding does it by first taking the block transform of a block of pixels and then individually coding the transform coefficients. Predictive coding does it by quantizing an error term formed as the difference between the new sample and a prediction of the new sample based on past coded outputs.

A fundamental result of Shannon's rate-distortion theory, the branch of information theory devoted to data compression, is that better performance can always be achieved by coding vectors (a group of values) instead of scalars (individual values).

This theory has had a limited impact on actual system design in the past because (1) the Shannon theory does not provide constructive design techniques for vector coders and (2) traditional scalar coders often yield satisfactory performance with enough adaptation and fine tuning. Only in the last decade has vector quantization (VQ) been greatly considered. A collection of excellent papers on vector quantization can be found in [12].

A vector quantizer is defined as a mapping Q of K-dimensional Euclidean space R^K into a finite subset Y of R^K, that is:

$$Q: R^K \text{ --->>} Y$$

where $Y = (x'_i; i = 1, 2, \ldots N)$, and x'_i is the ith vector in Y.

Y is the set of reproduction vectors and is called a VQ codebook or VQ table. N is the number of vectors in Y. In the encoder, each data vector x belonging to R^K is matched or approximated with a codeword in the codebook, and the address or index of that codeword is transmitted instead of the data vector itself. At the decoder, the index is mapped back to the codeword and the codeword is used to represent the original data vector. In the encoder and decoder, an identical codebook exists whose entries contain combinations of pixels in a block. Assuming the image block size is $(n \times n)$ pixels and each pixel is represented by m bits, theoretically, $(2^m)^{n \times n}$ types of blocks are possible. In practice, however, there are only a limited number of combinations that occur most often, which reduces the size of the codebook considerably. This is the basis of vector quantization. If properties of the human visual system are used, the size of codebook can be reduced further and fewer bits need to be used to represent the index of codebook entries.

We see that the principle of vector quantization is similar to that of the LZW algorithm: using an index or token to represent a block of data.

Fractal Image Coding

Another interesting development in the image compression area is *fractal image compression techniques* [13–15]. A fractal, in simplest terms, is an image of a texture or shape expressed as one or more mathematical formulas. In terms of fractal geometry, a fractal is a geometric form whose irregular details recur at different scales and angles, which can be described by affine or fractal transformations (formulas). Fractals have historically been used to generate images in applications such as flight-simulator scenes and special effects in motion pictures. Fractal formulas can now be used to describe almost all real-world pictures.

Fractal image compression is the inverse of fractal image generation; that is, instead of generating an image or figure from a given formula, fractal image compression searches for sets of fractals in a digitized image that describe and represent the entire image. Once the appropriate sets of fractals are determined, they are reduced (compressed) to very compact fractal transform codes or formulas. The codes are "rules" for reproducing the various sets of fractals that, in turn, regenerate the entire image. Because fractal transform codes require very small amounts of data to be expressed and stored as formulas, fractal compression results in very high compression ratios.

Fractal coding is highly asymmetric in that significantly more processing is required for searching and encoding than for decoding. This is because the encoding process involves many transformations and comparisons to search for sets of fractals, while the decoder simply generates images according to the fractal formulas received. For an example fractal coding scheme, refer to the technique proposed by Jacquin [14]. Lu [15] provides a thorough review on fractal-based image compression techniques.

Wavelet Compression

More recently, wavelet transforms have been used for image compression [37, 38]. The basic principle of wavelet compression is similar to that of DCT-based compression: to transform signals from the time domain into a new domain where essential parts of the signal are kept and coded to achieve data compression.

Practical Coding Systems

In a practical system, several of the coding techniques discussed above are often combined to achieve a high compression ratio at a fixed acceptable image quality. There are many combinations for different applications. One mature scheme used to code video data comprises following coding stages:

  (a) Spatial and temporal subsampling;
  (b) DPCM based on motion estimation and compensation;
  (c) Two-dimensional DCT;
  (d) Huffman coding;
  (e) Run-length coding.

This hybrid scheme is the basis of a number of currently proposed international standards discussed in this chapter.

The JPEG-Still Image Compression Standard

JPEG was the first international digital image compression standard for continuous-tone (multilevel) still images, both grayscale and color [16-18].

JPEG is now used widely in applications involving images. It has been implemented in both hardware and software. Although initially intended to compress still images, real-time JPEG encoding and decoding have been implemented to handle full-motion video. This application is called motion JPEG or MJPEG.

JPEG specifies four modes of operation:

  (1) Lossy sequential DCT-based encoding, in which each image component is encoded in a single left-to-right, top-to-bottom scan. This is called *baseline mode* and must be supported by every JPEG implementation.

(2) Expanded lossy DCT-based encoding, which provides enhancement to the baseline mode operation. One notable enhancement is progressive coding, in which the image is encoded in multiple scans to produce a quick, rough decoded image when the transmission bandwidth is low.
(3) Lossless encoding, in which the image is encoded to guarantee the exact reproduction.
(4) Hierarchical encoding, in which the image is encoded in multiple resolutions.

The baseline mode is most commonly used, so we briefly describe its compression process. The source image data is normally transformed into one luminance component Y and two chrominance components U and V. U and V are normally spatially-sampled in both the horizontal and vertical direction by a factor of 2 to take advantage of the lower sensitivity of human perception to the chrominance signals.

The original sample values are in the range $[0, 2^b-1]$, assuming b bits are used for each sample. These values are shifted into the range $[-2^{b-1}, 2^{b-1}-1]$, centering on zero. The new value range allows a low-precision calculation in the DCT. For baseline, 8 bits are used for each sample. Thus the original value range of $[0, 255]$ is shifted to $[-128, 127]$.

Then each component is divided into blocks of 8 x 8 pixels (Figure 2.7). A two-dimensional forward DCT (FDCT) is applied to each block of data. The result is an array of 64 coefficients with energy concentrated in the first few coefficients. These coefficients are then quantized using quantization values specified in the quantization tables. The quantization values can be adjusted to trade between compression ratio and compressed image quality. Quantization is carried out by dividing the DCT coefficients by the corresponding specified quantization value.

The quantized coefficients are zigzag scanned as shown in Figure 2.7, to obtain a one-dimensional sequence of data for Huffman coding. The first coefficient is called the DC coefficient, which represents the average intensity of the block. The rest of the coefficients (1 to 63) are called AC coefficients. The purpose of the zigzag scanning is to order the coefficients in increasing order of spectral frequencies. Since the coefficients of high frequencies (at the right bottom corner of the coefficient array) are mostly zero, the zigzag scanning will result in mostly zeros at the end of the scan, leading to higher Huffman and run-length coding efficiency.

The DC coefficient is DPCM coded relative to the DC coefficient of the previous block. AC coefficients are run-length coded. DPCM-coded DC coefficients and run-length-coded AC coefficients are then Huffman coded. The output of the entropy coder is the compressed image data.

JBIG

JBIG is an ISO standard. It specifies a lossless compression algorithm for binary (one bit/pixel) images. The intent of JBIG is to replace the current, less effective group 3 and group 4 fax algorithms. JBIG compression is based on a combination of predictive and arithmetic coding.

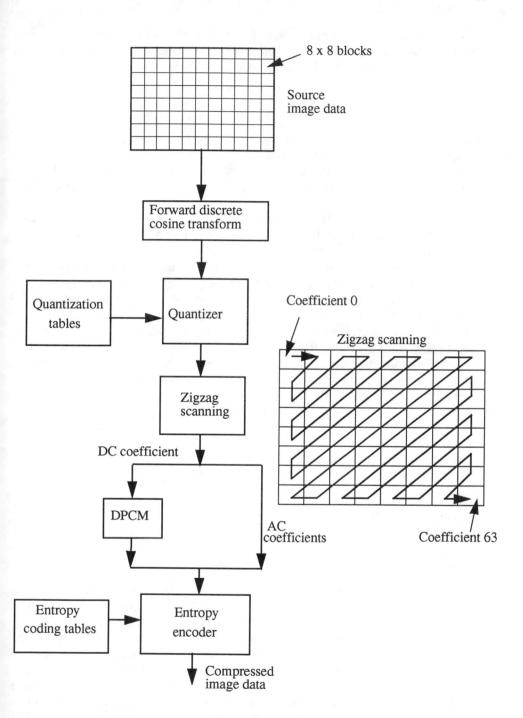

Figure 2.7 Sequential DCT-based encoding steps.

JBIG can also be used on grayscale or even color images for lossless compression by simply applying the algorithm 1 bit plane at a time. This works well up to about 6 bits per pixel, beyond which the JPEG lossless mode works better.

JPEG-2000

JPEG-2000 will be a new standard due to be published in March 2000 [19]. The new standard will have the following main features:

- It will provide a lower bit-rate mode of operation than the existing JPEG and JBIG standards that it will replace, and will provide better rate distortion and subjective image quality.
- It will be able to handle images larger than 64K x 64K pixels without having to use tiling, and will use a single decompression algorithm for all images to avoid the problems of mode incompatibility sometimes encountered with existing standards.
- It will be designed with transmission in noisy environments in mind, and not be inefficient when used to compress computer-generated images.
- It will specifically be designed to handle the mix of bilevel and continuous tone images required for interchanging and/or storing compound documents as part of document imaging systems in both lossless and lossy formats.
- It will allow for progressive transmission of images to allow images to be reconstructed with increasing pixel accuracy and spatial resolution. Images will be transmittable in real-time over low bandwidth channels to devices with limited memory space (e.g., a printer buffer).
- It will allow specific areas of an image to be compressed with less distortion than others.
- It will provide facilities for content-based description of the images, and mechanisms for watermarking, labeling, stamping, and encrypting images.
- The still images will be compatible with MPEG-4 moving images.

2.6 DIGITAL VIDEO

2.6.1 Digital Video Representation

Digital video is normally obtained by digitizing analog video. A digital video sequence consists of a number of frames or images that have to be played out at a fixed rate. The *frame rate* of a motion video is determined by three major factors. First, the frame rate should be high enough to deliver motion smoothly. It has been shown that when the frame rate is equal to or greater than 25 frames per second, most motion can be delivered smoothly. Second, the higher the frame rate, the higher the bandwidth required to transmit the video signal. If the frame rate is high, more images (frames) must be transmitted in the same amount of time, so higher bandwidth is required. Therefore, to use as low a bandwidth as possible and to deliver most scenes smoothly, 25 frames per second should be used. Third, when the phosphors in the display devices are hit by an electron beam, they emit light for a short time, typically for a few milliseconds. After this short time, the phosphors do not emit more light unless they are hit again by the electron beam. In another words, the image on the display disappears if it is not redisplayed (refreshed) after this short period. If the refresh interval is too large, the display has an annoying flickering appearance. Studies show that the display should be refreshed at least 50 times per second to prevent flicker. But if the frame rate is increased to 50 frames per second, the required transmission bandwidth increases substantially. To solve this problem, a display technique called *interlace* is used in current television systems. In interlace displays, more than one vertical scan is used to reproduce a complete frame. Each vertical scan is called a *field*. Broadcast television uses a 2:1 interlace: 2 vertical scan (fields) for a complete frame. With a 2:1 interlace, one vertical scan (called the *odd field*) displays all the odd lines of a frame, and then a second vertical scan (called the *even field*) displays the even lines. Therefore, at 25 frames per second, the field rate is 50 fields per second. Since the eye does not easily see small flickering objects, the 25-per-second repetition rate of any line is not seen as flicker, but rather the entire picture appears to be refreshed 50 times per second. Therefore, using an interlaced display, the same amount of bandwidth is used but flicker is avoided to a large extent.

Based on the above factors, two common frame rates are used in television broadcasting around the world. The 25 frames (50 fields) per second rate is used in television systems (PAL) in European countries, China, and Australia. The 30 frames (60 fields) per second rate is used in the television systems (NTSC) of North America and Japan. The field numbers 50 and 60 were chosen to match the frequencies of electricity power distribution networks in the respective countries to reduce interference to image display quality. For more on video technology, the reader is referred to [1, 20].

Thus, two major characteristics of video are that it has a time dimension and it takes a huge amount of data to represent. For example, a 10-minute video sequence with image size 512 pixels by 512 lines, pixel depth of 24 bits/pixel and frame rate 30 frames/s, requires 600*30*512*512*3 =13.8 GB storage. Therefore, video compression is essential.

2.6.2 Video Compression

Video is compressed by reducing redundancies and exploiting human perception properties. Digital video is a sequence of images and thus it also has spatial redundancies. In addition, neighboring images in a video sequence are normally similar. This similarity is called *temporal redundancy* and is removed by applying predictive coding between images. The image compression techniques described in the previous section are also used for video compression. In this section, we outline a technique to reduce temporal redundancies and then describe the existing video compression standards.

2.6.2.1 Motion Estimation and Compensation

Motion estimation and compensation exploit temporal redundancy in video. Motion within the pictures usually implies that the pixels in the previous picture are in a different position from the pixels in the current picture. In motion estimation and compensation techniques, each picture is divided into fixed-size blocks. A closest match for each block is found in the previous picture. The position displacement between these two blocks is called the *motion vector*. A difference block is obtained by calculating pixel-by-pixel differences. The motion vector and pixel difference block are then encoded and transmitted. The pixel difference is usually very small and it is usually more efficient to transmit the motion vector plus the difference than to transmit a description of the current block by itself [21-23].

2.6.2.2 MPEG

MPEG was established in 1988 in the framework of the Joint ISO/IEC Technical Committee (JTC 1) on Information Technology [24]. The group's mandate was to develop standards for coded representation of moving pictures, associated audio, and their combination when used for storage and retrieval on digital storage media (DSM). The DSM concept includes conventional storage devices, such as CD-ROMs, tape drives, Winchester disks, writable optical drives, as well as telecommunication channels such as ISDNs and local area networks (LANs).

The group had three original work items—coding of moving pictures and associated audio up to 1.5, 10, and 40 Mbps. These three work items were nicknamed MPEG-1, MPEG-2, and MPEG-3. The intention of MPEG-1 is to code VHS-quality video (360 x 280 pixels at 30 pictures per second) at the bit rate around 1.5 Mbps. The rate of 1.5 Mbits was chosen because the throughput of CD-ROM drives at that time was about that rate. The original intention of MPEG-2 was to code CCIR 601 digital-television-quality video (720 x 480 pixels at 30 frames per second) at a bit rate between 2 to 10 Mbps. The original intention of MPEG-3 was to code HDTV-quality video at a bit rate around 40 Mbps. Later on, it was realized that functionality supported by the MPEG-2 requirements covers MPEG-3 requirements, thus the MPEG-3 work item was dropped in July 1992. During the standardization process, it was also realized that there was a need for very-low-bit-rate and object-based coding for audiovisual information. Thus the MPEG-4 work item was proposed in May 1991 and approved in July 1993.

To date, MPEG has issued two standards: MPEG-1 in 1993 [9] and MPEG-2 in 1994 [25-27]. The MPEG-4 standard is expected to reach the international standard stage in 1999 [9].

The MPEG activities cover more than video compression, since the compression of the associated audio and the issue of audio-visual synchronization cannot be considered independently of video compression. The MPEG standard has three main parts: *MPEG-Video*, *MPEG-Audio* and *MPEG-Systems*. MPEG-Video deals with the compression of video signals. MPEG-Audio is concerned with the compression of a digital audio signal, as discussed in Section 2.4. MPEG-Systems deals with the issue of synchronization and multiplexing of multiple compressed audio and video bitstreams. In addition, there is a fourth part called *Conformance* that specifies the procedures for determining the characteristics of coded bitstreams and for testing compliance with the requirements stated in Systems, Video, and Audio.

Note that one of the most important features of the MPEG standards is that they only specify the syntax of coded bitstreams, so that decoders conforming to these standards can decode the bitstream. The standards do not specify how to generate the bitstream. This allows innovation in designing and implementing encoders.

MPEG standards, both MPEG-1 and MPEG-2, have found wide application in multimedia systems. This trend is going to continue. In the near future, MPEG standards and audio-visual applications will be inseparable. It has been proposed that MPEG-2 be used as the encoding standard for HDTV in Europe and the United States. In the following subsections we describe the MPEG-1 MPEG-2, and MPEG-4 standards. We also outline the objectives of MPEG-7.

MPEG-1

MPEG-1 was targeted at the encoding of video and associated audio at a bit rate of about 1.5 Mbps [9]. Note that while it is optimal to operate at this bit rate, MPEG-1 is not limited to this rate and may be used at higher or lower data rates.

MPEG-1 video uses a combination of motion compensation and DCT-based coding techniques. The major coding steps are as follows.
1. Input pictures are preprocessed (color space conversion and spatial resolution adjustment) to the specified source input format.
2. Picture types are determined for each picture (either, I, P, B, or D). The difficult challenge in the design of the MPEG algorithm was the following: on the one hand, to achieve a high compression ratio an interframe coding technique as well as intraframe coding should be used; on the other hand, the random access requirement of image retrieval is best satisfied with pure intraframe coding. To meet both these requirements in MPEG-1 video, some pictures are intraframe coded and others are interframe coded. MPEG-1 defines the following four types of pictures:

- **I-pictures** (intracoded pictures) are coded without reference to other pictures. They provide access points to the coded sequence where decoding can begin but are coded with only moderate compression. They also serve as reference pictures for predictive-coded pictures.
- **P-pictures** are predictive-coded pictures that are coded more efficiently using motion-compensated prediction from a past I-picture or P-picture and are generally used as a reference for further prediction.
- **B-pictures** are bidirectionally predictive-coded pictures that provide the highest degree of compression but require both past and future reference pictures for motion compensation. B-pictures are never used as references for prediction.
- **D-pictures** are DC-coded pictures that are coded without reference to other pictures. Of the DCT coefficients, only the DC ones are present. The D-pictures are not used in a sequence containing any other picture types. D-pictures are intended only for a fast-forward search mode.

I-pictures and P-pictures are generally called *reference pictures*, and P-pictures and B-pictures are generally called *predictive-coded pictures*. The organization of the three types of pictures in a video sequence is very flexible. The choice is left to the encoder and depends on the requirements of the application. Typically, an I-picture may occur every half-second to give reasonably fast random access, with two B-pictures inserted between each pair of I or P-pictures.

3. Each picture is divided into macroblocks of 16 x 16 pixels. Macroblocks in I-pictures are intracoded. Macroblocks in P-pictures are either intracoded or forward predictive-coded based on the previous I or P-picture, depending on coding efficiency. Macroblocks in B-pictures are intracoded, forward-predictive-coded, backward-predictive-coded, or bidirectionally-predictive-coded. For predictive-coded macroblocks (including BP, FP, and B-macroblocks), motion vectors are found and predictive errors are calculated.

4. The intracoded macroblocks and the predictive errors of the predictive-coded macroblocks are divided into six blocks of 8 x 8 pixels (4 luminance and 2 chrominance). A two-dimensional DCT is applied to each block to obtain transform coefficients, which are quantized and zigzag scanned.

5. The quantized transform coefficients and side information (e.g., picture types, macroblock address, and motion vectors) are coded using a combination of Huffman and run-length coding.

The standard does not specify the above encoding processes, though they are the expected functions to be performed by an encoder. The standard specifies the format of the output bitstream from the encoder, so that the decoder can parse the information encoded in the bitstream. The standard does not dictate how the encoder is implemented, so long as the output bitstream complies with the specified format.

MPEG-2

MPEG-2 is an extension of MPEG-1 to provide high-quality audio-visual encoding [25-27]. Although MPEG-2 uses the same concepts as MPEG-1, it has many improvements over MPEG-1. In the following, we outline the main improvements and differences in the three parts, Systems, Video, and Audio, respectively.

The function of MPEG-2 Systems is the same as that of MPEG-1 Systems: to specify coding formats for multiplexing audio, video, and other data into a form suitable for transmission or storage. Temporal relationships among these related media are also specified to enable synchronous decoding and playback at the decoder. MPEG-2 Systems, however, specifies two datastream formats: Program Stream and Transport Stream. The Program Stream is similar to the MPEG-1 Systems standard and is compatible with the MPEG-1 stream. The Program Stream is optimized for multimedia retrieval applications and for performing systems processing in software.

The Transport Stream can carry multiple programs simultaneously and is optimized for use in applications where data loss may be likely. The Transport Stream consists of fixed-length packets. The concept is similar to that of ATM cells, but the packet length is 188 bytes (including a 4-byte header) instead of the 53 bytes used by the ATM cell to improve bandwidth use. The Transport Stream is well suited for the transmission of digital television and videophone over fiber, satellite, ATM, and other networks.

MPEG-2 Video compression uses the same principle as MPEG-1 Video compression, with some notable extensions and improvements to support high-quality video. The major extensions are

1. MPEG-2 supports both interlaced and noninterlaced video. This is required to support interlaced video such as CCIR 601.
2. The videostream syntax allows picture sizes as large as 16,383 x 16,383 pixels.

3. The videostream syntax provides an indication of source composite video characteristics (e.g., PAL and NTSC) to facilitate postprocessing operations.
4. Scalable video is permitted in MPEG-2 Video: four scalable modes encode MPEG-2
videostream into different layers (base, middle, and high layers), mostly for priori-
tizing video data. There are two main purposes: first, important video data is placed
in high priority to avoid error. In case of data congestion, less important, low-priority data is dropped first and high priority data is kept so that a reasonable video
quality can still be reconstructed from this data. This is called *graceful degradation*.
Second, scalable video allows the decoder to selectively decode part of a video. For
example, if an HDTV video is coded in different layers, and one layer corresponds
to standard TV resolution, then a standard TV needs to decode only that layer to
receive a normal television program.

5. In MPEG-1 Video, the constrained parameters define a subset of parameters useful
for most MPEG-1 applications. In MPEG-2, a similar concept defines subset
parameters to limit the capability of a particular implementation. The MPEG-2
Video specification is intended to be generic in the sense that it serves a wide range
of applications, bit rates, resolution, qualities, and services. Applications cover,
among others, digital storage media, television broadcasting, and communications.
In the course of development of MPEG-2 Video, various requirements from typical
applications have been considered and the necessary algorithms have been developed, with integration into a single syntax. Hence, the MPEG-2 Video specification
will facilitate bitstream interchange among different applications.

Considering the practicality of implementing the full syntax of the specification, a
limited number of subsets of the syntax are also stipulated by a "profile" and "level." A
profile is a defined subset of the entire bitstream syntax. Within the bounds imposed by
the syntax of a given profile, it is still possible to have a very large variation in the performance of encoders and decoders depending on the values taken by parameters in the
bitstream. To deal with this problem, levels are defined within each profile. A level is a
defined set of constraints imposed on parameters in the bitstreams. Flags are provided in
the bitstream to indicate the profile and level used by it.

MPEG-4

MPEG-4 aims at providing standardized core technologies allowing efficient storage,
transmission, and manipulation of multimedia data [24].

The major feature of the visual part of MPEG-4 is that it provides tools for decoding
and representing atomic units of image and video content, called "video objects" (VOs).
An example of a VO could be a talking person (without background), which can be composed with other audiovisual objects (AVOs) to create a scene. Conventional rectangular
frames or images are handled as a special case of VOs.

MPEG-4 specifies coding and representation of both synthetic and natural VOs.
Synthetic VOs are treated as computer graphics suitable for rendering and animation. For
natural VOs, the shape or boundary of the object needs to be identified first. The shape
information and texture of the object are then encoded separately. The texture informa-

tion is encoded in the similar way to MPEG-1 video. It should be noted that MPEG-4 does not specify how to determine object boundaries. It is up to the MPEG-4 product developers to develop techniques for object segmentation.

With object-based coding, efficient compression and content-based scalability are possible. MPEG-4 is an important development in audiovisual coding - from pixel based coding to object-based coding. The object-based coding makes content-based indexing and retrieval of multimedia data achievable.

MPEG-7

The new member of the MPEG family, called "multimedia content description interface" (MPEG-7), will specify a standard set of descriptors that can be used to describe various types of multimedia information, to facilitate effective retrieval of multimedia information. MPEG-7 will also standardize ways to define other descriptors as well as structures (description schemes) for the descriptors and their relationships. This description (i.e., the combination of descriptors and description schemes) will be associated with the content itself, to allow fast and efficient searching for material of a user's interest. AV material that has MPEG-7 data associated with it can be indexed and searched. This 'material' may include still pictures, graphics, 3D models, audio, speech, video, and information about how these elements are combined in a multimedia presentation ("scenarios" composition information). Special cases of these general data types may include facial expressions and personal characteristics.

The MPEG-7 standard will build on other (standard) representations such as analog, PCM, MPEG-1, 2 and 4. One functionality of the standard is to provide references to suitable portions of them. For example, perhaps a shape descriptor used in MPEG-4 is useful in an MPEG-7 context as well, and the same may apply to motion vector fields used in MPEG-1 and MPEG-2.

MPEG-7 descriptors will not, however, depend on the ways the described content is coded or stored. It will be possible to attach an MPEG-7 description to an analog movie or to a picture that is printed on paper.

Even though the MPEG-7 description will not depend on the (coded) representation of the material, the standard in a way may build on MPEG-4, which provides the means to encode audiovisual material as objects having certain relations in time (synchronization) and space (on the screen for video, or in the room for audio). Using MPEG-4 encoding, it will be possible to attach descriptions to elements (objects) within the scene, such as audio and visual objects. MPEG-7 will allow different granularity in its descriptions, offering the possibility to have different levels of discrimination.

Because the descriptive features must be meaningful in the context of the application, they will be different for different user domains and different applications. This implies that the same material can be described using different types of features, tuned to the area of application. All these descriptions will be coded in an efficient way – efficient for search, that is.

The level of abstraction is related to the way the features can be extracted. Many low-level features can be extracted in fully automatic ways, whereas high-level features need (much) more human interaction.

MPEG-7 data may be physically located with the associated AV material, in the same data stream or on the same storage system, but the descriptions could also live somewhere else on the globe. When the content and its descriptions are not colocated, mechanisms that link AV material and their MPEG-7 descriptions are useful; these links should work in both directions.

It is important to note that MPEG-7 will standardize the description of multimedia contents and features. But it will not standardize the tools to extract features and the tools that use the description.

The MPEG-7 is expected to become an international standard in November 2001. Detailed information on MPEG development can be found on the MPEG home page [24].

Other Standards

In addition to MPEG, there are other video-related standards such as ITU-T H.261 and H.263. Their compression principle is similar to that of MPEG. They were developed for video conferencing and video telephony.

2.7 STANDARDS FOR COMPOSITE MULTIMEDIA DOCUMENTS

In the previous sections, we discussed individual media types and coding techniques. In this section, we briefly describe a number of standard formats of composite multimedia documents. Only the main concepts and functionality of each standard are mentioned. Detailed treatment of these standards is beyond the scope of this book. One major effect of the standards on multimedia information retrieval is that they provide some structural information that can be used to improve the accuracy of indexing and retrieval.

SGML
SGML is an international standard [28] which enables the description of structured information that is independent of how the information is processed. It provides a standard syntax for defining document type definitions (DTDs) of classes of structured information. Information is "marked up" according to a DTD, so that its structure is made explicit and accessible. The "markup" is checked against a DTD to ensure that it is valid, and that the structure of the information conforms to that of the class described by the DTD. HTML is a class of DTD of SGML. SGML and DTDs don't specify how the document should be handled or formatted, but having made the structure of the document explicit, they make many operations such as formatting, display, and retrieval possible.

ODA
ODA is an international standard that specifies how the logical and layout components of a document may be composed and interrelated. ODA also specifies an interchange format in which the layout and/or logical structures are embedded in a byte stream with the document content. The main purpose of the standard is to facilitate the open interchange of mixed-content documents. The logical and layout information can help in the information retrieval process.

Acrobat Portable Document Format

Adobe, Inc. has introduced a format called Acrobat Portable Document Format (PDF), which is proposed as a potential de facto standard for portable document representations [29]. Based on the Postscript page description language, Acrobat PDF is designed to represent the printed appearance, including logical and formatting structure, of a document that may include graphics and images as well as text. Unlike Postscript, however, Acrobat PDF allows data to be extracted from the document. It is thus a revisable format. Annotations, hypertext links, bookmarks, and structured documents in markup languages such as SGML are supported. Its supported functionality is similar to that of ODA.

Hypermedia/Time-Based Structuring Language (HyTime)

HyTime is an ISO standard for representing hypermedia documents using SGML [30]. HyTime specifies the document structure including the association of document elements with hyperlinks and the interrelation of document elements according to coordinate systems that can represent space, time, or any quantifiable dimension. It does not provide models for interaction and presentation format.

MHEG

MHEG is an ISO standard defining an object-oriented model for multimedia interchange [31, 32]. MHEG specifies a document format used to interchange information between independent systems. A multimedia application or document can be developed on any platform and in any format. Before the document is sent to another system or client it is converted into the MHEG format. At the client, the document in the MHEG format is converted (using an MHEG engine) into the format required by the local system for displaying or processing. In this way, a multimedia application or document can be used by many client systems.

2.8 MAJOR CHARACTERISTICS AND REQUIREMENTS OF MULTIMEDIA DATA AND APPLICATIONS

We have discussed various media types and formats. In this section, we summarize the major characteristics of these media. These characteristics have significant implications for the design of MIRSs and MMDBMSs.

2.8.1 Storage and Bandwidth Requirements

Storage requirement is measured in terms of bytes or megabytes. In the digital domain, bandwidth is measured as bit rate in bits per second (bps) or Megabits per second (Mbps). The base unit for storage is a byte and for bandwidth is a bit.

For images, we measure their storage requirement in terms of bytes or megabytes per image, calculated as shown in Section 2.5.2.

Single images obviously do not have a time dimension. If there is a time limit for each image transmission, however, the bandwidth requirement is calculated based on the storage requirement. In many applications, images must be displayed in synchrony with continuous media such as audio. In such cases, image transmission imposes strict timing and bandwidth requirements.

Both audio and video are time continuous. We normally characterize them in bits per second or Megabits per second. For audio, this number is calculated based on the sampling rate and the number of bits per sample. The bit rate for video is calculated in the same way. But we commonly calculate it from the amount of data in each image (called a frame) and the number of frames per second. The resulting number specifies the bit rate required of the transmission channel. If we want to store or retrieve digital audio and video, this number also specifies the transfer rate required of the storage devices. If we know the duration of the audio or video, the amount of storage required can be calculated.

Table 2.4 presents the bandwidth requirements of continuous media audio and video of different quality without compression. Figure 2.8 shows the storage requirements for common static media and continuous media of different durations. Note that these numbers are rough indications, assuming data is not compressed. Exact storage requirements depend on factors such as image size and color representations.

Table 2.4
Raw Bit Rate of Common Audio and Video Applications

Applications	*Data Rate (kbps)*
CD–Audio	1,411.2
DAT	1,536
Digital telephone	64
Digital radio, long-play DAT	1,024
Television-quality video	216,000
VHS-quality video	54,000
HDTV	864,000

From the above table and Figure 2.8 we see that uncompressed digital audio, image, and video require huge amounts of data for representation and very-high-network bandwidth for transmission. Using these values, we calculate that a hard disk of 1 GB can store only 1.5 hour of CD-audio or 36 seconds of television-quality video. This amount of data would require 800 seconds to be transferred at a disk transfer rate of 10 Mbps. A typical network bit rate is around a few Mbps to a few tens of Mbps and can merely support one television-quality video channel. Compression reduces the amount of data by 10 to 100 times depending on the techniques used and quality required. So even after compression, the storage and bandwidth requirements of multimedia data are still very high. This characteristic has an impact on storage, transmission, and processing.

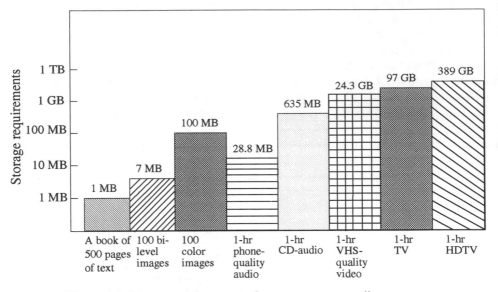

Figure 2.8 Storage requirements of some common media.

2.8.2 Semantic Structure of Multimedia Information

Digital audio, image, and video are just a series of sampled values, with no obvious semantic structure. This is in contrast to alphanumeric information, where each character is uniquely specified and identified by its ASCII code or other similar code. Based on this code, computers can search and retrieve relevant alphanumeric items from a database or document collection.

To facilitate information retrieval, features or contents have to be extracted from raw multimedia data. Thus feature extraction, organization of extracted features and similarity comparison between feature descriptions are major design issues of MIRSs.

2.8.3 Delay and Delay Jitter Requirements

Digital audio and video are time-dependent continuous media. This means that to achieve a reasonable quality playback of audio and video, audio samples and video samples (images) must be received and played back at regular intervals. For example, if an audio piece is sampled at 8 kHz, it must be played back at 8,000 samples per second. As continuous media have this time dimension, their correctness depends not only on the sample values, but also on the time samples play out. This is in contrast to static media, such as computer programs and data files, where correctness solely depends on the contents. Although it is desirable to receive these media as rapidly as possible, they are always correct and useful if their contents are correct.

In addition, MIRSs are interactive systems, requiring delay or system response time to be as short as possible.

2.8.4 Temporal and Spatial Relationships Among Related Media

In multimedia applications, multiple media types—including static and dynamic media—are involved in an application or presentation. To achieve the desired effects, the retrieval and transmission of these related media must be coordinated and presented so that their specified temporal relationships are maintained for presentation. In this context, the correct or desired temporal appearance or presentation of the media items is called *synchronization*. A synchronization scheme defines the mechanisms used to achieve the required degree of synchronization.

Work in multimedia synchronization is taking place in two areas. The first area aims to develop mechanisms and tools to let authors or users specify the required temporal relationships easily. The second area aims to guarantee the specified temporal relationships by overcoming the indeterministic nature of communications systems.

2.8.5 Subjectiveness and Fuzziness of the Meaning of Multimedia Data

In addition to diverse media types and features, multimedia data has another characteristic in that their meanings are subjective and fuzzy, complicating the design of MIRSs.

2.9 SUMMARY

An MIRS has to handle diverse media types and applications with special characteristics and requirements. These characteristics and requirements have major impacts on MIRS design, as briefly discussed below:

1. A proper data model needs to be designed and developed to represent these diverse media types and compositions of them.

2. Features of multiple abstraction levels need to be extracted and represented for indexing and retrieval.

3. It is required that multimedia data be compressed; it is also desirable that feature extraction, indexing and retrieval can be carried out on compressed data [36]. The compression schemes should also support flexible transmission, presentation, and browsing. JPEG 2000, MPEG 4, and MPEG 7 are standards moving in this direction.

4. Processors, networks and storage and associated software should not only have large capacities, but also provide quality of service guarantees to multimedia retrieval and presentations.

5. The user interface should be flexible and user-friendly, capable of handling diverse types of queries.

We discuss these issues and others in the subsequent chapters.

PROBLEMS

Problem 2.1

How is plain text normally represented? Explain how textual information can be identified and retrieved.

Problem 2.2

Explain the basic principle of Huffman coding.

Problem 2.3

Define audio and describe its main characteristics.

Problem 2.4

For a certain audio application, the required audio quality in terms of the SNR is 54 dB. How many bits are required to represent each audio sample to provide the required audio quality?

Problem 2.5

For CD-quality audio, we need to capture all audible sound and achieve an SNR of 96 dB. It has two channels to provide a stereo effect. List and explain the required sampling rate, the number of bits per sample, and the bit rate. If we need to store 2 hours of such audio, determine the storage requirement.

Problem 2.6

During the conversion of analog video into digital video, how are the sampling rate and quantization levels determined?

Problem 2.7

Contrast sample-based music and MIDI music in terms of their storage, indexing, and retrieval requirements.

Problem 2.8

Describe the principle of predictive compression techniques.

Problem 2.9

Explain the MPEG-Audio compression principle.

Problem 2.10

How are uncompressed digital audio, digital image, and digital video represented and stored?

Problem 2.11

Calculate the amount of data storage required for an image of 800 lines by 800 pixels with 24 bits per pixel.

Problem 2.12

Explain the basic principle of DCT-based image compression.

Problem 2.13

What is vector quantization? How does vector quantization achieve data compression?

Problem 2.14

Summarize the JPEG baseline compression process.

Problem 2.15

What are main capabilities of the proposed JPEG 2000? How do these features impact on MIRS design?

Problem 2.16

Describe the MPEG-1 video compression process. What are the main differences between JPEG and MPEG-1 video in terms of compression techniques?

Problem 2.17

What are main differences between MPEG-4 and MPEG-1 and 2? Why is MPEG-4 more suitable for multimedia indexing and retrieval?

Problem 2.18

Why was MPEG-7 proposed? What are the main purposes of MPEG-7?

Problem 2.19

Summarize the main characteristics and requirements of multimedia data and applications. Explain the implication of these characteristics and requirements on MIRS design.

FURTHER READING

The discussion on various topics has been brief in this chapter. Here we provide some pointers to further reading on digital media, compression techniques, and multimedia standards.

A good source on digital media is [33] which covers digital audio and video plus basic compression techniques. Sayood [34] provides a good coverage on data compression. The major multimedia compression standards are JPEG and MPEG. Good sources of JPEG are JPEG-faq (frequent asked questions) [35] and a book by Pennebaker and Mitchell [3]. Detailed information about MPEG can be found at its home page [24]. A comprehensive source is Rao and Hwang [39] which covers image, video, and audio compression techniques and standards.

REFERENCES

[1] Lu, G., *Communication and Computing for Distributed Multimedia Systems*, Norwood, MA: Artech House, 1996.

[2] Held, G., *Data Compression, 3rd ed.*, John Wiley & Sons, Ltd., 1991.

[3] Pennebaker, W. B. and J. L. Mitchell, *JPEG Still Image Data Compression Standard*, New York: Van Nostrand Reinhold, 1993.

[4] Pohlmann, K. C., *Principles of Digital Audio, Second Edition*, Howard W. Sams & Company, 1989.

[5] Buford, J. F. K., (contributing editor), *Multimedia Systems*, ACM Press, 1994.

[6] Loy, G., "Musicians Make a Standard: The MIDI Phenomenon," *Computer Music Journal*, Vol. 9, No.4, 1995, pp. 8-26.

[7] Bellamy, J., *Digital Telephony, 2nd ed.*, New York: John Wiley & Sons, Ltd., 1991.

[8] Pan, D., "A Tutorial on MPEG/Audio Compression," *IEEE Multimedia*, Vol. 2, No. 2, pp. 60–74, Summer 1995.

[9] ISO/IEC International Standard IS 11172, *Information Technology—Coding of Moving Pictures and Associated Digital Storage Media at Up to About 1.5 Mbits/s*, 1993.

[10] Clarke, R. J., *Transform Coding of Image*, Academic Press, 1984.

[11] Jain, A. K., P. M. Farrelle, and V. R. Algazi, "Image Data Compression," *Digital Image Processing Techniques*, (ed. M P Ekstrom), Academic Press Inc., pp. 172–226, 1984.

[12] Abut, H. (ed.), *Vector Quantization*, IEEE Press, 1990.

[13] Barnsley, M. F. and A. D. Sloan, " A Better Way to Compress Images," *Byte*, Jan. 1988, pp. 215-222.

[14] Jacquin, A. E., "A Novel Fractal Block-Coding Technique for Digital Images," *Proc. ICASSP*, 1990.

[15] Lu, G., "Fractal image compression," *Signal Processing: Image Communication*, Vol. 4, No. 4, pp. 327–343, Oct. 1993.

[16] Pennebaker, W. B., and J. L. Mitchell, *JPEG Still Image Data Compression Standard*, New York: Van Nostrand Reinhold, 1993.

[17] Wallace, G. K., "The JPEG Still Picture Compression Standard," *Communications of the ACM*, Vol. 34, No. 4, pp. 31–44, April 1991.

[18] Furht, B., "Survey of Multimedia Compression Techniques and Standards, Part 1: JPEG Standard," *Real-Time Imaging*, Vol. 1 No. 1, pp. 49–68, April 1995.

[19] Bryan, M., "Multimedia and Hypermedia Standard Activities", Available at: http://www2.echo.lu/oii/en/oiiaug96.html#JPEG2000

[20] Inglis, A. F., *Video Engineering*, McGraw-Hill, Inc., 1993.

[21] Jain, J. R., and A. K. Jain, "Displacement Measurement and its Application in Interframe Image Coding," *IEEE Trans. Comm.* COM-29, pp. 1799–1808, Dec. 1981.

[22] Netravali, A. N., and J. D. Robbins, "Motion Compensated Television Coding, Part-I," *Bell Systems Tech. J.* Vol. 58, No. 3, pp. 631–670, Mar. 1979.

[23] Musmann, H. G., P. Pirsch, and H. J. Grallert, "Advances in Picture Coding," *Proceedings of the IEEE*, Vol. 73, No. 4, April 1985.

[24] MPEG Home Page, http://drogo.cselt.stet.it/mpeg/

[25] ISO/IEC JTC1/SC29/WG11, *Generic Coding of Moving Pictures and Associated Audio: Systems*, International Standard, ISO/IEC 13818-1, Nov. 1994

[26] ISO/IEC JTC1/SC29/WG11, *Generic Coding of Moving Pictures and Associated Audio: Video*, Draft International Standard, ISO/IEC 13818-2, Nov. 1994

[27] ISO/IEC JTC1/SC29/WG11, *Generic Coding of Moving Pictures and Associated Audio: Audio*, International Standard, ISO/IEC 13818-3, Nov. 1994

[28] SoftQuad Inc., http://www.ncsa.uiuc.edu/SDG/Software/Mosaic/WebSGML.html

[29] Adobe Systems Inc., http://www.adobe.com/prodindex/acrobat/download.html

[30] Newcomb, S., N. Kipp, and V. Newcomp, "The HYTIME, Hypermedia Time based Document Structuring Language," *Communications of ACM*, Vol. 34, No. 11, 1991, pp. 67-83.

[31] Hofrichter, K., "MHEG 5 - Standardized Presentation Objects for the Set Top Unit Environment," Proceedings of European Workshop on Interactive Distributed Multimedia Systems and Services, Berlin, Germany, March 1996. Also published as *Lecture Notes in Computer Science*, Vol. 1045, Berthold Butscher, Eckhard Moeller and Herwart Pusch (eds.), Springer 96.

[32] MHEG-5 User Group, http://www.fokus.gmd.de/ovma/mug/

[33] Luther, A. C., *Principles of Digital Audio and Video*, Norwood, MA: Artech House 1997.

[34] Sayood, K., *Introduction to Data Compression*, Morgan Kaufmann Publishers, Inc., 1996.

[35] JPEG FAQ, http://www.cis.ohio-state.edu/hypertext/faq/usenet/jpeg-faq/top.html

[36] Lippman, A., and W. Butera, "Coding Image Sequence for Interactive Retrieval," *Communications of the ACM*, Vol. 32, No.7, pp. 852–860, July 1989.

[37] Mallat, S. G., "Multifrequency Channel Decompositions of Images and Wavelet Models," *IEEE Transactions on Acoustics, Speech, and Signal Processing*, Vol. 37, No. 12, pp. 2,094–2110, Dec. 1989.

[38] Polikar, R., *The Wavelet Tutorial*, http://www.public.iastate.edu/~rpolikar/WAVELETS/WTtutorial.html.

[39] Rao, K. R. and J. J. Hwang, *Techniques and Standards for Image, Video and Audio Coding*, Prentice Hall, 1997.

Chapter 3

Multimedia Database Design Issues

3.1 INTRODUCTION

In Chapters 1 and 2 we described why DBMSs cannot handle multimedia information effectively, the expected applications of MIRSs, and characteristics and requirements of data to be handled by MIRSs. This chapter describes design issues and requirements of MIRSs to meet application characteristics and requirements.

Section 3.2 gives an overview of a modular MIRS architecture. The main modules of an MIRS are the user interface, feature extractor, communication manager, indexing and search engine, and storage manager. The functions of these modules are explained by describing two main types of MIRS operations: database item insertion and retrieval.

The data model of an MIRS affects all aspects of MIRS design and operation. It determines how information is organized and stored, and what types of queries are supported. Section 3.3 describes the MIRS data model requirements, a general multimedia data model hierarchy, and a number of specific data models. It is assumed that the reader has basic knowledge of OO design. If the reader is not familiar with this, a number of references on OO design and programming are listed in the "Further Reading" section at the end of this chapter.

The user interface provides tools for the user to insert database items and issue queries, and presents the query results to the user. The user interface design is complicated by the diversity of media and features and fuzziness of meanings of multimedia data. Section 3.4 examines user interface design issues.

In MIRSs, features and attributes of multimedia data items are extracted and stored with the data items themselves. These features are organized using certain index structures for efficient retrieval. Retrieval is based on similarity measures between the query features and features of data items. Section 3.5 discusses issues and requirements of feature extraction, indexing, and similarity measures.

Multimedia retrieval and presentation should meet certain spatial and temporal constraints. These constraints are specified as quality of service (QoS) requirements of the multimedia objects or applications. Section 3.6 introduces the QoS concept and describes how QoS can be guaranteed in general. QoS guarantee is a systemwide issue. All subsystems, including operating systems, communication systems, and storage manager should work together to achieve the desired QoS.

Section 3.7 discusses other issues including data compression, data representation standardization, and query processing and retrieval. Section 3.8 summarizes the chapter.

3.2 MIRS ARCHITECTURE

MIRS architecture should be flexible and extensible to support diverse applications, query types, and contents (features). To meet these requirements, common MIRSs consist of a number of functional modules (library functions) or managers [1]. New managers can be added to extend the functionality of an MIRS. Existing managers can be deleted or replaced by new ones to update the functionality.

Another characteristic of MIRSs is that they are normally distributed, consisting of a number of servers and clients. This characteristic results from the large size of multimedia data (the duplication of databases for each user cannot be afforded) and the way multimedia information is used (it is often accessed by many users, such as in a digital library or a video-on-demand system).

Figure 3.1 shows the basic architecture of an MIRS. The major functional blocks are the user interface, feature extractor, communication managers (one in each of the clients and servers), indexing and searching engine, and storage manager. The main functions of

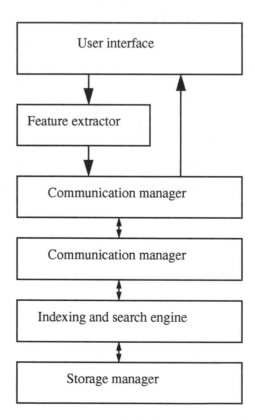

Figure 3.1 Architecture of an MIRS.

these managers or agents can be described through the operation scenario of an MIRS. Two major operations (phases) of an MIRS are insertion of new multimedia items and retrieval. During an insertion, the user specifies one or a group of multimedia items through the user interface. These items are stored files or input from other devices such as a microphone, a CD player, a VCR, or a video camera. The user can also draw an item as input. The contents or features of multimedia items are extracted either automatically or semiautomatically through the tools provided in the feature extractor. These features and the original items are sent to the server or servers via the communication managers. At the server(s), the features are organized (or inserted) according to a certain indexing scheme for efficient retrieval through the indexing and retrieval engine. The indexing information and the original items are stored appropriately via the storage manager.

During information retrieval, the user issues or specifies a query via the user interface. The query can be a file stored on local disk, or entered via input devices (including keyboard and mouse). The user interface also allows the user to browse through the items in the database and to use one of the browsed items as the query. If the query is not one of the items in the database, the main features of the query are extracted in the same way as item insertion. These features are passed to the server(s) through the communication managers. The indexing and search engine searches the database to find the items in the database that best match the query features. These items are retrieved by means of the storage manager and passed to the user interface by the communication managers. The user interface displays the list of items to the user.

The architecture shown in Figure 3.1 is the most basic one. Other functional blocks or managers may be needed in practice [1]. Other major managers and their functions are as follows:

- Thesaurus manager: keeps synonymous and other relations between information items;

- Integrity rule base: checks the integrity of a given application;

- Context manager: keeps the context of the application.

In the subsequent sections, we discuss major design issues for MIRSs including data modeling, user interface, feature extraction, indexing, QoS guarantees in communication, client and server, and storage manager.

3.3 DATA MODELS

3.3.1 Data Model Requirements

The role of a data model in DBMSs is to provide a framework (or language) to express the properties of the data items that are to be stored and retrieved using the system. The framework should allow designers and users to define, insert, delete, modify, and search database items and properties. In MIRSs and MMDBMSs, the data model assumes the additional role of specifying and computing different levels of abstraction from multimedia data.

Multimedia data models capture the static and dynamic properties of the database items, and thus provide a formal basis for developing the appropriate tools needed in using the multimedia data. The static properties could include the objects that make up the multimedia data, the relationships between the objects, and the object attributes. Examples of dynamic properties include those related to interaction between objects, operations on objects, user interaction, and so forth.

The richness of the data model plays a key role in the usability of the MIRS. Although the basic multimedia data types must be supported, they only provide the foundation on which to build additional features.

Multidimensional feature spaces are a characteristic of multimedia indexing. A data model should support the representation of these multidimensional spaces, especially the measures of distance in such a space.

In summary, an MIRS data model should meet the following main requirements:

1. The data model should be extensible, so that new data types can be added.
2. The data model should be able to represent basic media types and composite objects with complicated spatial and temporal relationships.
3. The data model should be flexible so that items can be specified, queried, and searched at different levels of abstraction.
4. The data model should allow efficient storage and search.

3.3.2 A General Multimedia Data Model

There is a general consensus that the MIRS data model should be based on OO principle and multilayer hierarchy [1–7]. OO design encapsulates code and data into a single unit called an object. The code defines the operations that can be performed on the data. The encapsulation promotes modularity and hides details of particular media and processing. More importantly, the OO approach provides extensibility by offering mechanisms for enhancing and extending existing objects.

A general MIRS data model is shown in Figure 3.2.

Object Layer

An object consists of one or more media items with specified spatial and temporal relationships. It is normally about only one central topic. An example of a multimedia object is a slide show (say introducing a tourist attraction) consisting of a number of images and accompanying audio.

The key issues are how to specify spatial and temporal relationships. Spatial relationships are specified by the displaying window size and position for each item. The common method for temporal specification is timeline-based specification in which the starting time and duration of each item are specified based on a common clock [8, 9]. Other methods include scrips and event-driven models [10, 11]. During presentation, the semantics of an object is maintained only when spatial and temporal relationships are maintained.

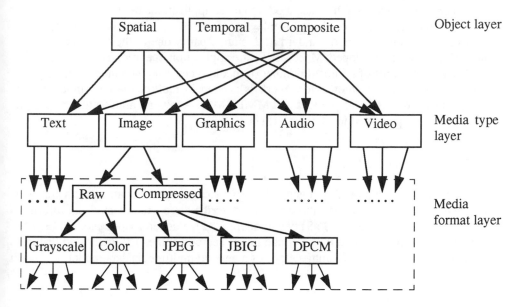

Figure 3.2 A general multimedia data model.

Media Type Layer

The media type layer contains common media types such as text, graphics, image, audio, and video. These media types are derived from a common abstract media class.

At this level, features or attributes are specified. Taking media type image as an example, the image size, color histogram, main objects contained, and so on are specified. These features are used directly for searching and distance calculations.

Media Format Layer

The media format layer specifies the media formats in which the data is stored. A media type normally has many possible formats. For example, an image can be in raw bit-mapped or compressed formats. There are also many different compression techniques and standards. The information contained in this layer is used for proper decoding, analysis and presentation.

Remaining Issues

Note that different applications may need different data models, due to the fact that different features and objects are used in different applications. But many applications can share a common base model if it is properly designed and new features and objects can be added on or derived from this base model to meet applications requirements.

At the moment, each of the above layers of the data model is not completely designed. There is no common standard in this area, partly due to the fact that no large scale MIRS has been developed. Most MIRSs are application-specific, focusing on a limited number of features of a limited number of media types. The data models, if any, are designed in an ad hoc fashion. More work is needed in multimedia data modeling to develop consistent large scale MIRSs and MMDBMSs. A general architecture or design of MMDBMSs is presented in Chapter 8 (Section 8.3).

3.3.3 Example Data Models

The model shown in Figure 3.2 is a general one. Currently, specific data models are used in different applications. In this subsection, we describe three examples: visual information management system (VIMSYS) data model [4, 12], a general video model [13, 14], and the schema structure used in the virage image search engine [15]. Ideas and features of these models are used in defining details of a general multimedia data model.

VIMSYS Data Model

The VIMSYS model is proposed specifically to manage visual information (images and video) [4, 12]. It consists of four layers (Figure 3.3): the representation layer, the image object layer, the domain object layer and the domain event layer. All objects in each layer have a set of attributes and methods.

Image representation layer
The representation layer contains image data and any transformation that results in an alternate image representation. Examples of transformations are compression, color space conversion, and image enhancement.

This layer is not very powerful at processing user queries; it can only handle queries that request pixel-based information. However, this layer provides the raw data for upper layers to extract and define higher level features.

Image object layer
The image object layer has two sublayers: the segmentation sublayer and the feature sublayer. The segmentation sublayer condenses information about an entire image or video into spatial or temporal clusters of summarized properties. These localized properties can be searched for directly. This sublayer relies heavily on image and video segmentation techniques.

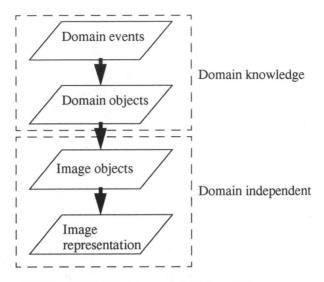

Figure 3.3 The VIMSYS data model. (After: [4]).

The feature sublayer contains features that are efficient to compute, organizable in a data structure, and amenable to a numeric distance computation to produce a ranking score. The common features are color distribution (histogram), object shape, and texture.

Domain object layer
A domain object is a user-defined entity representing a physical entity or a concept that is derived from one or more features in the lower layers. Examples of domain objects are "sunset" (a concept) and "heart" (a physical object). Domain knowledge is needed to derive domain objects.

Domain event layer
The domain event layer defines events that can be queried by the user. Events are defined based on motion (velocity of object movement), spatial and/or temporal relationships between objects, appearance and disappearance of an object, and so on. Event detection and organization mechanisms are needed to implement this layer.

A General Video Model

A commonly used video model consists of four levels: frame, shot, scene (or sequence), and episode (video document) [13, 14], as shown in Figure 3.4. A frame is an individual image in a video. A shot is a set of frames recorded by a camera in a single shooting. A scene is a set of shots with common semantics. An episode is a set of scenes in a specific sequence. It is a production unit, such as a television news program.

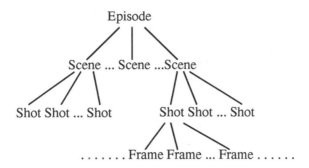

Figure 3.4 A general video model.

Attributes can be attached to each of these video levels. At the episode level, we can assign factual data such as title, author and creation date, and information related to the type of video such as a news program. A scene contains the common semantics shared among its shots. Shots are characterized by their key (representative) frames and other data such as main objects and shot date and location. Individual frames contain raw image data as well as image statistics such as color distribution.

Virage Image Schema Structure

The Virage image search engine provides an open framework for building content-based image retrieval systems [15]. The Virage engine schema structure consists of three levels: schema, primitives, and data types.

Note that a content-based information retrieval system creates an abstraction of the raw information in the form of features, and then operates only on these features. In image retrieval systems, five abstract data types are identified: values, distributions, indexed values, indexed distributions, and graphs. A value is a set of vectors that represent some global property of the image such as dominant colors. A distribution represents the statistic property of the image such as color distribution (histogram). An indexed value is a value local to a region of an image and is represented as an indexed set of vectors. An indexed distribution is a local pattern or distribution such as the intensity profile of a region of interest. A graph represents relational information such as the relative spatial position of two regions of interest in an image, and can be implemented in terms of the other four data types. Therefore, vectors form a uniform base type for features representing image content. The primary data type in the Virage engine is a collection of vectors. The main operations on this abstract data type are:

- Create collection: creates an empty collection of vectors;
- Create vector: extracts and creates a specific feature vector from the specified image using a specified feature extraction function;
- Extract: accesses an element of the collection;
- Distance: compares two vectors and returns a measure of distance between them

based on a specified distance function for the type of vector;
- Combine: creates a new vector by combining two given vectors;
- Delete vector: frees the memory associated with a particular vector;
- Delete collection: deletes the collection from memory.

The next level in the schema structure of the Virage engine is primitives. A primitive is defined as a collection of vectors representing a single category of image information. Thus a primitive is a semantically meaningful feature of an image, such as color, texture, and shape. A primitive is specified by its unique primitive identifier, a category name, and data retrieval and management functions.

At the highest level of the schema structure is a schema that is defined by a schema identifier and an ordered set of primitives. An application defines and use multiple schemas. At this level, functions for image insertion and content-based retrieval are provided.

3.4 USER INTERFACE DESIGN

The user uses, communicates, and interacts with the MIRS through the user interface. The user interface, therefore, to a large extent determines the usability of the MIRS. The main functions of the user interface are to allow the user to insert items into database and to enter queries, and to present to the user responses to queries. Thus a good user interface should meet the following requirements:
1. Provide tools for users to insert database items easily;
2. Provide tools for users to effectively and efficiently enter queries or inform the system their information needs;
3. Present query results to the user effectively and efficiently;
4. Be user-friendly.

There are many issues in meeting the first three requirements due to the characteristics of multimedia data and applications. In the following three subsections, we discuss these issues.

3.4.1 Database Population

In traditional DBMSs, each record has a fixed structure with a fixed number of attributes. Each record is inserted into the database manually by specifying these attributes using a language such as SQL. In MIRSs or MMDBMSs, database items can be in any media types and combinations of many media types. They don't have fixed structure and attributes. Therefore, the user interface should allow the user to specify various types of input, compose multimedia objects, and specify attribute types to be extracted and indexed. The general user interface requirements for insertion are similar to those of query by example discussed in the next subsection.

Multimedia information processing and feature extraction are computationally intensive and can take from a few seconds for a simple object to a few hours for a complicated object like a movie. Thus it is desirable to be able to specify operations on a group of objects. This is only possible when the feature extraction is fully automated.

3.4.2 Query Support

Multimedia queries are diverse and fuzzy. They are diverse because the user can specify queries in many different ways and in different media types. They are fuzzy because users may know what they are looking for but cannot describe it exactly, or their information needs are not exactly defined (they recognize items they want when they see them). To meet the requirements of these characteristics, tools for searching, browsing, and query refinement should be provided.

Search

Search is the basic task of all database management systems. In the context of MIRSs, there are two types of search: search by specification and search by example. In search by specification, users normally use a number of key words and parameters to describe the main features or attributes of their information needs. The first three query types discussed in Chapter 1 can be implemented using this search strategy.

A difficult issue is how to map the users' high-level description in natural language into actual multimedia data patterns that are measurable. For example, the user may specify the query as "red car." Assume that the images in the database are not fully annotated but the system keeps color histograms and shapes of objects of images. The questions are: what pixel value or value range should be used to describe "red," and what shape should be used to describe "a car"? To make such searches effective, the system through the user interface should provide detailed guidelines on query specifications.

The above mapping problem can be alleviated by providing search by example. In search by example, the user interface allows the user to specify a query in different media types or a combination of different media. The query becomes an example object and the system is asked to search for items that are similar to the example object. In the above example, the user would draw a shape like a car and paint it with the required color. The system would then compute the color histogram and shape parameters of the query and search for items with similar color histogram and shape parameters. To support this type of query, the user interface should provide a variety of input tools such as a microphone, graphics tool, video camera, scanner, and multimedia authoring tools. The user should also be able to use the existing items in the database as queries. This would be supported by the browsing capability.

Browsing

Sometimes users do not know exactly what they want but can recognize what they what when they see it. This type of information need can be met by browsing. Browsing also supports the search-by-example capability. There are three methods used to initiate browsing. The first method is to start with a very vague query and then the user can navigate through the items based on the results. The second method requires that the information in the database be organized according to some criteria (such as date and topic) so that the user can browse based on this organization. In the third method, a number of items randomly chosen from the database are presented and the user can use them as the starting point for browsing. If the user does not find any interesting items to follow, the user can request that another set of random items be presented.

To effectively support browsing, information items should be properly organized and some small representative "icons" for information items (instead of the items themselves) should be constructed and displayed in the browsing mode. For images, we use thumbnail images. For video, we can use a representative frame or 3D movie icons that shows both spatial and temporal content of the movie [16, 17]. The representation and transmission issues for browsing are similar to those of "Result Presentation" Section to be discussed.

Effective hyperlinks help users in browsing. In fact, most users heavily rely on browsing and navigation through hyperlinks to locate useful information in environment such as the World Wide Web (WWW).

Query refinement

Most initial multimedia queries are fuzzy or not exact. The user interface should provide tools for users to refine their queries based on the results of the initial query. Query refinement is normally done based on users' feedback on the relevance of the initial results. When the users see an item close to what they are looking for they can incorporate features of that item into their new query. After a few iterations, it is likely that users will find relevant items if they do exist in the database. Domain knowledge and user profile can be used to help query refinement.

Relevance feedback is especially useful in multimedia applications, as the users can tell if an image or audio segment is relevant to their needs almost instantly.

In practice, locating multimedia information is a combination of search, browsing, and query refinement.

3.4.3 Result Presentation

An MIRS presents query results to the user through the user interface. There are many design issues in result presentation. First, the user interface should be able to present all media types and maintain their spatial and temporal relationships. Maintaining the spatial and temporal relationships is mainly an issue of QoS guarantee, which is discussed in Section 3.6 and Chapter 10.

Second, the result information may be contained in many long audio segments, large images, or long videos. The issue is how to extract (construct) and present essential information for users to browse and select. In other words, techniques are required to construct an information landscape (or structure) so that the user can tell very quickly what is available. Thumbnail images and movie icons as mentioned previously are important tools.

Third, the system response time should be short. The response time is determined by both the communication subsystem and database search efficiency. One technique to shorten the perceived response time is progressive decoding and display where data is decoded and displayed while it is received progressively rather than decoded and displayed only when all data has been received [18].

Fourth, the result presentation should facilitate relevance feedback and query refinement as the result may not be final, as discussed earlier.

3.5 FEATURE EXTRACTION, INDEXING, AND SIMILARITY MEASURE

As mentioned previously, features and attributes of information items in the MRIS are extracted, parametrized, and stored together with items themselves. Features and attributes of queries are also extracted in a similar way if they are not explicitly specified. The system searches the database for items with similar features and attributes based on certain similarity metrics. To expedite the search process, the features and attributes are organized into a certain indexing structure. In this section, we discuss the main issues and requirements in feature extraction, indexing, and similarity measurement. The details on feature extraction for individual media types, indexing structure, and similarity measurement will be covered in Chapters 4, 5, 6, 7, 8, and 11.

3.5.1 Feature Extraction

Multimedia information items in the database are normally preprocessed to extract features and attributes. During the retrieval process, these features and attributes are searched and compared instead of the information items themselves. Therefore the quality of feature extraction determines the retrieval effectiveness; if a feature is not extracted from an item, that item will not be retrieved for the queries specifying that feature. This is one of the main differences between DBMSs and MIRSs. In DBMSs, all attributes are given and complete, while in MRISs, features and attributes are extracted based on expected query types and are normally not complete.

Feature extraction should meet the following requirements:
1. Features and attributes extracted should be as complete as possible to represent the contents of the information items.
2. The features should be represented and stored compactly. Complicated and large features will defeat the purpose of feature extraction; it would be faster to search and compare information items themselves.
3. The computation of distance between features should be efficient, otherwise the system response time would be too long.

Generally, there are four levels of features and attributes: metadata, text annotation, low-level content features, and high-level content features. Metadatas include the formal or factual attributes of multimedia objects such as author name, creation date, and title of the object. Note that metadata does not describe or interpret the content of the object. These attributes are handled using DBMS techniques. Note also that some of the literature uses metadata to refer to features of all four levels [3].

Text annotation is the text description of object content. The annotation can be in the form of a number of keywords or a long free-text description. Indexing and retrieval based on text annotation can be handled by IR techniques discussed in the next chapter. Although text annotation has the limitations of subjectiveness and incompleteness, it is still a powerful and commonly used method. We should use text annotation together with other features in multimedia applications. Its limitations can be partially overcome by using relevance feedback to refine the text annotation. At the moment, text annotation is a tedious manual process. Semiautomatic and efficient tools should be developed to help this process. Domain knowledge and a thesaurus are useful in achieving high IR performance.

The low-level content features capture data patterns and statistics of a multimedia object, and possibly spatial and temporal relations between parts of the object. Different media have different low-level content features. In audio, low-level features include average loudness, frequency distribution, and silence ratio. Image low-level features include color distributions, texture, object shapes and spatial structure. Video low-level features include temporal structure as well as those of images. We discuss details of audio, image, and video feature extraction and retrieval in Chapters 5, 6, and 7, respectively. The main advantage of using low-level features is that they can be extracted automatically.

High-level feature extraction attempts to recognize and understand objects. Except for text and speech recognition, it is generally difficult to recognize and understand audio pieces and visual objects. But any breakthrough will be a great help to multimedia information indexing and retrieval. In specific applications where the number of objects is limited, it is useful and may be possible to describe and recognize common objects. For example, it is estimated that in over 95% of all video the primary camera subject is a human or a group of humans [19]. It would be very useful for systems to recognize and interpret humans. Initially, the recognition and interpretation process may be semiautomatic.

Retrieval based on the last two types of features is called content-based retrieval. A system should use all four levels of features so that flexible user queries can be supported. These features complement each other and make the object description more complete. For example, text annotation is good at capturing abstract concepts such as feelings (happy, sad, etc.) but is not capable of describing complicated data patterns such as irregular shapes and textures. On the other hand, low-level content features can capture these data patterns but cannot describe abstract concepts.

When a multimedia object has multiple media types, the relationships and interactions between these media should be used to help feature extraction, interpretation, and retrieval. Some media types are easier to understand and interpret than others and we can use the understanding of one or more media types to help understand and extract feature from other media types. For example, if a multimedia object consists of a video stream and a speech track, we can apply speech recognition to gain knowledge about the object and use this knowledge to segment and extract features and objects from the video stream.

Note that MPEG-7, discussed in the previous chapter, will standardize the descriptions of features, but will not specify how these features can be extracted.

3.5.2 Indexing Structure

After feature extraction, we need to use indexing structures to organize these features so that retrieval is efficient. As we have seen, many features are required to represent an object and each feature may need multiple parameters to represent. For example, color distribution is normally represented by a histogram with many color bins. The indexing structures used in DBMS are not suitable for content-based features.

Indexing in MIRSs should be hierarchical and take place at multiple levels. The highest level may be the application classification. The second indexing level may be on the different levels of features as discussed in the previous subsection. Different indexing may be needed for different features. The third indexing level may be on spatial and temporal relationships between objects. We discuss details of indexing issues in Chapter 9.

3.5.3 Similarity Measurement

Multimedia retrieval is based on similarity instead of exact match between queries and database items. The similarity is calculated based on extracted features and attributes and is in a form of one or more values. However, the relevance of retrieval results are judged by human beings. Therefore the main requirement of similarity measurement is that the calculated similarity values should conform to human judgment. Types of features used to describe the objects also play an important role in meeting this requirement. Similarity measurement is also complicated by the fact that the human judgment is subjective and context dependent. All these factors make retrieval evaluation complicated and important. We discuss retrieval performance measurement in Chapter 11.

3.6 QoS GUARANTEES IN CLIENTS, SERVERS, AND COMMUNICATION SYSTEMS

MIRSs are normally distributed. Multimedia objects are retrieved from servers and transported to the client for presentation. As discussed earlier, multimedia data imposes diverse and stringent requirements on multimedia systems. They require high bandwidth, large storage space and high transfer rate, delay and jitter bound, and temporal and spatial synchronization. Different media and applications have different requirements. These requirements have to be satisfied for the entire communication or presentation session across the entire system.

To provide a uniform framework to specify and guarantee these diverse requirements, QoS has been introduced [20, 21]. QoS is a set of requirement parameters. There is no universally agreed set of parameters. But common requirement parameters encompass the requirements mentioned above, including bandwidth (transfer rate), delay and jitter bound, and synchronization requirements. These parameters are normally specified in two grades: the preferable quality and the acceptable quality.

QoS is a contract negotiated and agreed among multimedia applications and the multimedia system (service provider). When an application needs to start a session, it submits a request with the required QoS to the system. The system will either reject or accept the request, possibly with some negotiation to lower the application requirements. When the system accepts the request, a contract between the system and application is signed and the system must provide the required QoS. This guarantee can be in one of three forms: a hard or deterministic guarantee, a soft or statistical guarantee, and best effort. In a deterministic guarantee, the required QoS is satisfied fully. A statistical guarantee provides a guarantee with a certain probability of p. In the best effort policy, there is no guarantee at all; the application is executed for as long as it takes. This is the traditional system-sharing policy.

The guarantee must be end-to-end or system-wide. A typical multimedia system consists of three major components: hosts (including clients and servers) under the control of the operating system, the storage manager, and the transport or communications system. The transport system includes the transport protocol and the underlying network architecture.

QoS can only be guaranteed when the required system resources are properly managed. System resources include CPU cycles, memory, bandwidth, and so forth. Each system component should have a resource manager, which monitors the current usage of resources and the resources available. When it receives a new session request, it will carry out an *admission test*. If available resources are sufficient to support the new request and admission of the new session does not interfere with existing sessions, the new session will be admitted. Otherwise, a new set of QoS parameters may be suggested to the application based on the available resources. If the suggestion is acceptable to the application, the new session is started. In all other cases, the new session is rejected.

QoS research is still very new and many research issues remain. Examples of these issues are: how to convert QoS parameters into resource requirements and how to schedule sessions so that more sessions can be supported given a fixed amount of resources. In essence, multimedia communication is about guaranteeing QoS of multimedia applications while using system resources efficiently.

In Chapter 10, we discuss QoS guarantees in key subsystems of MIRSs, including the operating system, networking, and storage servers.

3.7 OTHER ISSUES

We discussed several main design issues of MIRSs in the previous sections. In this section we briefly describe issues related to data compression, multimedia data representation standardization, and query processing and retrieval.

3.7.1 Multimedia Data Compression

The main aim of multimedia data compression has been to compress data as much as possible without considering retrieval and presentation aspects. Most audio, image, and video files are compressed using certain techniques and standards. In order to extract features from these files, they must be decompressed first. This approach is computationally inefficient as compression and decompression may need to be done several times in the feature extraction process, and inefficient in storage as compressed files and features extracted are stored separately. Therefore, there is a need for compression techniques that allow feature extraction directly from compressed data and in which compression is based on objects rather than individual sample values. There have been attempts to perform image index and retrieval from DCT, vector quantization, and wavelet compressed data [22–25]. But the results are not very promising. Ultimately, if we can effectively convert bitmapped images (graphics) into vector graphics, we achieve both a high compression ratio and easy retrieval. Model based image and video compression is a step in this direction [26, 27]. MPEG-4 and JPEG 2000, discussed in Chapter 2, are standardization efforts in combining compression and retrieval.

Another aspect of data compression we should consider is suitability for transmission and presentation. In many applications, a number of thumbnail images are first displayed on a screen or in a window for the user to browse. If the user is interested in a particular image, he/she selects the image and a higher resolution version of the image is retrieved and displayed. Conventionally, we can realize this type of application in the following two methods.

In the first method, images of different sizes derived from the same image are created, sequentially compressed, and stored in the server independently. Images of the requested sizes are sent to the client for display. For example, thumbnail image data is transmitted for the initial display (browsing), and full-size image data is sent upon subsequent requests.

In the second method, images are sequentially compressed and stored in their original size only. Upon request, full-size image data is transmitted to the client regardless of the client requirement. In most cases the client will reduce the transmitted image data to a smaller size for the initial display. If the user wishes to view the full size of selected image(s), full-size image data is transmitted again.

These two methods are not efficient in terms of the usage of storage space and network bandwidth. In the first method, some storage space is wasted because images of different sizes derived from the same image are highly correlated. Some network bandwidth is also wasted because the server has to send data corresponding to a complete image even when the client already has the data corresponding to a smaller version of the image. In the second method, usage of storage space is efficient as only one version of each image is stored. However, a significant amount of network bandwidth is wasted because the server has to send the full-size image data although the client may just need a thumbnail image. Transmitting the full-size image data also causes extra transmission delay.

To solve the above problems, scalable, progressive and/or hierarchical compression techniques, such as specified in JPEG and MPEG-4 should be used [18, 28, 29]. They not only save storage space and network bandwidth, but also improve response time as images are transmitted, decoded, and displayed progressively, instead of being decoded and displayed only when all data is available.

3.7.2 Data Representation Standardization

In the feature extraction and comparison processes, it is assumed that the raw sample values for each individual media are obtained in same way and have the same meaning. In practice, this assumption is not true. For example, audio pieces may be recorded at different amplification levels, so direct comparison of sample values from different audio pieces are meaningless. Similarly, image pixel values from different images may have different meanings due to the use of different gamma correction values and color systems used [20, 30]. Therefore, information affecting sample values should be included in the file header and sample values adjusted accordingly during feature extraction. At the moment, common audio and image formats do not include this information. Alternatively, there should be a standard representation for each medium. This not only makes sample values have the same meaning, but also simplifies the decoding and presentation process since it avoids the need to decode and handle many different representations and formats.

3.7.3 Query Processing and Retrieval

There are many issues related to query processing and retrieval. First, there is a need for formal multimedia query language. There is an effort with SQL/MM [31], but its capability is currently limited. Second, a multimedia query may use a number of features. Each feature produces a ranked list. The issue is how to obtain a combined rank list from these individual lists. Which feature is more important than others? The third issue is related to system integration. Information is represented by a number of media types. However, the users are interested in the information regardless of the media types. How can different media types and handling techniques be integrated to present the information effectively to the user?

3.8 SUMMARY

This chapter discussed the main design issues and requirements in MIRS architecture, data modeling, user interface, feature extraction, indexing, feature similarity measures, QoS guarantees, data compression, data representation standardization, and query processing and retrieval. We cover most of these issues in greater detail in the following chapters.

PROBLEMS

Problem 3.1

Design a general MIRS architecture. Explain and justify your design.

Problem 3.2

Describe roles of data models in MIRSs. What are the differences between the data model requirements of DBMSs and MIRSs?

Problem 3.3

Discuss the suitability of the object-oriented approach to multimedia data modeling.

Problem 3.4

Read references [8] and/or [9]. Using an example, describe the timeline-based temporal specification method.

Problem 3.5

Design an abstract class called media. Then define media types text, graphics, audio, and image as derived classes of the abstract class media.

Problem 3.6

Design a data model for an image management system, based on a reasonable assumption of its capabilities.

Problem 3.7

Describe the main functions of the user interface of an MIRS. What are the main issues and requirements in implementing these functions?

Problem 3.8

Why is feature extraction necessary? How may the feature extraction quality affect the retrieval performance of an MIRS?

Problem 3.9

What is QoS? What are the three types of QoS guarantees?

Problem 3.10

Describe the general principle to provide QoS guarantees.

Problem 3.11

Describe the features of an ideal multimedia compression scheme for MIRS applications.

Problem 3.12

Read references [20] and [30]. Explain how different image representations may affect image retrieval performance.

FURTHER READING

Object-oriented concepts and analysis and design for multimedia databases are covered in detail in [32]. Gibbs and Tsichritzis [2] provide class definitions for most media types and an object-oriented multimedia framework.

Many design issues of visual information management systems are discussed in reports of the *NSF Workshop on Visual Information Management Systems* [33] and the *NSF-ARPA Workshop on Visual Information Management Systems* [19].

REFERENCES

[1] Narasimhalu, A. D., "Multimedia Databases," *Multimedia Systems*, No.4, 1996, pp.226-249.

[2] Gibbs, S. J., and Dionysios C. Tsichritzis, *Multimedia Programming - Objects, Environments and Frameworks*, Addison-Wesley, 1995.

[3] Prabhakaran, B., *Multimedia Database Management Systems*, Kluwer Academic Publishers, 1997.

[4] Jain, R. and Amarnath Gupta. "Computer Vision and Visual Information Retrieval," In *Festschrift for Prof. Azriel Rosenfeld*. IEEE Computer Soc., 1996.

[5] Nwosu, K. C., Bhavani Thuraisingham and P. Bruce Berra, "Multimedia Database Systems - A New Frontier," *IEEE Multimedia*, July-September 1997, Vol. 4, No. 3, pp. 21-23

[6] Adjeroh, D. A., and Kinsley C. Nwosu, "Multimedia Database Management - Requirements and Issues," *IEEE Multimedia*, July-September 1997, Vol. 4, No.3, pp.24-33

[7] Pazandak, P., and Jaideep Srivastava, "Evaluating Object DBMSs for Multimedia," *IEEE Multimedia*, July-September 1997, Vol. 4, No.3, pp.34-49

[8] Lu, G., et al., "Temporal Synchronization Support for Distributed Multimedia Information Systems," *Computer Communications*, Vol. 17, No. 12, Dec. 1994, pp. 852–862.

[9] *QuickTime*, Software Product, Apple Computer, Inc., 1991.

[10] Buchanan, M. C., and P. Z. Zellweger, "Automatic Temporal Layout Mechanisms," *Proceedings of ACM Multimedia'93*, Anaheim, CA, August 1–6, 1993, pp. 341–350

[11] Little, T. D. C., and A. Ghafoor, "Spatio-Temporal Composition of Distributed Multimedia Objects for Value-Added Networks," *IEEE Computer*, Oct. 1991, pp. 42–50.

[12] Bach, J. R., S. Paul, and R. Jain, "A Visual Information Management System for the Interactive Retrieval of Faces," *IEEE Trans. Knowledge and Data Engineering*, Vol.5, No.4, 1993, pp.619-628.

[13] Swanberg, D., C. F. Shu, and R. Jain, "Knowledge Guided Parsing in Video Databases," *Proceedings of Storage and Retrieval for Image and Video Databases*, San Jose, California, Feb., 1993, *SPIE Proceedings*, Vol. 1908, pp. 13-24.

[14] Zhang, H. J., A. Kankanhalli, and S. W. Smoliar, "Automatic Parsing of Full-Motion Video," *Multimedia Systems*, Vol.1, July 1993, pp. 10-28.

[15] Bach, J. R. et al., "The Virage Image Search Engine: An Open Framework for Image Management," *Proceedings of Storage and Retrieval for Image and Video Databases IV*, San Jose, California, 1-2 Feb. 1996, SPIE, Vol. 2670, pp. 76-87.

[16] Tonomura, Y., A. Akutsu, Y. Taniguchi, and G. Suzuki, "Structured Video Computing," *IEEE Multimedia Magazine*, Fall 1994, pp. 34-43.

[17] Smoliar, S. W., H. J. Zhang, S. L. Koh, and G. Lu, "Interacting with Digital Video," *Proceedings of IEEE Regino 10's Ninth Annual International Conference*, 22-26 August 22-26, 1994, pp. 852-856.

[18] Lu, G., and H. Lu, "Applications of JPEG Progressive Coding Mode in Distributed Multimedia Sys-

tems," *Proceedings of Multimedia Modelling '95*, Nov.14-17, 1995, Singapore, pp. 309-321.

[19] Jain, R., A. P. Pentland, and D. Petkovic, "Workshop Report: NSF-ARPA Workshop on Visual Information Management Systems," available at http://www-vision.ucsd.edu/papers/vimsReport95.html

[20] Lu, G., *Communication and Computing for Distributed Multimedia Systems*, Artech House, 1996.

[21] Vogel, A. et al., "Distributed Multimedia and QoS: a Survey," *IEEE Multimedia*, Vol. 2, No. 2, Summer 1995, pp. 10-19.

[22] Jacobs, C. E., A. Finkelstein, and D. H. Salesin, "Fast Multiresolution Image Querying," *Proceedings of ACM Computer Graphics '95*, Aug. 6-11, 1995, Los Angeles, CA, pp. 277-286.

[23] Idris, F., and S. Panchanathan, "Storage and Retrieval of Compressed Images," *IEEE Trans. on Consumer Electronics*, Vol. 41, No. 3, Aug. 1995, pp. 937-941.

[24] Shneier, M., and M. Abdek-Mottaleb, "Exploiting the JPEEG Compression Scheme for Image Retrieval," *IEEE Trans. on pattern Analysis and Machine Intelligence*, Vol.18, No.8, Aug. 1996, pp. 849-853.

[25] So, S., C. Leung, and P. Tse, "A Comparative Evaluation of Algorithms Using Compressed Data for Image Indexing and Retrieval," *Proceedings of International Conference on Computational Intelligence and Multimedia Applications*, Feb. 9-11, 1998, Churchill, Victoria, Australia, pp. 866-872.

[26] Hotter, M., "Object-Oriented Analysis-Synthesis Coding Based on Moving Two-Dimensional Objects," *Signal Processing: Image Communication*, Vol. 2, No. 4, Dec. 1990, pp. 409- 428.

[27] Pearson, D., "Texture Mapping in Model-Based Image Coding," *Signal Processing: Image Communication*, Vol. 2, No. 4, Dec. 1990, pp. 377-395.

[28] Lu, G., and C. Goh, "Hierarchical Image Coding for Efficient Usage of Storage Space and Network Bandwidth," *3rd Asia-Pacific Conference on Communications*, December 7-10, 1997, Sydney, Australia, pp. 1180-1184.

[29] Koenen, R., "Overview of the MPEG-4 Version 1 Standard," March 1998, available at http://drogo.cselt.stet.it/mpeg/public/w2196.htm

[30] Lu, G., "Image Retrieval Based on Color," *Proceedings of Storage and Retrieval for Image and Video Databases IV*, San Jose, CA, Feb. 1-2, 1996, SPIE Vol. 2670, pp. 310-320.

[31] International Organization for Standardization, *SQL Multimedia and Application Packages (SQL/MM) Project Plan*, ftp://jerry.ece.umassd.edu/isowg3/sqlmm/BASEdocs/projplan.txt

[32] Khoshafian, S., and A. B. Baker, *Multimedia and Image Databases*, Morgan Kaufmann Publishers, Inc., 1996.

[33] Jain, R., "NSF Workshop on Visual Information Management Systems," *SIGMOD Record*, Vol.22, No.3, Sept. 1993, pp. 57-75.

Chapter 4

Text Document Indexing and Retrieval

4.1 INTRODUCTION

This chapter is devoted to text document retrieval techniques, commonly called IR techniques. IR techniques are important in multimedia information management systems for two main reasons. First, there exist a large number of text documents in many organizations such as libraries. Text is a very important information source for an organization. To efficiently use information stored in these documents, an efficient IR system is needed. Second, text can be used to annotate other media such as audio, images, and video, so conventional IR techniques can be used for multimedia information retrieval.

The two major design issues of IR systems are how to represent documents and queries and how to compare similarities between document and query representations. A retrieval model defines these two aspects. The four commonly used retrieval models are exact match, vector space, probabilistic, and cluster-based. The most common exact match technique is the Boolean model.

In Section 4.2, we describe the main differences between IR systems and DBMSs, and the general information retrieval process.

Although different retrieval models use different document representation or indexing, the indexing process used is similar. Section 4.3 discusses the general automatic document indexing process and the Boolean retrieval model. Sections 4.4 to 4.6 discusses vector space, probabilistic, and cluster-based retrieval models, respectively.

To improve retrieval performance, natural language processing and artificial intelligence techniques are used. In Section 4.7, we briefly describe the applications of these two areas in IR.

Due to the ambiguity and variations of natural language, it is almost impossible to retrieve all relevant items and reject all irrelevant items, so measurement of IR effectiveness is important. Section 4.8 is devoted to the performance measurement issue. Section 4.9 briefly compares performance of different retrieval techniques.

IR techniques are popular because they are now used in search engines of the WWW. In Section 4.10, we describe the basic architecture of the WWW, general issues of resource discovery in the WWW, the main differences between IR systems and WWW search engines, the implications of these differences to the WWW search engine design, and an example WWW search engine.

Section 4.11 summarizes the chapter.

4.2 DIFFERENCES BETWEEN IR SYSTEMS AND DBMS

An understanding of differences between IR systems and DBMS is helpful to understanding IR techniques.

A DBMS contains homogeneous structured records. Each record is characterized by a set of attributes, and the values of the attributes attached to particular records describe these records unequivocally and completely. In IR systems, records are not structured. They do not contain fixed attributes. They are just normal text documents. These documents can be indexed with a number of keywords, document descriptors, or index terms. Each index term is assumed to describe the text content only to some extent, not completely or unequivocally, and large numbers of different index terms may be attached to each particular document or text. Because text-retrieval operations depend directly on the content representations used to describe the stored records, a substantial effort must be devoted to analyzing the content of the stored documents and dealing with the generation of the keywords and indices.

In a DBMS the retrieval is based on an exact match between the query and the attribute values of records. Each retrieved record contains the precise attribute values specified in the query (and possibly other attribute values not mentioned in the query), while each nonretrieved record exhibits at least one mismatch between attribute values attached to the query and those attached to the records. In IR systems, it may not be useful to insist on an exact match between the query and document terms for particular documents to be retrieved. Instead, the retrieval of an item may depend on a sufficient degree of coincidence between the sets of terms attached to queries and documents, produced by some approximate or partial matching method. Further, the same term may have different meaning. In other words, items retrieved in DBMS are definitely relevant to the query and useful to the user. But in IR systems, items considered relevant to the query by the system may not be relevant and useful to the user.

The basic document retrieval process is shown in Figure 4.1. As shown on the right side of the figure, the documents are processed off-line to obtain document representations. These representations are stored together with documents themselves. During retrieval (left side of the figure), the user issues a query that is processed (on-line) to obtain its representation. Then the query representation is compared with the document representations. Documents deemed relevant by the system are retrieved and presented to the user, who evaluates the returned documents and decides which ones are actually relevant to the information need. A good IR system should then allow the user to provide relevance feedback to the system. The system uses this information to modify query, query representation, and/or document representations. Another retrieval is done based on the modified query and document representations. If necessary, the retrieval-feedback process is iterated a few times. Note that not all IR systems support the user relevance feedback process.

Different IR models use different methods for query and document representation, similarity comparison and/or relevance feedback. We discuss Boolean, vector space, probabilistic, and clustering models in the following sections.

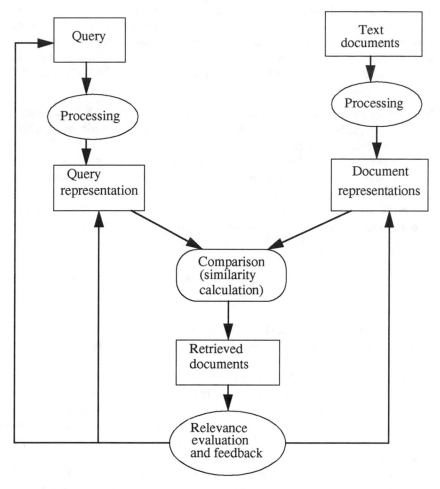

Figure 4.1 Information retrieval process.

4.3 AUTOMATIC TEXT DOCUMENT INDEXING AND BOOLEAN RETRIEVAL MODEL

4.3.1 Basic Boolean Retrieval Model

The aim of an IR system is to retrieve relevant items from a document database in response to users' queries. Most of the commercial IR systems today can be classified as Boolean IR systems or text-pattern search systems. Text-pattern search queries are strings or regular expressions. During retrieval, all documents are searched and those containing the query string are retrieved. Text-pattern systems are more common for searching small document databases or collections. A well known example of text pattern search is the *grep* family of tools in the UNIX environment.[1]

In the Boolean retrieval system, documents are indexed by sets of keywords. (The indexing process will be discussed later.) Queries are also represented by a set of keywords joined by logical (Boolean) operators that supply relationships between the query terms. Three types of operators are in common use: OR, AND, and NOT. Their retrieval rules are as follows:

- The OR operator treats two terms as effectively synonymous. For example, given the query (term 1 OR term 2), the presence of either term in a record (or a document) suffices to retrieve that record.
- The AND operator combines terms (or keywords) into term phrases; thus the query (term 1 AND term 2) indicates that both terms must be present in the document in order for it to be retrieved.
- The NOT operator is a restriction, or term-narrowing, operator that is normally used in conjunction with the AND operator to restrict the applicability of particular terms; thus the query (term 1 AND NOT term 2) leads to the retrieval of records containing term 1 but not term 2.

4.3.2 File Structure

A fundamental decision in the design of IR systems is which type of file structure to use for the underlying document database. File structures used in IR systems include flat files, inverted files, signature files, and others such as PAT trees and graphs [1].

Using a flat-file approach, one or more documents are stored in a file, usually as ASCII or EBCDIC text. Documents are not indexed. Flat-file searching is usually done via pattern searching. In UNIX, for example, one can store a document collection one document per file in a UNIX directory. These files can be searched using pattern searching tools such as "grep" and "awk." This approach is not efficient, because for each query the entire document collection must be searched to check the query text pattern.

Signature files contain signatures (bit patterns) that represent documents. There are many ways to generate signatures for documents. The query is also represented by a signature that is compared with the document signature during retrieval.

A commonly used file structure is an inverted file that is a kind of indexed file. The inverted file concept and retrieval operations based on inverted files are described next.

Inverted Files

In an inverted file, for each term a separate index is constructed that stores the record identifiers for all records containing that term. An inverted file entry usually contains a keyword (term) and a number of document-IDs. Each keyword or term and the document-IDs of documents containing the keyword are organized into one row. An example of an inverted file is shown below:

---

1. In Unix, command "*grep* string-pattern file-names" will search for the string-pattern in specified files and print the lines that contain the string-pattern.

Term 1: Record 1, Record 3
Term 2: Record 1, Record 2
Term 3: Record 2, Record 3, Record 4
Term 4: Record 1, Record 2, Record 3, Record 4

where Term i (i being 1, 2, 3, or 4) is the ID number of index term i, Record i (i being 1, 2, 3, or 4) is the ID number of record i or document i.

The first row means that Term 1 is used in Record 1 and Record 3. The other rows have analogous meanings. Using an inverted file, searching and retrieval is fast. Only rows containing query terms are retrieved. There is no need to search for every record in the database.

Retrieval rules using the Boolean model based on inverted files are as follows:

- For the Boolean AND query, such as (Term i AND Term j), a merged list is produced for rows i and j of the inverted file and all duplicated records (those containing both Term i and Term j) are presented as output. Using the above inverted file as an example, for query (Term 1 and Term 3), the output is Record 3.
- For an OR query, such as (Term i OR Term j), the merged list is produced for rows i and j and all distinct items of the merged list are presented as output. Using the above inverted file as an example, for query (Term 1 OR Term 2), the output is: Record 1, Record 2, Record 3.
- For a NOT query, such as (Term i AND NOT Term j), the output is items appearing in row i but not in row j. Using the above inverted file as an example, for query (Term 4 AND NOT Term 1), the output will be: Record 2, Record 4. For query (Term 1 AND NOT Term 4), the output is nil.

Extensions of the Inverted File Operation

So far we have ignored two important factors in document indexing and retrieval: term positions and the significance of terms (term weights) in documents. In AND queries, all records containing both terms are retrieved, regardless of their positions in the documents. Each term is of equal importance, regardless of their occurring frequencies in documents. To improve retrieval performance, these two factors must be taken into account. We discuss term weight later. In the following we discuss position constraints.

The relationships specified between two or more terms can be strengthened by adding nearness parameters to the query specification. When nearness parameters are included in a query specification, the topic is more specifically defined, and the probable relevance of any retrieved item is larger.

Two possible parameters of this kind are the *within sentence* and *adjacency* specification:

- (Term i *within sentence* Term j) means that terms i and j occur in a common sentence of a retrieved record.
- (Term i *adjacent* Term j) means that Terms i and j occur adjacently in the retrieved documents.

To support this type of query, term location information must be included in the inverted file. The general structure of the extended inverted file is

Term *i*: Record no., Paragraph no., Sentence no., Word no.

For example, if an inverted file has the following entries:

information: R99, 10, 8, 3; R155, 15, 3, 6; R166, 2, 3, 1
retrieval: R77, 9, 7, 2; R99, 10, 8, 4; R166, 10, 2, 5

then as a result of query *(information within sentence retrieval)*, only document R99 will be retrieved.

In the above example, terms "information" and "retrieval" appear in the same sentence of document R99. So it is very likely the record is about information retrieval. Although document R166 contains both "information" and "retrieval," they are at different places of the document, so the document may not be about information retrieval. It is likely that the terms "information" and "retrieval" are used in different contexts.

4.3.3 Term Operations and Automatic Indexing

We mentioned that documents are indexed with keywords, but we have not described how the indexing is actually done. We discuss the operations carried out on terms and an automatic indexing process next.

A document contains many terms or words. But not every word is useful and important. For example, prepositions and articles such as "of," "the," and "a" are not useful to represent the contents of a document. These terms are called *stop words*. An excerpt of common stop words is listed in Table 4.1. During the indexing process, a document is treated as a list of words and stop words are removed from the list. The remaining terms or words are further processed to improve indexing and retrieval efficiency and effectiveness. Common operations carried out on these terms are stemming, thesaurus, and weighting.

Stemming is the automated conflation (fusing or combining) of related words, usually by reducing the words to a common root form. For example, suppose that words "retrieval," "retrieved," "retrieving," and "retrieve" all appear in a document. Instead of treating these as four different words, for indexing purposes these four words are reduced to a common root "retriev." The term "retriev" is used as an index term of the document. A good description of stemming algorithms can be found in Chapter 8 of [1].

With stemming, the index file will be more compact and information retrieval will be more efficient. Information recall will also be improved because the root is more general and more relevant documents will be retrieved in response to queries. But the precision may be decreased as the root term is less specific. We discuss performance measurement in recall and precision in Section 4.8.

Table 4.1
Excerpt of Common Stop Words

A	ALTHOUGH	ANYONE
ABOUT	ALWAYS	ANYTHING
ACROSS	AMONG	ANYWHERE
AFTER	AMONGST	ARE
AFTERWARDS	AN	AROUND
AGAIN	AND	AS
AGAINST	ANOTHER	AT
ALL	ANY	BE
ALSO	ANYHOW	BECOME

Another way of conflating related terms is with a thesaurus that lists synonymous terms and sometimes the relationships among them. For example, the words "study," "learning," "schoolwork," and "reading" have similar meanings. So instead of using four index terms, a general term "study" can be used to represent these four terms. The thesaurus operation has a similar effect on retrieval efficiency and effectiveness as the stemming operation.

Different indexing terms have different frequencies of occurrence and importance to the document. Note that the occurring frequency of a term after stemming and thesaurus operations is the sum of the frequencies of all its variations. For example, the term frequency of "retriev" is the sum of the occurring frequencies of the terms "retrieve," "retrieval," "retrieving," and "retrieved," The introduction of term-importance weights for document terms and query terms may help the distinguish terms that are more important for retrieval purposes from less important terms. When term weights are added to the inverted file, different documents have different similarities to the query and the documents can be ranked at retrieval time in decreasing order of similarity.

An example of inverted file with term weights is shown below:
Term1: R1, 0.3; R3, 0.5; R6, 0.8; R7, 0.2; R11, 1
Term2: R2, 0.7; R3, 0.6; R7, 0.5; R9, 0.5
Term3: R1, 0.8; R2, 0.4; R9, 0.7

The first row means that weight of term 1 is 0.3 in Record 1, 0.5 in Record 3, 0.8 in Record 6, 0.2 in Record 7 and 1 in Record 11. Other rows can be read similarly.

Boolean operations with term weights can be carried out as follows:

- For the OR query, the higher weight among records containing the query terms is used as the similarity between the query and documents. The returned list is ordered in decreasing similarity. For example, for query (Term 2 OR Term 3), we have R1 = 0.8, R2 = 0.7, R3 = 0.6, R7 = 0.5, R9 = 0.7, therefore the output order is R1, R2, R9, R3, and R7.

- For the AND query, the lower weight between the common records matching query terms is used as the similarity between the query and the documents. For example, for the query (Term 2 AND Term 3), we have R2 = 0.4, R9 = 0.5. Therefore the output is R9 and R2.

- For the NOT query, the similarity between the query and the documents is the difference between the common entries in the inverted file. For example, for query (Term 2 AND NOT Term 3), we have R2 = 0.3, R3 = 0.6, R7 = 0.5, R9 = 0, therefore the output is R3, R7, and R2.

We discussed how the use of term weights can help rank the returned list. Ranked return is very important because if the first few items are most similar or relevant to the query, they are normally the most useful to the user. The user can just look at the first few items without going through a long list of items. Now let us look at how to determine term weights for different index terms.

The assignment of index terms to documents and queries is carried out in the hope of distinguishing documents that are relevant for information users from other documents.

In a particular document, the more often a term appears, the more important the term and the higher the term weight should be.

In the context of an entire document collection, if a term appears in almost all documents, the term is not a good index term, because it does not help in distinguishing relevant documents from others.

Therefore good index terms are those that appear often in a few documents but do not appear in other documents. Term weight should be assigned taking into account both term frequency (tf_{ij}) and document frequency (df_j). The commonly used formula to calculate term weight is

$$W_{ij} = tf_{ij} * \log (N/df_j)$$

where W_{ij} is the weight of term j in document i, tf_{ij} is the frequency of term j in document i, N is the total number of documents in the collection, df_j is the number of documents containing term j. The above weight is proportional to term frequency and inverse document frequency. Thus the above formula is commonly called $tf.idf$.

Based on the above formula, if a term occurs in all documents in the collection ($df_j = N$), the weight of the term is zero (i.e., the term should not be used as an index term because use of the term is not able to differentiate documents). On the other hand, if a term appears often in only a few documents, the weight of the term is high (i.e., it is a good index term).

4.3.4 Summary of Automatic Document Indexing

The aim of indexing is to find the best terms to represent each document so that documents can be retrieved accurately during the retrieval process. The automatic indexing process consists of the following steps:

1. Identify words in the title, abstract, and/or document;

2. Eliminate stop words from the above words by consulting a special dictionary, or stop list, containing a list of high-frequency function words;
3. Identify synonyms by consulting a thesaurus dictionary. All terms with similar meanings are replaced with a common word;
4. Stem words using certain algorithms by removing derivational and inflectional affixes (suffix and prefix);
5. Count stem frequencies in each document;
6. Calculate term (stem) weights;
7. Create the inverted file based on the above terms and weights.

4.4 VECTOR SPACE RETRIEVAL MODEL

4.4.1 Basic Vector Space Retrieval Model

The concept of Boolean retrieval model is simple and used in most commercial systems. However, it is difficult to formulate Boolean queries and the retrieval results are very sensitive to query formulation. Query term weights are normally not used as queries are often very short. To overcome these problems, alternative retrieval models – vector space, probabilistic and cluster-based models – have been proposed. This section discusses the vector space model and the following two sections deals with the other two models.

The vector space model assumes that there is a fixed set of index terms to represent documents and queries. A document D_i and a query Q_j are represented as

$D_i = [T_{i1}, T_{i2}, ..., T_{ik}, ... , T_{iN}]$

$Q_j = [Q_{j1}, Q_{j2}, ..., T_{jk}, ... , Q_{jN}]$

where T_{ik} is the weight of term k in document i, Q_{jk} is the weight of query k in query j, and N is the total number of terms used in documents and queries.

Term weights T_{ik} and Q_{jk} can be binary (i.e., either 1 or 0), or tf.idf or weights obtained by other means.

Retrieval in the vector space model is based on the similarity between the query and the documents. The similarity between document D_i and query Q_j is calculated as follows:

$$S(D_i, Q_j) = \sum_{k=1}^{N} T_{ik} \cdot Q_{jk}$$

To compensate for differences in document sizes and query sizes, the above similarity can be normalized as follows:

$$S(D_i, Q_j) = \frac{\displaystyle\sum_{k=1}^{N} T_{ik} \cdot Q_{jk}}{\sqrt{\displaystyle\sum_{k=1}^{N} T_{ik}^2 \cdot \sum_{k=1}^{N} Q_{jk}^2}}$$

This is the well known cosine coefficient between vectors D_i and Q_j. During retrieval, a ranked list in descending order of similarity is returned to the user. For example, if four documents and a query are represented as the following vectors:

$D_1 = [0.2, 0.1, 0.4, 0.5]$
$D_2 = [0.5, 0.6, 0.3, 0]$
$D_3 = [0.4, 0.5, 0.8, 0.3]$
$D_4 = [0.1, 0, 0.7, 0.8]$
$Q = [0.5, 0.5, 0, 0]$

then the similarities between the query and each of the document are as follows:

$S(D_1, Q) = 0.31$
$S(D_2, Q) = 0.93$
$S(D_3, Q) = 0.66$
$S(D_4, Q) = 0.07$

The system will return the documents in the order D_2, D_3, D_1, and D_4.

The main limitation of the vector space model is that it treats terms as unrelated and it only works well with short documents and queries.

4.4.2 Relevance Feedback Techniques

As we mentioned, items relevant to the query according to the system may not actually be relevant to the query as judged by the user. Techniques that employ users' relevance feedback information have been developed to improve system effectiveness. Relevance feedback takes users' judgments about the relevance of documents and uses them to modify query or document indexes.

Query Modification

Query modification based on user relevance feedback uses the following rules:

- Terms occurring in documents previously identified as relevant are added to the original query, or the weight of such terms is increased.

- Terms occurring in documents previously identified as irrelevant are deleted from the query, or the weight of such terms is reduced.

The new query is submitted again to retrieve documents. The above rules are expressed as follows:

$$Q^{(i+1)} = Q^{(i)} + \alpha \sum_{D^i \in Rel} D^i - \beta \sum_{D^i \in NonRel} D^i$$

where $Q^{(i+1)}$ is the new query, $Q^{(i)}$ is the current query, D^i is a collection of documents retrieved in response to $Q^{(i)}$, the first summation is done on all relevant documents within D^i, and the second summation is done on nonrelevant documents with D^i.

Experiments show that the performance is improved by using this technique. The principle behind this approach is to find similar documents to the ones already judged as relevant to the query. Documents relevant to the query should be similar to each other.

Document Modification

In query modification based on user relevance feedback, queries are modified using the terms in the relevant documents. Other users do not benefit from this modification. In document modification based on the user's relevance feedback, document index terms are modified using query terms, so the change made affects other users. Document modification uses the following rules based on relevance feedback:

- Terms in the query, but not in the user-judged relevant documents, are added to the document index list with an initial weight.
- Weights of index terms in the query and also in relevant documents are increased by a certain amount.
- Weights of index terms not in the query but in the relevant documents are decreased by a certain amount.

When subsequent queries similar to the queries used to modify the documents are issued, performance is improved. But this approach may decrease the effectiveness if the subsequent queries are very different from those used to modify the documents.

4.5 PROBABILISTIC RETRIEVAL MODEL

The probabilistic retrieval model considers term dependencies and relationships. It is based on the following four parameters:

P(rel): the probability of relevance of a document
P(nonrel): the probability of nonrelevance of a document

a$_1$: the cost associated with the retrieval of a nonrelevant document

a$_2$: the cost associated with the nonretrieval of a relevant document

Since the retrieval of a nonrelevant document carries a loss of a$_1$P(nonrel) and the rejection of a relevant document carries a loss of a$_2$P(rel), the total loss caused by a given retrieval process will be minimized if a document is retrieved whenever

$$a_2 P(rel) \geq a_1 P(nonrel)$$

The main issue of the probabilistic retrieval model is how to estimate P(rel) and P(nonrel). This is normally done by assuming a certain term occurrence distribution in documents. We will not discuss the derivation of these parameters further. Interested readers are referred to [2–4].

The probabilistic model provides an important guide for characterizing retrieval processes. However, it has not improved retrieval effectiveness greatly, due to the difficulties of obtaining P(rel) and P(nonrel).

4.6 CLUSTER-BASED RETRIEVAL MODEL

In the information retrieval models discussed so far, similar documents may not be in close proximity in the file system. In such a file organization, it is difficult to implement browsing capability. Retrieval effectiveness and efficiency are low because not all relevant items may be retrieved and whole document space has to be searched. To overcome these disadvantages, document clustering – grouping similar documents into clusters – was introduced. In the following we briefly describe cluster generation methods and cluster-based retrieval techniques. The coverage is quite brief, focusing on basic principles. Interested readers are referred to [2, 3] for details about these topics.

4.6.1 Cluster Generation

There are two general approaches to cluster generation. The first one is based on all pairwise document similarities and assembles similar items into common clusters. The second uses heuristic methods that do not require pairwise document similarities to be computed.

In the approach based on pairwise similarities, each document is represented as a document vector as in the vector space model. Then the similarity between each pair of documents is calculated. During the clustering process, each document is initially placed into a class by itself and then two most similar documents based on the pairwise similarities are combined into a cluster. The similarities between the newly formed cluster and other documents are calculated then the most similar documents (including the cluster) are combined into a new cluster. The combining process continues until all documents are grouped into a supercluster. This is called an hierarchical, agglomerative clustering process.

The hierarchical clustering methods are based on all pairwise similarities between documents and are relatively expensive to perform. But these methods produce a unique set of well formed clusters for each set of documents.

In contrast, heuristic clustering methods produce rough cluster arrangements rapidly and at relatively little expense. The simplest heuristic process, called a one-pass procedure, takes the the documents to be clustered one at a time in arbitrary order. The first document taken is placed in a cluster of its own. Each subsequent document is then compared with all existing clusters, and is placed into an existing cluster if it is sufficiently similar to that cluster. If the document is not similar enough to any existing cluster, the document is placed in a new cluster of its own. This process continues until all documents are clustered. The cluster structure generated this way depends on the order in which documents are processed and is uneven. Some control mechanisms are required to produce usable clusters.

4.6.2 Cluster-Based Retrieval

When clusters are formed, document search and retrieval is effective and efficient. Each cluster has a representative vector, normally its centroid. A cluster centroid is typically calculated as the average vector of all documents of the cluster (i.e., the weight of centroid term i is defined as the average of the weights of the ith terms of all documents).

During document retrieval, the query vector is compared with the centroids of clusters. After the cluster with highest similarity to the query vector is identified, there are two alternatives. In the first, all documents in the cluster are retrieved. This option is normally taken when clusters are small. In the second alternative, the query vector is compared with each document vector in the cluster and only the most similar documents are retrieved.

4.7 NONTRADITIONAL IR METHODS

The main issues of IR are how to represent documents and information needs (queries) accurately and then how to match users' information needs with documents. It is obvious that these two processes need to be improved to improve IR performance. A number of new techniques have been proposed to achieve this. In this section we briefly describe natural language processing (NLP) and concept- (or knowledge-) based IR retrieval techniques [3, 4].

Traditional IR retrieval models rely on statistical occurrences of terms as a basis for retrieval. There are a number of problems with the methods based on term occurrences only. First, individual words do not contain all the information encoded in language. The order of words provides a lot information. The same words in a different order may have totally different meanings. Second, one word may have multiple meanings. This is called polysemy. Third, a number of words may have a similar meaning. This is called synonymy. Fourth, phrases have meanings beyond the sum of individual words. Overall, natural language is ambiguous. To improve IR performance, the system should be able to understand the natural language. NLP attempts automatic natural language understanding. The application of NLP techniques to IR improves retrieval performances.

Another way to improve IR performance is to use domain knowledge. In a knowledge-based IR model, information specific to a domain, called domain knowledge, is used to model concepts (terms), events, and relationships among concepts and events [5]. For example, terms "multimedia," "audio," "video," 'images," "information," "indexing," and "retrieval" are all associated with the topic "multimedia information retrieval," with different weights. If we build a complete relationship tree with weights attached to different terms for this topic, documents with one or more these terms will have different combined weights or similarities to the topic. Retrieval can be based on these similarities.

Knowledge about the user, such as his/her preference and background, can also be used to improve IR performance. For example, if the system knows that the user is a tennis fan and the user issued a query "sports news," the system will give higher weights to news items about tennis than to other sports.

Those who are interested in nontraditional IR using NLP, domain knowledge and user profile are referred to references [3-5, 13-16].

4.8 PERFORMANCE MEASUREMENT

Information retrieval performance is normally measured using three parameters: retrieval speed, recall, and precision. These three parameters are largely determined by the indexing scheme and similarity measurement used. The meaning of speed is obvious and the higher the speed, the better the performance. This parameter measures efficiency.

Recall and precision are collectively used to measure the effectiveness of a retrieval system. Recall measures the capacity to retrieve relevant information items from the database. It is defined as the ratio between the number of relevant items retrieved and the total number of relevant items in the database. During performance testing, the total number of relevant items in the database for each testing query should be determined first by an expert in the domain. The higher the recall, the better the performance.

Precision measures the retrieval accuracy. It is defined as the ratio between the number of relevant items retrieved and the total number of retrieved items. If considered in isolation, the higher the precision, the higher the retrieval performance. In practice, recall and precision are considered together. It is normally the case that the higher the recall, the lower the precision. This is because in the process of trying to retrieve all relevant items to a query some irrelevant items are also retrieved, reducing the precision. A system with high recall but low precision means that the system will return a long list of items, many of which are irrelevant. On the other hand, a system with high precision but low recall means that many items relevant to the query are not retrieved. Thus a good retrieval system should balance the recall and precision. So to compare the performance between two information retrieval systems, both recall and precision should be compared. One technique to do this is to determine precision values with recall values ranging from 0 to 1 and to plot a recall-precision graph for each system, as shown in Figure 4.2. The system with the graph further from the origin has the higher performance. The following example shows calculation of recall and precision.

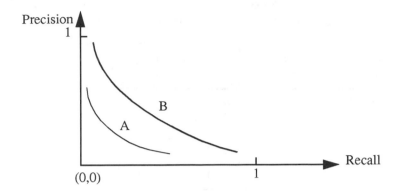

Figure 4.2 Recall-precision graphs. A system with the graph further from
the origin has higher performance. So the system with graph B
is better than the system with graph A.

Suppose a database has 1,000 information items in total, out of which 10 are relevant to a
particular query. The system returned the following list in response to the query:

R, R, I, I, R, R, I, I, R, I, R, R, I, I, R

where the Rs denote items relevant to the query judged by the user and the Is denote
items judged irrelevant by the user. Note that all items returned are deemed relevant by
the system, but only some of them are actually relevant to the query as judged by the
user.

Recall-precision pairs are calculated by considering the different number of items
returned as shown in Table 4.2.

We see that the more the items returned, the higher the recall and the lower the precision. In performance evaluation, recall-precision pairs are calculated at fixed intervals
of recall. For instance, precision is calculated when the recall value is at 0.1, 0.2, 0.3, ...,
0.9, 1.0. Experiments with many queries should be carried out. The precision values at
the same recall value are then averaged to obtain a set of average recall-precision pairs
for the system. At a fixed recall value, the higher the precision, the higher the system
performance.

The index affects both recall and precision as well as system efficiency. If the index
does not capture all the information about items, the system is not able to find all the
items relevant to queries, leading to a lower recall. If the index is not precise, some irrelevant items are retrieved by the system, leading to a lower precision.

Similarity measurement is extremely important and should conform to human judgment. Otherwise, the precision of the system will be low. As shown in the above example, when some returned items are judged not relevant to the query by the user, the
retrieval precision is decreased.

Table 4.2
Recall and Precision Calculation

Number of items returned	Recall	Precision
1	1/10	1/1
2	2/10	2/2
3	2/10	2/3
4	2/10	1/2
5	3/10	3/5
6	4/10	4/6
7	4/10	4/7
8	4/10	4/8
9	5/10	5/9
10	5/10	5/10
11	6/10	6/11
12	7/10	7/12
13	7/10	7/13
14	7/10	7/14
15	8/10	8/15

4.9 PERFORMANCE COMPARISON AMONG DIFFERENT IR TECHNIQUES

Studies have been carried out to evaluate the retrieval performance of different techniques [4, 6]. The following are some of the findings:
- Automatic indexing is as good as manual indexing, but performance will be better if a combination of automatic and manual indexing is used.
- When similar queries are used, the retrieval performance of partial match techniques is better than exact match techniques (Boolean model).
- The probabilistic model and vector space model have similar retrieval performance.
- Cluster-based retrieval techniques and the probabilistic model have similar retrieval performance, but they retrieve different documents.
- Assuming all relevant documents are not found on the first pass, the use of relevance feedback will improve the retrieval performance.
- During query formulation and relevance feedback, significant user input produces

higher retrieval performance than no or limited user input.
- The use of domain knowledge and user profile significantly improves the retrieval performance.

4.10 WWW SEARCH ENGINES

The WWW is currently one of the most popular applications of the Internet. It can be perceived as a collection of interlinked documents distributed around the world. The main purpose of this section is to discuss how a user can retrieve relevant documents from the WWW using tools called search engines. We first introduce the basic concepts of the WWW, discuss the main differences between traditional IR systems and WWW search engines, and then describe an example search engine.

4.10.1 A Brief Introduction to the WWW

A basic understanding of hypertext and hypermedia is required to understand the WWW. Hypertext is a way of organizing information that allows nonsequential access. A hypertext document is made up of a number of *nodes* and *links*. A node usually represents a single concept or idea. It is a container of information. Links connect related nodes. An area within the content of a node indicating the existence of a link is called an *anchor*. Anchors are normally highlighted in a special way (e.g., underlined or color shaded) or represented by a special symbol. Selecting the anchor activates the link and brings up the destination node. Note that many people do not distinguish between links and anchors. To them a highlighted area in a hypertext document is a link. Figure 4.3 shows an example hypertext document. It shows three of many nodes of a document about Monash University. Initially, the first node with general information on Monash is shown. The underlined words are anchors indicating that there are links leading to more information about the underlined items. If the user wants to find more information on any underlined item, he or she can simply select the link associated with the anchor. For example, if he or she selects "campuses" hoping to find more about these campuses, the system brings up node 2 with information on the campuses. Again there are a number of anchors that the reader can select. For example, if the user selects "Gippsland," node 3 is brought up. We see that with hypertext it is easy to retrieve related information.

To summarize, hypertext is an approach to information management in which data is stored in a network of nodes connected by computer-supported links. The modifier "computer supported" is very important. In traditional printed text, we can think of footnotes and references as links. These links are not computer supported and information pointed to by these links cannot be retrieved quickly. Thus hypertext capability is achieved through use of the storage, fast-searching, and fast-retrieval abilities of computers.

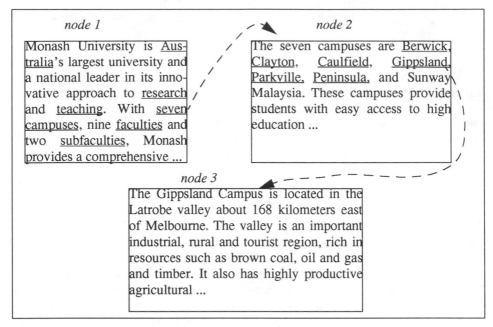

Figure 4.3 An example hypertext document.

Hypermedia is an extension of hypertext in that anchors and nodes can be any type of media such as graphics, images, audio, and video as well as text. For example, if the hypertext document in the above example is extended into hypermedia, a picture of a map may be used indicate the locations of the campuses and sound and video clips may be used to make the presentation more effective.

The WWW is the geographical extension of hypermedia in that the destination anchor or node of a link can be located anywhere on the network. So a WWW document is distributed and different parts of the document are stored at different locations on the network. In the above example, for instance, the information for individual campuses is maintained and stored on servers at the respective campuses. The locations of these nodes are almost transparent to the user. As in hypermedia, the user just selects the anchor and the associated nodes are brought up. We say it is almost transparent because if the network connecting the selected node is slow or busy, the user may find that it takes longer to bring up the node than when the node is stored locally. Thus it may not be entirely transparent.

In principle, the network for linking nodes can be any type of network. However, due to the popularity and wide availability of the Internet, the current WWW runs on the Internet. So the WWW is the integration of hypermedia and the Internet.

Figure 4.4 shows the architecture of the WWW. The main components of the WWW are server, client, and the connection between the server and the client. Note that although only one server is shown in the diagram, the user may access multiple servers in any information retrieval session.

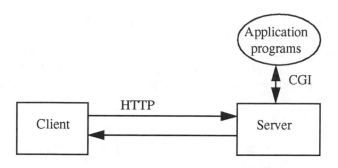

Figure 4.4 A simplified configuration of the WWW.

The user interacts with the client or *browser* through a user interface. In a typical session, the user enters the document request through the interface. The client then sends the request to the appropriate server. The server processes the request and retrieves and sends the requested document to the client if the server has the document and the client has permission to access the document. The received document is presented to the user by the client.

When the user's request is related to a specific application such as searching a database, the server passes the request to an application program through the common gateway interface (CGI). The result of processing the request is passed back to the server which then sends it to the client.

WWW documents are formatted using Hypertext Markup Language (HTML). HTML structures the document in a standard way so that clients can interpret and display the document correctly.

The communication between the client and server is carried out using Hypertext Transport Protocol (HTTP). HTTP is a reliable protocol built on top of TCP/IP. In other words, the HTTP guarantees the logical correctness of the communication but does not provide a timeliness guarantee.

The term WWW has two meanings. First, it refers to a set of concepts and protocols including HTTP and HTML. Second, it refers to a space of digitized information. The success of the WWW is largely due to user-friendly browsers that provide easy access to information on the Internet. In addition to native HTML documents, we can access other servers, such as a file transfer protocol (FTP) server and gopher, through the Web browser.

The WWW is now a popular tool to disseminate and retrieve information. We do not attempt to cover all technical aspects of the WWW. There is a large amount of literature on the WWW on-line and in printed form. Here we look at one important issue of the WWW – how to find useful information.

4.10.2 Resource Discovery

Resource discovery refers to the process of finding and retrieving information on the Internet. As the number of users and the amount of information on the Internet grow rapidly, how to find relevant information becomes very important. There are millions of users and millions of servers managing and storing information in one form or another. How do we know the information that we want exists on the Internet? If it exists, how do we know the location of the documents and how can we retrieve them? These are some of the issues of resource discovery.

Let us first look at how locations of documents in the WWW and the Internet in general are specified. On the Internet, document locations are specified using uniform resource locators (URL). The general format of URLs is as follows:

Protocol://Server-name[:port]/Document-name

The URL has three parts. The first part specifies the Internet protocol used to access the document. The protocols that can be used include "ftp," "http," "gopher," and "telnet."

The second part of the URL identifies the name of the document server, such as "www-gscit.fcit.monash.edu.au." This is the standard Internet domain specification. The example server name means that the server is called "www-gscit," which is in domain "fcit" (Faculty of Computing and Information Technology) of "monash" (Monash University) of "edu" (education sector) of "au" (Australia). Each server name has a corresponding Internet Protocol (IP) address. So if the IP address is known we can use it directly instead of the machine name string. If the server is run on a nondefault port[1] (for the WWW, the default port is 80), we need to specify the port being used. The final part of the URL represents the file name of the document to be retrieved. The file name must be complete, including the full path name.

The following are two example URLs:

http://www-gscit.fcit.monash.edu.au/gindex.html
ftp://ftp.monash.edu.au/pub/internet/readme.txt

The first URL refers to a document called gindex.html in the default directory of server "www-gscit.fcit.monash.edu.au" accessible using HTTP. The second URL refers to a file called readme.txt in the directory "/pub/internet" of the server "ftp.monash.edu.au" accessible using ftp.

Internet documents are uniquely specified with URLs. Now, how can we know that the file we want exists, and what is its corresponding URL?

There are two general ways to find and retrieve documents on the Internet: organizing/browsing and searching. Organizing refers to the human-guided process of deciding how to interrelate information, usually by placing documents into some sort of a hierarchy. For example, documents on the Internet can be classified according to their subject areas. One subject area may have multiple levels of subareas. Browsing refers to the cor-

---

1. A host can run multiple applications (including clients and servers) at the same time. Ports can be thought of as internal communications addresses associated with different applications.

responding human-guided activity of exploring the organization and contents of a resource space or to the human activity of following links or URLs to see what is around there. Searching is a process where the user provides some description of the resources being sought, and a discovery system locates information that matches the description, usually using the IR techniques discussed in the previous section.

Browsing is a slow process for information finding. It depends heavily on the quality of information's organization. It may be difficult to find all relevant information, and users can get disoriented and lost in the information space.

Searching is more efficient than browsing, but it relies on the assumption that information is indexed. There are currently many servers in the Internet that provide searching facilities. These servers use a program called a *crawler* to visit major information servers around the world and to index information available on these servers. The indexing technique used is similar to that used in IR discussed earlier in this chapter. In this case the document identifiers are the URLs of the documents. These searching servers also rely on the document creator to inform them about the contents and URLs of documents they created. So these searching servers provide pointers to documents on the Internet.

In practice both browsing and searching are used in information discovery. The user may first browse around to find a suitable search engine to use. Then he or she issues a query to the server. There may be many documents returned in response to each query. These documents are normally ranked according to the similarity between the query and documents. The user has to determine which documents are useful by browsing.

Resource discovery on the Internet is an extended case of IR. In this case, documents are distributed across many servers on the Internet, making information organization, indexing, and retrieval more challenging. In the following, we describe the main differences between WWW search engines and IR systems, their implications to WWW search engine design, and an example WWW search engine.

4.10.3 Major Differences Between IR Systems and WWW Search Engines

The basic role of WWW search engines is similar to that in an IR system: to index documents and retrieve relevant documents in response to users' queries. But their operating environment differs significantly, leading to many challenges in designing and developing a WWW search engine. The major differences are:
  1. WWW documents are distributed around the Internet while documents in an IR system are centrally located;
  2. The number of WWW documents is much greater than that of an IR system;
  3. WWW documents are more dynamic and heterogeneous than documents in an IR system;
  4. WWW documents are structured with HTML while the documents in an IR system are normally plain text;
  5. WWW search engines are used by more users and more frequently than IR systems.

We discuss these differences and their implications to the WWW search engine design.

4.10.3.1 WWW Documents are Distributed

In the WWW, documents are stored on a huge number of servers located around the world. Before these document can be analyzed and indexed, they have to be retrieved from these distributed servers. The component in a WWW search engine performing this function is called a crawler, robot, or spider [7, 8].

The spider visits WWW servers and retrieves HTML documents based on a URL database. URLs can be submitted by the Web documents' authors, from embedded links in Web documents, or from databases of name servers.

The retrieved documents are sent to an indexing engine for analysis and indexing. Most current spiders only retrieve HTML documents. Images, video, and other media are ignored.

It is sometimes not possible to crawl the entire WWW. So a search engine must decide which WWW documents are visited and indexed. Even if crawling the entire WWW is possible, it is advantageous to visit and index more "important" documents first because a significant amount of time is required to obtain and index all documents. Cho, Garcia-Molina, and Page defined several importance metrics and proposed a number of crawling order schemes [9]. Their experimental results show that a crawler with a good ordering scheme can obtain important pages significantly faster than one without.

4.10.3.2 The Number of WWW Documents is Large

There are millions of WWW servers around the world and each server stores many HTML documents. This large scale has many implications for search engine resources (CPU speed, bandwidth, storage) and retrieval strategies.

A simple calculation shows the resource requirements of a WWW search engine. Suppose a total of 100 million documents need to be retrieved and indexed by a search engine and it takes 1 second to retrieve, analyze and index each document. It would then take 1,157 days for the search engine to complete the task! This is simply unacceptable. To overcome this problem, most search engines are built around multiple powerful computers with huge main memory, huge disk, fast CPUs, and high bandwidth Internet connections. For example, AltaVista[1] has 16 AlphaServer 8400 5/300s, each with 6 GB of memory, with 100 Mbps Internet access [10]. It is claimed that it can visit and retrieve 6 million HTML documents per day.

Another effect of the large number of documents is on retrieval strategies. The returned list must be ranked, with more relevant items being listed first. Otherwise, it would be hard for the user to find the relevant items from the long return list. Indexing and retrieval should be designed to take into account the fact that retrieval precision is more important than recall. This is to reduce the return list and make the first few items more relevant to the user's needs. Also, the low recall problem can be alleviated by the fact that retrieved relevant documents may have links to other relevant items.

---

1. AltaVista is a trademark of Digital Equipment Corporation.

4.10.3.3 WWW Documents are Dynamic and Heterogeneous

Web pages are heterogeneous and dynamic. They are developed by a wide range of people according to different standards and cover diverse topics. They are also constantly updated and changed without notice. These facts have significant implications for search engine design:

First, a huge vocabulary must be used to cope with the large number and diversity of documents.

Second, it is difficult to make use of domain knowledge to improve retrieve effectiveness as documents are from many different domains.

Third, document frequency cannot be obtained by calculating the term weight as the Web database is built progressively and is never complete.

Fourth, the vector space model is not suitable because document size varies and this model favors short documents.

Fifth, the index must be updated constantly as the documents change constantly.

Sixth, the search engine must be robust to cope with the unpredictable nature of documents and Web servers.

4.10.3.4 WWW Documents are Structured

Web pages are normally structured according to HTML. There are tags to indicate different types of text such as document title, section title, different fonts, and links to other pages. A search engine can make use of this information to assign different weights to different types of text, leading to high retrieval effectiveness. We describe how this information is used using an example search engine in Section 4.10.4.

4.10.3.5 WWW Search Engines are Heavily Used

Web search engines are used frequently by many diverse users. This means that the user interface must be easy for novices to use and must provide advanced features for advanced users to improve the retrieval effectiveness. In addition, the search engine must efficiently serve many users simultaneously with a reasonable response time. This requires both powerful machines and appropriate index structures.

4.10.3.6 Other Issues

In addition to the above characteristics and implications, there are many other issues in designing and developing Web search engines.

First, the designers have to decide whether the search engine has a central storage (i.e., whether indexed Web pages should be stored centrally in the search engine or be discarded after indexing and users have to retrieve them from their original servers). The decision has a number of implications. If Web pages are centrally stored, a large amount of storage is required. As Web pages are constantly updated, the central storage may not have the latest version of the document. In addition, there is a copyright issue. Is it legal to collect Web pages and distribute them? On the other hand, if the Web pages are not centrally stored after indexing, the original documents or even servers may not exit any more when the user tries to retrieve indexed documents.

Second, search engines are heavily commercialized. The search engine may favor the Web pages of its sponsors, leading to low objective retrieval effectiveness.

Third, retrieval effectiveness can be manipulated by Web page designers. For example, most search engines rank documents based on word occurrence. The more often the word occurs in a document, the higher the relevance of the document to the query containing that word. A Web page designer can use this knowledge to "improve" the rank of the page by repeating the word or phrase many times in the document title or body.

Fourth, the result of a search may give a wrong impression regarding the availability of required information. For example, a user needing information on a particular topic may wrongly conclude that there is no such information available on-line if the search engine returns with "no match is found," although the information actually exists. This may be due to the fact that indexing by the search engine is not complete, the retrieval effectiveness is very low, and/or the query is not well formulated.

Fifth, most likely, different search engines return totally different lists to the same query. There is currently no comparison among common search engines in terms of completeness and effectiveness.

4.10.4 General Structure of WWW Search Engines

Design details differ from one search engine to another. However, all search engines have three major elements. The first is the spider, crawler, or robot. The spider visits a Web page, reads it, and then follows links to other pages within the site. The spider may return to the site on a regular basis, such as every month or two, to look for changes.

Everything the spider finds goes into the second part of a search engine, the index. The index, sometimes called the catalog, is like a giant book containing a copy of every Web page that the spider finds. If a Web page changes, then this book is updated with new information. Sometimes it can take a while for new pages or changes that the spider finds to be added to the index. Thus, a Web page may have been "spidered" but not yet "indexed." Until it is indexed – added to the index – it is not available to those searching with the search engine.

Search engine software is the third part of a search engine. This is the program that sifts through the millions of pages recorded in the index to find matches to a search and rank them in order of what it estimates is most relevant. Different search engines use different similarity measurement and ranking functions. However, they all use term frequency and term location in one way or another.

All search engines have the basic parts described above, but there are differences in how these parts are tuned. That is why the same search on different search engines often produces different results.

4.10.5 An Example Search Engine

There are many search engines available on the WWW. For commercial reasons, their design details are rarely publicized. But their main working principles are the same. In this subsection, we describe a research prototype search engine, called Google [11, 12]. In the following we first provide an overview of the Google architecture and then describe a number of major components in some detail.

4.10.5.1 Architecture Overview of Google

Figure 4.5 shows the high level architecture of Google. It has two interfaces to the Internet. One is used for crawlers to visit and fetch documents from WWW servers distributed around the world, while the other is used to serve users' search requests. Its operation can be described in two phases: Web crawling (downloading Web pages) and indexing, and document searching.

During the Web crawling and indexing phase, the URL server sends lists of URLs to be fetched to the crawlers. To improve the crawling speed, several distributed crawlers run simultaneously. The Web pages (or documents) fetched by the crawlers are passed to the compression server, which compresses and stores Web pages in the repository. The indexer reads compressed Web pages, uncompresses and parses them. Based on word occurrences, word positions, and word properties such as font size and capitalization, the indexer generates a forward index file that is sorted by DocID. DocID is the ID number assigned to each Web page. In addition, the indexer also parses out all the links in every Web page and stores important information, including link source and destinations, and the text of the link (anchor text), in an anchor file.

The URL resolver reads URLs from the anchor file and converts relative URLs into absolute URLs. It extracts anchor text and puts it into the forward index, associated with the DocID that the anchor points to. It also generates a links database that contains pairs of documents linked by each link. PageRanks for all the documents are then calculated, based on the link database.

The indexer and URL resolver also generate a document information (Doc Infor) file that contains information about each document including DocID, URL, whether crawled, and a pointer to the repository. Uncrawled URLs are fed to the URL server, waiting to be crawled.

The sorter generates an inverted index file from the forward index file. The inverted index is sorted by WordID.

As a result of the crawling and indexing phase, entries for each Web page are created in the forward index, inverted file, document information file, and PageRank file.

During the document searching phase, the user enters a query from a Web browser. The query is normally a number of keywords. It is transmitted to the Google Web server which in turn passes the query to the Google searcher. The searcher retrieves relevant information from the forward index, inverted file, document information file, and PageRank file and ranks documents according to their similarity to the query. The ranked list is returned to the user who selects the Web pages to be retrieved from the repository and displayed.

In the following, we describe some of the main components or functions of the Google search engine.

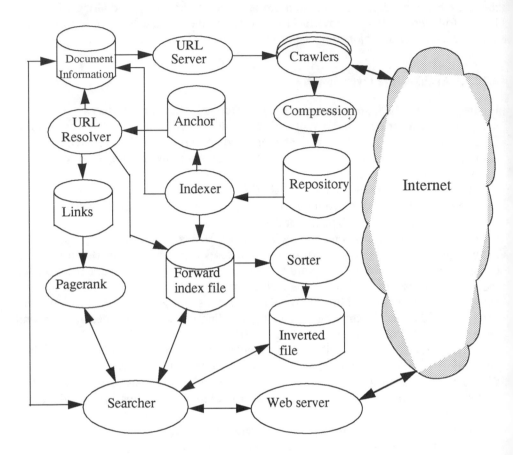

Figure 4.5 The Google architecture.

4.10.5.2 Web Crawling

The two technical issues of Web crawling are performance and reliability. To improve performance, Google runs a number of crawlers (typically 3) at the same time. Each crawler keeps about 300 connections open at once. At peak speeds, the system can crawl over 100 Web pages per second using four crawlers. As a major bottleneck of Web crawling is domain name server (DNS) lookup, each crawler maintains its own DNS cache so it does not need to do a DNS lookup before crawling each document.

Reliability is a very important practical issue as a crawler needs to visit millions of diverse Web pages. These pages may use different versions of HTML, may not confirm to the HTML standards, have many typos, and be in different development stages. Careful design, testing, and monitoring of the crawling process is required.

4.10.5.3 PageRanks and Anchor Text

Google improves retrieval effectiveness by using information present in Web page structure. The two main features used in Google are PageRank and Anchor text.

Pagerank is introduced based on an intuition that a page is important if there are many other pages that have links pointing to it and/or if one or more important pages have links pointing to it. The PageRank of page A is defined as:

$$PR(A) = (1-d) + d(PR(T_1)/C(T_1) + ... + PR(T_n)/C(T_n))$$

where d is a damping factor between 0 and 1, T_1 to T_n are Web pages that have links pointing to A, $C(T_n)$ is the number of links going out of page T_n.

$PR(A)$ is calculated using a simple iterative algorithm. It was reported that Page-Ranks for 26 million Web pages can be computed in a few hours on a medium size workstation [12]. PageRank is a good way to prioritize the results of Web keyword searches, leading to higher retrieval precision.

The second main feature of Google is that it considers anchor text in both source and destination pages. As anchor text is part of the source document, most search engines consider it implicitly. In Google, anchor text has more importance (higher weight) than normal text. In addition, it has a significant weight in the destination document. This approach has a number of advantages. First, anchor text is normally made up of important terms or concepts, otherwise the author would not bother to add a link to the text for further information. Second, anchor text normally provides a good description of the destination document. Third, this approach makes it possible to return Web pages that have not been crawled.

4.10.5.4 Searching

When the Google Web server receives a user's query, it is passed to the searcher. The searcher parses the query and converts it into WordIDs.

In the forward and inverted index files, many types of information about each word is stored. The information includes position in a document and type of text (title, anchor, URL, font size, etc.). Different types of text have different weights. Word proximity is computed based on word positions. The closer the words, the higher the weight. An initial score is then calculated for each document based on types of text, occurrence of each type, and word proximity. The final score is obtained by combining the initial score with the PageRank. The return list is displayed in the descending order of the final score.

4.11 SUMMARY

The main design issue of IR systems is how to represent documents and queries and then how to compare the similarity between the document and query representations. We have described a number of common techniques (called retrieval models) that address this issue.

The retrieval effectiveness of IR systems is yet to be improved. A promising approach is to use domain knowledge and NLP to automatically understand documents and queries. This is not surprising considering how human beings determine if a document is relevant or useful.

WWW search engines are similar to IR systems but present many other challenging issues. Current WWW search engines search text only (HTML) documents. It is expected that future search engines will be able to search various media including text, image, video, and audio by integrating IR techniques with the content-based multimedia retrieval techniques discussed in the following chapters.

PROBLEMS

Problem 4.1

What is an information retrieval model? List four common retrieval models.

Problem 4.2

What is indexing in IR? Explain how indexing performance affects overall retrieval performance.

Problem 4.3

Why are conventional IR techniques important in multimedia information retrieval?

Problem 4.4

In the Boolean IR retrieval model, explain what documents are retrieved in response to the query "keyword 1 AND keyword 2."

Problem 4.5

In the Boolean IR retrieval model, explain what documents are retrieved in response to the query "keyword 1 OR keyword 2."

Problem 4.6

In the Boolean IR retrieval model, describe what criteria the retrieved document should meet in response to the query "term 1 AND NOT term 2."

Problem 4.7

What is an inverted file? Why is it commonly used in IR systems?

Problem 4.8

Explain how the term position information can be used to improve retrieval precision.

Problem 4.9

What are stop words, stemming, and thesaurus conflation? Why are they used in the document indexing process?

Problem 4.10

Explain the function of the term weight in IR systems. How is the term weight commonly determined?

Problem 4.11

What are the criteria for a good indexing term? What are the implications of these criteria?

Problem 4.12

Explain how documents and queries are represented and how similarity between documents and queries is calculated in the vector space model.

Problem 4.13

In the vector space model, assume a document is represented as D = [0.6, 0.8, 0, 0.2] and a query is represented as Q = [0.4, 0.6, 0.1, 0]. Find the similarity between the document and the query using the Cosine coefficient formula.

Problem 4.14

What are the relevance feedback techniques used in IR? Explain how query modification using relevance feedback can improve retrieval performance.

Problem 4.15

Describe a common document cluster generation method. Explain the advantage of cluster-based IR.

Problem 4.16

Intuitively, how can we improve IR effectiveness?

Problem 4.17

What are the common parameters for measuring the performance of a multimedia information retrieval system?

Problem 4.18

Explain the terms recall and precision as used for measuring the effectiveness of an information retrieval system. Why do they have to be used together?

Problem 4.19

Assume there are 10 items relevant to a query in a database of 2,000 items. The system returned the following list in response to the query: R, R, I, R, I, R, R, I, R, R. Calculate recall-precision pairs for recall values at 0.1, 0.2, 0.3, ..., 0.9, and 1.

Problem 4.20

Explain how documents are identified in the WWW.

Problem 4.21

Discuss the similarity and differences between IR systems and WWW search engines.

Problem 4.22

There are many search engines on the WWW. Think of three queries to be used for search. Issue each of these three queries to at least three different search engines. Compare and explain the search results.

FURTHER READING

The ACM has a special interest group in IR called ACM-SIGIR. The ACM-SIGIR holds annual conferences addressing all aspects of IR. Conference proceedings are published as special issues of ACM-SIGIR Forum.

Most information about WWW search engines is available on-line, but it is normally not very technical due to commercial reasons. Some technical information can be obtained from the proceedings of annual International World Wide Web Conference. The latest one was held in Brisbane, Australia, 14-18 April 1998. The proceedings are on-line at http://www7.conf.au.

REFERENCES

[1] Frakes, W. B., and R. Baeza-Yates (Ed.), *Information Retrieval: Data Structures and Algorithms*, Prentice Hall, 1992.

[2] Salton, G., and M. J. McGill, *Introduction to Modern Information Retrieval*, McGraw-Hill Book Company, 1983.

[3] Salton, G., *Automatic Text Processing - The Transformation, Analysis, and Retrieval of Information by Computers*, Addison-Wesley Publishing Company, 1989

[4] Hersh, W. R., *Information Retrieval - A Health Care Perspective*, Springer- Verlag New York, Inc., 1996

[5] Chua, T. S., et al., "A Concept-based Image Retrieval System," *Proceedings of 27th Annual Hawaii International Conference on System Science*, Maui, Hawaii, January 4-7 1994, Vol. 3, pp 590-598.

[6] Croft, W. B., *Information Retrieval and Hypertext*, ITI Symposium Tutorial Notes, 9 July 1993, Singapore.

[7] Koster, M., "The Web Robots FAQ," http://info.webcrawler.com/mak/projects/robots/faq.html

[8] Koster, M., "Robots in the Web: Threat or Treat?" http://info.webcrawler.com/mak/projects/robots/threat-or-treat.html

[9] Cho, J., H. Garcia-Molina, and L. Page, "Efficient Crawling Through URL Ordering," available at : http://www-db.stanford.edu/~cho/crawler-paper/

[10] Home page of AltaVista, http://www.altavista.yellowpages.com.au/av/content/about.html

[11] Stanford University, Google Home Page , http://google.stanford.edu/

[12] Brin S., and L. Page, "The Anatomy of a Large-Scale Hypertextual Web Search Engine," *Proceedings of the Seventh International World Wide Web Conference*, April 14-18, 1998, Brisban Australia. Also available at: http://www7.conf.au/programme/fullprog.html

[13] Croft, W. B., H. Turtle, and D. Lewis, "The Use of Phrases and Structured Queries in Information Retrieval," *Proceedings of ACM SIGIR Conference*, 1991, pp.32-45.

[14] P. M. Tong, P. M., et al., "Conceptual Information Retrieval Using RUBIC," *Proceedings of ACM SIGIR Conference*, 1987, pp.247-263.

[15] Ponte, J. M., and W. B. Croft, "A Language Modelling Approach to Information Retrieval," *Proceedings of ACM SIGIR Conference 1998*, pp. 275-281.

[16] Mitain, S., and B. Kosko, "Neural Fuzzy Agents that Learn a User's Preference Map," *Proceedings of IEEE International Forum on Research and Technology Advances in Digital Libraries*, May 7-9, 1997, Washington, DC, pp. 25-35.

Chapter 5

Indexing and Retrieval of Audio

5.1 INTRODUCTION

In Chapter 2 we learned that digital audio is represented as a sequence of samples (except for structured representations such as MIDI) and is normally stored in a compressed form. The present chapter is devoted to the automatic indexing and retrieval of audio.

Human beings have amazing ability to distinguish different types of audio. Given any audio piece, we can instantly tell the type of audio (e.g., human voice, music, or noise), speed (fast or slow), the mood (happy, sad, relaxing, etc.), and determine its similarity to another piece of audio. However, a computer sees a piece of audio as a sequence of sample values. At the moment, the most common method of accessing audio pieces is based on their titles or file names. Due to the incompleteness and subjectiveness of the file name and text description, it may be hard to find audio pieces satisfying the particular requirements of applications. In addition, this retrieval technique cannot support queries such as "find audio pieces similar to the one being played" (query by example).

To solve the above problems, content-based audio retrieval techniques are required. The simplest content-based audio retrieval uses sample to sample comparison between the query and the stored audio pieces. This approach does not work well because audio signals are variable and different audio pieces may be represented by different sampling rates and may use a different number of bits for each sample. Because of this, content-based audio retrieval is commonly based on a set of extracted audio features, such as average amplitude and frequency distribution.

The following general approach to content-based audio indexing and retrieval is normally taken:

- Audio is classified into some common types of audio such as speech, music, and noise.
- Different audio types are processed and indexed in different ways. For example, if the audio type is speech, speech recognition is applied and the speech is indexed based on recognized words.
- Query audio pieces are similarly classified, processed, and indexed.
- Audio pieces are retrieved based on similarity between the query index and the audio index in the database.

The audio classification step is important for several reasons. First, different audio types require different processing and indexing retrieval techniques. Second, different audio types have different significance to different applications. Third, one of the most important audio types is speech and there are now quite successful speech recognition techniques/systems available. Fourth, the audio type or class information is itself very useful to some applications. Fifth, the search space after classification is reduced to a particular audio class during the retrieval process.

Audio classification is based on some objective or subjective audio features. Thus before we discuss audio classification in Section 5.3, we describe a number of major audio features in Section 5.2. In our discussion, we assume audio files are in uncompressed form.

One of the major audio types is speech. The general approach to speech indexing and retrieval is to first apply speech recognition to convert speech to spoken words and then apply traditional IR on the recognized words. Thus speech recognition techniques are critical to speech indexing and retrieval. Section 5.4 discusses the main speech recognition techniques.

There are two forms of musical representation: structured and sample-based. We describe general approaches to the indexing and retrieval in Section 5.5.

In some applications, a combination of multiple media types are used to represent information (multimedia objects). We can use the temporal and content relationships between different media types to help with the indexing and retrieval of multimedia objects. We briefly describe this in Section 5.6.

Section 5.7 summarizes the chapter.

5.2 MAIN AUDIO PROPERTIES AND FEATURES

In this section, we describe a number of common features of audio signals. These features are used for audio classification and indexing in later sections. Audio perception is itself a complicated discipline. A complete coverage of audio features and their effects on perception is beyond the scope of this book. Interested readers are referred to [1, 2].

Audio signals are represented in the time domain (time-amplitude representation) or the frequency domain (frequency-magnitude representation). Different features are derived or extracted from these two representations. In the following, we describe features obtained in these two domains separately. In addition to features that can be directly calculated in these two domains, there are other subjective features such as timbre. We briefly describe these features, too.

5.2.1 Features Derived in the Time Domain

Time domain or time-amplitude representation is the most basic signal representation technique, where a signal is represented as amplitude varying with time. Figure 5.1 shows a typical digital audio signal in the time domain. In the figure, silence is represented as 0. The signal value can be positive or negative depending on whether the sound pressure is above or below the equilibrium atmospheric pressure when there is silence. It is assumed that 16 bits are used for representing each audio sample. Thus the signal value ranges from 32767 (2^{15}-1) to -32767.

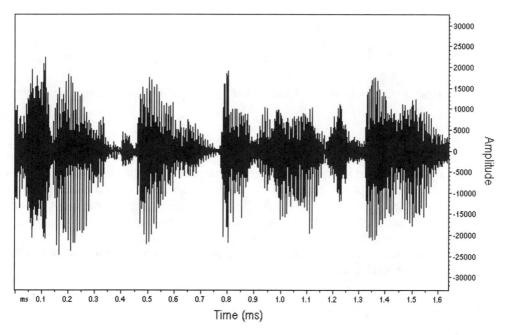

Figure 5.1 Amplitude-time representation of an audio signal.

From the above representation, we can easily obtain the average energy, zero crossing rate, and silence ratio.

Average energy
The average energy indicates the loudness of the audio signal. There are many ways to calculate it. One simple calculation is as follows:

$$E = \frac{\sum_{n=0}^{N-1} x(n)^2}{N}$$

where E is the average energy of the audio piece, N is the total number of samples in the audio piece, and $x(n)$ is the sample value of sample n.

Zero crossing rate
The zero crossing rate indicates the frequency of signal amplitude sign change. To some extent, it indicates the average signal frequency. The average zero crossing rate is calculated as follows:

$$ZC = \frac{\sum\limits_{n=1}^{N} |\mathrm{sgn}\,x(n) - \mathrm{sgn}\,x(n-1)|}{2N}$$

where sgnx(n) is the sign of $x(n)$ and will be 1 if $x(n)$ is positive and -1 if $x(n)$ is negative.

Silence ratio

The silence ratio indicates the proportion of the sound piece that is silent. Silence is defined as a period within which the absolute amplitude values of a certain number of samples are below a certain threshold. Note that there are two thresholds in the definition. The first is the amplitude threshold. A sample is considered quiet or silent when its amplitude is below the amplitude threshold. But an individual quiet sample is not considered as a silent period. Only when the number of consecutive quiet samples is above a certain time threshold are these samples considered to make up a silent period.

The silence ratio is calculated as the ratio between the sum of silent periods and the total length of the audio piece.

5.2.2 Features Derived From the Frequency Domain

Sound Spectrum

The time domain representation does not show the frequency components and frequency distribution of a sound signal. These are represented in frequency domain. The frequency domain representation is derived from the time domain representation according to the Fourier transform. The Fourier transform can be loosely described as any signal can be decomposed into its frequency components. In the frequency domain, the signal is represented as amplitude varying with frequency, indicating the amount of energy at different frequencies. The frequency domain representation of a signal is called the spectrum of the signal. We look at an example spectrum first and then briefly describe how the spectrum is obtained using the Fourier transform.

Figure 5.2 shows the spectrum of the sound signal of Figure 5.1. In the spectrum, frequency is shown on the abscissa and amplitude is shown on the ordinate. From the spectrum, it is easy to see the energy distribution across the frequency range. For example, the spectrum in Figure 5.2 shows that most energy is in the frequency range 0 to 10 kHz.

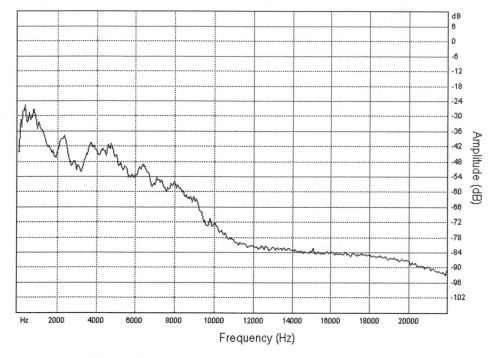

Figure 5.2 The spectrum of the sound signal in Figure 5.1.

Now let us see how to derive the signal spectrum, based on the Fourier transform. As we are interested in digital signals, we use the DFT, given by the following formula:

$$X(k) = \sum_{n=0}^{N-1} x(n)e^{-jn\omega_k}$$

where $\omega_k=2\pi k/N$, $x(n)$ is a discrete signal with N samples, k is the DFT bin number.

If the sampling rate of the signal is f_s Hz, then the frequency f_k of bin k in herz is given by:

$$f_k = f_s\frac{\omega_k}{2\pi} = f_s\frac{k}{N}$$

If $x(n)$ is time-limited to length N, then it can be recovered completely by taking the inverse discrete Fourier transform (IDFT) of the N frequency samples as follows:

$$x(n) = \frac{1}{N}\sum_{k=0}^{N-1} X(k)e^{jn\omega_k}$$

The DFT and IDFT are calculated efficiently using an algorithm called the Fast Fourier transforms (FFT).

As stated above, the DFT operates on finite length (length N) discrete signals. In practice, many signals extend over a long time period. It would be difficult to do a DFT on a signal with very large N. To solve this problem, the short time Fourier transform (STFT) was introduced. In the STFT, a signal of arbitrary length is broken into blocks called *frames* and the DFT is applied to each of the frames. Frames are obtained by multiplying the original signal with a window function. We will not go into details of the STFT here. Interested readers are referred to [3–5]. Typically, a frame length of 10 to 20 ms is used in sound analysis.

In the following, we describe a number of features that can be derived from the signal spectrum.

Bandwidth

The bandwidth indicates the frequency range of a sound. Music normally has a higher bandwidth than speech signals. The simplest way of calculating bandwidth is by taking the frequency difference between the highest frequency and lowest frequency of the non-zero spectrum components. In some cases "nonzero" is defined as at least 3 dB above the silence level.

Energy Distribution

From the signal spectrum, it is very easy to see the signal distribution across the frequency components. For example, we can see if the signal has significant high frequency components. This information is useful for audio classification because music normally has more high frequency components than speech. So it is important to calculate low and high frequency band energy. The actual definitions of "low" and "high" are application dependent. For example, we know that the frequencies of a speech signal seldom go over 7 kHz. Thus we can divide the entire spectrum along the 7 kHz line: frequency components below 7 kHz belong to the low band and others belong to the high band. The total energy for each band is calculated as the sum of power of each samples within the band.

One important feature that can be derived from the energy distribution is the spectral *centroid*, which is the midpoint of the spectral energy distribution of a sound. Speech has low centroid compared to music. The centroid is also called *brightness*.

Harmonicity

The second frequency domain feature of the sound is harmonicity. In harmonic sound the spectral components are mostly whole number multiples of the lowest, and most often loudest frequency. The lowest frequency is called *fundamental frequency*. Music is normally more harmonic than other sounds. Whether a sound is harmonic is determined by checking if the frequencies of dominant components are of multiples of the fundamental frequency.

For example, the sound spectrum of the flute playing the note G4 has a series of peaks at frequencies of:

400 Hz, 800 Hz, 1200 Hz, 1600 Hz, and so on.

We can write the above series as:

f, $2f$, $3f$, $4f$, and so on.

where $f = 400$ Hz is the fundamental frequency of the sound. The individual components with frequencies of nf are called *harmonics* of the note.

Pitch

The third frequency domain feature is pitch. Only period sounds, such as those produced by musical instruments and the voice, give rise to a sensation of pitch. Sounds can be ordered according to the levels of pitch. Most percussion instruments, as well as irregular noise, don't give rise to a sensation by which they could be ordered. Pitch is a subjective feature, which is related to but not equivalent to the fundamental frequency. However, in practice, we use the fundamental frequency as the approximation of the pitch.

5.2.3 Spectrogram

The amplitude-time representation and spectrum are the two simplest signal representations. Their expressive power is limited in that the amplitude-time representation does not show the frequency components of the signal and the spectrum does not show when the different frequency components occur. To solve this problem, a combined representation called a spectrogram is used. The spectrogram of a signal shows the relation between three variables: frequency content, time, and intensity. In the spectrogram, frequency content is shown along the vertical axis, and time along the horizontal one. The intensity, or power, of different frequency components of the signal is indicated by a gray scale, the darkest part marking the greatest amplitude/power.

Figure 5.3 shows the spectrogram of the sound signal of Figure 5.1. The spectrogram clearly illustrates the relationships among time, frequency, and amplitude. For example, we see from Figure 5.3 that there are two strong high frequency components of up to 8 kHz appearing at 0.07 and 1.23 ms.

We determine the regularity of occurrence of some frequency components from the spectrogram of a signal. Music spectrogram is more regular.

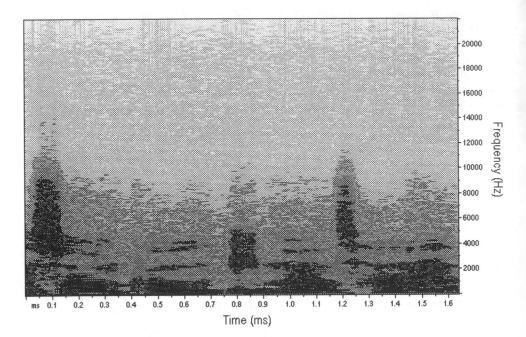

Figure 5.3 Spectrogram of the sound signal of Figure 5.1.

5.2.4 Subjective Features

Except for pitch, all the features described above can be directly measured in either the time domain or the frequency domain. There are other features that are normally subjective. One such feature is timbre.

Timbre relates to the quality of a sound. Timbre is not well understood and defined. It encompasses all the distinctive qualities of a sound other than its pitch, loudness, and duration. Salient components of timbre include the amplitude envelope, harmonicity, and spectral envelope.

5.3 AUDIO CLASSIFICATION

We have mentioned five reasons why audio classification is important in Section 5.1. In this section, we first summarize the main characteristics of different types of sound, based on the features described in the previous section. We broadly consider two types of sound – speech and music, although each of these sound types can be further divided into different subtypes such as male and female speech, and different types of music. We then present two types of classification frameworks and their classification results.

5.3.1 Main Characteristics of Different Types of Sound

In the following we summarize the main characteristics of speech and music. They are the basis for audio classification.

Speech
The bandwidth of a speech signal is generally low compared to music. It is normally within the range 100 to 7,000 Hz. Because speech has mainly low frequency components, the spectral centroids (also called brightness) of speech signals are usually lower than those of music.

There are frequent pauses in a speech, occurring between words and sentences. Therefore, speech signals normally have a higher silence ratio than music.

The characteristic structure of speech is a succession of syllables composed of short periods of friction (caused by consonants) followed by longer periods for vowels [6]. It was found that during the fricativity, the average zero-crossing rate (ZCR) rises significantly. Therefore, compared to music, speech has higher variability in ZCR.

Music
Music normally has a high frequency range, from 16 to 20,000 Hz. Thus, its spectral centroid is higher than that of speech.

Compared to speech, music has a lower silence ratio. One exception may be music produced by a solo instrument or singing without accompanying music.

Compared to speech, music has lower variability in ZCR.

Music has regular beats that can be extracted to differentiate it from speech [7].

Table 5.1 summarize the major characteristics of speech and music. Note that the list is not exhaustive. There are other characteristics derived from specific characteristics of speech and music [8].

Table 5.1
Main Characteristics of Speech and Music

Features	Speech	Music
Bandwidth	0 – 7 kHz	0 – 20 khz
Spectral centroid	Low	High
Silence ratio	High	Low
Zero-crossing rate	More variable	Less variable
Regular beat	None	Yes

5.3.2 Audio Classification Frameworks

All classification methods are based on calculated feature values. But they differ in how these features are used. In the first group of methods, each feature is used individually in different classification steps [9, 10], while in the second group a set of features is used together as a vector to calculate the closeness of the input to the training sets [8, 11]. We discuss these two types of classification frameworks.

Step-by-Step Classification

In step-by-step audio classification, each audio feature is used separately to determine if an audio piece is music or speech. Each feature is seen as a filtering or selection criterion. At each filtering step, an audio piece is determined as one type or another. A possible filtering process is shown in Figure 5.4. First, the centroid of all input audio pieces is calculated. If an input has a centroid higher than a preset threshold, it is deemed to be music. Otherwise, the input is speech or music because not all music has high centroid. Second, the silence ratio is calculated. If the input has a low silence ratio, it is deemed to be music. Otherwise, the input is speech or solo music because solo music may have a very high silence ratio. Finally, we calculate ZCR. If the input has very a high ZCR variability, it is speech. Otherwise, it is solo music.

In this classification approach, it is important to determine the order in which different features are used for classification. The order is normally decided based on computational complexity and the differentiating power of the different features. The less complicated feature with high differentiating power is used first. This reduces the number of steps that a particular input will go through and reduces the total required amount of computation.

Multiple features and steps are used to improve classification performance. In some applications, audio classification is based on only one feature. For example, Saunders [6] used ZCR variability to discriminate broadcast speech and music and achieved an average successful classification rate of 90% [6]. Lu and Hankinson [12] used the silence ratio to classify audio into music and speech with an average success rate of 82%.

Feature-Vector-Based Audio Classification

In feature-vector-based audio classification, values of a set of features are calculated and used as a feature vector. During the training stage, the average feature vector (reference vector) is found for each class of audio. During classification, the feature vector of an input is calculated and the vector distances between the input feature vector and each of the reference vectors are calculated. The input is classified into the class from which the input has least vector distance. Euclidean distance is commonly used as the feature vector distance. This approach assumes that audio pieces of the same class are located close to each other in the feature space and audio pieces of different classes are located far apart in the feature space. This approach can also be used for audio retrieval, discussed in Section 5.5.

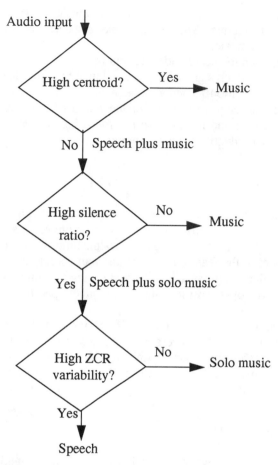

Figure 5.4 A possible audio classification process.

Scheirer and Slaney [8] used 13 features including spectral centroid and ZCR for audio classification. A successful classification rate of over 95% was achieved. Note that because different test sound files were used in [6], [8], and [12], it is not meaningful to compare their results directly.

5.4 SPEECH RECOGNITION AND RETRIEVAL

Now that we have classified audio into speech and music, we can deal with them separately with different techniques. This section looks at speech retrieval techniques, and the next section deals with music.

The basic approach to speech indexing and retrieval is to apply speech recognition techniques to convert speech signals into text and then to apply IR techniques for indexing and retrieval. In addition to actual spoken words, other information contained in speech, such as the speaker's identity and the mood of the speaker, can be used to enhance speech indexing and retrieval. In the following, we describe the basic speech recognition and speaker identification techniques.

5.4.1 Speech Recognition

In general, the automatic speech recognition (ASR) problem is a pattern matching problem. An ASR system is trained to collect models or feature vectors for all possible speech units. The smallest unit is a phoneme. Other possible units are word and phrases. During the recognition process, the feature vector of an input speech unit is extracted and compared with each of the feature vectors collected during the training process. The speech unit whose feature vector is closest to that of the input speech unit is deemed to be the unit spoken.

In this section, we first present the basic concepts of ASR and discuss a number of factors that complicate the ASR process. We then describe three classes of practical ASR techniques. These classes are dynamic time warping, hidden Markov models (HMMs), and artificial neural network (ANN) models. Among these techniques, those based on HMMs are most popular and produce the highest speech recognition performance.

5.4.1.1 Basic Concepts of ASR

An ASR system operates in two stages: training and pattern matching. During the training stage, features of each speech unit is extracted and stored in the system. In the recognition process, features of an input speech unit are extracted and compared with each of the stored features, and the speech unit with the best matching features is taken as the recognized unit. Without losing generality, we use a phoneme as a speech unit. If each phoneme can be uniquely identified by a feature vector independent of speakers, environment and context, speech recognition would be simple. In practice, however, speech recognition is complicated by the following factors:

- A phoneme spoken by different speakers or by the same speaker at different times produces different features in terms of duration, amplitude, and frequency components. That is, a phoneme cannot be uniquely identified with 100% certainty.
- The above differences are exacerbated by the background or environmental noise.
- Normal speech is continuous and difficult to separate into individual phonemes because different phonemes have different durations.
- Phonemes vary with their location in a word. The frequency components of a vowel's pronunciation are heavily influenced by the surrounding consonants [13].

Because of the above factors, the earlier ASR systems were speaker dependent, required a pause between words, and could only recognize a small number of words.

The above factors also illustrate that speech recognition is a statistical process in which ordered sound sequences are matched against the likelihood that they represent a particular string of phonemes and words. Speech recognition must also make use of knowledge of the language, including a dictionary of the vocabulary and a grammar of allowable word sequences.

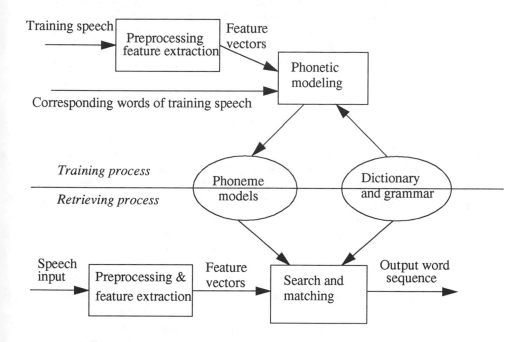

Figure 5.5 A general ASR system (after [13]).

Figure 5.5 shows a general model of ASR systems. The first stage is training (top part of Figure 5.5). In this stage, speech sequences from a large number of speakers are collected. Although it is possible to carry out speech recognition from the analog speech signals, digital signals are more suitable. So these speech sequences are converted into digital format. The digitized speech sequences are divided into frames of fixed duration. The typical frame size is 10 ms. Feature vectors are then computed for each frame. Many types of features are possible, but the most popular ones are the mel-frequency cepstral coefficients (MFCCs). MFCCs are obtained by the following process:

1. The spectrum of the speech signal is warped to a scale, called the mel-scale, that represents how a human ear hears sound.
2. The logarithm of the warped spectrum is taken.
3. An inverse Fourier transform of the result of step 2 is taken to produce what is called the cepstrum.

The phonetic modeling process uses the above obtained feature vectors, a dictionary containing all the words and their possible pronunciations, and the statistics of grammar usage to produce a set of phoneme models or templates. At the end of the training stage we have a recognition database consisting of the set of phoneme models, the dictionary, and grammar.

When speech is to be recognized (bottom part of Figure 5.5), the input speech is processed in a similar way as in the training stage to produce feature vectors. The search and matching engine finds the word sequence (from the recognition database) that has the feature vector that best matches the feature vectors of the input speech. The word sequence is output as recognized text.

Different techniques vary in features used, phonetic modeling, and matching methods used. In the following we describe three techniques based on dynamic time warping, HMMs, and ANNs.

5.4.1.2 Techniques Based on Dynamic Time Warping

As we have mentioned, each speech frame is represented by a feature vector. During the recognition process, the simplest way to find the distances between the input feature vector and those in the recognition database is to compute the sum of frame to frame differences between feature vectors. The best match is the one with the smallest distance. This simple method will not work in practice, as there are nonlinear variations in the timing of speeches made by different speakers and made at different times by the same speaker. For example, the same word spoken by different people will take a different amount of time. Therefore, we cannot directly calculate frame to frame differences.

Dynamic time warping normalizes or scales speech duration to minimize the sum of distances between feature vectors that most likely match best. Figure 5.6 shows an example of dynamic time warping. Although the spoken words of the reference speech and the test speech are the same, these two speeches have different time durations before time warping (Figure 5.6(a)), and it is difficult to calculate the feature differences between them. After time warping (Figure 5.6(b)), however, they are very similar and their distance can be calculated by summing the frame to frame or sample to sample differences.

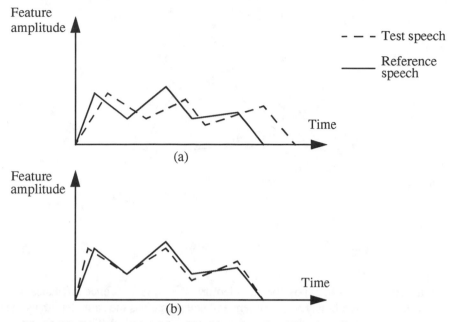

Figure 5.6 A Dynamic time warping example: (a) before time warping; (b) after time warping.

5.4.1.3 Techniques Based on Hidden Markov Models

Techniques based on HMMs are currently the most widely used and produce the best recognition performance. A detailed coverage of HMMs is beyond the scope of this book. The interested reader is referred to [14, 15] for details. In the following, we describe the basic idea of using HMMs for speech recognition.

Phonemes are fundamental units of meaningful sound in speech. They are each different from all the rest, but they are not unchanging in themselves. When one phoneme is voiced, it can be identified as similar to its previous occurrences, although not exactly the same. In addition, a phoneme's sound is modified by its neighbors' sounds. The challenge of speech recognition is how to model these variations mathematically.

We briefly describe what HMMs are and how they can be used to model and recognize phonemes.

An HMM consists of a number of states, linked by a number of possible transitions (Figure 5.7). Associated with each state are a number of symbols, each with a certain occurrence probability associated with each transition. When a state is entered, a symbol is generated. Which symbol to be generated at each state is determined by the occurrence probabilities. In Figure 5.7, the HMM has three states. At each state, one of four possible symbols, x_1, x_2, x_3 and x_4, is generated with different probabilities, as shown by $b_1(x)$, $b_2(x)$, $b_3(x)$ and $b_4(x)$. The transition probabilities are shown as a_{11}, a_{12}, and so forth.

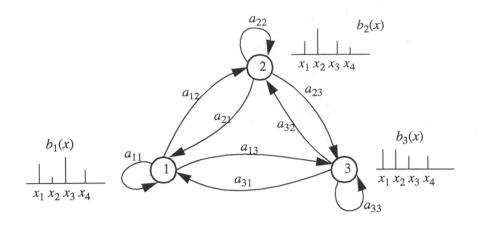

Figure 5.7 An example of an HMM.

In an HMM, it is not possible to identify a unique sequence of states given a sequence of output symbols. Every sequence of states that has the same length as the output symbol sequence is possible, each with a different probability. The sequence of states is "hidden" from the observer who sees only the output symbol sequence. This is why the model is called the hidden Markov model.

Although it is not possible to identify the unique sequence of state for a given sequence of output symbols, it is possible to determine which sequence of state is most likely to generate the sequence of symbols, based on state transition and symbol generating probabilities.

Now let us look at applications of HMMs in speech recognition. Each phoneme is divided into three audible states: an introductory state, a middle state, and an exiting state. Each state can last for more than one frame (normally each frame is 10 ms). During the training stage, training speech data is used to construct HMMs for each of the possible phonemes. Each HMM has the above three states and is defined by state transition probabilities and symbol generating probabilities. In this context, symbols are feature vectors calculated for each frame. Some transitions are not allowed as time flows forward only. For example, transitions from 2 to 1, 3 to 2 and 3 to 1 are not allowed if the HMM in Figure 5.7 is used as a phoneme model. Transitions from a state to itself are allowed and serve to model time variability of speech.

Thus, at the end of the training stage, each phoneme is represented by one HMM capturing the variations of feature vectors in different frames. These variations are caused by different speakers, time variations, and surrounding sounds.

During speech recognition, feature vectors for each input phoneme are calculated frame by frame. The recognition problem is to find which phoneme HMM is most likely to generate the sequence of feature vectors of the input phoneme. The corresponding phoneme of the HMM is deemed as the input phoneme. As a word has a number of phonemes, a sequence of phonemes are normally recognized together. There are a number of algorithms, such as forward and Viterbi algorithms, to compute the probability that an HMM generates a given sequence of feature vectors. The forward algorithm is used for recognizing isolated words and the Viterbi algorithm for recognizing continuous speech [15].

5.4.1.4 Techniques Based on Artificial Neural Networks

ANNs have been widely used for pattern recognition. An ANN is an information processing system that simulates the cognitive process of the human brain. An ANN consists of many neurons interconnected by links with weights. Speech recognition with ANNs consists of also two stages: training and recognition. During the training stage, feature vectors of training speech data are used to train the ANN (adjust weights on different links). During the recognition stage, the ANN will identify the most likely phoneme based on the input feature vectors. For more details of ANNs and their applications to ASR, the reader is referred to [16].

5.4.1.5 Speech Recognition Performance

Speech recognition performance is normally measured by recognition error rate. The lower the error rate, the higher the performance. The performance is affected by the following factors:

1. Subject matter: this may vary from a set of digits, a newspaper article, to general news.
2. Types of speech: read or spontaneous conversation.
3. Size of the vocabulary: it ranges from dozens to a few thousand words.

As techniques based on HMMs perform best, we briefly list their performance when the above factors vary (Table 5.2)

Table 5.2

Error Rates for High Performance Speech Recognition (Based on [13])

Subject Matter	Type	Vocabulary, No. of Words	Word Error Rate (%)
Connected digits	Read	10	<0.3
Airline travel system	Spontaneous	2,500	2
Wall Street Journal	Read	64,000	7
Broadcast news	Read/spontaneous (mixed)	64,000	30
General phone call	Conversation	10,000	50

The above table shows that speech recognition performance varies greatly. For many specific applications, it is quite acceptable. However, the recognition performance for general applications is still very low and unacceptable.

5.4.2 Speaker Identification

While speech recognition focuses on the content of speech, speaker identification or voice recognition attempts to find the identity of the speaker or to extract information about an individual from his/her speech [17]. Speaker identification is potentially very useful to multimedia information retrieval. It can determine the number of speakers in a particular setting, whether the speaker is male or female, adult or child, a speaker's mood, emotional state and attitude, and other information. This information, together with the speech content (derived from speech recognition) significantly improves information retrieval performance.

Voice recognition is complementary to speech recognition. Both use similar signal processing techniques to some extent. However they differ in the following aspect. Speech recognition, if it is to be speaker-independent, must purposefully ignore any idiosyncratic speech characteristics of the speaker and focus on those parts of the speech signal richest in linguistic information. In contrast, voice recognition must amplify those idiosyncratic speech characteristics that individualize a person and suppress linguistic characteristics that have no bearing on the recognition of the individual speaker. Readers are referred to [17] for details of voice recognition.

5.4.3 Summary

After an audio piece is determined to be speech, we can apply speech recognition to convert the speech into text. We can then use IR techniques discussed in Chapter 4 to carry out speech indexing and retrieval. The information obtained from voice recognition can be used to improve IR performance.

5.5 MUSIC INDEXING AND RETRIEVAL

We discussed speech indexing and retrieval based on speech recognition in the previous section. This section deals with music indexing and retrieval. In general, research and development of effective techniques for music indexing and retrieval is still at an early stage. As mentioned in Chapter 2, there are two types of music: structured or synthetic and sample based music. We briefly describe the handling of these two types of music.

5.5.1 Indexing and Retrieval of Structured Music and Sound Effects

Structured music and sound effects are represented by a set of commands or algorithms. The most common structured music is MIDI, which represent music as a number of notes and control commands [18]. A new standard for structured audio (music and sound effects) is MPEG-4 Structured Audio, which represents sound in algorithms and control languages [19].

These structured sound standards and formats are developed for sound transmission, synthesis, and production. They are not specially designed for indexing and retrieval purposes. The explicit structure and notes description existing in these formats make the retrieval process easy, as there is no need to do feature extraction from audio signals.

Structured music and sound effects are very suitable for queries requiring an exact match between the queries and database sound files. The user can specify a sequence of notes as a query and it is relatively easy to find those structured sound files that contain this sequence of notes. Although an exact match of the sequence of notes is found, the sound produced by the sound file may not be what the user wants because the same structured sound file can be rendered differently by different devices.

Finding similar music or sound effects to a query based on similarity instead of exact match is complicated even with structured music and sound effects. The main problem is that it is hard to define similarity between two sequences of notes. One possibility is to retrieve music based on the pitch changes of a sequence of notes [20]. In this scheme, each note (except for the first one) in the query and in the database sound files is converted into pitch change relative to its previous note. The three possible values for the pitch change are U(up), D(down), and S(same or similar). In this way, a sequence of notes is characterized as a sequence of symbols. Then the retrieval task becomes a string-matching process. This scheme was proposed for sample-based sound retrieval where notes must be identified and pitch changes must be tracked with some algorithms that we will discuss in the next subsection. But this scheme is equally applicable to structured sound retrieval, where the notes are already available and pitch change can be easily obtained based on the notes scale.

5.5.2 Indexing and Retrieval of Sample-Based Music

There are two general approaches to indexing and retrieval of sample-based music. The first approach is based on a set of extracted sound features [21], and the second is specifically based on pitches of music notes [20, 22]. We briefly describe these two approaches separately.

Music retrieval based on a set of features

In this approach to music retrieval, a set of acoustic features is extracted for each sound (including queries). This set of N features is represented as an N-vector. The similarity between the query and each of the stored music pieces is calculated based on the closeness between their corresponding feature vectors. This approach can be applied to general sound including music, speech, and sound effects.

A good example using this approach is the work carried out at Muscle Fish LLC [21]. In this work, five features are used, namely loudness, pitch, brightness, bandwidth, and harmonicity. These features of sound vary over time and thus are calculated for each frame. Each feature is then represented statistically by three parameters: mean, variance, and autocorrelation. The Euclidean distance or Manhattan distance between the query vector and the feature vector of each stored piece of music is used as the distance

124

between them.

This approach can be used for audio classification, as discussed earlier. It is based on the assumption that perceptually similar sounds are closely located in the chosen feature space and perceptually different sounds are located far apart in the chosen feature space. This assumption may not be true, depending on the features chosen to represent the sound.

Music retrieval based on pitch

This approach is similar to pitch-based retrieval of structured music. The main difference is that the pitch for each note has to be extracted or estimated in this case [20, 22]. Pitch extraction or estimation is often called pitch tracking. Pitch tracking is a simple form of automatic music transcription that converts musical sound into a symbolic representation [23, 24].

The basic idea of this approach is quite simple. Each note of music (including the query) is represented by its pitch. So a musical piece or segment is represented as a sequence or string of pitches. The retrieval decision is based on the similarity between the query and candidate strings. The two major issues are pitch tracking and string similarity measurement.

Pitch is normally defined as the fundamental frequency of a sound. To find the pitch for each note, the input music must first be segmented into individual notes. Segmentation of continuous music, especially humming and singing, is very difficult. Therefore, it is normally assumed that music is stored as scores in the database. The pitch of each note is known. The common query input form is humming. To improve pitch tracking performance on the query input, a pause is normally required between consecutive notes.

There are two pitch representations. In the first method, each pitch except the first one is represented as pitch direction (or change) relative to the previous note. The pitch direction is either U(up), D(down), or S (similar). Thus each musical piece is represented as a string of three symbols or characters.

The second pitch representation method represents each note as a value based on a chosen reference note. The value is assigned from a set of standard pitch values that is closest to the estimated pitch. If we represent each allowed value as a character, each musical piece or segment is represented as a string of characters. But in this case, the number of allowed symbols is much greater than the three that are used in the first pitch representation.

After each musical piece is represented as a string of characters, the final stage is to find a match or similarity between the strings. Considering that humming is not exact and the user may be interested in find similar musical pieces instead of just the same one, approximate matching is used instead of exact matching. The approximate matching problem is that of string matching with k mismatches. The variable k is determined by the user of the system. The problem consists of finding all instances of a query string $Q=q_1q_2q_3...q_m$ in a reference string $R=r_1r_2r_3...r_n$ such that there are at most k mismatches (characters that are not the same). There are several algorithms that were developed to address the problem of approximate string matching [21, 22].

Both the systems of Muscle Fish LLC [21] and the University Waikato [22] produced good retrieval performance. But the performance depends on the accuracy of pitch tracking of hummed input signals. High performance is only achieved when a pause is inserted between consecutive notes.

5.6 MULTIMEDIA INFORMATION INDEXING AND RETRIEVAL USING RELATIONSHIPS BETWEEN AUDIO AND OTHER MEDIA

So far, we have treated sound independently of other media. In some applications, sound appears as part of a multimedia document or object. For example, a movie consists of a sound track and a video track with fixed temporal relationships between them. Different media in a multimedia object are interrelated in their contents as well as by time. We use this interrelation to improve multimedia information indexing and retrieval in the following two ways.

First, we can use knowledge or understanding about one medium to understand the contents of other media. We have used text to index and retrieve speech through speech recognition. We can in turn use audio classification and speech understanding to help with the indexing and retrieval of video. Figure 5.8 shows an multimedia object consisting of a video track and a sound track. The video track has 26 frames. Now we assume the sound track has been segmented into different sound types. The first segment is speech and corresponds to video frames 1 through 7. The second segment is loud music and corresponds to video frames 7 through 18. The final segment is speech again and corresponds to video frames 19 through 26. We then use the knowledge of the sound track to do the following on the video track. First, we segment the video track according to the sound track segment boundaries. In this case, the video track is likely to have three segments with the boundaries alined with the sound track segment boundaries. Second, we apply speech recognition to sound segments 1 and 3 to understand what was talked about. The corresponding video track may very likely have similar content. Video frames may be indexed and retrieved based on the speech content without any other processing. This is very important because in general it is difficult to extract video content even with complicated image processing techniques.

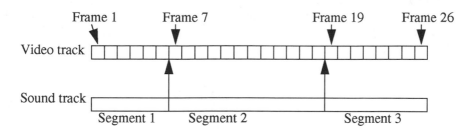

Figure 5.8 An example multimedia object with a video track and a sound track.

The second way to make use of relationships between media for multimedia retrieval is during the retrieval process. The user can use the most expressive and simple media to formulate a query, and the system will retrieve and present relevant information to the user regardless of media types. For example, a user can issue a query using speech to describe what information is required and the system may retrieve and present relevant information in text, audio, video, or their combinations. Alternatively, the user can use an example image as query and retrieve information in images, text, audio, and their combinations. This is useful because there are different levels of difficulty in formulating queries in different media.

We discuss the indexing and retrieval of composite multimedia objects further in Chapter 9.

5.7 SUMMARY

This chapter described some common techniques and related issues for content-based audio indexing and retrieval. The general approach is to classify audio into some common types such as speech and music, and then use different techniques to process and retrieve the different types of audio. Speech indexing and retrieval is relatively easy, by applying IR techniques on words identified using speech recognition. But speech recognition performance on general topics without any vocabulary restriction is still to be improved. For music retrieval, some useful work has been done based on audio feature vector matching and approximate pitch matching. However, more work is needed on how music and audio in general is perceived and on similarity comparison between musical pieces. It will also be very useful if we can further automatically classify music into different types such as pop and classical.

The classification and retrieval capability described in this chapter is potentially important and useful in many areas, such as the press and music industry, where audio information is used. For example, a user can hum or play a song and ask the system to find songs similar to what was hummed or played. A radio presenter can specify the requirements of a particular occasion and ask the system to provide a selection of audio pieces meeting these requirements. When a reporter wants to find a recorded speech, he or she can type in part of the speech to locate the actual recorded speech. Audio and video are often used together in situations such as movie and television programs, so audio retrieval techniques may help locate some specific video clips, and video retrieval techniques may help locate some audio segments. These relationships should be exploited to develop integrated multimedia database management systems.

PROBLEMS

Problem 5.1

Explain why it is not practical to compare the distance between two audio files by summing the differences between corresponding samples of those two files.

Problem 5.2

Describe a general approach to content-based audio indexing and retrieval. Justify the approach you described.

Problem 5.3

Read reference [6]. Describe the algorithm used to discriminate between speech and music.

Problem 5.4

(a) Write a program to calculate the silence ratio of audio files in .wav format. You may need to adjust the values of the two thresholds described in Section 5.2.1 experimentally. (b) Apply your program to a few music and speech files. Describe and explain your observations.

Problem 5.5

Is it possible to tell whether an audio signal is music or speech from its spectrum? Justify your answer.

Problem 5.6

(a) Describe the basic principles of ASR. (b) Why is it difficult to develop a high performance ASR systems for general applications?

Problem 5.7

For multimedia indexing and retrieval purposes, what information in addition to spoken words should be extracted and recorded from the speech recognition process?

Problem 5.8

Contrast speech recognition and voice recognition.

Problem 5.9

Read reference [20]. (a) Describe the proposed music retrieval method. (b) Explain its limitations, if any.

128

Problem 5.10

Explain why it is important to use an integrated approach (using multiple media types and features) to the indexing and retrieval of multimedia objects. Use an example in your explanation.

REFERENCES

[1] Moore, B. C. J., *An Introduction to Psychology of Hearing*, Academic Press, 1997.

[2] Bregman, A. S., *Auditory Scene Analysis - The Perception Organization of Sound*, The MIT Press, 1990.

[3] Lynn, P. A. and Wolfgang Fuerst, *Introductory Digital Signal Processing with Computer Applications*, John & Wiley & Sons, 1989.

[4] Polikar, R., "The Wavelet Tutorial," http://www.public.iastate.edu/~rpolikar/WAVELETS/WTtutorial.htm

[5] Peevers, A. W., "A Real Time 3D Signal Analysis/Synthesis Tool Based on the Short Time Fourier Transform," http://cnmat.CNMAT.Berkeley.EDU/~alan/MS-html/MSthesis.v2_ToC.html

[6] Saunders, J., "Real-Time Discrimination of Broadcast Speech/Music," *Proceedings ACASSP'96*, Vol. 2, pp. 993-996.

[7] Scheirer, E. D., "Tempo and Beat Analysis of Acoustic Music Signals," http://sound.media.mit.edu/~eds/papers/beat-track.html

[8] Scheirer, E. D., and M. Slaney, "Construction and Evaluation of a Robust Multifeature Speech/Music Discriminator," *Proceedings of the 1997 International Conference on Acoustics, Speech, and Signal Processing (ICASSP)*, Munich, Germany, April 21-24, 1997. Also available at http://web.interval.com/papers/1996-085/index.html

[9] Patel, N. V., and Ishwar K. Sethi, "Audio Characterization for Video Indexing," *SPIE Proceedings*, Vol. 2670, 1996, pp. 373-384.

[10] Pfeiffer, S., S Fischer, and W. Effelsberg, "Automatic Audio Content Analysis," http://www.informatik.uni-mannheim.de/informatic/pi4/projects/MoCA/

[11] Foote, J. T., "A Similarity Measure for Automatic Audio Classification," *Pro. AAAI 1997 Spring Symposium on Intelligent Integration and Use of Text, Image, Video and Audio Corpora*, Stanford, Palo Alto, CA, march 1997.

[12] Lu, G., and T. Hankinson, "A Technique towards Automatic Audio Classification and Retrieval," *Proceedings of International Conference on Signal Processing*, Oct. 12-16, 1998, Beijing, China.

[13] Comerford, R., J. Makhoul, and R. Schwartz, "The Voice of the Computer is Heard in the Land (and It Listens too!)", *IEEE Spectrum*, Vol. 34, No. 12, Dec. 1997, pp. 39-47

[14] Rabiner, L. R., "A Tutorial on Hidden Markov Models and Selected Applications in Speech Recognition," *Proceedings of the IEEE*, Vol.77, No.2, Feb. 1989.

[15] Rabiner, L. R., and Biing-Hwang Juang, *Fundamentals of Speech Recognition*, Prentice Hall, 1993.

[16] Morgan, D. P., and C. L. Scofield, *Neural networks and Speech Processing*, Kluwer, 1991.

[17] Klevans, R. L., and Robert D. Rodman, Voice Recognition, Norwood, MA: Artech House, 1997.

[18] Gibbs, S. J., and Dionysios C. Tsichritzis, *Multimedia Programming - Objects, Environments and Frameworks*, Addison-Wesley Publishing Company, 1995.

[19] Scheirer, E. D., "The MPEG-4 Structured Audio Standard," *Proc. IEEE ICASSP 1998*, also available at http://sound.media.mit.edu/papers.html

[20] Ghias, A. et al., "Query by Humming - Musical Information Retrieval in an Audio Database," *Proceedings of ACM Multimedia 95*, November 5-9, 1995, San Francisco, California.

[21] Wold, E. et al., "Content-Based Classification, Search, and Retrieval of Audio," *IEEE Multimedia*, Fall 1996, pp.27-36.

[22] McNa, R. J., et al., "The New Zealand Digital Library MELody inDex," *D-Lib Magazine*, May 1997, available at http://mirrored.ukoln.ac.uk/lis-journals/dlib/dlib/dlib/may97/meldex/05written.html

[23] Scheirer, E. D., "Using Musical Knowledge to Extract Expressive Performance Information from Audio Recordings," available at http://sound.media.mit.edu/papers.html

[24] Martin, K. D., "Automatic Transcription of Simple Polyphonic Music: Robust Front End Processing," *M.I.T. Media Laboratory Perceptual Computing Section Technical Report*, No. 399, 1996, available at http://sound.media.mit.edu/papers.html

Chapter 6

Image Indexing and Retrieval

6.1 INTRODUCTION

We discussed text and audio indexing and retrieval in Chapters 4 and 5, respectively. This chapter deals with image indexing and retrieval. More research has been carried out in image indexing and retrieval than in audio and video indexing and retrieval. A number of practical techniques and commercial products in image indexing and retrieval are now available. This chapter focuses on image feature extraction and image similarity or distance calculation based on extracted feature vectors. The organization of feature vectors for efficient searching and retrieval is discussed in Chapter 9.

There are many approaches to image indexing and retrieval. Section 6.2 briefly describes four main approaches, which are based on structured attributes, object-recognition, text, and low-level image features. The first approach, attribute-based, uses traditional database management systems for image indexing and retrieval. The second approach is not mature yet as it relies on automatic object recognition. Thus, the remaining sections focus on the third and fourth approaches.

Text-based image retrieval uses traditional IR for image indexing and retrieval. Since we covered IR in Chapter 4, Section 6.3 highlights some significant differences between text document retrieval and image retrieval based on text description.

The low-level content-based approach to image indexing and retrieval requires the extraction of low level image features. The common features used are color, object shape, and texture. We describe representations of these features and image similarity calculations based on these features in Sections 6.4, 6.5, and 6.6, respectively.

As most images are stored in compressed form, it would be advantageous if we could derive image features directly from compressed image data. Section 6.7 looks into a number of image indexing and retrieval techniques based on compressed image data.

In addition to the techniques discussed in Sections 6.2 to 6.7, there are other techniques for image indexing and retrieval. Section 6.8 briefly describes some of them.

An individual feature will not be able to describe an image adequately. For example, it is not possible to distinguish a red car from a red apple based on color alone. Therefore, a combination of features is required for effective image indexing and retrieval. Section 6.9 discusses a number of integrated image retrieval techniques.

To avoid too detailed information on color representation in the main text, this is described in Appendix 6A at the end of the chapter.

6.2 DIFFERENT APPROACHES TO IMAGE INDEXING AND RETRIEVAL

There are four main approaches to image indexing and retrieval. In the first, image contents are modeled as a set of attributes extracted manually and managed within the framework of conventional database management systems. Queries are specified using these attributes. Many images have predefined attributes that can be stored with them. Examples of these attributes are image file name, image category, date of creation, subject, author, and image source. Thus images can be indexed and retrieved using a powerful relational database model based on these attributes [1]. The major drawback of this approach is that the attributes may not be able to describe the image contents completely, and the types of queries are limited to those based on these attributes. Attribute-based retrieval is advocated and advanced primarily by database researchers.

The second approach depends on an integrated feature-extraction/object-recognition subsystem. This subsystem automates the feature extraction and object recognition. However, automated approaches to object recognition are computationally expensive, difficult, and tend to be domain specific. This approach is advanced primarily by image-interpretation researchers.

The third approach uses free text to describe (annotate) images and employs IR techniques to carry out image retrieval. Text can describe the high-level abstraction contained in images. Since there is no structure or attributes to limit the description, it is less domain-specific and the text description can be added incrementally. It has the drawbacks of incompleteness and subjectiveness, but these can be partially overcome by using relevance feedback and domain knowledge [2].

The fourth approach uses low-level image features such as color and texture to index and retrieve images. The advantage of this approach is that the indexing and retrieval process is carried out automatically and is easily implemented. It has been shown that this approach produces quite good retrieval performance.

The second and fourth approaches are called *content-based image retrieval*, as the retrieval is based on pictorial contents. But the second approach is currently not practical for general applications. In the following we describe text-based and low-level, feature-based image retrieval techniques. There are many low-level features that can be used for image indexing and retrieval. We describe techniques based on color, shape, and texture. In practice, text-based and low-level, feature-based techniques are combined to achieve high-retrieval performance.

6.3 TEXT-BASED IMAGE RETRIEVAL

In text-based image retrieval, images are described with uncontrolled or free text. Queries are in the form of keywords or free text with or without Boolean operators. The retrieval uses conventional information retrieval techniques based on similarity between the query and the text description of images. The basic IR techniques are described in Chapter 4. There are, however, two significant differences between text-based image retrieval and conventional text document retrieval.

First, in a text-based image retrieval system, the text description has to be entered (or an existing caption used). Text annotation is normally (except in very domain-specific applications) a manual process because high-level image understanding is not possible. So annotation is a very important aspect of text-based image retrieval techniques. The issues in annotation are how to do it efficiently and how to describe the image contents completely and consistently. Domain knowledge or an extended thesaurus should be used to overcome the completeness and consistency problems. Relationships between words or terms will also be considered. For example, "child," "man," and "woman" are subclasses of the more general terms "people" and "human being." Consider that a user issues a query using the keyword "human being," intending to retrieve all images containing human beings. Without using the thesaurus, images described with "people," "person," "man," "woman," and "child" are not retrieved although they are actually what the user is looking for. With the thesaurus, images with these terms are retrieved, leading to high recall and possibly high precision. When building a domain-specific image retrieval system, domain-specific knowledge is introduced to further improve performance [2].

Second, the text description may not be complete and may be subjective. Thus the use of a knowledge base and relevance feedback is extremely important for text-based image retrieval. Relevance feedback is very effective as users can determine whether the image is relevant very quickly. Also, since the original text description may not be complete, we can use relevance feedback to modify the description to make it more complete and accurate.

The advantage of text-based image retrieval techniques is that it captures high level abstractions and concepts, such as "smile" and "happy," contained in images. These concepts are difficult to capture using content-based image retrieval techniques. The limitation is that some lower level features such as texture and irregular shapes are difficult to describe using text. Also, a text-based image retrieval system cannot accept pictorial queries (such as "Retrieve images similar to this one"). These limitations are overcome by content-based image retrieval techniques based on color, shape, and texture.

6.4 COLOR-BASED IMAGE INDEXING AND RETRIEVAL TECHNIQUES

Color-based image indexing and retrieval is the most commonly used content-based image retrieval technique. The concepts involved are simple and are easily implemented. In this section we first look at the basic color-based image indexing and retrieval technique. We then examine its limitations and describe ways to overcome these limitations.

6.4.1 The Basic Color-Based Image Retrieval Technique

The idea of color-based image retrieval techniques is to retrieve from a database images that have perceptually similar colors to the user's query image or description [3-7]. There are many techniques proposed, but their main ideas are similar. Each image in the database is represented using three primaries or channels of the color space chosen. The most common color space used is red, green, and blue (RGB). Each color channel is discretized into m intervals. So the total number of discrete color combinations (called bins) n is equal to m^3. For example, if each color channel is discretized into 16 intervals, we have 4,096 bins in total. A color histogram $H(M)$ is a vector $(h_1, h_2, ..., h_j, ..., h_n)$, where element h_j represents the number of pixels in image M falling into bin j. This histogram is the feature vector to be stored as the index of the image.

During image retrieval, a histogram is found for the query image or estimated from the user's query. The distances between the histograms of the query image and images in the database are measured. Images with a histogram distance smaller than a predefined threshold are retrieved from the database and presented to the user. Alternatively, the first k images with smallest distance are retrieved.

Many histogram distance measurements have been proposed. The simplest distance between images I and H is the L-1 metric defined as:

$$d(I, H) = \sum_{l=1}^{n} |i_l - h_l|$$

where i_l and h_l is the number of pixels falling in bin l in image I and H, respectively. The other commonly used distance measurement is Euclidean distance.

We use an example to show how the basic color-based image retrieval technique works. Suppose we have three images of 8x8 pixels and each pixel is in one of eight colors C_1 to C_8. Image 1 has 8 pixels in each of the eight colors, Image 2 has 7 pixels in each of colors C_1 to C_4, and 9 pixels in each of colors C_5 to C_8. Image 3 has 2 pixels in each of colors C_1 and C_2, and 10 pixels in each of colors C_3 to C_8. Then we have the following three histograms:

$H_1 = (8, 8, 8, 8, 8, 8, 8, 8)$
$H_2 = (7, 7, 7, 7, 9, 9, 9, 9)$
$H_3 = (2, 2, 10, 10, 10, 10, 10, 10)$

The distances between these three images are:
$d(H_1, H_2) = 1+1+1+1+1+1+1+1 = 8$
$d(H_1, H_3) = 6+6+2+2+2+2+2+2 = 24$
$d(H_2, H_3) = 5+5+3+3+3+1+1+1+1 = 23$

Therefore, images 1 and 2 are most similar and images 1 and 3 most different according to the basic technique.

6.4.2 Improvements to the Basic Technique

The basic color-based image retrieval technique has a number of limitations. In this section, we discuss these limitations and present ways to overcome them.

6.4.2.1 Making Use of Similarity Among Colors

The first limitation of the basic color-based image retrieval technique is that the similarity between different colors (and bins) is ignored. Suppose all images have N pixels (if they do not, they are normalized to have the same number of pixels N), then the distance between two images is always less than or equal to $2N$. Their distance will be maximal if two images have no common colors after color discretization. This means that two images with perceptually similar color but with no common color will have maximum distance according to the basic color-based image retrieval method. This is an undesirable feature in practical applications for the following reasons. First, in many applications, users are not only interested in images with exactly same colors as the query, but in images with perceptually similar colors. In most cases, the user requirement is not exact. Second, image colors may change slightly due to noise and variations in illumination. (This is related to the color constancy issue [3, 4]; we do not discuss it further here.) The basic technique may not be able to retrieve perceptually similar images due to these changes. For example, if we have two bins representing color ranges $1 - 10$ and $11 - 20$ (assuming colors with closer values are more similar), then color 10 will be classified into bin 1, color 11 in bin 2, and color 20 in bin 2. In effect, we are saying color 11 is the same as color 20 but totally different from color 10. This is obviously incorrect.

Many approaches have been proposed to overcome the above problem. The first approach takes into account contributions of perceptually similar colors in the distance or similarity calculation. Note that image distance and similarity have an inverse relationship. If the distance is small, the similarity is high, and vice versa. The similarity measurement used by Niblack et al. [5] is as follows. Let X be the query histogram and Y the histogram of an image in the database, both normalized. The bin-to-bin similarity histogram Z is computed. Then the similarity between X and Y is given by

$$\|Z\| = Z^T A Z$$

where A is a symmetric color similarity matrix with

$$a(i, j) = 1 - d(c_i, c_j)/d_{\max}$$

where c_i and c_j are the ith and jth color bins in the color histogram, and $d(c_i, c_j)$ is the color distance in the mathematical transform to Munsell (MTM) color space, and $d_{\max}$ is the maximum distance between any two colors in the color space. The similarity matrix A accounts for the perceptual similarity between different pairs of colors. If two colors are very different, $d(c_i, c_j)$ will be close to $d_{\max}$ and $a(i, j)$ will be close to 0, leading to almost 0 contribution to image similarity. On the other hand, if two colors are very similar, $d(c_i, c_j)$ will be close to 0 and $a(i, j)$ will be close to 1, leading to a high contribution to image similarity.

A similar approach has been taken by Chan [8], where histogram values are adjusted based on color similarity when calculating image distance. For example, if image 1 has two bins bin 1 and bin 2 having values 300 and 0, respectively, the value in bin 2 is adjusted to $300w$, where w ranges from 0 to 1 depending on the color similarity between bin 1 and bin 2. If image 2 also has two bins, bin 1 and bin 2 having values 0 and 300, respectively, the value in bin 1 is adjusted to $300w$. The distance between these two images is $600(1-w)$. If bin 1 and bin 2 represent very similar colors, w is close to 1, so the distance between these two images is much smaller than 600. On the other hand, if bin 1 and bin 2 represent two very different colors, w is close to 0, so the distance between these two images is close to 600. This is a much better outcome than that of the basic method in which bin values are not adjusted and the resulting distance is always 600, although bin 1 and bin 2 may represent perceptually very similar colors.

The second approach to avoiding the calculation of bin-to-bin distance without considering color similarity is to use a cumulative histogram [7]. The cumulative histogram $CH(M) = (ch_1, ch_2, \ldots, ch_n)$ of image M is defined in terms of the color histogram $H(M)$:

$$ch_i = \sum_{j \le i} h_j$$

To calculate image distances, the L1-metric or Euclidean distance between cumulative histograms is used. This approach avoids calculating image distance based on bin-to-bin distance. The drawback of this approach is that the cumulative histogram values may not reflect the perceptual color similarity. This is especially true in cases when i is large, where very different colors are classified into the same cumulative bin.

The third approach is to use a perceptually weighted histogram (PWH) [9]. When calculating PWH, representative colors in the color space chosen are determined. The number of the representative colors is equal to the required number of histogram bins. These representative colors are uniformly distributed in the color space. While building a histogram, the 10 perceptually most similar representative colors are found for each pixel. The distance between the pixel and the 10 representative colors are calculated. Then weights inversely proportional to the color distances are assigned to these 10 representative colors. Compared to the techniques proposed in [5] and [8], the PWH technique considers color similarity when building histograms while those techniques only consider color similarity during the distance calculation. Thus some color similarity information is lost in those techniques. For example, suppose we have three color values 10, 11, and 22, and two bins with value range of 1 to 10 and 11 to 20, respectively. The PWH method assigns appropriate weights to bin 1 and bin 2 for each of these colors based on its perceptual similarity to the representative color of each bin. However, in the techniques of [5] and [8], color 10 will be classified entirely in bin 1, and colors 11 and 20 entirely in bin 2. Only during retrieval is similarity between bin 1 and bin 2 considered. But at this stage, there is no way to know if the value in bin 1 is contributed by color 1 or color 10. Similarly there is no way to know which colors contributed to bin 2. Thus the PWH-method is advantageous as perceptual similarity is built into the PWH. It has been shown that the PWH based method results in better image retrieval performance than the basic color-based image retrieval technique [9].

6.4.2.2 Making Use of Spatial Relationships Among Pixels

The second major limitation of the basic color-based image retrieval technique is that it ignores spatial relationships among pixels. For example, the two images in Figure 6.1 have the same histogram according to the basic color-based image index technique, leading to the wrong conclusion that these two images are the same.

To overcome this limitation, it has been proposed that each image be segmented into a fixed number of regions and a histogram calculated for each region [10-12]. During retrieval, histograms of corresponding regions are compared.

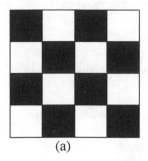
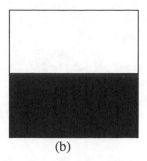

(a)   (b)

Figure 6.1 An example showing two different images that have the same basic histogram.

Another limitation related to the above limitation is the masking effect of the background [13]. As mentioned previously, a color histogram shows the number of pixels that are in each color bin. Therefore, if there is a large block of color j, h_j will be large. Colors of small blocks will have low representation in the histogram. That is, the histogram is biased towards the colors of large blocks.

A large number of images consist of two distinctive parts: foreground (main objects of the image) and background. Background normally has regular colors and a large number of pixels. In this case, if two images have the same or similar background colors, their histograms will be similar and the images will be considered similar during retrieval, although they may have very different foregrounds in which the user is primarily interested. We can think of this problem as background masking foreground in color histograms, leading to difficulty in retrieving images with relevant foreground. For example, suppose we have three images: the first image is a red car on black background (road), the second image is a red car on brown background (showroom carpet), and the third image is a blue car on the same brown background. The basic image retrieval technique will consider the second image more similar to the third image than to the first image. This is obviously incorrect when the user is interested in finding cars with the same or similar color.

To solve the above problem, Lu and Phillips proposed to derive separate histograms for foreground and background [13]. The segmentation into foreground and background is not required to be accurate, although the more accurate the better. The foreground is the minimum rectangle containing the main objects of the image. This segmentation can be done automatically by determining the pixel value transitions in both the horizontal and vertical directions. Alternatively, the foreground rectangle can be drawn by the user during the indexing and retrieval processes. In this way, each image in the database is indexed by a foreground histogram and a background histogram. The histogram of the whole image can be obtained easily from these two histograms.

During image retrieval, the user has the following options and can decide which one to use depending on his/her requirements and the image type.

- Option 1: Each of the query image and images in database is represented by a single histogram. This is the basic retrieval method.
- Option 2: The query is based on the foreground histogram and the foreground histo-

grams in the database are searched and compared. The retrieval is based on the similarity between the query foreground histogram and the foreground histograms of the images in the database.

- Option 3: The query is based on the background histogram and the background histograms in the database are searched and compared. The retrieval is based on the similarity between the query background histogram and the background histograms of the images in the database.
- Option 4: Both background and foreground histograms are used and the user selects the weight to be used for these two histograms in calculating similarity.

Experimental results show that the above proposed method improves image retrieval performance [13].

6.4.2.3 Making Use of the Statistics of Color Distribution

The third limitation of the basic image retrieval technique is that the chosen color space is uniformly quantized, although image pixel colors are not uniformly distributed in the color space. Wan and Kuo [14] studied color distribution and proposed to quantize colors nonuniformly: color regions where pixels are highly populated in the color space are quantized more finely than others.

6.4.2.4 Better Color Representation

As color-based image retrieval techniques operate based on pixel values that represent different colors, it is essential that an appropriate color representation is used. There are many different color spaces and images originating from different sources can be represented differently. Thus two important questions to ask are: Which color space is best suited for color distance calculation and thus image retrieval, and do the pixel values of different images mean the same thing? We briefly address color spaces and variations of image representation separately in the following. Detailed discussion of these two topics is covered in Appendix 6A at the end of this chapter.

Different Color Spaces

A color space defines how colors are represented. There are many different color spaces. The most commonly used color space is based on RGB primaries. However, RGB color space is device-dependent, meaning that the displayed color depends on not only the RGB values but also the device specifications. There are a number of RGB color space standards, such as the CCIR REC.709 and SMPTE "C" primaries (details on these are in Appendix 6A). They differ in how the reference white and three primaries are defined in the device-independent color space CIE XYZ. Color representations can be converted among different RGB and CIE XYZ color spaces when the definitions for the reference white and three primaries are known.

The second feature of RGB spaces is that they are not perceptually uniform, meaning that the calculated distance in a RGB space does not truly reflect perceptual color difference. Two colors can be quite far apart in a RGB space, but they can be perceptually similar, and vice versa.

For the above reasons, RGB color spaces are not very suitable for color-based image retrieval. The commonly used alternatives are CIE Luv, CIELab, HSI (hue, saturation, and intensity) and HVC (hue, value, and chroma). The first two are uniform color spaces. The latter two have characteristics that are used by human beings to distinguish one color from another. These color spaces (RGB, CIE Luv, CIELab, HSI, and HVC) can be converted to and from each other when RGB color spaces are properly defined. Interested readers are referred to Appendix 6A for details.

It is not clear which color space is best suited for color-based image retrieval, as there has been no comprehensive test carried out using all these color spaces on a common large image collection.

Variations of Image Representation

Given a stored digital image in RGB format, it is commonly not possible to interpret the image data correctly for the following reasons. First, it is likely that the definition of the RGB color space (reference white and three primaries) is not provided, so there is no way to determine the image data in terms of device-independent color spaces. (This is similar to the case where temperature is specified in degrees without mentioning Celsius or Fahrenheit. How hot is 50 degrees?) Second, image data is normally scaled by the image capturing device by a so-called gamma correction value (see Appendix 6A for details). Different capturing devices use different gamma correction values. (Imagine different scales that use different calibrations. Different readings are produced on different scales for the same weight!) Third, images can be taken in different illumination, resulting in very different image data for the same or similar objects.

For the above reasons, distance calculation and image data comparison among images from different sources may not be reliable, leading to low image retrieval performance. We use examples to illustrate this in the following.

Effects of Different Image Representations on Retrieval Performance

In color-based image retrieval, it is implied that all images are represented in the same color space and their pixel values mean the same thing. In practical large-image database applications, this assumption is not true. Images may be captured at different times, using different devices, and may be represented differently. For example, images may be collected and digitized over a long time period, or may be contributed by somebody on the Internet, making it likely that these images are represented differently.

Color comparison based on the "face values" of the image data may result in a wrong conclusion. In the case of image retrieval, the retrieval performance may be poor.

Currently most image file formats, such as plain raster format, JPEG, and GIF, do not carry information about gamma values, chromaticity of primaries, and white reference. This causes the wrong interpretation of image pixel values, leading to poor image retrieval performance and image display quality. This situation is changing: TIFF 6.0

[15] and SMPTE DPX [16] contain tags to specify these parameters. But until a common color image interchange format is adopted and widely used, wrong interpretations of image code values will have serious effects on image retrieval performance and image display quality. In the following, we use examples to show the effects of different gamma values and color systems on histograms and their distance.

Given a typical image (we use a picture of a TV announcer as an example), we calculate and draw histograms assuming different gamma values and different RGB systems are used. Each pixel was originally represented by 24 bits: 8 bits for each of the RGB components. We discretize each color component to 4 bits (i.e., 16 intervals for each component). To make examples simple, we use only one color component to calculate the histogram. In this case, we have only 16 bins instead of 4,096 bins in total. The image size is 512 x 480 pixels. So the possible maximum distance between histograms for this image size is 491,520.

In the first case, we first assume a gamma correction value of 1/2 is used and obtain a base histogram as shown in solid graph in Figure 6.2(a). We want to find out what the histogram would be like if we assume a gamma correction value of 1/2.5 is used. In order to compare with the base histogram, we have to convert the pixel values represented in the gamma correction value 1/2 to pixel values represented in the gamma correction value 1/2.5. The dotted graph in Figure 6.2(a) shows the histogram of the same image obtained assuming a gamma correction value of 1/2.5. In the histogram calculation, we assume that the color systems used are the same. Using the histogram distance measurement L-1, the distance between these two histograms is 127,780 (or 26% of the maximum distance). This means that given the same image data, the histogram varies greatly depending on the assumption of gamma values used.

Similarly, the dotted curve in Figure 6.2(b) is the histogram obtained assuming the CCIR Rec. 709 Primaries are used, and the solid curve is the histogram of the same image obtained assuming the SMPTE "C" Primaries are used. We assume that the gamma correction value and white reference used are the same. Using the histogram distance measurement L-1, the distance between these two histograms is 106,634 (or 22% of the maximum distance).

From the examples, we see that different representations and interpretations of image data have serious effects on image retrieval performance. In a large image database, representations of images within the database and between the query and images in the database can be different. Different color representations have two implications for image retrieval performance. First, images with different dominant colors originally could have similar histograms due to different representations. This results in the retrieval of irrelevant images, leading to low retrieval precision. Second, images with the same or similar dominant colors originally could have different histograms due to different representations. Thus, relevant images may not be retrieved, leading to low retrieval recall. If the appropriate correction transformations are not carried out, the image retrieval performance will be poor.

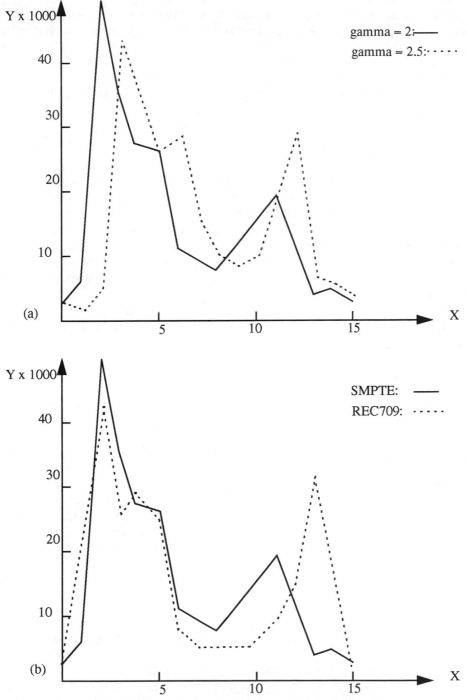

Figure 6.2 (a) Effects of different gamma values on histograms;
(b) Effects of different color spaces on histograms.

In reality, the correction transformation from one color representation to another may not be carried out because image files do not carry the information (gamma value, chromaticities of reference white and primaries) needed to carry out the transformations. This indicates that there is a need for a common image interchange format incorporating this information. This would help not only to improve image retrieval performance but also to improve image display quality and the performance of other image processing operations.

6.5   IMAGE RETRIEVAL BASED ON SHAPE

Another important low-level image feature is the shape of objects contained in the image. For retrieval based on shapes, images must be segmented into individual objects using certain methods, possibly a semiautomatic method as reported in [43]. Although image segmentation is an important and interesting topic, we do not discuss it further. After segmentation, the basic issue of shape-based image retrieval is shape representation and similarity measurement between shape representations. A good shape representation and similarity measurement for recognition and retrieval purposes should have the following two important properties:

- Each shape should have a unique representation, invariant to translation, rotation, and scale;
- Similar shapes should have similar representations so that retrieval can be based on distances among shape representations.

The first property is required to identify objects of different sizes and at different position and orientations.

Image retrieval systems are normally based on best-match techniques instead of exact match techniques. During the retrieval process, the user selects an example image or draws a shape that he or she is interested in. The image is then presented to the retrieval system. The system retrieves images containing similar shapes and presents them to the user in the order of decreasing similarity. Thus it is important that similar shapes have similar measures; the distance between similar shapes should be smaller than that between dissimilar shapes. In other words, the similarity measure between shape representations should conform to human perception. Different shape representations vary in their success in meeting these two properties.

The following subsections describe a number of approaches to shape description and similarity measurements.

6.5.1 Definitions of Common Terms and Some Simple Shape Measurements

The following are some important terms associated with shape description:
- Major axis: the straight line segment joining the two points on the boundary furthest away from each other.
- Minor axis: the straight line perpendicular to the major axis, and of such length that a rectangle with sides parallel to major and minor axes that just encloses the bound-

ary can be formed using the lengths of the major and minor axes.
- Basic rectangle: the above rectangle formed with the major and minor axes as its two sides is called the basic rectangle.
- Eccentricity: the ratio of the major to the minor axis is called eccentricity of the boundary.

The above shape measurements provide a rough shape representation. Thus they can be used for shape indexing and retrieval. However, as they alone don't describe shape adequately, they are normally used together with other shape representations. For example, the Query By Image Contents (QBIC[1]) system of IBM uses shape area, circularity, orientation of the major axis, and moment invariants for shape indexing and retrieval [5].

6.5.2 Invariant Moments

Moments have been used to identify images and have been used in a number of image retrieval systems [5, 17-19]. For a digital image $f(x, y)$, the moment of order $(p + q)$ is defined as

$$m_{pq} = \sum_x \sum_y x^p y^q f(x, y)$$

where x, y is the pixel position in the image, and $f(x,y)$ is the pixel intensity.

If $\bar{x}$ and $\bar{y}$ are defined as

$$\bar{x} = m_{10}/m_{00} \text{ and } \bar{y} = m_{01}/m_{00}$$

then the central moments are expressed as

$$\mu_{pq} = \sum_x \sum_y (x - \bar{x})^p (y - \bar{y})^q f(x, y)$$

The central moments of up to order 3 are defined as follows:

$$\mu_{00} = m_{00}$$
$$\mu_{10} = 0$$
$$\mu_{01} = 0$$
$$\mu_{20} = m_{20} - \bar{x} m_{10}$$
$$\mu_{02} = m_{02} - \bar{y} m_{01}$$
$$\mu_{11} = m_{11} - \bar{y} m_{10}$$

---

1. QBIC is a trademark of IBM Corporation.

$$\mu_{30} = m_{30} - 3\bar{x}m_{20} + 2m_{10}\bar{x}^2$$

$$\mu_{12} = m_{12} - 2\bar{y}m_{11} - \bar{x}m_{02} + 2\bar{y}^2 m_{10}$$

$$\mu_{21} = m_{21} - 2\bar{x}m_{11} - \bar{y}m_{20} + 2\bar{x}^2 m_{01}$$

$$\mu_{03} = m_{03} - 3\bar{y}m_{02} + 2\bar{y}^2 m_{01}$$

The normalized central moment of order $(p + q)$, denoted by η_{pq}, is defined as

$$\eta_{pq} = \frac{\mu_{pq}}{\mu_{00}^{\gamma}}$$

where $\gamma = \dfrac{(p + q)}{2} + 1$ for $p + q = 2, 3, \ldots$

It has been shown that the following seven moments are invariant to translation, rotation, and scale change [19]:

$$\phi_1 = \eta_{20} + \eta_{02}$$

$$\phi_2 = (\eta_{20} - \eta_{02})^2 + 4\eta_{11}^2$$

$$\phi_3 = (\eta_{30} - 3\eta_{12})^2 + (3\eta_{21} - \eta_{03})^2$$

$$\phi_4 = (\eta_{30} + \eta_{12})^2 + (\eta_{21} + \eta_{03})^2$$

$$\phi_5 = (\eta_{30} - 3\eta_{12})(\eta_{30} + \eta_{12})[(\eta_{30} + \eta_{12})^2 - 3(\eta_{21} + \eta_{03})^2]$$
$$+ (3\eta_{21} - \eta_{03})(\eta_{21} + \eta_{03})[3(\eta_{30} + \eta_{12})^2 - (\eta_{21} + \eta_{03})^2]$$

$$\phi_6 = (\eta_{20} - \eta_{02})[(\eta_{30} + \eta_{12})^2 - (\eta_{21} + \eta_{03})^2] + 4\eta_{11}(\eta_{30} + \eta_{12})(\eta_{21} + \eta_{03})$$

$$\phi_7 = (3\eta_{21} - 3\eta_{30})(\eta_{30} + \eta_{12})[(\eta_{30} + \eta_{12})^2 - 3(\eta_{21} + \eta_{03})^2]$$
$$+ (3\eta_{12} - \eta_{30})(\eta_{21} + \eta_{03})[3(\eta_{30} + \eta_{12})^2 - (\eta_{21} + \eta_{03})^2]$$

The above seven moments are used for shape description. The Euclidean distance between two shape descriptions is used as the distance between the two shapes. However, it has been shown that similar moments do not guarantee similar shapes and some of the above moments are similar and some are different for visually different shapes [5, 18]. Therefore, the performance of moment-based shape indexing and retrieval is not very high [20].

6.5.3 Fourier Descriptors Method

In the Fourier descriptor-based method, a shape is first represented by a feature function called a shape signature. A discrete Fourier transform is applied to the signature to obtain Fourier descriptors (FD) of the shape. These FDs are used to index the shape and for calculation of shape [20-25].

The discrete Fourier transformation of a shape signature $f(i)$ is given by

$$F_u = \frac{1}{N} \sum_{i=0}^{N-1} f(i) \cdot \exp\left[\frac{-j2\pi ui}{N}\right]$$

for $u=0$ to $N-1$, where N is the number of samples of $f(i)$.

There are a number of types of shape signatures. The commonly used signatures are curvature based, radius based, and boundary coordinates based. It has been found that shape classification performance based on these three signatures does not differ significantly [25]. The radius-based signature is simplest to implement.

Radius-based signature consists of a number of ordered distances from the shape centroid to boundary points (called radii). The radii are defined as

$$r_i = \sqrt{(x_c - x_i)^2 + (y_c - y_i)^2}$$

where (x_c, y_c) are the coordinates of the centroid and (x_i, y_i) for $i = 0$ to 63 are the coordinates of the 64 sample points along the shape boundary. The boundary points are sampled such that the number of pixels along the boundary between each two neighboring points is the same.

Shape radii and thus their transformations are translation invariant. Note that shapes are not orientation normalized before the shape radii are used. The normalization is achieved by ignoring the phase values of the FDs. Shape rotation is reflected in the phase information of F_u and the magnitude of F_u, i.e., $|F_u|$, is invariant to rotation. $|F_0|$ reflects the energy of the shape radii, thus $|F_u|/|F_0|$ will be scale invariant. Therefore, we use the following feature vector, which is invariant to translation, rotation, and scale, to index the shape:

$$x = \left[\frac{|F_1|}{|F_0|}, \ldots, \frac{|F_{63}|}{|F_0|}\right]$$

The distance between shapes is calculated as the Euclidean distance between their feature vectors.

Why should we use FDs as the shape index instead of radii directly? The main reason is that the direct representation is very sensitive to small changes and noise, leading to very poor retrieval performance. If 64 radius lengths are directly used as an index, it would be very difficult to do scale and rotation normalization. It may appear that we can achieve rotation normalization by identifying the shortest (or longest) radius and achieve scale normalization by fixing the length of the shortest radius. But this normalization is not stable as a small change on the boundary may affect the position of shortest radius and the positions of sample points, leading to very different indexes and large distances between shapes due to the small change. The purpose of using FDs is to convert the sensitive radius lengths into the frequency domain where the data is more robust to small changes and noise. This is because FDs capture the general features and form of the shape instead of each individual detail.

6.5.4 Histogram of Significant Edges

The shape information contained in an image can also be described on the basis of its significant edges [26]. A histogram of edge directions is used to represent the shape features. The distance between histograms is calculated using the L-1 metric. Since matching the histograms of the edge directions is inherently not rotation or scale invariant, a normalization process is needed. The scale invariance problem is solved by normalizing histograms with respect to the number of edge points in the image. Rotation of an image only shifts the histogram bins, so a match across all possible shifts (a function of bin quantization level) is used to solve the rotation invariance problem. This approach is slow and the first normalization is questionable, as the number of edges in an image is not directly proportional to the scale of the image.

6.5.5 Ordered List of Interest Points

Mehrotra and Gary proposed the use of an ordered list of *boundary points* or *interest points* to describe shapes [27]. Given a shape F with n interest points, a pair is chosen to form a *basis vector*. The basis vector is normalized as a unit vector along the x-axis. All other interest points of the shape are transformed to this coordinate system, as shown in Figure 6.3. The shape F is then described by the coordinate set $((x1, y1), ..., (xn, yn))$, where (xi, yi) are the normalized coordinates of the ith interest point.

By normalizing the basis vector, the representation is scale invariant. To achieve rotation invariance, all vectors formed by connecting two adjacent points are used as basis vectors in turn. In this way, a shape is described by a number of coordinate sets, the number of coordinate sets being equal to $n - 1$, where n is the number of the interest points.

The query features are described in the same way as the shapes in the database. The distance between the query and the shapes in the database is calculated as the Euclidean distance between coordinate sets.

In this approach, indexes (coordinate sets) are large so retrieval is slow. Also, it is not clear how the distance is calculated when the numbers of interest points are different for different shapes.

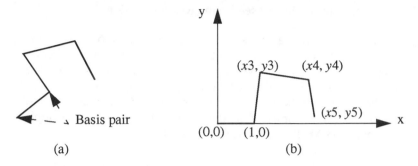

Figure 6.3 Example of interest point description: (a) original image
feature; (b) interest points in the normalized coordinate system.

6.5.6 Elastic Template Matching

In elastic template matching (ETM) [28], the query shape is deformed to match each shape in the database as closely as possible. The similarity between the query shape and each of the database shapes is determined based on the following five parameters. The first parameter measures how well the deformed query shape overlaps the database shape. The second and third parameters measure the amount of energy needed to achieve the above overlapping. The fourth parameter measures the complexity of the query shape. The final parameter measures the correlation between the original query shape and the deformed query shape.

A neural network is then used to obtain a single similarity value from these five parameters.

6.5.7 Region-Based Shape Representation and Similarity Measure

The shape similarity measurements based on shape representations described above do not conform to human perception in general. Studies have compared shape similarity measurements using algebraic moments, spline curve distance, cumulative turning angle, sign of curvature, and Hausdorff-distance with the human similarity judgment [20]. It was found that the computational similarity based on these measurements does not match very well with human judgment.

In the following we describe a region-based shape representation and similarity measure, which has been reported to have promising retrieval performance [24, 29]. The discussion of this method is more detailed than other methods for the following two reasons. First, this method has been shown to have high retrieval performance. Second, we use this method as an example to show the complete process of feature representation, normalization, and distance measurement.

6.5.7.1 Basic Idea of Region-Based Shape Representation

Given a shape, we overlay a grid space over it (see Figure 6.4). The grid space, which consists of fixed size square cells, is just big enough to completely cover the shape. Some grid cells are fully or partially covered by the shape and some are not. We assign a 1 to the cell with at least 15% of pixels covered by the shape, and a 0 to each of the other cells. We then read these 1s and 0s from left to right and top to bottom to obtain a binary sequence for the shape. For example, the shape in Figure 6.4 can be represented by the binary sequence 11100000 11111000 01111110 01111111.

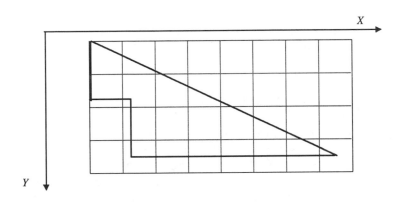

Figure 6.4 Generation of binary sequence for a shape.

We see that the smaller the cell size, the more accurate the shape representation and the more the storage and computation requirements. A good compromise for the cell size is around 10x10 to 20x20 pixels.

The above representation is compact, easy to obtain, and translation invariant but it is not invariant to scale and rotation. Thus the binary sequence is normalized for scale and rotation, if we want to use it for shape representation.

6.5.7.2 Rotation Normalization

The purpose of rotation normalization is to place shapes in a unique common orientation. We rotate the shape so that its major axis is parallel with the x-axis. There are still two possibilities for the shape placement: one of the furthest points can be on the left or on the right. This is caused by $180°$ rotation. For example, The shape in Figure 6.4 can be placed in one of the two orientations as shown in Figure 6.5.

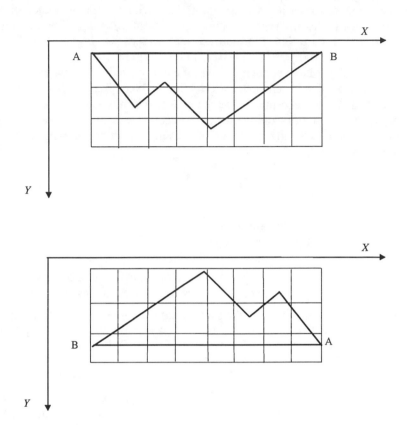

Figure 6.5 Two possible orientations with the major axis along the x direction.

Two different binary sequences are needed to represent these two orientations. As the binary sequences are used to index of the shapes in the retrieval system, storing two for each shape needs twice the storage space. To save storage space, we obtain and store only one of the binary sequences. Which one to use is not important and is determined by the implementation. The two orientations are accounted for during retrieval time by representing the query shape using two binary sequences that are compared to each shape index stored in the database.

6.5.7.3 Scale Normalization

To achieve scale normalization, we proportionally scale all shapes so that their major axes have the same fixed length. In [24, 29], the fixed length used is 192 pixels.

6.5.7.4 Unique Shape Representation – Shape Index

After rotation and scale normalization and selection of a grid cell size, we obtain a unique binary sequence for each shape assuming that each has a unique major axis. This binary sequence is used as the representation or index of the shape. For example, the index of shape in Figure 6.4 (normalized into shapes in Figure 6.5) is either 1111111101111111000011000 or 0011111011111111111111111.

As we use a grid just large enough to cover the normalized shape, when the cell size is decided, the number of grid cells in the x direction is fixed. The number of cells in the y direction depends on the eccentricity of the shape, the maximum number being the same as that in x direction. For example, when grid cell size is 24x24 pixels, the number of cells in the x direction is 8 and the number of cells in Y direction can range from 1 to 8, depending on shape eccentricity.

6.5.7.5 Similarity Measure

The next issue is how to measure similarity between shapes based on their indexes. As the index indicates the cell positions covered by a shape, it is natural to define the distance between two shapes as the number of cell positions not commonly covered by these two shapes. Rotation through 180° and other shape operations is considered later. Based on the shape eccentricities, there are the following three cases for similarity calculation:

- If two normalized shapes have the same basic rectangle, we bitwise compare the indexes of these two shapes, and the distance between them is equal to the number of positions having different values. For example, if shapes A and B have the same eccentricity of 4 and binary sequences 11111111 11100000 and 111111111111100, respectively, then the distance between A and B is 3.

- If two normalized shapes have very different basic rectangles (i.e, they have very different minor axis lengths), there is no need to calculate their similarity as we can safely assume that these two shapes are very different. For example, if the eccentricities of shapes A and B are 8 and 2, respectively (i.e., the lengths of minor axes are 1 and 4 cells), then we can assume that these two shapes are quite different and there is no value in retrieving the shape. The difference threshold between minor axes depends on applications and cell size. Normally, if the lengths of the minor axes of two shapes differ by more than 3 cells, these two shapes are considered quite different.

- If two normalized shapes have slightly different basic rectangles, it is still possible these two shapes are perceptually similar. We add 0s at the end of the index of the shape with shorter minor axis, so that the extended index is of the same length as that of the other shape. The distance between these two shapes is calculated as in the first case. For example, if the length of the minor axis and binary sequence of shape A are 2 and 11111111 11110000 and the length of the minor axis and binary sequence of shape B are 3 and 11111111 111111000 11100000, respectively, then we extend the binary number for shape A to 11111111 11110000 00000000. The distance between A and B is 4.

To facilitate the above similarity calculation during retrieval, shape eccentricity is stored together with the unique binary sequence. They together form the index of a shape.

6.5.7.6 Other Shape Operations

In addition to the 180° rotation of shapes, the other two operations that result in perceptually similar shapes are horizontal and vertical flips. Figure 6.6 shows the two shapes resulting from these two operations on the shape in Figure 6.5(a). These two shapes are perceptually similar to the shape in Figure 6.4.

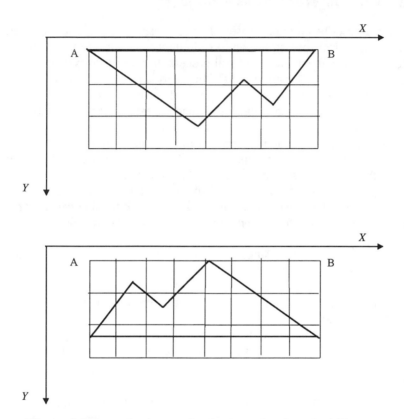

Figure 6.6 Example shapes after horizontal and vertical flips.

To take into account of these two operations and yet to save storage space, we still store one index for each shape but we generate four binary sequences for each query shape during retrieval. In this case, perceptually similar shapes resulting from 180° rotation and horizontal and vertical flips are retrieved.

6.5.7.7 Handling Multiple Major Axes

In the above discussion, we assumed that each shape has only one major axis. In practice, a shape may have multiple major axes of equal length. The same shape may result in different binary numbers depending on which major axis is used for rotation normalization.

To solve this problem, rotation normalization is done along each major axis and binary numbers for each normalization are used as a shape index. The distance between two shapes is the minimum distance between each pair of binary numbers of these two shapes.

6.5.7.8 Summary of Index and Retrieval Processes

In the above we described a region-based shape representation invariant to translation, scale, rotation and mirror operations, and its similarity measure. In this subsection, we summarize the shape indexing and retrieval process. In a retrieval system, all shapes in the database are indexed. During retrieval, the query shape is also indexed. Then the query index is compared with shape indexes in the database to retrieve similar shapes.

Each shape in the database is processed and indexed as follows (assuming each shape has only one major axis):

- The major and minor axes and eccentricity of each shape are found.
- The shape is rotated to place the major axis along the x direction, and the shape is scaled so that the major axis is of a standard fixed length.
- A grid space with fixed cell size is overlaid on top of the normalized shape.
- The 1s are assigned to cells covered by the shape and 0s to other cells. By reading these 1s and 0s from left to right and top to bottom, we obtain a binary sequence for the shape.
- The binary sequence and the length of the minor axis are stored as the index of the shape.

During retrieval, the following steps are used to represent the query shape and carry out similarity comparisons.

1. The query shape is represented by its minor axis length and binary sequences using the same procedure as in the above indexing process. But note there are four binary sequences for each query to take into account $180°$ rotation and the horizontal and vertical flip operations.
2. For efficiency reasons, these four binary sequences are only compared with binary sequences of shapes in database with the same or similar eccentricities.
3. The distance between the query and a shape in the database is calculated as the number of positions with different values in their binary sequences.
4. The similar shapes are displayed or retrieved in increasing order of shape distance.

The above outlined approach is simple and similar to the way we normally compare shapes. To compare two shapes, we prefer that they are of same or similar size (scale normalization). Then we rotate one of the shapes over the other so that they have the same orientation (rotation normalization). Finally we determine how much they differ based on how much they do not overlap. The region-based approach incorporates all of these steps.

6.5.7.9 Retrieval Performance

We use an example to show whether the distance measure of the region-based method conforms with human perception. Table 6.1 shows the distance among 7 queries in Figure 6.8 (labeled as a to g) and 20 shapes in Figure 6.7 (numbered as 1 to 20). In general, the results obtained conform with human perception. Of course, human perception of shape similarity among some shapes is sometimes subjective and application dependant.

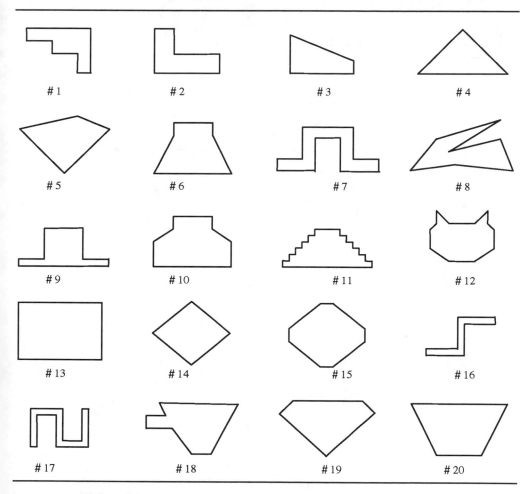

Figure 6.7 Twenty example shapes.

154

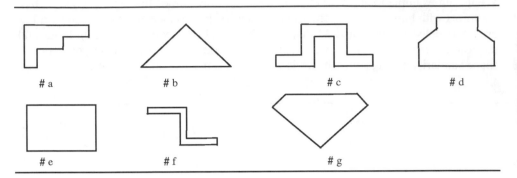

a   # b   # c   # d

e   # f   # g

Figure 6.8 Seven query shapes.

Table 6.1
Distances Between the Seven Queries and Twenty Shapes

	a	b	c	d	e	f	g
1	0	104	46	76	37	44	65
2	33	65	69	80	38	61	56
3	17	81	33	96	48	37	60
4	104	0	87	76	71	100	37
5	72	62	75	41	53	78	61
6	98	55	104	50	110	103	77
7	46	87	0	86	79	44	60
8	54	88	32	117	89	40	69
9	32	84	34	101	55	52	65
10	76	76	86	0	72	93	76
11	40	76	50	89	47	64	59
12	105	68	121	65	69	90	80
13	37	71	79	72	0	71	66
14	108	55	116	64	74	91	69
15	123	71	132	62	88	137	62
16	44	100	44	93	71	0	63
17	54	92	71	109	49	50	91
18	54	51	52	54	62	69	36
19	65	37	60	76	66	63	0
20	91	38	109	65	81	86	70

The retrieval performance of the region-based method was also compared with that of FD-based, moment-based, ETM, and QBIC shape retrieval. It was reported that the region-based method has similar retrieval effectiveness to that of ETM and higher effectiveness than that of the FD-based, moment-based and QBIC methods, and it is more efficient than all other methods [24, 29].

6.6   IMAGE RETRIEVAL BASED ON TEXTURE

Texture is an important image feature, but it is difficult to describe and its perception is subjective to a certain extent. Many methods have been proposed in the computer vision literature. So far one of the best texture specifications is the one proposed by Tamura et al. [30]. To find a texture description, they conducted psychological experiments. The aim of their study was to make the description conform to human perception as closely as possible. In their specification, texture is described by six features: coarseness, contrast, directionality, line likeness, regularity, and roughness. A description of the quantitative computation of these features is beyond the scope of this book. In the following we give qualitative descriptions of these six features:

- *Coarseness*: Coarse is opposite to fine. Coarseness is the most fundamental texture feature and to some people texture means coarseness. The larger the distinctive image elements, the coarser the image. So, an enlarged image is coarser than the original one.
- *Contrast*: The contrast is measured using four parameters: dynamic range of gray levels of the image; polarization of the distribution of black and white on the gray-level histogram or ratio of black and white areas; sharpness of edges; and period of repeating patterns.
- *Directionality*: It is a global property over the given region. It measures both element shape and placement. The orientation of the texture pattern is not important: two patterns that differ only in orientation have the same degree of directionality.
- *Line likeness*: This parameter is concerned with the shape of a texture element. Two common types of shapes are linelike and bloblike.
- *Regularity*: This measures variation of an element placement rule. It is concerned with whether the texture is regular or irregular. Different element shape reduces regularity. A fine texture tends to be perceived as regular.
- *Roughness*: This measures whether the texture is rough or smooth. It is related to coarseness and contrast.

Most texture-based image retrieval systems use the computation measure proposed in [30]. But not all six features are used. In the QBIC system, texture is described by coarseness, contrast, and directionality [5]. In Chan [8], texture is described by coarseness and contrast. Retrieval is based on similarity instead of exact match. Both systems are reported to have good retrieval performance based on texture.

Other common texture representations used in the literature are:

- Fractal dimension: it has been observed that the fractal dimension is relatively insensitive to image scaling and shows a strong correlation with human judgment of surface roughness. Fractal dimension characterizes the geometrical complexity of a set. An image can be viewed as a set of three dimensions: the first two corresponding to pixel position and the third pixel intensity. The rougher the image, the higher the fractal dimension of the image. Thus fractal dimensions can be used to describe the texture of images [31].

- Fourier coefficients: the Fourier coefficients (FC) of an image describe how fast the pixel intensities of the image change. Thus FC values can be used to indicate the roughness of images. Dadd and Ables proposed to use the average non-DC FC values calculated over different frequencies to describe the texture of an image [32]
- Color distribution statistics: Color distribution statistics, such as the first, second, and third moments of the color distribution can roughly indicate the texture of an image [33].

6.7 IMAGE INDEXING AND RETRIEVAL BASED ON COMPRESSED IMAGE DATA

The techniques discussed so far derive feature vectors (indexes) from uncompressed image data (i.e., directly from pixel values). As most images are stored in compressed form, it would be useful if we could directly derive feature vectors from compressed image data. A number of research activities have been carried out in this area. The three common compression techniques investigated for image indexing and retrieval are DCT, wavelet, and vector quantization (VQ).

6.7.1 Image Indexing and Retrieval Based on DCT Coefficients

Since most images are compressed using JPEG, it is natural to exploit the feasibility of carrying out indexing and retrieval based on JPEG compressed data. However, due to the use of entropy coding at the last stage of JPEG coding, it is difficult to derive semantics directly from the JPEG compressed data. Thus the common approach is to do reverse entropy coding and carry out indexing and retrieval based on the quantized DCT coefficients [34].

As the DC components of DCT coefficients reflect average energy of pixel blocks and AC components reflect pixel intensity changes, it is theoretically possible to index and retrieve images directly based on DCT coefficients. However, the index or representation would not be compact as the number of DCT coefficients is equal to the number of pixels. Therefore, it has been proposed to use only some of the coefficients [34]. The proposed method works as follows:

1. $2k$ subimages or windows (W_1, ..., W_{2k}) are selected from the image. The windows are nonoverlapping areas covering the entire image or just a small part of the image. Each window size must be a multiple of 8 pixels in each dimension to coincide with the boundary of JPEG 8x8 blocks.
2. These $2k$ windows are grouped into k pairs. The windows in each pair are labeled as window 1 and window 2, respectively.
3. For each window, a representative block whose components are the average of corresponding components of all blocks in the window is found.

4. The two representative blocks of each pair of windows are compared component by component, resulting in 64 bits of 1s and 0s. A 1 is obtained when a component in window 1 is larger than the corresponding component in window 2. A 0 is obtained otherwise.

5. Thus each image is represented by k strings of 64 bits each.

6. During retrieval, the query image is also represented as k strings of 64 bits each, using the same steps as above.

7. The difference between the query image and each of the stored images is calculated as the sum of differences between corresponding bits for all k strings.

No detailed results are reported. But we identify a number of limitations of the above scheme. First, the choice of windows affects the performance dramatically, as the objects of interest may be located anywhere in images. There is no detailed guideline on how windows are chosen. Second, the proposed scheme treats all DCT frequency components equally although different DCT frequency components have different significance to the image's appearance. In general, lower frequency components are more important than higher frequency components.

6.7.2 Image Indexing and Retrieval Based on Wavelet Coefficients

The basic ideas of wavelet transforms and the Fourier transform are similar. In the Fourier transform, a signal is decomposed into a number of sinusoids of different frequencies. In a wavelet transform, a signal is decomposed into a number of the chosen base function and its variations, called wavelets. The result of the wavelet compression is a sequence of wavelet coefficients.

To index an image based on wavelet compressed data, it is proposed that only a selected number of coefficients are used [35, 36]. The selected coefficients are quantized into -1 (if the coefficient is a large negative number), 0, or 1 (it the coefficient is a large positive number). This sequence of -1, 0, and 1 is used as the index of the image. During image retrieval, the query image is also represented by a sequence of -1, 0, and 1. The distance between two images is calculated as the weighted sum of differences of corresponding numbers in the two sequences. The weights are used to differentiate the significance of different coefficient positions.

It is reported that the retrieval performance based on wavelet coefficients is lower than that of the basic color-based image retrieval technique described in Section 6.4 [35, 36]. The common problem of the techniques based on DCT coefficients and wavelet coefficients is that it is hard to relate different coefficient values with image perception, despite the fact that image information is contained in the transform domain.

6.7.3 Image Indexing and Retrieval Based on VQ Compressed Data

The third compression technique that is investigated for its suitability for image index and retrieval is VQ. As described in Chapter 2, VQ has the attractive feature that a compressed image is represented as a sequence of numbers, each of which identifies a codevector (a pixel pattern) in the codebook. That is, the VQ compressed image consists of codevectors identified by the numbers. The codevectors are directly displayed in the decompressed image. As the compressed data is directly related to the pixel patterns in the image, image indexing and retrieval based on VQ compressed data should be feasible.

Indris and Panchanathan proposed a method of image retrieval based on VQ compressed data [37]. A codevector usage map for each is built that indicates if a codevector is used by an image. Image distance is calculated based on the differences between usage maps. Because the usage map dose not show how many times a particular codevector is used by an image during the compression process, two totally different images can have the same image map, leading to lower retrieval precision.

Recently, Teng proposed an alternative method of image retrieval based on VQ compressed data [38]. After VQ compression, each block of pixels is represented by an codevector index number. For a given image, we calculate the number of occurrences of each index to obtain an index histogram $H(v_1, v_2, ..., v_i, ..., v_n)$, where v_i is the number of times code vector i is used by the image, and n is the total number of code vectors in the codebook.

During image retrieval, an index histogram is calculated for the query image. Let us call the histogram $H(q_1, q_2, ..., q_i, ..., q_n)$. Then the distance between the query image Q and an image V is calculated as follows:

$$d(Q, V) = \sum_{i=1}^{n} |q_i - v_i|$$

Images are ranked in ascending order of the calculated distance. The larger the calculated distance between two images, the greater the difference between the two images.

The above image indexing and retrieval process is very similar to the basic color-histogram-based image retrieval technique described in Section 6.4. The main difference is that in the VQ-based method, the histogram represents the numbers of different codevectors used by an image, while the basic histogram represents the numbers of pixels with the same color. In comparison, image retrieval based on VQ compressed data has the following advantages over the basic color-histogram-based method:

1. During the indexing process, no decompression is required.
2. The number of blocks is significantly less than the number of pixels, leading to more efficient indexing and retrieval.
3. The VQ-based method should provide higher image retrieval effectiveness. This is because the similarity is based on a block of pixels instead of individual pixels. Thus the VQ-based method overcomes the problem in cases where two blocks of pixels based on individual pixels have the same or similar histograms, but the overall appearance of these two blocks are totally different.

The experimental results show that the VQ-based method proposed by Teng has higher retrieval performance than the basic color-based method [38].

6.8 OTHER IMAGE INDEXING AND RETRIEVAL TECHNIQUES

The image indexing and retrieval techniques discussed above are normally called low-level, content-based image retrieval techniques. The common characteristic of these techniques is that they derive a feature vector for each image and the similarity or distance between two images is calculated based on their corresponding feature vectors. Normally, images cannot be reconstructed from these feature vectors, except for the region-based shape representation. These feature vectors are compact representations of images, but incorporate no understanding of the contents or objects within images. This section briefly describes two high-level, content-based image retrieval techniques. They are called high-level techniques because the contents or objects are explicitly identified.

6.8.1 Image Retrieval Based on Model-Based Compression

In model based image compression, an image, normally an object, is represented by a mathematical model (i.e., an object is represented by a number of parameters or mathematical equations [39, 40]). As very little data is required to represent these parameters and equations, a very high compression can be achieved. Also, this compression technique is very suitable for content-based image retrieval. We can use the parameters or values defining the equations as the object indexes. Image similarity is calculated from the differences between these parameters.

One of the model-based compression techniques is fractal or IFS-based coding described in Chapter 2. In this technique, an image is represented by a set of affine transforms that are defined by parameters such as translation, scaling, and rotation. Thus we can use these parameters as image indexes. In addition, these transforms have the attractive property that similar parameters represent similar images. Thus image distances can be calculated based on the parameter differences. The main problem with this approach is that it is difficult to find affine transforms for general images, and one image can be represented by different sets of affine transforms [41].

6.8.2 Image Retrieval Based on Spatial Relationship

In many applications, such as geographic information systems (GISs), spatial relationships between objects are the criteria for image retrieval. Example queries are "find images containing a lake next to a mountain" and "find images containing a highway that is to the left of a forest." For these types of applications, objects and their spatial relationships have to be determined. Readers are referred to the GIS literature [42] for details.

6.9 INTEGRATED IMAGE INDEXING AND RETRIEVAL TECHNIQUES

We have described image retrieval based on structured attributes, free text, color, shape, and texture. These features capture different contents and abstractions of images. Structured attributes and free text capture high-level contents and abstractions of images. But they are partial or incomplete and subjective. They support attribute or text-based queries, but cannot support pictorial queries. Image retrieval techniques based on color, shape, and texture capture low-level features of images. They support pictorial queries in the form of drawing and example images. But they have difficulty in accommodating text-based queries, and they cannot capture high-level abstractions contained in images. Therefore, the strengths of text-based and content-based image retrieval techniques complement each other. In addition, techniques based on a single low-level feature are not adequate for image retrieval. For example, a color-based technique considers a red apple and red car to be the same. Thus a number of low level features must be combined in a practical image retrieval system. A practical system must integrate as many useful features as possible. We briefly describe four integrated image retrieval systems in the following.

In addition to using multiple image features, integrated techniques normally use relevance feedback in the retrieval process.

6.9.1 QBIC

The QBIC system was developed by the IBM Corporation. It allows a large image database to be queried by visual properties such as colors, color percentages, texture, shape, and sketch, as well as by keywords [5, 43-45]. The visual properties are taken from an example (query) image. Color features are represented by histograms and perceptual similarity among color bins is considered during image similarity calculation. Texture features are represented by the coarseness, contrast, and directionality. Shape features are described by area, circularity, eccentricity, major axis orientation, and a set of algebraic moment invariants. Sketch features are based on edge information in the sketch.

Normally any one visual property can be used in a query. But any visual property can be combined with keywords to form a composite query.

QBIC capabilities have been incorporated into IBM's DB2 Universal Database product. QBIC software and demonstrations are available at http://wwwqbic.almaden.ibm.com/.

6.9.2 Virage Image Search Engine

The Virage Image Search Engine is a product of Virage, Inc. (http://www.virage.com). It provides an open framework for image management [46]. The Virage Engine expresses visual features as image primitives. Primitives can be very general, such as color, shape and texture, or domain specific, such as face and cancer cell features.

Information about the image search engine and other related products is available at Virage, Inc.'s home page http://www.virage.com.

6.9.3 WebSEEK

WebSEEK is one of the content-based visual query prototypes systems developed at Columbia University [47-49]. It is specially designed for searching for images and video on the WWW. In WebSEEK, the images are analyzed in two separate automatic processes. The first process extracts and indexes visual features, such as color histograms and texture. The second process parses associated text and classifies images into subject classes in a customized image taxonomy. There are more than 2,000 image classes in the taxonomy. Example classes are sports, travel, plants, and their subclasses.

More than 650,000 unconstrained images and video clips from various sources are indexed in the initial prototype implementation. Users search for images by navigating through subject categories (classes) or by using content-based search tools.

One main feature of WebSEEK is the integration of visual features and text. The feasibility of the approach is demonstrated via a large WWW-based testbed.

An enhanced prototype called VisualSEEK was also developed. VisualSEEK enhances the search capability by integrating spatial queries (like those used in GIS) and visual feature queries. Users ask the system to find images that include regions of matched features and spatial relationships.

WebSEEK can be accessed from http://www.ctr.columbia.edu/webseek/.

6.9.4 ImageRover WWW Search Engine

ImageRover is also specially designed to search for images on the WWW [50]. Visual features used include color, edge orientation, texture, and shape. The main difference between ImageRover and other systems is that it uses relevance feedback. Relevance feedback enables the user to iteratively refine a query via the specification of relevant items. By including the user in the loop, better search performance is achieved.

To some extent, other systems such as QBIC and WebSEEK also use relevance feedback – the user can use one of the displayed images that is retrieved in response to the initial user query as the new query image. But ImageRover uses a special relevance feedback algorithm. The user can select multiple images (obtained from the initial query) as relevant. The algorithm then calculates the combined feature vector from these images. The combined feature vector is used as the new query.

PROBLEMS

Problem 6.1

Describe the four common approaches to image retrieval. What are their strengths and weaknesses?

Problem 6.2

A text-based image retrieval system is essentially an IR system. Are there any differences between these two types of systems? If so, what are they?

Problem 6.3

Describe the operating principles of the basic color-based image retrieval technique.

Problem 6.4

What do you think are the two main limitations of the basic color-based image retrieval techniques? Describe methods to overcome these limitations.

Problem 6.5

Read reference [7]. Discuss the pros and cons of the proposed cumulative histogram-based image retrieval method.

Problem 6.6

Explain how different color representations of images can affect image retrieval performance.

Problem 6.7

What are the criteria for a good shape representation suitable for image indexing and retrieval?

Problem 6.8

Describe three common shape representations. Examine their strengthes and weaknesses based on the criteria described in Problem 6.7.

Problem 6.9

In the Fourier descriptor-based shape representation method, we derive FDs from a shape signature such as radii and then use normalized FDs for shape indexing and retrieval. Why do we prefer FDs over shape signatures for shape indexing and retrieval? Use an example in your explanation.

Problem 6.10

Derive the unique binary sequences for shapes #1 and #3 in Figure 6.7 and calculate the distance between these two shapes. Make appropriate assumptions for grid size and standard length of the major axis.

Problem 6.11

Examine Table 6.1. Is there any distance that does not conform with perceptual judgment? If so, explain why it occurs.

Problem 6.12

What features are commonly used to describe texture? What features are important for image indexing and retrieval?

Problem 6.13

What are advantages of image indexing based on compressed image data over that based on raw (uncompressed) image data?

Problem 6.14

Contrast the image indexing and retrieval techniques based on VQ compressed data and the basic color-based image indexing and retrieval technique.

Problem 6.15

To achieve high retrieval performance, a system combining techniques based on text, color, shape, and texture should be used. The QBIC system as reported in [5, 43–45] is such a system. Try to use the demonstration system at the URL http://wwwq-bic.almaden.ibm.com/ to retrieve images by formulating your own queries. Discuss your observations.

Problem 6.16

Try WebSEEK at http://www.ctr.columbia.edu/webseek/. Compare the QBIC system and WebSEEK in terms of retrieval effectiveness and user-friendliness based on your observations.

APPENDIX 6A   COLOR REPRESENTATIONS

Image data (a collection of pixel values) represents the color of pixels. Many operations, such as image retrieval, are based on pixel values or color representation. Correct representation and handling of color could improve the performance of these operations. In this appendix, we describe the details of color representation.

6A.1 Color Properties

Visible light is electromagnetic radiation with a spectrum wavelength ranging approximately from 400 to 780 nm. Light of different wavelengths produces different color sensations. Figure 6A.1 shows perceived colors for different wavelengths. The three basic physical properties of color radiation are luminance, hue, and saturation. The corresponding perceptual terms are brightness, color, and purity [51-53].

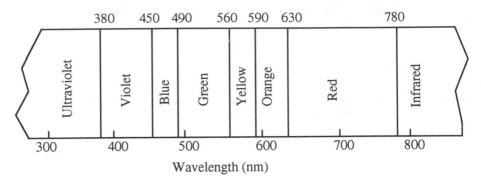

Figure 6A.1 Color perceptions of different wavelengths.

Luminance is the attribute of a visual sensation according to which an area appears to emit more or less light. Human vision has a nonlinear perceptual response to brightness: a source having a luminance of only 18% of a reference luminance appears about half as bright. As mentioned earlier, an observer can detect an intensity difference between two patches when their intensities differ by more than 1%.

Hue is the attribute of a visual sensation according to which an area appears to be similar to one of the perceived colors red, yellow, green, and blue, or a combination of any two of them. The colors that appear in nature are normally polychromatic; that is, they are mixture of many wavelengths. Each natural color has a dominant wavelength that establishes the visual perception of its hue, but it may contain radiation components with wavelengths that extend over the entire visible spectrum. White or gray light results when the radiation at all wavelengths is present in approximately equal amounts.

Saturation is the colorfulness of an area judged in proportion to its brightness. The appearance of any color can be duplicated by a mixture of white or gray light with a pure spectrum color (the dominant wavelength) in the proper proportion. The ratio of the magnitude of the energy in the spectrum component to the total energy of the light defines its purity or saturation. A pure color has a saturation of 100%, while the saturation of white or gray light is zero.

6A.2 Color Specification Systems

To communicate color images and video, color must be specified by a certain method. This subsection describes a number of color specification systems or color spaces and the conversions between these systems.

Device-Independent Color Specification

The three basic physical properties of a color are specified by its spectral power distribution (SPD), a plot of its radiant energy versus wavelength. Color is the visual sensation to light of different SPDs. For example, Figure 6A.2 shows the SPD of a red color. SPD is the most accurate method to specify color. However, the SPD format does not describe the relationship between the physical properties of color and its visual perception. It is not always the most useful format for specifying color—numerical criteria are often more convenient.

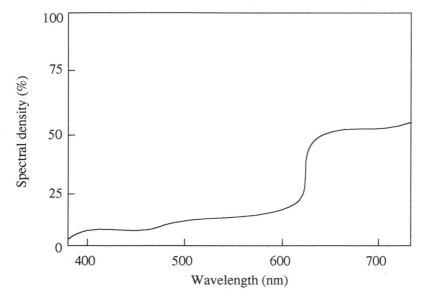

Figure 6A.2 SPD of a red color.

The Comite Internationale de l'Eclairage, or International Commission on Illumination (CIE) system defines how to map an SPD to a triple-numeral-component that are mathematical coordinates in a color space. The CIE has defined a human "standard observer" based on measurements of the color-matching abilities of the average human eye. Using data from measurements, a system of three stimuli, XYZ, was developed in which all visible colors are represented using only positive values of X, Y, and Z. The Y is identical to luminance; X and Z give color information. This forms the basis of the CIE 1931 XYZ color system, which is fundamental to all colorimetry. It is completely device independent, and the X, Y, and Z values are normally defined to lie in the range $[0, 1]$.

In practice, colors are rarely specified in XYZ terms; it is far more common to use chromaticity coordinates that are independent of the luminance Y. The chromaticity coordinates, x and y, are calculated from the tristimulus values X, Y, and Z using the following equations:

$$x=X/(X+Y+Z) \tag{6A.1}$$
$$y=Y/(X+Y+Z) \tag{6A.2}$$

The plot of the chromaticity coordinates of visible light is known as the CIE Chromaticity Diagram (Figure 6A.3). The coordinates of spectral (monochromatic) colors are located on the horseshoe-shaped curve around the periphery of the diagram. Their wavelengths in nanometers are indicated on the curve. All visible colors are located within the area bounded by the spectral curve and the line joining coordinates corresponding to wavelengths 380 and 800 nm.

Based on the chromaticity diagram, colors are specified using *xyY*. Tristimulus values are derived from the *xyY* values using the following equations:

$$X = x*Y/y \tag{6A.3}$$

and

$$Z = (1-x-y)*Y/y \tag{6A.4}$$

The main advantage of CIE XYZ, and any color space or definition based on it, is that it is completely device independent. The main disadvantage with CIE-based spaces is the complexity of implementing them. In addition, they are not user intuitive.

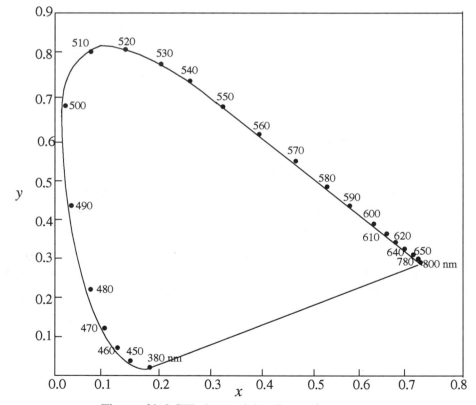

Figure 6A.3 CIE chromaticity diagram.

Relationships Between CIE XYZ and Other Color Spaces

According to the tristimulus theorem, any color can be obtained by mixing three primary colors in an appropriate proportion. Primary colors are independent in the sense that a primary color cannot be obtained by mixing the other two primary colors. Another criterion for choosing primary colors is that they should be able to represent as many colors as possible. Three primary colors are sufficient to represent all colors because there are three types of color receptors (called cones) in a human eye. Stimulation of these three types of receptors generates the color sensation.

To uniquely specify a color space based on three primary colors, such as red, green, and blue, we need to specify the chromaticities of each primary color and a reference white point as in Table 6A.1.

Table 6A.1
Parameters Required to Specify a Primary Color Space

Color component	x	y
Red	x_r	y_r
Green	x_g	y_g
Blue	x_b	y_b
White	x_n	y_n

Remember that $R=G=B=Y=1$ for the reference white point. For a particular color space, $x_r, y_r, x_g, y_g, x_b, y_b, x_n$, and y_n are constants. Different color spaces have different sets of constants. We discuss this further in later subsections. These four points (three primary colors and reference white) can be drawn in the chromaticity diagram (Figure 6A.4). The extent of the colors that can be produced from a given set of RGB primaries is given in the chromaticity diagram by a triangle whose vertices are the chromaticities of the primaries. This extent is called the gamut of the color space. The XYZ and any other color space can be converted to each other using a linear transformation. We use RGB color space as an example here.

According to Grassman's law, we have the following general conversion equation between XYZ and RGB:

$$\begin{bmatrix} X \\ Y \\ Z \end{bmatrix} = \begin{bmatrix} A1 & A2 & A3 \\ A4 & A5 & A6 \\ A7 & A8 & A9 \end{bmatrix} \times \begin{bmatrix} R \\ G \\ B \end{bmatrix} \tag{6A.5}$$

Transforming the above equation, we have

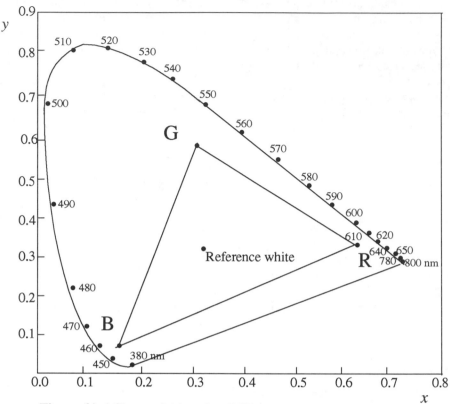

Figure 6A.4 Chromaticities of an RGB system.

$$\begin{bmatrix} R \\ G \\ B \end{bmatrix} = \begin{bmatrix} B1 & B2 & B3 \\ B4 & B5 & B6 \\ B7 & B8 & B9 \end{bmatrix} \times \begin{bmatrix} X \\ Y \\ Z \end{bmatrix} \tag{6A.6}$$

A1 to A9 and B1 to B9 are constant when the chromaticities of RGB and reference white are specified. They are obtained by solving the above equations using equations (6A.3) and (6A.4) under the following conditions:

(1) When $R=1$, $G=B=0$, we know the chromaticity of R: x_r, y_r
(2) When $G=1$, $R=B=0$, we know the chromaticity of G: x_g, y_g
(3) When $B=1$, $R=G=0$, we know the chromaticity of B: x_b, y_b
(4) When $R=G=B=1$, we know $Y=1$, and the chromaticity of reference white: x_n, y_n.

For example, the CCIR 601-1 recommendation specifies the following parameter: $x_r=0.67$, $y_r=0.33$, $x_g=0.21$, $y_g=0.71$, $x_b=0.14$, $y_b=0.08$, $x_n=0.31$, and $y_n=0.32$, so we have

$$\begin{bmatrix} X \\ Y \\ Z \end{bmatrix} = \begin{bmatrix} 0.6069 & 0.1735 & 0.2003 \\ 0.2989 & 0.5866 & 0.1145 \\ 0.0000 & 0.0661 & 1.1162 \end{bmatrix} \times \begin{bmatrix} R \\ G \\ B \end{bmatrix}$$

(6A.7)

and

$$\begin{bmatrix} R \\ G \\ B \end{bmatrix} = \begin{bmatrix} 1.910 & -0.532 & -0.288 \\ -0.985 & 1.999 & -0.028 \\ 0.058 & -0.118 & 0.898 \end{bmatrix} \times \begin{bmatrix} X \\ Y \\ Z \end{bmatrix}$$

(6A.8)

Different color spaces have different chromaticities for the three primary colors and reference white, and hence different relationships with CIE XYZ.

Uniform Color Spaces

In Figure 6A.4, the chromaticity of G is some distance away from the chromaticity of wavelength 510 nm. It would seem that many colors cannot be reproduced using the RGB primaries. This conclusion is incorrect, because the *xyY* color space is not a *uniform color space*: the human visual system is not equally responsive to distances in the chromaticity diagram. In a uniform color space, equal distances approximately represent equal perceived color differences. The CIE specified two approximate uniform color spaces: CIEL*u*v* (or *LUV*) and CIEL*a*b* (or *LAB*) [52]. The conversion between *XYZ* and $L^*u^*v^*$ is as follows:

$L^* = 116(Y/Y_n)^{1/3} - 16$ for $Y/Y_n > 0.008856$ (6A.9)

$L^* = 903.3(Y/Y_n)$ for $Y/Y_n <= 0.008856$ (6A.10)

$u^* = 13L^*(u' - u'_n)$ (6A.11)

$v^* = 13L^*(v' - v'_n)$ (6A.12)

with

$u' = 4X/(X+15Y+3Z)$ $v' = 9Y/(X+15Y+3Z)$

$u'_n = 4X_n/(X_n+15Y_n+3Z_n)$ $v'_n = 9Y_n/(X_n+15Y_n+3Z_n)$

where X_n, Y_n, and Z_n are the X, Y, and Z of the chosen reference white.

The conversion between *XYZ* and $L^*a^*b^*$ is as follows:

L^* is the same as in equation (A.9).

$a^* = 500[(X/X_n)^{1/3} - (Y/Y_n)^{1/3}]$ (6A.13)

$b^* = 200[(Y/Y_n)^{1/3} - (Z/Z_n)^{1/3}]$ (6A.14)

Uniform color spaces are useful in color measurement and image retrieval based on color, where pixel value differences should reflect perceived color differences.

A.3 Different Color Representations

In multimedia systems, the RGB representation is most commonly used. A digital image is represented by three two-dimensional arrays corresponding to its red, green, and blue color components. To most people, if all images are represented in RGB, then they are represented in the same color space and can be used and compared directly, no matter where these images are from. In reality, pixel values in the RGB representation may have different meanings. There are two main causes for these differences:

(1) The gamma correction values used may be different for images captured using different devices;
(2) As discussed earlier, to uniquely specify a color space, the chromaticities of the three primary colors and a reference white must be specified. In practice, many varieties of RGB color space are used and their chromaticities are rarely specified, leading to confusion, poor image display quality, and poor image retrieval performance.

In the following subsections, we discuss issues of gamma correction and different RGB color spaces.

Gamma Correction

Due to the characteristics of the electronics of the cathode ray tube (CRT) and the grid of an electron gun, the intensity of light generated by a CRT is not a linear function of the applied signal. A CRT has a power-law response to applied voltage: the light intensity produced at the face of the display is proportional to the applied voltage raised to the power of between 2.2 and 2.5. This power value is called *gamma* [51, 54-56]. The luminance produced by a CRT and the voltage (V') applied to the CRT have the following relationship:

$$Luminance = (V')^{\text{gamma}} \tag{6A.16}$$

Gamma was originally used to refer to the nonlinearity of a CRT. But it has been generalized to refer to the nonlinearity of an entire system or any subsystem. The gamma of a system (or an image) is calculated by multiplying the gammas of its individual series of components from the image capture stage through to the display. Figure 6A.5 shows three common power functions. Note that the voltage range is in [0,1]. When the gamma value is larger than 1, x is always larger than or equal to y. When the gamma value is less than 1, y is always larger than or equal to x.

To compensate for the nonlinearity of a CRT, gamma correction with a power of less than 1 is performed so that the overall gamma of an imaging system is close to 1. Ideally, gamma correction performs the following transformation:

$$V' = (V)^{1/\text{gamma}} \tag{6A.17}$$

where V is the voltage generated by a camera sensor that is linear to the brightness of the scene.

Equations (6A.16) and (6A.17) are called *transfer functions* with the powers of gamma and 1/gamma. The gamma correction value is the reciprocal of gamma. The image capture and display process has the following transfer stages:

1. The camera sensor converts the light into an electrical voltage linearly;
2. Gamma correction transfers the linear voltage into a nonlinear voltage with a power of 1/gamma;
3. The CRT converts the nonlinear voltage into linear light with a power of gamma.

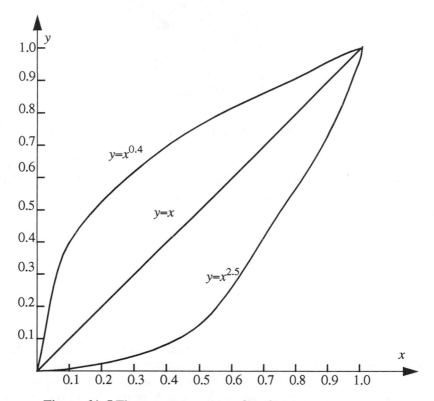

Figure 6A.5 Three common power functions.

The entire system is linear or almost linear. Conventionally, linear voltage (before gamma correction) uses a notation without prime. Nonlinear voltage (after gamma correction) uses a notation with a prime, as in equations (6A.16) and (6A.17).

An image gamma of 1 would indicate that the system is precisely reproducing the gray scale of the scene. This is the technical ideal, but deliberate distortions may be introduced for aesthetic reasons and for different viewing conditions.

If gamma is greater than unity, the image will appear sharper, but the scene contrast range that can be reproduced is reduced. If gamma is increased sufficiently, the image will be a silhouette with only blacks and whites. Reducing the gamma has a tendency to make the image appear soft and "washed out," as shown in Figure 6A.6. These effects can be explained using the curves in Figure 6A.5: when gamma is larger than 1, all x values below 0.5 are transferred to close to 0, leading to an either "black" or "white" effect. But when gamma is smaller than 1, y increases very fast at low x, leading to very few black pixels, thus images appear soft.

Figure 6A.6 The image appears soft when the gamma is reduced.

For color images and video, the linear voltages R, G, and B representing primary colors red, green, and blue are converted into nonlinear voltages R', G', and B' (normally by capturing devices). The color CRT converts R', G', and B' into linear light red, green, and blue to reproduce the original color. Note that R, G, and B are normally in the range [0, 1]. But in digital form, each component is normally represented as an integer in the range of [0, 255]. Thus we have

$$R' = 255R^{1/\text{gamma}} \tag{6A.18}$$

$$G' = 255G^{1/\text{gamma}} \tag{6A.19}$$

$$B' = 255B^{1/\text{gamma}} \tag{6A.20}$$

The constant 255 in the above equations is added in the ADC process. During image display, it is removed in the DAC process. Because gamma corrections are often performed in cameras, pixel values are commonly represented by nonlinear voltages. (Therefore, strictly speaking, prime notations should be used for all pixel values.)

It is now obvious that if two images were captured with two cameras with different gamma correction values, the pixel values of these two images represent colors differently. For example, if the gamma correction values of two cameras were 0.4 and 0.5, respectively, a pixel with $R'G'B'$ values of (100, 200, 100) in the first image would have a color proportional to linear voltages RGB of (0.096, 0.545, 0.096). But a pixel with the same $R'G'B'$ values of (100, 200, 100) in the second image would have a color proportional to linear voltages RGB of (0.154, 0.615, 0.154). Therefore, pixel values alone cannot determine the color of the pixel—we also need to know the gamma correction value used for capturing the image. In practice, the gamma correction value is seldom specified within the image or video data.

One common source of images is digitized video. It is assumed that the display has a gamma of 2.5, so video cameras should have a gamma correction value of 1/2.5. But for aesthetic reasons, an overall gamma of 1.1. or 1.2 is used for the entire system [55]; so

NTSC uses a gamma correction value of 1/2.2, or 0.45. In reality, a video camera can use a gamma correction value of anything between 1/2 to 1/2.5. So the same pixel values may correspond to different color intensities, depending on the gamma correction value used.

Another source of digital images is a scanner. The gamma correction values used for scanners also vary. It depends on the software used with the scanner. Some software may perform operations similar to the gamma correction to suit some specific display platform or for some specific purpose. Some images are scanned from negative films, which have a gamma of 0.6 for the film industry and 3.0 for color printing. Computer imaging systems generally assume an output gamma in the range of 1.4 to 2.2 and perform the gamma correction accordingly. Recent software lets the user specify any gamma from 0.5 to 5 [54].

Some images may be computer generated, in which case no gamma correction is applied to pixel values. Some images may have already been preprocessed for other purposes and later used in a multimedia system. The gamma correction value used may be unknown, and can be anything between 1 to 3.

The above discussion indicates that there is no standard for the gamma correction values to be used. If two images are from different sources or are captured using different devices, there is a good chance that they use different gamma correction values. This means that their pixel values should be interpreted according to the gamma value used. Otherwise, the image display quality is poor and comparisons between the pixel values of different images is meaningless.

Different RGB Systems or Color Spaces

As described in Section 6A.2, an RGB color space "floats" within the chromaticity diagram. Pixel values are just values relative to the three primary colors. If these three primary colors and a reference white are not specified within the chromaticity diagram, pixel values are meaningless. However, in practice, these parameters are seldom specified, although a number of RGB color spaces (systems) have been defined and are in use.

The common color spaces used in the television industry are the Federal Communication Commission of America (FCC) 1953 Primaries, the Society of Motion Picture and Television Engineers (SMPTE) "C" Primaries, the European Broadcasting Union (EUB) Primaries, and the CCIR Rec. 709 Primaries. The reference white most commonly used is the CIE D65, but other reference whites, such as CIE Illuminant A, are sometimes used. For details on these topics of colorimetry, refer to [52, 53, 57]. The main point to make here is that there are different RGB systems in use. In practice, the actual chromaticities are determined by sensors in cameras, phosphors in CRTs, and their illuminant used. To add to the confusion, color films use different RGB systems from those used in the television industry.

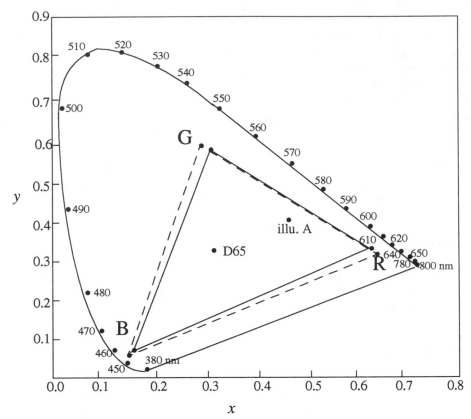

Figure 6A.7 Chromaticities of CCIR Rec. 709 and SMPTE "C" Primaries and D65 and Illuminant A. The triangle with solid lines is the gamut of the SMPTE "C" Primaries, and the triangle with dashed lines is the gamut of the CCIR Rec. 709.

As an example of different RGB primaries and illuminants, Figure 6A.7 shows the CCIR Rec. 709 Primaries, the SMPTE "C" Primaries, and the white points of CIE D65 and CIE Illuminate A.

Different RGB systems can be converted to each other using a linear transformation, when the white references being used are known. The transformation is derived using (6A.7). For example, when D65 is used for both CCIR Rec. 709 and SMPTE "C," they can be converted using the following formula:

$$
\begin{bmatrix} R709 \\ G709 \\ B709 \end{bmatrix} = \begin{bmatrix} 0.939555 & 0.050173 & 0.010272 \\ 0.017775 & 0.965795 & 0.016430 \\ -0.001622 & -0.004371 & 1.005993 \end{bmatrix} \begin{bmatrix} Rc \\ Gc \\ Bc \end{bmatrix} \tag{6A.21}
$$

where $R709$, $G709$, and $B709$ are the linear R, G, and B components in the CCIR Rec. 709 system, and Rc, Gc, and Bc are the linear R, G, and B components in the SMPTE "C" system. This conversion is carried out in the linear voltage domain; that is, pixel values must be converted into linear voltages before using (6A.21). For example, assume that two images are captured using the same gamma correction value of 2.2 and white reference D65, but with different primaries: the first in the SMPTE "C" primaries and the second in the CCIR Rec. 709 primaries. Then the pixel values (100, 200, 100) in the first system will produce the same color as the pixel values (108, 200, 108) in the second system. When different gamma correction values and reference whites are used, the difference between pixel values corresponding to the same color will be much larger.

We can look at (6A.21) from another perspective: if the image is captured using a camera with SMPTE "C" primaries and displayed on a CRT with CCIR Rec. 709 primaries, we have to convert pixel values Rc', Gc', and Bc' into linear voltages Rc, Gc, and Bc. Rc, Gc, and Bc are then converted into $R709$, $G709$, and $B709$, which are then converted into pixel values $R709'$, $G709'$, and $B709'$. $R709'$, $G709'$, and $B709'$ are used to drive the CCIR Rec. 709 CRT to produce the correct color. If the primaries of the camera and/or the CRT are not known, the above conversion cannot be carried out and the color will not be reproduced correctly.

From the above discussion, it is clear that without appropriate specification of the chromaticities of the primaries and the reference white used, the pixel values of an image cannot be interpreted correctly. This leads to poor display quality and inappropriate comparison of the pixels of different images.

REFERENCES

[1] Ogle, V. E., "Chabot: Retrieval From a Relational Database of Images," *Computer*, September 1995, pp. 40–48.

[2] Chua, T. S., et al., "A Concept-Based Image Retrieval System," *Proceedings of 27th Annual Hawaii International Conference on System Science*, Maui, HI, Jan. 4-7, 1994, Vol. 3, pp. 590–598.

[3] Swain, M. J., and D. H. Ballard, "Color Indexing," *Int. J. Comput. Vision*, vol. 7, 1991, pp. 11–32.

[4] Finlayson, G. D., *Color Object Recognition*, MSc Thesis, Simon Fraser University, 1992.

[5] Niblack, W., et al., "QBIC Project: Querying Images by Content, Using Color, Texture, and Shape," *Proceedings of the Conference Storage and Retrieval for Image and Video Databases*, Feb. 2–3, 1993, San Jose, CA, SPIE Proceedings Series, Vol. 1908, 1993, pp. 173–187.

[6] Gong, Y., H. Zhang, and C. Chuan, "An Image Database System With Fast Image Indexing Capability Based on Color Histograms," *Proceedings of IEEE 10's Ninth Annual International Conference*, Singapore, 22-26 August 1994, pp.407-411.

[7] Stricker, M., and M. Orengo, "Similarity of Color Images", *Proceedings of Conference on Storage and Retrieval for Image and Video Database III*, Feb. 9-10, 1995, San Jose, California, SPIE Vol. 2420, pp. 381-392.

[8] Chan, S. K., *Content-based Image Retrieval*, Master Thesis, Department of Information Systems and Computer Science, National University of Singapore, 1994.

[9] Lu, G., and J. Phillips, "Using Perceptually Weighted Histograms for Color-Based Image Retrieval," *Proceedings of International Conference on Signal Processing*, Oct. 12-16, 1998, Beijing, China, pp. 1150-1153.

[10] Stricker, M., and A. Dimai, "Color Indexing with Weak Spatial Constraints," *Proceedings of Confer-

176

ence on Storage and Retrieval for Image and Video Database IV, Feb. 1-2, 1996, San Jose CA, SPIE Vol. 2670, pp.29-40.

[11] White, D. A., and R. Jain, "ImageGREP: Fast Visual Pattern Matching in Image Databases," Technical Report of Visual Computing Laboratory, University of California, San Diego, CA, 1997, 12 pages.

[12] H. Lu, B. Ooi, and K. Tan, "Efficient Image Retrieval by Color Contents," *Proceedings of First International Conference on Applications of Databases*, June 21-23, 1994, Vadstena, Sweden, pp.95-108.

[13] Lu, G., J. Phillips, and S. Rahman, "Techniques to Improve Color Based Image Retrieval Performance," *Proceedings of International Symposium on Audio, Video, Image Processing and Intelligent Applications*, August 17-21, 1998, Baden-Baden, Germany, pp. 57-61.

[14] Wan, X., and C. J. Kuo, "Color Distribution Analysis and Quantization for Image Retrieval," *Proceedings of Conference on Storage and Retrieval for Image and Video Database IV*, Feb. 1-2, 1996, San Jose California, SPIE Vol. 2670, pp. 8-16.

[15] TIFF Revision 6.0, Aldus Corporation, 1992.

[16] Proposed Standard SMPTE 268M, "File Format for Digital Moving Picture Exchange (DPX)," *SMPTE Journal*, Vol. 102, Aug. 1993, pp. 760–766.

[17] Gonzalez, R. C., and P. Wintz, *Digital Image Processing*, 2nd ed., Addison-Wesley, 1987.

[18] Mohamad, D., G. Sulong, and S. S. Ipson, "Trademark Matching Using Invariant Moments," *Proceedings of Second Asian Conference on Computer Vision*, Dec. 5-8, 1995, Singapore, pp. I–439–444.

[19] Hu, M. K., "Visual Pattern Recognition by Moment Invariants," *IRE Trans. Info. Theory*, vol. IT-8, Feb. 1962, pp. 179–187.

[20] Scassellati, B., S. Alexopoulos, and M. Flickner, "Retrieving Images by 2D Shape: a Comparison of Computation Methods With Human Perceptual Judgements," *Storage and Retrieval for Image and Video Databases II*, SPIE Proceedings, Vol. 2185, 1994, pp. 2-14.

[21] Chellappa, R., and R. Bagdazian, "Fourier Coding of Image Boundaries", *IEEE Transactions on Pattern Analysis and Machine Intelligence*, Vol.6, 1984, pp. 102-105.

[22] Dudani, A. S., K. J. Breeding, and R. B. McGhee, "Aircraft Identification by Moment Invariants," *IEEE Transactions on Computers*, C-26(1), January 1977, pp. 39-46.

[23] Persoon, E., and K. S. Fu, "Shape Discrimination Using Fourier Descriptors," *IEEE Transactions on Systems, Man and Cybernetics*, SMC-7(3), March 1977, pp. 170-179.

[24] Sajjanhar, A., and G. Lu, "Indexing 2D Non-Occluded Shape for Similarity Retrieval," *SPIE Conference on Applications of Digital Image Processing XX*, Vol. 3164, July 30 – August 1, 1997, San Diego, USA, pp. 188-197.

[25] Kauppinen, H., T. Seppanen, and M. Pietikainen, "An Experimental Comparison of Autoregressive and Fourier-Based Descriptors in 2D Shape Classification," *IEEE Transactions on PAMI*, Vol.17, No. 2, Feb. 1995, pp. 201-207.

[26] Jain, A. J., and A. Vailaya, "Image Retrieval Using color and Shape," *Proceedings of Second Asian Conference on Computer Vision*, Dec. 5-8, 1995, Singapore, pp. II–529–533.

[27] Mehrotra, R., and J. E. Gary, "Similar-Shape Retrieval in Shape Data Management," *Computer*, Sept. 1995, pp. 57–62.

[28] Bimbo, A. D., and P. Pala. "Visual Image Retrieval by Elastic Template Matching of User Sketches," *IEEE transactions on Pattern Analysis and Machine Intelligence*, Vol. 19, No. 2, 1997, pp. 121-132.

[29] Sajjanhar, A., and G. Lu, "A Grid Based Shape Indexing and Retrieval Method," *Australian Computer Journal*, Special Issue on Multimedia Storage and Archiving Systems, Vol. 29, No.4, November 1997, pp. 131-140.

[30] Tamura, H., S. Mori, and T. Yamawaki, "Texture Features Corresponding to Visual Perception," *IEEE Transactions on Systems, Man, and Cybernetics*, Vol. 8, No. 6, 1978, pp. 460–473.

[31] Chaudhuri, B. B., and N. Sarkar, "Texture Segmentation Using Fractal Dimension," *IEEE Trans. on Pattern Analysis and Machine Intelligence*, Vol. 17, No. 1 Jan. 1995, pp. 72-77.

[32] Dadd, M., and Jon Ables, "A Multi-Invariant Difference Measure for Grey-Scale Texture," *Proceedings of IEEE TENCON 1997*, pp. 267-270.

[33] Swain, M. J., Charles H. Frankel, and Mei Lu, "View-based Techniques for Searching for Objects and Texture," *Proceedings of Second Asian Conference on Computer Vision*, Dec 5-8, 1995, Singapore, pp. II-534 - II-538.

[34] Shenier, M., and Mohamed Abdel-Mottaleb, "Exploiting the JPEG Compression Scheme for Image Retrieval," *IEEE Trans. On Pattern Analysis and Machine Intelligence*, Vol. 18, No.8, August, 1996, pp.849-853.

[35] Jacobs, C. E., Adam Finkelstein, and David, H. Salesin, "Fast Multiresolution Image Querying," *Proceedings of SIGGRAPH'95*, Los Angels, CA, Aug. 6-11, 1995, pp. 277-286.

[36] Chen, C., and R. Wilkinson, "Image Retrieval Using Multiresolution Wavelet Decomposition," *Proceedings of International Conference on Computational Intelligence and Multimedia Applications*, Feb. 9-11, 1998, Monash University, Australia, pp. 824-829.

[37] Idris, F., and S. Panchanathan, "Algorithms for Indexing of Compressed Images," *Proceedings of International Conference on Visual Information Systems*, Melbourne, Feb. 1996, pp.303-308.

[38] Teng, S., "Image Compression, Indexing and Retrieval Based on Vector Quantization," Technical report, 1998, Gippsland School of Computing and Information Technology, Monash University.

[39] Lippman, A., "Feature Sets for Interactive Images," *Communications of ACM*, Vol. 34, No.4, April 1991, pp. 93-102.

[40] Vasconcelos, N,. and A. Lippman, "Library-based Coding: A Representation for Efficient Video Compression and Retrieval," *Proceedings of Data Compression Conference*, March 25-27, 1997, Snowbird, Utah, pp. 121-130.

[41] Cohen, H. A., "The Application of IFS to Image Analysis," *Proceedings of IEEE International Conference on Image Processing*, Sept. 5-8, 1989, Singapore, pp. 583-587.

[42] Samet, II., *Applications of Spatial Data Structures: Computer Graphics, Image Processing, and GIS*, Addison-Wesley, 1989.

[43] Ashley, J., et al., "Automatic and Semiautomatic Methods for Image Annotation and Retrieval in QBIC," *Proceedings of the Conference on Storage and Retrieval for Image and Video Databases III*, San Jose, CA, Feb. 9–10, 1995, SPIE Proceedings Series, Vol. 2420, pp. 24–35.

[44] Flickner, M. et al., "Query by Image and Video Content: The QBIC System," *Computer*, Sept. 1995, pp. 23-32.

[45] Niblack, W., et al., "Updates to the QBIC System," *Proceedings of Conference on Storage and Retrieval for Image and Video Databases VI* (SPIE Proceedings Vol. 3312), Jan. 28-30, 1998, San Jose, California, pp. 150-161.

[46] Bach, J. R., "The Virage Image Search Engine: An Open Framework for Image Management," *Proceedings of Conference on Storage and Retrieval for Image and Video Databases IV* (SPIE Proceedings Vol. 2670), Feb. 1-2, 1996, San Jose, California, pp. 76-87.

[47] Smith, J. R., and S.-F. Chang, "Visually Searching the Web for Content," *IEEE Multimedia Magazine*, July-Sept. 1997, pp. 12-19.

[48] Smith, J. R., and S.-F. Chang, "Tools and Techniques for Color Image Retrieval," *Proceedings of Conference on Storage and Retrieval for Image and Video Databases IV* (SPIE Proceedings Vol. 2670), Feb. 1-2, 1996, San Jose, California, pp. 426-437.

[49] Chang, S.-F., and John R. Smith, "Finding Images/Video in Large Archives," *D-Lib Magazine*, Feb. 1997, Available at: http://www.dlib/org/dlib/february97/columbia/02chang.html.

[50] Taycher, L., M. La Cascia, and S. Sclaroff, "Image digestion and Relevance Feedback in the ImageRover WWW Search Engines," *Proceedings of the Second International Conference on Visual Information Systems*, San Diego, Dec. 15-17, 1997, pp. 85-91.

[51] Inglis, A. F., *Video Engineering*, McGraw-Hill, Inc., 1993.

[52] Hunt, R. W. G., *Measuring Colour*, Ellis Horwood Limited, 1989.

[53] Judd, D. B., and G. Wyszecki, *Color in Business, Science and Industry*, 3rd ed., John Wiley & Sons, 1975.

[54] Patterson, R., "Gamma Correction and Tone Reproduction in Scanned Photographic Images," *SMPTE Journal*, pp. 377–385, June 1994.

[55] Poynton, C. A., "Gamma and its Disguises: The Nonlinear Mappings of Intensity in Perception, CRTs, Film, and Video," *SMPTE Journal*, pp. 1099–1108, Dec. 1993.

[56] DeMarsh, L., "TV Display Phosphors/Primaries–Some History," *SMPTE Journal*, pp.1095–1098, Dec. 1993.

[57] Hall, R., *Illumination and Color in Computer Generated Imagery*, Springer-Verlag, 1989.

Chapter 7

Video Indexing and Retrieval

7.1 INTRODUCTION

We studied indexing and retrieval of text, audio, and images in Chapters 4, 5, and 6. This chapter deals with the indexing and retrieval of video. Video is information rich [1, 2]. A complete video may consist of subtitles (text), sound track (both speech and nonspeech), and images recorded or played out continuously at a fixed rate. So we can consider video as a combination of text, audio, and images with a time dimension. In addition, some metadata, such as the video title and author/producer/director, are associated with a video. Therefore, the following methods are used for video indexing and retrieval:

- Metadata-based method: Video is indexed and retrieved based on structured metadata using traditional DBMSs [3, 4]. Common metadata are the video title, author/producer/director, date of production, and types of video .

- Text-based method: Video is indexed and retrieved based on associated subtitles using the IR techniques discussed in Chapter 4 [4]. Transcripts and subtitles normally already exist in many types of video such as news program and movies, eliminating the need for manual annotation. Temporal information should be included to associate text with related frames.

- Audio-based method: Video is indexed and retrieved based on associated soundtracks using the methods discussed in Chapter 5. Audio is segmented into speech and nonspeech groups. Speech recognition is applied to the speech signal to obtain the spoken words. We then index and retrieve video based on these spoken words using IR techniques. If we identify the meaning of nonspeech signals, we gain some information about the video from the sound effect. Again, temporal information should be included to associate the sound with frames.

- Content-based method: There are two general approaches to content-based video indexing and retrieval [5-9]. In the first approach, we treat the video as a collection of independent frames or images, and use the image indexing and retrieval methods discussed in Chapter 6 for video indexing and retrieval. The problem with this approach is that it ignores the temporal relationships among video frames, and a huge number of images need to be processed. The second approach divides video sequences into groups of similar frames, and indexing and retrieval is based on representative frames for these groups (called shots, to be defined later). This approach is called shot-based video indexing and retrieval, and is the focus of this chapter.

- Integrated approach: Two or more of the above methods can be combined to provide more effective video indexing and retrieval [4, 9]. We briefly describe integrated approaches in this chapter and will discuss further in the next chapter.

The remaining sections of the chapter are organized as follows. Section 7.2 gives an overview of shot-based video indexing and retrieval. The main steps in shot-based video indexing and retrieval are segmenting video sequences into shots, finding representative frames (r frames) for each of the shots, and indexing and retrieving the video based on these r frames. Section 7.3 describes a number of techniques for video segmentation. Section 7.4 discusses ways of determining r frames, and indexing and retrieval based on r frames.

One important aspect of video retrieval is how to represent video compactly yet accurately for browsing and results presentation. We describe a number of video representations and abstract tools in Section 7.5.

Section 7.6 summarizes the chapter.

7.2 OVERVIEW OF SHOT-BASED VIDEO INDEXING AND RETRIEVAL

A video sequence consists of a sequence of images taken at a certain rate. A long video (say, over 30 minutes), contains many frames. If these frames are treated individually, indexing and retrieval are not efficient. Fortunately, video is normally made of a number of logical units or segments (see Chapter 3 for common video models). We call these segments *video shots*. A shot is a short sequence of contiguous frames having one or more of the following features:

1. The frames depict the same scene;
2. The frames signify a single camera operation;
3. The frames contain a distinct event or an action such as the significant presence of an object;
4. The frames are chosen as a single indexable entity by the user.

For example, in a news video, each news item corresponds to a shot. In a film, frames taken in the same scene and featuring the same group of people correspond to a shot.

In many applications, it is required not only to identify which video contains the required information, but also to identify which part of the video contains the required information. Browsing through a video to look for some specific information is very time consuming, so automatic methods for locating shots containing the required information are needed. Shot-based video indexing and retrieval consists of the following main steps:

- The first step is to segment the video into shots. This step is commonly called video temporal segmentation, partition, or shot detection.
- The second step is to index each shot. The common approach used in this step is to first identify key frames or representative frames (r frames) for each shot, and use the image indexing method described in Chapter 6 to index these r frames.
- The third step is to apply a similarity measurement between queries and video shots and retrieve shots with high similarities. This is achieved using the image retrieval methods described in Chapter 6, based on indexes or feature vectors obtained in the second step.

7.3 Video Shot Detection or Segmentation

Segmentation is a process for dividing a video sequence into shots. Consecutive frames on either side of a camera break generally display a significant quantitative change in content. Therefore, what is required is some suitable quantitative measure that captures the difference between a pair of frames. Then if the difference exceeds a given threshold, it may be interpreted as indicating a segment boundary. Hence, establishing suitable difference metrics and techniques for applying them are the key issues in automatic partitioning.

A camera break is the simplest transition between two shots. More sophisticated camera operations include dissolve, wipe, fade-in, and fade-out. Such special effects involve much more gradual changes between consecutive frames than does a camera break. Since these quantitative changes are too small to be detected by a single threshold, a more sophisticated approach is required.

In the following subsections, we first describe the basic shot detection techniques or algorithms. We then discuss techniques to deal with special cases such as gradual transitions and compressed video.

7.3.1 Basic Video Segment Techniques

The key issue of shot detection is how to measure the frame-to-frame differences. A number of difference measures between frames have been proposed [5-7, 10]. The most simple measure is the sum of pixel-to-pixel differences between neighboring frames. If the sum is larger than a preset threshold, a shot boundary exists between these two frames. This method is not effective and many false shot detections will be reported. This is because two frames within one shot may have large pixel-to-pixel difference due to object movement from frame to frame.

To overcome the limitation of the first method, the second method measures color histogram distance between neighboring frames. The principle behind this method is that object motion causes little histogram difference. If a large difference is found, it is quite certain that a camera break occurred.

Let $H_i(j)$ denote the histogram for the ith frame, where j is one of the G possible gray levels. Then the difference between the ith frame and its successor is given by the following formula:

$$SD_i = \sum_j |H_i(j) - H_{i+1}(j)|$$

If SD_i is larger than a predefined threshold, a shot boundary is declared.

For color video, the above basic technique is modified to take into account color components. A simple but effective approach is to compare histograms based on a color code derived from the R, G, and B components. In this case, j in the above equation denotes a color code instead of gray level. To reduce the computation, we choose only two or three most significant bits of each color component to compose a color code. For example, if three bits for each component are used, the histogram has a total of 512 bins.

The third method is a modification of the second method. The frame distance is calculated as follows:

$$SD_i = \sum_j \frac{(H_i(j) - H_{i+1}(j))^2}{H_{i+1}(j)}$$

This measurement is called χ^2 test.

In the above shot detection techniques, selection of appropriate threshold values is a key issue in determining the segmentation performance. A threshold must be assigned so that it tolerates variations in individual frames but detects actual boundaries. Normally the threshold is chosen as the mean of the frame-to-frame difference plus a small tolerance value [6]. In [11], the thresholds are determined based on a statistical model for frame-to-frame differences.

7.3.2 Detecting Shot Boundaries with Gradual Change

Each of the above shot detection techniques relies on a single frame-to-frame difference threshold for shot detection. Ideally, the difference threshold is chosen so that all shot boundaries are detected and there is no false detection. In practice, the above basic techniques cannot not detect shot boundaries when the change between frames are gradual. On the other hand, since the above basic technique does not consider spatial color distribution, it will not recognize a boundary between two frames of two different scenes but with the similar color histograms. Different techniques are needed to overcome these two problems.

Videos produced with the techniques of fade-in, fade-out, dissolve, and wipe operations have much more gradual changes between shot boundaries than a camera break. Fade-in is when a scene gradually appears. Fade-out is when a scene gradually disappears. Dissolve is when one scene gradually disappears while another gradually appears. Wipe is when one scene gradually enters across the frame while another gradually leaves.

The difference values within a fade-in, fade-out, dissolve, and wipe operation tend to be higher than those within a shot but significantly lower than the shot threshold. In these situations, a single threshold does not work, because to capture these boundaries, the threshold must be lowered significantly, causing many false detections. To solve this problem, Zhang et al. developed a twin-comparison technique that can detect normal camera breaks and gradual transitions [6]. The twin-comparison technique requires the use of two difference thresholds: the threshold T_b used to detect normal camera breaks, and a second lower threshold T_s to detect the potential frames where a gradual transition may occur. During the shot boundary detection process, consecutive frames are compared using one of the difference measures as described in the previous section. If the difference is larger than T_b, a shot boundary is declared. If the difference is smaller than T_b but larger than T_s, the frame is marked as a potential transition frame. We then add the frame-to-frame differences of potential transition frames occurring consecutively. If the accumulated frame-to-frame differences of consecutive potential transition frames is larger than T_b, a transition is declared and the consecutive potential transition frames are treated as a special segment. Note that the accumulated difference is only computed when the frame-to-frame difference is larger than T_s consecutively. That is, in a transition, all frame-to-frame differences (between current and previous frames) should be larger than T_s but less than T_b.

In general, it is hard to correctly determine gradual transitions. Boreczky and Rowe did a comparison among a number of shot detection methods [10]. The success rate of correctly detecting gradual transition is below 16%. Trying to improve the success rate, Yu and Wolf proposed a shot detection technique based on wavelet transformation [12]. Their technique is based on the assumption that during fade-in, fade-out, and dissolve, the high frequency component of the image is reduced. However, no detailed performance comparison has been carried out.

7.3.3 Preventing False Shot Detection

While gradual transitions create the problem of detecting boundaries that cannot be detected by a simple quantitative measurement, operations such as panning and zooming by the camera can lead to gradual changes that may be falsely interpreted as segment boundaries, since they tend to cause successive difference values of the same order as those of gradual transitions. Motion analysis techniques are currently being employed to avoid the problem of such "false segmenting." The specific feature that serves to detect camera movements is *optical flow* [6]. The motion vectors that represent optical flow are computed by a block-matching method developed for motion compensation coding. The distribution of motion vectors resulting from camera panning should exhibit a single strong modal value that corresponds to the movement of the camera. On the other hand, the field of motion vectors resulting from zooming converges or diverges at the focus center.

Another common reason for false detection of shots is illumination change. Illumination can be changed in many ways, such as an actor walking into a spotlight, a cloud moving across the sky, or using special lighting effects. All these changes may cause the frame-to-frame distance to be larger than the shot threshold, leading to a false shot detection. To overcome this problem, Wei, Drew, and Li proposed to normalize color images before carrying out shot detection [13]. The proposed frame-to-frame distance is also different from those discussed above. Their shot detection scheme works as follows:

1. To reduce the effect of lighting changes, each of the R, G, and B channels of each frame is normalized separately using the following formulas:

$$R_i' = \frac{R_i}{\sqrt{\sum_{i=1}^{N} R_i^2}}$$

$$G_i' = \frac{G_i}{\sqrt{\sum_{i=1}^{N} G_i^2}}$$

$$B_i' = \frac{B_i}{\sqrt{\sum_{i=1}^{N} B_i^2}}$$

where R_i, G_i and B_i are the original color components of the image pixels; R_i', G_i', and B_i' are the normalized color components of the image pixels; N is the number of pixels in the image.

2. Normalized pixel values are converted into chromiticity using the following formulas:

$$r_i = \frac{R_i'}{R_i' + G_i' + B_i'}$$

$$g_i = \frac{G_i'}{R_i' + G_i' + B_i'}$$

3. A combined histogram for r and g is built for each image.
4. As the combined histogram is indexed by two parameters r and g, it can be viewed as a type of image, called a chromaticity histogram image (CHI).
5. The resolution of each CHI is reduced to 16x16 using wavelet-based compression technique.
6. A two-dimensional DCT is applied to the reduced CHI to obtain 256 DCT coefficients.
7. Only 36 significant DCT coefficients are selected from the 256 coefficients.
8. Shot and gradual transition are determined based on the distances between frames calculated from their corresponding 36 coefficients.

It was reported that this method produced higher shot detection performance than other methods [13].

7.3.4 Other Shot Detection Techniques

Ideally, the frame-to-frame distances used for shot detection should have the following distribution. They should be close to zero with very little variation within a shot and be significantly larger than those between shots. With this type of distribution, there will be no shot misdetection. However, the frame-to-frame distances of common videos do not have this type of distribution due to object and camera motion and other changes between frames. To improve the shot detection performance, Otsuji and Tonomura proposed to use a filter to remove the effects of object and camera motion so that the distribution of the frame-to-frame distances is close to the idea distribution [14].

While most shot detection methods are directly based on the color or intensity histograms, Zabih, Miller, and Mai [15] proposed a shot detection method based on edge detection. In the proposed method, edge detection is performed on each image frame. After certain normalization, the percentage of edges that enter and exit between the two frames was computed. Shot boundaries were declared when the percentage was over a pre-set threshold. Dissolves and fades were identified by looking at the relative values of the entering and exiting edge percentages. They reported that their method was more accurate at detecting cuts than methods based on color or intensity histograms.

Advanced cameras that can record their position, time, and orientation onto video signals are emerging in the consumer market. This extra information can be used in video segmentation and understanding.

7.3.5 Segmentation of Compressed Video

Most video is stored in compressed form. Thus it would be advantageous to carry out video segmentation and indexing directly based on compressed data. This situation is parallel to that of image indexing and retrieval.

Based on MPEG Compressed Video

As MPEG is the most common video compression technique/standard, most proposed video segmentation methods work on MPEG compressed video. The two types of information used for video segmentation are DCT coefficients and motion information.

In MPEG (including MPEG 1 and MPEG 2), DCT is applied to each I block and differential block. Therefore, the DCT coefficients for each block are easily obtained from MPEG video streams (for differential blocks, the DCT coefficients are obtained by adding differential DCT coefficients and DCT coefficients of the reference frame/s). Among the 64 DCT coefficients of each block, the first coefficient, called the direct current (DC) coefficient, represents the average intensity of that block. A DC image is formed by combining the DC coefficients of each block. The DC image is 64 times smaller than the original image, but contains the main feature of the original image. Therefore, many researchers have proposed to perform video segmentation based on DC images. The frame-to-frame distance measures discussed in Section 7.3.1 can still be used. But distance calculations based on DC images are much faster as they are much smaller than the original frames [9].

Another type of information that is used for video segmentation is motion information, which is used in the following two ways. First, we determine camera operations such as panning and zooming based on directional information of motion vectors, as discussed in Section 7.3.3. Second, we perform shot detection based on the number of bidiretionally coded macroblocks in B frames. As described in Chapter 2, macroblocks in B frames can be intracoded (coded without reference to macroblocks in other frames), forward predictively coded based on the previous reference picture (I- or P-picture), or bidirectionally coded based on the previous and next reference pictures, depending on the coding efficiency. If a B frame is in the same shot as its previous and next reference pictures (i.e., if there is not significant change among these pictures), most macroblocks can be most efficiently coded using bidirectional coding. Therefore, if the number of bidirectional coded macroblocks is below a certain threshold, it is likely that a shot boundary occurs around the B frame [16]. However, this method cannot determine the exact location of the shot boundary, as this can occur anywhere between the B frame and its next reference frame.

Based on VQ Compressed Video

In the previous chapter we described an image indexing and retrieval method based on VQ codevector histograms. This method can be extended to carry out video segmentation [17]. If the frame-to-frame codevector histogram distance is larger than a preset threshold, a shot boundary is declared. A gradual transition is detected if the distance between the current frame and the first frame of the current shot is larger than a second threshold.

In [17], a χ^2-metric was used for distance calculation between two codevector histograms. It is reported that the VQ-based segmentation method has higher shot detection performance than methods based on DCT coefficients.

7.4. VIDEO INDEXING AND RETRIEVAL

The previous section is mainly about preprocessing for video indexing: segmenting video sequences into shots. The next step is to represent and index each shot so that shots can be located and retrieved quickly in response to queries. The most common way is to represent each shot with one or more key frames or representative frames (r frames). Retrieval is then based on similarity between the query and r frames. We discuss this approach in Section 7.4.1.

Video indexing and retrieval can be based on other information and features. We briefly describe methods based on motion information, objects, metadata, and annotation in Sections 7.4.2 to 7.4.5. Section 7.4.6 describes an integrated approach combining all of the above methods for effective video retrieval.

7.4.1 Indexing and Retrieval Based on r Frames of Video Shots

The most common way of creating a shot index is to use a representative frame to represent a shot. An r frame captures the main contents of the shot. Features of this frame are extracted and indexed based on color, shape, and/or texture, as in the case of image retrieval. During retrieval, queries are compared with indices or feature vectors of this frame. If this frame is deemed similar or relevant to the query, it is presented to the user. If the user finds this frame relevant, he or she can play out the shot it represents. Thus selection of a representative frame is very important as it is used as an index or visual cue for the whole shot.

There are a number of ways to choose the representative frame. If the shots are quite static, any frame within the shot can be used as the representative frame. But when there is panning or a lot of object movement in the shot, other methods should be used. We have to address two issues regarding r frame selection. The first issue is how many r frames should be used in a shot and the second issue is how to select these r frames within a shot.

A number of methods have been proposed to address the first issue – determining the number of r frames to be used for each shot. Some common methods are as follows:

- The first method uses one r frame per shot. The limitation of this method is that it does not consider the length and content changes of shots.
- To partially overcome this limitation, the second method assigns the number of r frames to shots according to their length [18, 19]. If the length of a shot is equal to or less than one second, only one r frame is assigned to the shot. If the length of a shot is longer than one second, one r frame is assigned to each second of video. The second method takes into account the length of shots, but ignores shot contents.
- The third method divides a shot into subshots or scenes and assigns one r frame to each subshot. Subshots are detected based on changes in contents. The contents are determined based on motion vectors [20], optical flow [21], and frame-to-frame difference [11].

After we have determined the number of r frames to be used for each shot, we have to decide how these r frames are selected. According to the above three methods of determining the number of r frames for each shot, we have three possibilities: one r frame per shot, one r frame per second, and one r frame per subshot. In the following discussion, we use the general term "segment" to refer to a shot, a second of video, or a subshot depending on which method is used to determine the number of r frames for each shot. In this case, one r frame per segment must be selected. The following are common methods to select an r frame for each segment:

- In the first method, the first frame of each segment is normally used as the r frame. This choice is based on the observation that cinematographers attempt to "characterize" a segment with the first few frames, before beginning to track or zoom to a closeup. Thus the first frame of a segment normally captures the overall contents of the segment.
- In the second method, an average frame is defined so that each pixel in this frame is the average of pixel values at the same grid point in all frames of the segment. Then the frame within the segment that is most similar to this average frame is selected as the representative frame of the segment.
- In the third method, the histograms of all the frames in the segment are averaged. The frame whose histogram is closest to this average histogram is selected as the representative frame.
- The fourth method is mainly used for segments captured using camera panning. Each image or frame within the segment is divided into background and foreground objects. A large background is then constructed from the background of all frames, and then the main foreground objects of all frames are superimposed onto the constructed background [8].

Another r frame selection approach addresses the both issues of determining the number of r frames for each shot and selecting these r frames. The first frame of each shot is automatically used as an r frame. Then each of the subsequent frames in the shot are compared with the previous r frame. If the distance is larger than a preset threshold, that frame is marked as a new r frame. The problem with this approach is that the final number of r frames is unpredictable. We can end up with a huge number of r frames or simply too few r frames. To solve this problem, an upper limit of r frames is set and the number of r frames are assigned to shots proportional to their amount of content [11]. The amount of content is measured based on the sum of frame-to-frame differences in each shot.

There is no thorough comparison among these methods over a given video database, so it is hard to say which method is the best. In general, the choice of r frame selection method is application dependent.

7.4.2 Indexing and Retrieval Based on Motion Information

Indexing and retrieval based on r frames treats video as a collection still images and ignores temporal or motion information contained in the video. Thus to complement the r frame-based approach, video indexing and retrieval methods based on motion information have been proposed.

Motion information is normally derived from optical flow or motion vectors. In [22], the following parameters are used for motion indexing:
- Motion content: This is a measure of the total amount of motion within a given video. It measures the action content of the video. For example, a talking head video has a very small motion content measure while a violent explosion or a car crash typically has high motion content.
- Motion uniformity: This is a measure of the smoothness of the motion within a video as a function of time. For example, a smooth panning shot has a high value of motion smoothness, while a video with a staggered pan has a low value.
- Motion panning: This captures the panning motion (left to right or right to left motion of the camera). A smooth pan shot scores higher than a zoom shot.
- Motion tilting: This is a measure of the vertical motion component of the motion within a video sequence. Panning shots have a lower value than a video with large amount of vertical motion.

The above motion parameters are associated with an entire video stream or a video shot.

In [23], motion information is determined for each r frame. Thus r frames are indexed-based on both image contents and motion information. Motion information is derived as follows. A fixed number of pairs of subimages or windows is decided for all r frames. Two bits are used to store motion for each window pair. These 2 bits are assigned as follows:
- Bits are set to 00 if there is no motion in both windows (i.e., the magnitude of the motion vector is smaller than a certain threshold);
- Bits are set to 01 if there is no motion in the first window, but there is motion in the second window;

- Bits are set to 10 if there is motion in the first window, but not in the second window;
- Bits are set to 11 if there is motion in both windows.

7.4.3 Indexing and Retrieval Based on Objects

The major drawback with shot-based video indexing and retrieval is that while the shot is cinematically the smallest unit in a video sequence, it does not lend itself directly to a content-based representation. The content can drastically change within a single shot, or it might stay virtually constant over a series of successive shots. Determining "content change" thus emerges as a key question to be addressed in devising a content-based indexing scheme.

Any given scene is a complex collection of parts or objects; the location and physical qualities of each object, as well as their interaction with others, define the content of the scene. If one could find a way to distinguish individual objects throughout the sequence, and carry out the indexing process based on information about each object, the indexing strategy would be able to capture the changes in content throughout the sequence. Object-based indexing schemes have been proposed to do just that.

In a still image, object segmentation and identification is normally difficult. But in a video sequence, an object moves as a whole. So we can group pixels that move together into an object. Object segmentation can be quite accurate by using this idea [5, 24, 25]. These segmented objects can be used to index the video. If we track an object's motion, we can construct a description of that motion for use in subsequent retrieval of the video shot. There is also the value of identifying the object once it has been extracted. Even without sophisticated identification techniques, we can construct an icon from the extracted object that may serve as a valuable visual index cue.

Object-based video indexing and retrieval can be carried out easily when video is compressed using the MPEG-4 object-based coding standard [26]. An MPEG-4 video session (VS) is a collection of one or more VOs. A VO consists of one or more video object layers (VOLs). Each VOL consists of an ordered sequence of snapshots in time called the video object planes (VOP). A VOP is a semantic object in the scene containing shape and motion information. Accompanying each VOP is the composition that indicates where and when each VOP is to be displayed. Ferman, Gunsel, and Tekalp [26] proposed to index MPEG-4 compressed video using the following parameters: the birth and death frames of individual objects, global motion characteristics/camera operations observed in the scene, representative key frames that capture the major transformations each object undergoes, and the dominant motion characteristics of each object throughout its lifetime. Note that MPEG-4 specifies how objects are represented in the compressed bitstreams. But it does not specify how objects are segmented and detected. It is up to the developers of an MPEG-4 encoder to design and implement object tracking and segmentation techniques.

7.4.4 Indexing and Retrieval Based on Metadata

Metadata for video is available in some standard video formats. Video indexing and retrieval can be based on this metadata using conventional DBMSs [11]. For example, the program specific information (PSI) of MPEG-2 systems defines four tables that contain the necessary information to demultiplex and present program via a transport stream. Other information like copyright and language can be obtained from the program map table.

Digital video broadcasting (DVD), the European standard for transmission of digital services, is now being adopted in other countries. It uses MPEG-2 for video compression and transmission. To provide identification of services and events for the user, additional metadata is provided by the DVD standard in the service information table (DVD-SI). The DVD-SI is organized into six tables. The most useful for video indexing are the service description table and the event information table, which contain items such a title, video type (e.g., movie), and directors.

7.4.5 Indexing and Retrieval Based on Annotation

Video can be indexed and retrieved based on annotation using the IR techniques described in Chapter 4. Annotation is important as it can capture the high-level contents of video. Annotation is obtained in the following three ways:

First, video can be manually interpreted and annotated. This is a time-consuming task, but is still widely used because automatic high-level video content understanding is currently not possible for general video. Therefore efforts have been made to simplify the manual annotation process [27-29]. There are two aspects of this work. One is to provide a well-defined framework for manual entry. The second is to make use of domain knowledge of specific types of video to make the annotation semiautomatic.

Second, many videos have associated transcripts and subtitles that can be directly used for video indexing and retrieval.

Third, if subtitles are not available, speech recognition can be applied to the sound track to extract spoken words, which can then be used for indexing and retrieval. This approach is still very challenging because speech and nonspeech are normally mixed in soundtracks, and there is background music and/or noise in speech signals, leading to a lower recognition rate.

7.4.6 Integrated Approach to Video Indexing and Retrieval

Video is information rich. One single feature or technique cannot capture all of the content of a video. Thus an integrated approach combining all above techniques should be used in a practical system. Furthermore, the indexing and retrieval systems are likely to be application dependent, emphasizing certain aspects based on application requirements. We discuss integration issues further in the next chapter on multimedia information indexing and retrieval.

Another often-used video retrieval technique is by *browsing*. To facilitate browsing and retrieval result presentation, video should be represented using some structures and abstraction. We discuss effective video representation and abstraction in the next section.

7.5 EFFECTIVE VIDEO REPRESENTATION AND ABSTRACTION

Video sequences are rich in information, large in storage requirements, and have a time dimension. Thus it is extremely useful to have effective video representation and abstraction tools so that video content can be represented compactly. The challenge is how to show the main contents of videos in a limited display space. Such tools have the following three main applications.

The first application is video browsing. One of the most effective methods of determining whether a video is relevant and for locating a relevant video segment is browsing. The traditional video operations (play, fast forward, and fast reverse) that are used for browsing are sequential and thus time consuming. Compact representation of video allows the user to see the main video contents quickly without going through the video sequentially.

The second application is for presentation of video retrieval results. A retrieval system normally returns a number of videos or video shots in response to a user query. Compact video representation allows the results to be displayed in a limited display window, and allows the user to determine quickly which videos or shots are interesting without going through the entire return list.

The third application is to reduce network bandwidth requirements and delay. Video databases or servers are normally accessed by remote users through network connections. Before the users download or play a video, they determine which video to download or play by browsing. Compact video representation not only makes quick browsing possible, but also reduces the network bandwidth and delay because the compact representation is normally many times smaller than the video itself, even if the video is compressed.

In the following, we describe a number of ways of organizing and compactly representing videos.

7.5.1 Topical or Subject Classification

When dealing with a large amount of information, one of the most effective ways to organize it is based on subject classification. This strategy has been proven in traditional library systems, and many large on-line search engines such as Yahoo and Infoseek. Subject classification facilitates browsing. Once the user has selected a topic of interest, searching tools are used to search for relevant items. Thus subject classification allows the combination of two powerful information retrieval approaches: browsing and search. Browsing narrows down search space and thus enables the subsequent search to produce high retrieval accuracy.

For video organization, two levels of topical or subject classification are used. The first level classification divides different videos into different subject classes, while the second level classification divides the shots of each individual video into different subclasses or topics.

Most WWW search engines use the first-level subject classification. Figure 7.1 shows a portion of the subject classification used in WebSEEK [30-32]. If there is text associated with the video, subject classification is carried out automatically based on a key-term dictionary. It has been reported that the correct classification rate is very high (over 90%) [30].

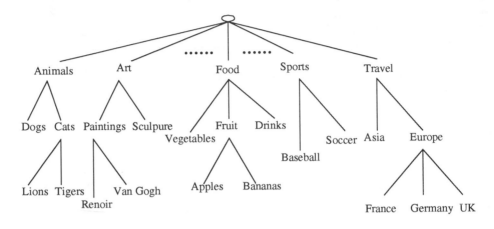

Figure 7.1 Part of an image and video subject taxonomy. (After [30].)

Many videos are very well structured based on topic. For example, news programs are commonly structured into home news, international news, finance, sport, and weather. Movies are commonly structured according to time, event, place, and so on. So it would be useful to group video shots according to their topic or scope. For example, a travel promotional video of a country can be divided into sections according to places of interest. A promotional video for a university can be organized according to faculties and departments.

With video classification, the user either directly views the relevant video segments or searches relevant video segments with a chosen subject or topic. Video classification not only provides an overview of the available information, but also helps navigation, browsing, and searching.

7.5.2 Motion Icon or Video Icon

We use thumbnails to represent still images for browsing and result presentation. Since video has an additional temporal dimension, thumbnails are not adequate to represent it. Thus motion icons (micons) were introduced [33-35]. A micon has three dimensions (Figure 7.2). The front face of the micon shows the first frame or any representative image of the video, and the depth indicates the duration and some motion information about the video. A micon can be thought of a volume of pixels. Instead of displaying the frames of a video one by one, the frames are stacked together with two sides of the icon showing the pixels along the horizontal and vertical edges of each frame. Some spatial-temporal information can be perceived from these two side planes. For example, we can easily tell that shot boundaries occur at frame 200 and 370 in Figure 7.2. Note that not all frames of a video are required to be used in a micon.

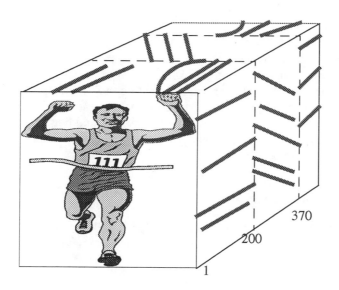

Figure 7.2 An illustration of a micon.

A number of operations can be implemented on a micon [33]. The first operation is browsing. When the user moves the cursor along the side of the micon, the frame that is pointed to is displayed on the front face. This operation provides a quick viewing of the video. The second operation is vertical or horizontal slicing. The micon is cut vertically or horizontally to gain some spatial and temporal information. Smoliar et al. [33, 34] showed that the foot movement in a dance video can be seen from a horizontal slice. The third operation is extracting a subicon. The user specifies the frame range from the micon, and the subicon corresponding to the frame range is lifted from the micon.

A micon can be used to represent a complete video sequence, or one or more video shots. For a long video sequence, only r frames are used in the micon. For a short video sequence or video shot, all frames can be used in the micon.

7.5.3 Video Streamer

A video streamer is similar in appearance to a micon [33, 34]. The only significant difference is the representation of time. In a micon, the earliest event is at the front of the volume with increasing time proceeding "into the screen." In the video streamer, the front face is always the most recent frame. The video streamer is normally used for video display. Its advantage is that the spatial-temporal information shown on the side panels serves as a reminder of past frames and provides a perspective of the video's progress. In a normal two-dimensional display, the past frames disappear completely. The video streamer can be used to facilitate manual shot detection when the automatic shot detection is not 100% accurate.

7.5.4 Clipmap

A clipmap is a window containing a collection of three-dimensional micons, each of which represents a shot or a group of similar shots [34]. The first r frame of the shot is displayed on the front face of the micon. In addition to providing a useful interface for the results of retrieval queries, clipmaps also serve as an interactive tool for index construction. In this capacity, the clipmap plays a role in examining camera shots similar to that of a light table in examining photographic slides. Such a display is very useful for manually sorting the video segments into different categories.

7.5.5 Hierarchical Video Browser

To be able to browse a video sequence efficiently is important. A hierarchical video browser is such a video browsing and management tool (Figure 7.3) [34, 36, 37].

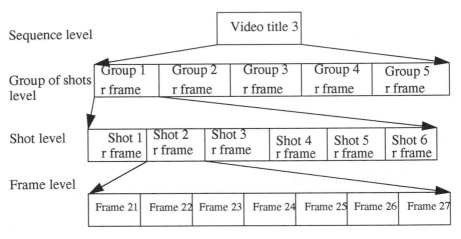

Figure 7.3 A hierarchical video browser.

A hierarchical video browser consists of a number of levels, from the video title, to groups of shots, to shots, and to individual frames. Representative frames are displayed at each level. Subsequent levels are displayed when selected. Using the hierarchical video browser, the user can find relevant shots or frames quickly. For example, in Figure 7.3, the user first selected video 3 based on the title and cover frame and a collection of video shot groups were displayed to the user. Based on the visual information displayed in each video shot group, the user found group 1 interesting and selected it. All the shots in group 1 were displayed with an r frame for each shot. The user then selected shot 2 and all frames in shot 2 were displayed. Normally after very few interactions, the user is able to locate the video sections of interest.

7.5.6 Storyboard

A storyboard is a collection of representative frames that faithfully represent the main events and action in a video [9]. It is similar to the clipmap when used for providing an overview of a video. The main difference is that a clipmap shows three-dimensional micons but a storyboard shows only representative frames. A storyboard is 2 orders of magnitude smaller (in storage requirements) than the corresponding compressed entire video. This greatly reduces the bandwidth and delay required to deliver the information over a network for quick preview or browsing.

When constructing a storyboard, r frames are first found for each shot as described earlier. During display, a user can select different viewing granularities. For example, one can display just one r frame per shot, or all r frames from a particular shot. The coarser granularity is used for browsing long videos.

7.5.7 Mosaicking

Frames of a shot normally show different parts of a scene. Mosaicking uses some algorithms to combine information from a number of frames to show a complete scene. For example, if we take a video of a large building in a close range, each frame only covers a small part of the building. We have to pan the video camera left to right and/or top to bottom to cover the complete building. As each frame only covers a small part of the building, none of them can effectively represent the video shot. Mosaicking solves this problem by constructing the complete building in a mosaic image from all frames of the video shot. The mosaic image is then used to represent the shot. For details of how to create mosaic images, the reader is referred to [38].

Shot representation using mosaic images is more effective and efficient. However, it is hard to generate mosaic images.

7.5.8 Scene Transition Graph

The scene transition graph (STG) is a directed graph structure that compactly captures both the content and temporal flow of video [39, 40]. It is similar in concept to hypertext used for text document representation. An STG consists of a number of nodes connected by directed edges. Each node is represented by a typical image and represents one or more video shots. Directed edges indicate the content and temporal flow of the video.

An STG offers a condensed view of the story content, serves as the summary of the clip represented, and allows nonlinear access to video content. For example, given an STG of a movie clip, a user first gets an overview of the movie by looking at different nodes and the flow. He/she selects any node to look into the contents (images and sound) represented by it.

STGs serve as a valuable tool for both the analysis of video structure and presentation of a high-level visual summary for video browsing applications. The challenge is how to automatically generate effective STGs.

Related to the work on STGs is automatic object tracking for video hypermedia authoring [41]. Video hypermedia systems enable users to retrieve information related to an object by selecting it directly in a video sequence.

7.5.9 Video Skimming

High-level video characterization, compaction, and abstraction so that video contents are represented concisely and accurately is called video skimming [42]. Some of the above representation techniques such as storyboards and STGs are considered as video skimming. To provide effective video skimming, text and sound as well as video content should be used to gain understanding of the video contents [43].

7.6 SUMMARY

This chapter has focused on content-based video indexing and retrieval and compact video representation. The most current content-based video indexing and retrieval techniques follow the following steps. The video is first segmented into shots. r frames are identified for each shot. Indexing and retrieval is then done based on features of these r frames. Although these techniques have made a significant step towards automatic content-based video management, they only handle low-level features. High-level features such as temporal events and interaction between objects within a video are still hard to identify and extract. One current approach to this problem uses detailed structured manual annotation. We discuss this approach further in the next chapter. More research is required to achieve automatic video indexing and retrieval based on high-level features and concepts.

PROBLEMS

Problem 7.1

What are the main video characteristics and common information types associated with video? Describe the general approaches to video indexing and retrieval based on those characteristics and associated information.

Problem 7.2

What are video shots? Discuss the general principles of shot detection.

Problem 7.3

Describe the main steps in shot-based video indexing and retrieval.

Problem 7.4

Implement the first and second shot detection techniques of Section 7.3.1 and then test the implementation on a video sequence by using appropriate thresholds. Discuss your observation in terms of shot detection performance.

Problem 7.5

Obtain a copy of [6]. Study the twin-comparison shot detection algorithm and discuss the strengths and weaknesses of this algorithm.

Problem 7.6

Discuss the advantages and disadvantages of shot detection techniques that work directly with MPEG compressed video streams.

Problem 7.7

Describe three r frame selection methods. Compare their strengths and weaknesses.

Problem 7.8

Motion is an important part of video content. But motion information is hard to extract and is thus not used fully for video indexing and retrieval. Explain the reason behind this situation.

Problem 7.9

Read [5]. Describe the proposed object segmentation technique.

Problem 7.10

Describe three common compact video representation methods. Discuss their suitability in different application scenarios.

REFERENCES

[1] Hjelsold, R., et al, "Searching and Browsing a Shared Video Database," Chapter 4 in *Multimedia Database Systems: Design and Implementation Strategies* (K. C Nwosu, B. Thuraisingham and P. B. Berra, Eds.), Kluwer Academic Publishers, 1996.

[2] Lu, G., *Communication and Computing for Distributed Multimedia Systems*, Artech House, 1996.

[3] Campbell, S. T., and S. M. Chung, "Database Approach for the Management of Multimedia Informa-

tion," Chapter 2 in *Multimedia Database Systems: Design and Implementation Strategies* (K. C Nwosu, B. Thuraisingham and P. B. Berra, Eds.), Kluwer Academic Publishers, 1996.

[4] Rowe, L. A., J. S. Boreczky, and C. A. Eads, "Indexes for User Access to Large Video Databases," *Proceedings of the Conference on Storage and Retrieval for Image and Video Databases II*, San Jose, CA, Feb. 7–8, 1994, SPIE Proceedings Series, Vol. 2185, pp.150-161.

[5] Nagasaka, A,. and Y. Tanaka, "Automatic Video Indexing and Full-Video Search for Object Appearances," *Proceedings of 2nd Working Conference on Visual Database Systems*, 1991, pp. 119–133.

[6] Zhang, H., A. Kankanhalli, and S. W. Smoliar, "Automatic Partitioning of Full-Motion Video," *Multimedia Systems*, Vol. 1, No. 1, 1993, pp. 10–28.

[7] Zhang, H., S. W. Smoliar, and Y. H. Tan, "Towards Automating Content-based Video Indexing and Retrieval," *Proceedings of the First International Conference on Multimedia Modelling*, Nov. 9–12, 1993, Singapore, pp. 193–206.

[8] Flickner, M., et al., "Query by Image and Video Content: The QBIC System," *Computer*, Sept. 1995, pp. 23–32.

[9] Niblack, W., et al., "Update to the QBIC System," *Proceedings of the Conference on Storage and Retrieval for Image and Video Databases VI*, San Jose, CA, Jan. 28-30, 1998, SPIE Proceedings Series, Vol. 3312, pp.150-161.

[10] Boreczky, J. S,. and L. A. Rowe, "Comparison of Video Shot Boundary Detection Techniques," *Proceedings of the Conference on Storage and Retrieval for Image and Video Databases IV*, San Jose, CA, Feb. 1–2 1996, SPIE Proceedings Series, Vol. 2670, pp.170-179.

[11] Hanjalic, A., et al., "Automation of Systems Enabling Search on Stored Video Data," *Proceedings of the Conference on Storage and Retrieval for Image and Video Databases V*, San Jose, CA, Feb. 13–14 1997, SPIE Proceedings Series, Vol. 3022, pp.427-438.

[12] Yu, H. H., and W. Wolf, "Multiresolution Video Segmentation Using Wavelet Transformation," *Proceedings of the Conference on Storage and Retrieval for Image and Video Databases VI*, San Jose, CA, Jan. 28-30, 1998, SPIE Proceedings Series, Vol. 3312, pp.176-187.

[13] Wei, J., M. S Drew, Z. N. Li, "Illumination-Invariant Video Segmentation by Hierarchical Robust Thresholding," *Proceedings of the Conference on Storage and Retrieval for Image and Video Databases VI*, San Jose, CA, Jan. 28-30, 1998, SPIE Proceedings Series, Vol. 3312, pp.188-201.

[14] Otsuji, K., and Y. Tonomura, "Projection Detecting Filter for Video Cut Detection," *Proceedings of ACM Multimedia*, Anaheim, California, Aug. 1-6, 1993, pp.251- 258.

[15] Zzabih, R., J. Miller, and K. Mai, "A Feature-Based Algorithm for Detecting and Classifying Scene Breaks," *Proc. ACM Multimedia 95*, San Francisco, CA, Nov. 1995, pp.189-200.

[16] Wei, Q., H. Zhang, and Y. Zhong, "Robust Approach to Video Segmentation Using Compressed Data," *Proceedings of the Conference on Storage and Retrieval for Image and Video Databases V*, San Jose, CA, Feb. 13–14 1997, SPIE Proceedings Series, Vol. 3022, pp.448-456.

[17] Idris, M. F,. and S. Panchanathan, "Indexing of Compressed Video Sequences," *Proceedings of the Conference on Storage and Retrieval for Image and Video Databases IV*, San Jose, CA, Feb. 1–2 1996, SPIE Proceedings Series, Vol. 2670, pp.247-253.

[18] La Cascia, M., and E. Ardizzone, "JOCOB: Just A Content-Based Query System for Video Databases," *Proceedings of ICASSP'96*, pp.1216-1219.

[19] Ardizzone, E., and M. La Casia, "Automatic Video Database Indexing and Retrieval," *Journal of Multimedia Tools and Applications*, Vol. 4, 1997, pp. 29-56.

[20] Kobla, V., et al, "Compressed Domain Video Indexing Techniques Using DCT and Motion Vector Information in MPEG Video," *Proceedings of the Conference on Storage and Retrieval for Image and Video Databases V*, San Jose, CA, Feb. 13–14 1997, SPIE Proceedings Series, Vol. 3022, pp. 200-211.

[21] Wolf, W., "Key Frame Selection by Motion Analysis," *Proceedings of ICASSP'96*, pp.1228-1231.

[22] Hampapur, A., et al., "Virage Video Engine," *Proceedings of the Conference on Storage and Retrieval for Image and Video Databases V*, San Jose, CA, Feb. 13–14 1997, SPIE Proceedings Series, Vol. 3022,

pp.188-198.

[23] Dimitrova, N,. and M. Abdel-Mottaleb, "Content-Based Video Retrieval by Example Video Clip," *Proceedings of the Conference on Storage and Retrieval for Image and Video Databases V*, San Jose, CA, Feb. 13–14 1997, SPIE Proceedings Series, Vol. 3022, pp.59-70.

[24] Kim, Y.-W., and Y-S Ho, "Video Segmentation Using Spatio-Temporal Information," *Proceedings of IEEE TENCON'97*, pp.785-788.

[25] Meier, T., and K. N. Ngan, "Automatic Video Sequence Segmentation Using Object Tracking," *Proceedings of IEEE TENCON'97*, pp.283-286.

[26] Ferman, A. M., B. Gunsel, and A. M. Tekalp, "Object-Based Indexing of MPEG Compressed Video," *Procceddings of SPIE Conference on Visual Communications and Image Processing '97*, SPIE Proceeding, Vol. 3024, pp. 953-963.

[27] England, P., et al., "I/Browse: The Bellcore Video Library Toolkit," *Proceedings of the Conference on Storage and Retrieval for Image and Video Databases IV*, San Jose, CA, Feb. 1–2 1996, SPIE Proceedings Series, vol. 2670, pp.254-264.

[28] Elmagarmid, A. K., et al., *Video Database System*, Kluwer Academic Publishers, 1997.

[29] Saur, D. D., "Automated Analysis and Annotation of Basketball Video," *Proceedings of the Conference on Storage and Retrieval for Image and Video Databases V*, San Jose, CA, Feb. 13–14 1997, SPIE Proceedings Series, Vol. 3022, pp.176-187.

[30] Smith, J. R., and S.-F. Chang, "Visually Searching the Web for Content," *IEEE Multimedia Magazine*, July-Sept. 1997, pp. 12-19.

[31] Smith, J. R., and S.-F. Chang, "Tools and Techniques for Color Image Retrieval," *Proceedings of Conference on Storage and Retrieval for Image and Video Databases IV* (SPIE Proceedings Vol. 2670), Feb. 1-2, 1996, San Jose, California, pp. 426-437.

[32] Chang, S.-F., and John R. Smith, "Finding Images/Video in Large Archives," D-Lib Magazine, Feb. 1997, Available at: http://www.dlib/org/dlib/february9//columbia/02chang.html.

[33] Smoliar, S. W., et al., "Interacting with Digital Video," *Proceedings of IEEE Region 10's Ninth Annual International Conference*, Singapore, Aug. 22–26, 1994, pp.852-856.

[34] Smoliar, S. W.. and H. Zhang, "Content-Based Video Indexing and Retrieval," *IEEE Multimedia Magazine*, Summer 1994, pp. 62-72.

[35] Tonomura, Y., "Video handling Based on Structured Information for Hypermedia Systems," *Proceedings of International Conference on Multimedia Information Systems*, Singapore, 1991, pp.333-344.

[36] Zhang, H., et al., "An Integrated System for Content-Based Video Retrieval and Browsing," *Pattern Recognition*, Vol. 30, No. 4, pp.643-658.

[37] Zhong, D., H. Zhang, and S-F Chang, "Clustering Methods for Video Browsing and Annotation," *Proceedings of the Conference on Storage and Retrieval for Image and Video Databases IV*, San Jose, CA, Feb. 1–2 1996, SPIE Proceedings Series, Vol. 2670, pp.239-246.

[38] Kreyβ, J., et al., "Video Retrieval by Still-Image Analysis with ImageMiner," *Proceedings of the Conference on Storage and Retrieval for Image and Video Databases V*, San Jose, CA, Feb. 13–14 1997, SPIE Proceedings Series, Vol. 3022, pp. 36-44.

[39] Yeung, M. M., et al., "Video Browsing using Clustering and Scene Transition on Compressed Sequence," *Proc. Multimedia Computing and Networking*, Feb. 1995, SPIE Vol. 2417, pp.399-413.

[40] Yeo, B.-L., and M. M. Yeung, "Classification, Simplification and Dynamic Visualization of Scene Transition Graphs for Video Browsing," *Proceedings of the Conference on Storage and Retrieval for Image and Video Databases V*, San Jose, CA, Jan. 28-30, 1998, SPIE Proceedings Series, Vol. 3312, pp. 60-70.

[41] Kanda, J., et al., "Video Hypermedia Authoring using Automatic Object Tracking," *Proceedings of the Conference on Storage and Retrieval for Image and Video Databases V*, San Jose, CA, Jan. 28-30, 1998, SPIE Proceedings Series, Vol. 3312, pp. 108-116.

[42] Aigrain, P., H. Zhang, and D. Petkovic, "Content-Based Representation and Retrieval of Visual Media:

A State-of-the-Art Review," *Journal of Multimedia Tools and Applications*, Vol. 3, 1996, pp. 179-202.

[43] Wactlar, H. D., et al., "Lessons Learned from Building a Terabyte Digital Video Library," *Computer*, Vol.32, No. 2, Feb. 1999, pp. 66-73.

Chapter 8

Integrated Multimedia Indexing and Retrieval

8.1 INTRODUCTION

We discussed techniques for indexing and retrieval of text, audio, image, and video separately in Chapters 4 to 7. In this chapter, we focus on the integration of these techniques for multimedia information indexing and retrieval.

There are three general approaches to audio, image, and video indexing and retrieval. The first approach is directly based on low-level audio, image, and video features (such as pitch, color, and texture). This approach is called content-based indexing and retrieval. The second approach indexes and retrieves audio, image, and video based on structured attributes such as the title and date. The third approach uses annotation to index and retrieve audio, image, and video. The annotation can be unstructured free text or a structured description capturing spatial and temporal relationships. Free text annotation is derived from existing transcripts, subtitles, speech recognition, and manual entry.

To be effective, a multimedia information indexing and retrieval system should integrate the above approaches, for the following three main reasons:

- First, media do not normally appear in isolation. They usually coexist within an information unit to reinforce each other to convey a message. For example, images appear together with captions, and video frames appear together with a soundtrack. Thus access to a multimedia information unit should be based on indexes derived from multiple media.
- Second, different indexing and retrieval approaches have different strengths and weaknesses and complement each other. The content-based approach captures low-level features such as color distribution and texture that are difficult to describe using structured attributes and annotations. However, it cannot capture high-level abstraction and concepts such as names, feelings and temporal and spatial relationships that are easily captured using structured attributes and annotations. Within the content-based approach, different features capture different aspects of information content. Therefore, different features and different approaches should be integrated in one system to effectively index and retrieve multimedia information units.
- Third, we have different levels of difficulty in using different retrieval approaches. It is normally easy to issue queries based on attributes and keywords to search a multimedia database. The content-based approach is normally implemented using query by examples, sketches, or humming. But example images and audio pieces are not always on hand, and we may know what we are looking for but are unable to draw or hum it properly. Thus we can use keywords and/or attributes to retrieve an

initial list, and then issue content-based queries based on the initial returned items, possibly in combination with keywords and attributes. Furthermore, attributes can be used to narrow the content-based search space – only items satisfying the specified attributes are searched. This combination of different approaches for information search is illustrated in the following example. Suppose the user wants to look for images of carpets with a certain color and pattern and does not have an example image. The user starts the search by issuing a search based on the keyword "carpet," and it is likely that the system will return a list of icons of various of carpet images. The user then browses through the list and selects an image similar to what he or she wants, and uses it as a content query to search based on color and texture. After a few iterations, it is most likely that the required images will be found if they exist in the database.

The following sections of this chapter are organized as follows. Section 8.2 summarizes multimedia information unit indexing and retrieval by integrating techniques based on multiple features and media. Section 8.3 presents a general architecture for integrated multimedia information indexing and retrieval. Section 8.4 discusses some user interface design requirements and techniques. Section 8.5 describes three example multimedia information indexing and retrieval systems. Section 8.6 summarizes this chapter.

Other issues, such as data structures for efficient retrieval, storage, and transmission of multimedia information are discussed in the next three chapters.

8.2 INTEGRATED INDEXING AND RETRIEVAL TECHNIQUES

In most multimedia applications, individual media such as structured data, text, audio and image appear in combinations as integrated information units instead of appearing individually. We call these units multimedia objects (MMOs). Some media types are purposely added to facilitate the indexing and retrieval of other more difficult media. The media hierarchy according to the level of difficulty for handling is: structured data, free text, audio, images, and video. Normally media types that are easier to handle are added to help the indexing and retrieval of more difficult media. For example, free text is normally added as annotation to images and video to better use information contained in these media.

To effectively index and retrieve MMOs, each of the involved media and their temporal, spatial, and semantic relationships are exploited. Although there are numerous MMO types with varying media compositions, the following are three common MMO types with their component media:

Type 1:
  • Structured attributes;
  • Free text;
  • Audio.

Type 2:
  • Structured attributes;
  • Free text;
  • Audio;

- Image.

Type 3:
  - Structured data;
  - Free text;
  - Audio ;
  - Video.

In the following, we describe indexing and retrieval for the above three MMOs. To some extent, we discussed integrated audio, image, and video indexing and retrieval in sections of the previous chapters, such as 5.6, 6.2, 6.3, 6.9, and 7.4, so the description in this section will be brief. We also briefly discuss media translation, which refers to semantic mapping between different media types.

8.2.1 Integrated Audio Indexing and Retrieval

In Chapter 5, we described a general framework for content-based audio indexing and retrieval. Audio pieces are segmented into speech, music, and other types of sound. For speech, we apply speech recognition to obtain the spoken words and then apply traditional IR techniques on these words to index and retrieve the speech. For music, we calculate features such as pitch for indexing and retrieval. Automatic understanding of music is currently difficult to achieve.

The above general framework can be supplemented by indexing and retrieval based on structured data and free text annotation. It is usual that many structured data is associated with audio pieces. Common structured data include attributes such as the file name, file creator, speaker, performer, creation date, file format, and type of music. These attributes are managed by relational database systems and used to retrieve relevant audio pieces. This retrieval is treated as a filtering stage to narrow down the search space. The user can then browse the retrieved audio files, search based on spoken words, or search based on pitch patterns. For many applications, high-level attribute-based retrieval may be sufficient to meet the requirements.

For some long and complicated soundtracks, segmentation is essential, so that only relevant audio segments are retrieved and played. Each segment can be annotated with free text. Annotation is important when high-level semantics or concepts are to be captured. At the moment, annotation is the only way to capture high-level concepts such as excited speech and light music. Note that time information should be encoded in the annotation so that it is directly linked to the appropriate position on a soundtrack.

Therefore, integrated audio indexing and retrieval should combine the techniques based on contents (audio physical features), structured attributes, and free text annotation. Users select the appropriate search strategy based on their requirements and background.

8.2.2 Integrated Image Indexing and Retrieval

The case for integrated image indexing and retrieval is similar to that of audio indexing and retrieval. Images are indexed and retrieved based on low-level features, as described in Chapter 6. Structured attributes and free text annotation are also used for image indexing and retrieval. In addition, images are sometimes accompanied by speech commentaries. Thus images are indexed and retrieved based on recognized spoken words within the speech commentaries.

8.2.3 Integrated Video Indexing and Retrieval

After video segmentation, a similar approach to that of image indexing and retrieval can be used for integrated video indexing and retrieval. However, video is very information rich. A typical video sequence lasts for many minutes and contains many objects with complex spatial and temporal relationships. Thus to support queries related to objects and their relationships, detailed annotation describing all necessary temporal and spatial information as well as high-level semantics is required. Many researchers have worked on video annotation [1-4]

Annotations are obtained in three ways. First, transcripts for some videos already exist and can be used as annotation. Second, we can use automatic music and speech detection and recognition on the video soundtrack to obtain annotation automatically [5-9]. Third, detailed annotation may be entered manually by a domain expert [2, 10]. This approach is most tedious and time-consuming, but may be very comprehensive and thus useful.

8.2.4 Merging of Results Obtained Based on Individual Features

When a retrieval is based on a combination of features, the common approach is to obtain a ranked return list based on each of the features, and then to combine these lists to obtain a final list to be presented to the user. Because different similarity or distance measurements are used for different features, the similarity values or rankings associated with different return lists have different value ranges and different meanings. In addition, different features may have different significance to the user for similarity judgment. Therefore, a difficult but critical issue is how to merge the retrieval results from each individual feature to obtain a combined return list that is ranked according to the returned items' relevance to the query.

The common solution to the above issue is to normalize the similarity calculations so that the resulting similarity values for different features are within the same range, commonly from 0 to 1 [27, 29]. After this normalization, ranking the final merged list is simply based on the sum of each item's similarities from all returned lists. When the user chooses to have different weights for different features, the normalized similarity values are adjusted proportionally according to the chosen weights. We use an example to illustrate the merging process.

Suppose the following are two ranked lists based on feature 1 and feature 2

Feature 1 (C:0.8, G:0.6, A:0.5, M:0.4, H:0.2)

Feature 2 (A:0.7, C:0.5, N:0.4, D:0.3, P:0.1)

where letters denote retrieved items and the associated numbers are the normalized similarity measures of the item for the given feature.

When the user chooses the same weight of 50% for each of the two features, the merged ranked list is as follows:

Merged (C:0.65, A:0.6, G:0.3, M:0.2, N:0.2, D:0.15, H:0.1, P:0.05)

However, when the user's preferred weights are 30% for feature 1 and 70% for feature 2, then the merged ranked list is as follows:

Merged (A:0.64, C:0.59, N:0.28, D:0.21, G:0.18, M:0.12, P:0.07, H:0.06)

When returned lists are long, the order in the merged list is important because the user tends to investigate only the first few items.

8.2.5 Media Translation

In some cases, the user is interested in relevant information regardless of the media types. Thus all relevant information, whether it is in the form of text, audio, image and video should be presented to the user even though the query is in the form of structured attributes, free text, image, audio or video or their combination. That is, semantically related media components should be mapped or linked to each other. At the moment, retrieval works in one direction in the media hierarchy (i.e., when presented with a query in a simple medium in the media hierarchy more difficult media can be retrieved but not vice versa). For example, we can use a text query to retrieve images but cannot use an image query to retrieve text documents. To support this type of capability, content or information among media types should be linked. As high-level understanding of audio, image, and video is not possible at the moment, we rely on annotation to provide the media mapping or linking.

8.3 A GENERAL ARCHITECTURE OF MULTIMEDIA INFORMATION MANAGEMENT

In this section we describe a general architecture for integrated multimedia information management. A database architecture is normally designed based on a chosen data model. The most common data models used for multimedia are the object-oriented and object-relational models [31–37]. In the architecture described in this section, the basic information unit is modeled by a multimedia object that consists of any number of different media with semantic, spatial, and temporal relationships. Each object contains a presentation method based on these relationships and is indexed by a number of features.

Figure 8.1 shows the general architecture of an integrated multimedia database management system. The user interface is used to edit and annotate multimedia objects, issue queries and present retrieval results. We discuss some user interface design issues in the next section.

During the database population phase, features of each multimedia object to be inserted are analyzed and extracted. The extracted feature vectors are stored in the appropriate feature indexes. Each feature vector has a pointer to the original multimedia object that is stored in the separate data store. The different media types of a multimedia object are stored in different types of storage or stored in the same storage. The most important requirement is that multimedia objects should be stored in a way such that continuous multimedia presentation is supported. We discuss multimedia data storage in Chapter 10.

After feature extraction, structured data or attributes are stored and managed by a relational database. The text index stores and manages textual information using chosen IR techniques such as those based on inverted files and the vector space model. Textual information is derived from various sources such as text documents, free text annotations of audio, image and video, and recognized spoken words from speech.

Most features (including text when the vector space model is used) are represented as multidimensional vectors. We discuss data structures to store these vectors for efficient retrieval in the next chapter.

The pitch, color, shape, and texture indices are self-explanatory. The spatial and temporal relationship indices need some explanation. As automatic extraction of spatial and temporal objects and events and their relationships is not generally possible at present, we assume these objects and relationships are obtained by manual annotation. Thus the spatial relationship index will store and manage names of spatial objects and their locations, and is organized in an enhanced inverted file. Similarly, the temporal relationship index stores and manages the names of temporal objects and their number of occurrences and can be organized in an enhanced inverted file. Spatial information is specified by the coordinates of each object's centroid. The following is an example entry in the inverted file of spatial relationships:

Object 3: MMO2(40, 70), MMO7(80, 120)

which reads as "Object 3 appears in MMO2 and MMO7 with its centroid at coordinates (40, 70) and (80, 120), respectively." Spatial relationships between objects appearing in the same MMO are worked out during retrieval based on information contained in the inverted file.

Temporal information about each object is specified by the appearance and disappearance times of the object relative to the beginning of the MMO. The following is an example entry in the inverted file of temporal relationships:

Object 4: MMO5(2, 9), MMO9(7, 15)

which reads as "Object 4 appears in MMO5 from 2 to 9 seconds relative to the start of MMO5, and in MMO9 from 7 to 15 seconds relative to the start of MMO9." Temporal relationships between objects appearing in the same MMO are worked out during retrieval based on the information contained in the inverted file.

During retrieval, features of the query are extracted and compared with corresponding stored features. A combined ranked list is presented to the user. The list normally consists of a number of multimedia object names or icons. When required, the original multimedia objects are retrieved and presented continuously to the user.

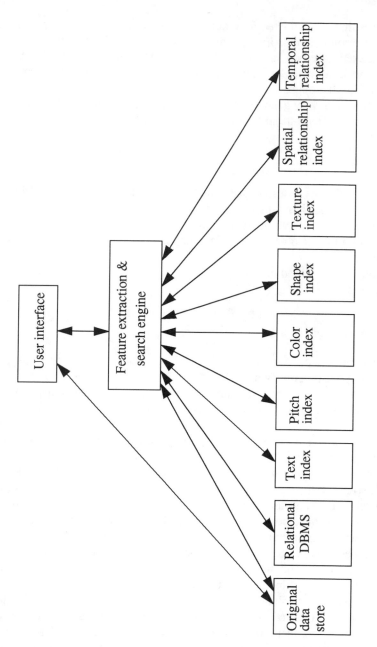

Figure 8.1 General architecture of a multimedia database system.

The features that are extracted for stored multimedia objects and queries depend on object and query composition. For example, when an MMO contains an image and speech, it is indexed based on structured attributes, text from recognized spoken words and/or manual annotation, color, shape, texture, and/or spatial relationships between objects appearing in the image.

This architecture is very general and is easily adapted or extended for most applications. Different applications are likely to use different features.

8.4 USER INTERFACE

We have discussed the main design issues for user interfaces in Chapter 2. We summarize some of the main requirements and techniques in this section.

The user interface has the following main functions:
- To support multimedia object authoring, composition, annotation, and insertion into the database;
- To facilitate searching and browsing;
- To present search results.

Multimedia authoring and annotation

There are many multimedia authoring tools available. The preferred ones are graphic-based that let users easily specify spatial and temporal relationships among multimedia object components. Note that most multimedia objects used in multimedia databases are simple information units such as an image with accompanying text, and a video sequence with accompanying sound. Very complicated and elaborate authoring tools commonly used for highly interactive multimedia presentation and courseware development are not required for authoring basic multimedia objects.

Annotation tools are very important during multimedia database population. These tools should let users easily enter structured attributes and free text descriptions, as well as annotation on spatial and temporal relationships among multimedia object components. Many such tools have been proposed [2-4]. But as most of them are very application dependent, we do not describe them further.

Based on object composition, the system should automatically determine what features are extracted and inserted into the database. For example, if the object to be inserted is an image with accompanying text and structured attributes, the system indexes the object based on structured attributes, free text, color, texture, shape, and possibly the spatial layout of the image. Extraction of most features such as color and texture can be carried out automatically. Extraction of other features such as shape may require human intervention. Thus some tools must be provided to the user to carry out these processes.

Search and browsing

The most common approach to information retrieval is search by issuing a query. Because of the complexity of and multiple features contained in multimedia objects, the

following query types and their combinations should be supported:
- SQL queries for retrieval based on structured attributes;
- Queries specified by certain query languages with multimedia capabilities. There is a lot of research activity put into developing and standardizing such languages. Such activities include extending SQL to handle multimedia objects [11, 12], and developing specific languages to handle complicated data types and spatial and temporal relationships [3, 4].
- Queries based on keywords connected with logic operators;
- Queries with free text;
- Queries by example multimedia objects;
- Queries by humming ;
- Queries by sketch;
- Queries by specifying feature values.

It will be challenging to design a user interface with all of the above capabilities without cluttering the screen and disorienting the user. Most current systems use a subset of the above queries and don't integrate different query types well (although a number of query types are provided, only one type of query can be used at any time). The user interfaces and query types supported are specific to particular applications. We show a number of examples in the next section.

Due to the ambiguity and vagueness of a typical user's information requirements, browsing is a useful mode of multimedia information retrieval. To facilitating browsing, tools such as hyperlinking [13], information classification and structuring, micons, and storyboards are very useful. We described some of these tools for video handling in the previous chapter.

Result presentation and relevance feedback

Retrieval results should be presented in such a way that the user can quickly see if an item is relevant by using visual icons and information compaction. More importantly, the system should allow the user to refine or reformulate queries based on the initial returned items. A multimedia information search is an iterative and progressive process [14]. Some advanced systems incorporate user preferences and can learn from previous information search processes [9, 15, 16].

8.5 EXAMPLE SYSTEMS

Many image and/or video indexing and retrieval systems, such as QBIC [17-20], SWIM[21], Virage image and video engines [22, 23], and WebSEEK and VisualSEEK [24-26] have been developed in the past few years. In this section, we describe three systems, focusing on their user interfaces and their integration of different media and features.

8.5.1 QBIC

QBIC is a set of technologies and associated software that allows a user to search, browse, and retrieve images and video from large collections [17-20]. The following two main techniques are used for content-based image indexing and retrieval:

- Image indexing and retrieval based on color: two improvements have been made over the basic histogram-based method. The first improvement is that perceptual color similarities between color bins are incorporated in the calculation of the similarity between color histograms, as discussed in Section 6.4.2.1. The second improvement is that some spatial relationships between pixels are considered by dividing the entire image into subimages, and distances between corresponding subimages of two images are calculated, as discussed in Section 6.4.2.2. This is to help find images having particular color patterns at certain positions.
- Image indexing and retrieval based on texture: three parameters – coarseness, contrast, and directionality – are used to describe the texture feature, as discussed in Section 6.6.

There are two approaches to handling video [20]. First, each video frame is treated independently and is indexed and retrieved using image retrieval techniques, as discussed above. Second, a shot-based technique is used where video sequences are segmented into shots and each shot is represented by one or more r frames. Indexing and retrieval can then be based on these r frames, as discussed in Sections 7.3 and 7.4. For browsing and result presentation, a video storyboard is used, as discussed in Section 7.5.6.

A number of visual features can be used together in a query, although only one visual feature is used in a query in the demonstrations (see below). Composite queries are formed by combining keywords and visual features.

Several on-line demonstrations of QBIC technology are available at *http://wwwq-bic.almaden.ibm.com*. Figure 8.2 shows an example display from one of the demonstrations. Once the demonstration is started, 12 images (icons) are randomly chosen from the image collection and displayed. The user then performs any of the following functions as indicated by buttons on each image icon:

- Click I to view the full image and the associated keyword list for the image;
- Click C to search images with similar color percentages;
- Click L to search images with similar color layout (sensitive to color position);
- Click T to search images with similar global texture;
- Click S to search images with a special multipass filter (similar to color layout).

If the images contain keyword information, the user searches the images by keywords as well, by entering any keyword in the keyword entry box located at the top of the image display area. If the user simply hits return after entering a keyword, QBIC returns a set of randomly selected images that contain the keyword entered. If the user hits any button on an image after entering a keyword, QBIC searches the images based on the feature the button corresponds to and on the keyword entered. Keyword search is useful in constraining the search domain. Note that the keyword search implemented in QBIC does not use different weights for different keywords based on their significance and returns images in random order (not ranked).

In addition to the above capabilities, the QBIC system can search for images based on a user specified color percentage (Custom Color % Query), user sketch (Custom Paint Query), and structured attributes such as date and author (Query by Properties). The user can also browse the image collection by asking the system to display images randomly chosen from the image collection.

Figure 8.2 The main user interface of the QBIC system.

8.5.2 An Integrated WWW Image Search Engine Developed at Monash University

As more and more images are used in HTML documents on the WWW, many image search engines have been developed specifically for finding images on the WWW. But most are commercial products and details of their implementation are not available. In this section, we describe an Integrated WWW Image Search Engine (IWISE) developed by a research group in Monash University [27]. The system searches images based on a combination of free-text description and image color features. Users start their search process by issuing a text query. From the initial returned images, they select images for content-based queries. The final returned images are based on combined matching scores of the text-based and content-based searching, incorporating the user's preference weighting.

The key issues in designing the integrated image retrieval system were how to use the structure of HTML documents to achieve effective text-based image retrieval, how to implement the color-based image retrieval technique, and how to combine the retrieval results of these two techniques to obtain meaningful final results. In the following, we describe these three issues.

Text-based image indexing and retrieval

Text-based image retrieval is based on traditional IR techniques. However, to improve retrieval performance we make use of the structure of HTML documents. This is because words or terms appearing at different locations of an HTML document have different levels of importance or relevance to related images. Therefore, term weights should be assigned based on term positions and frequency.

Terms are classified into the following groups based on their locations. The numbers in parentheses are their assigned weights, reflecting their importance for image retrieval.

- Metadata (0.2). Terms found in the description or keywords fields of metadata in documents are associated equally with all images in the document.
- Title (0.2). Terms found in the HTML page title are associated with equal weight to all images in the document.
- Heading (0.2). The terms in the most recent heading prior to each image are associated with that image.
- Same paragraph (0.3). Terms found within the same paragraph as an image link tag are associated specifically to that image.
- Image URL (0.4). The URL is split and terms of alphabetic characters are extracted from the file name and path. For example, the URL: http://www-mugc.cc.monash.edu.au/transport/cars/holden/commodore.jpg will have the terms transport, cars, holden, and commodore extracted.
- Alternate text (0.4). Terms found in the alt component of an image link tag are associated specifically with that image.
- Anchor text (0.4). Terms found between the <a ...> and </a> anchor tags for referenced images are associated with the referenced image.
- Other terms (0.2). Terms found external to HTML tags are associated equally with all images linked to the HTML document.

The final weight of each term for each image is the sum of weights assigned based on its frequency and location in which it appears. However, a problem arises from a straightforward calculation of weights. HTML documents with terms in only a few of the designated locations will have lower weights in comparison to HTML documents with text in most or all locations. Consider two HTML documents on the topic of trains. One document contains no text other than a single heading "Pictures of Trains." Another document consists of text throughout all eight of the locations. Using straightforward addition of term weights, the former document will be poorly represented with term weights, despite the fact that the heading, and in particular the term "trains" is likely to describe the linked images well. To solve this problem, a weighting redistribution algorithm was designed to allocate the weights of the missing locations to other locations.

Another problem with the straightforward weight calculation is that excessive repetition of a term in the same location distorts the term weight. To solve this problem, weights are assigned to a term appearing many times in the same location (group) as follows. For the first appearance, the full location or group weight is assigned. The second appearance has a weight of half that of the first appearance. The third appearance has only a quarter of the weight of the first appearance, and so forth. This strategy discourages authors from repeating terms purposely to increase the hit rate while increasing relevance for legitimate multiple appearances of terms.

Color-based image indexing and retrieval

Perceptually weighted color histograms (PWH) are used for image indexing and retrieval. We have discussed PWH in Chapter 6. It has been shown that the PWH-based method produces better retrieval performance than the basic histogram-based method [30].

Image retrieval combining text and color-based methods

The text-based and color-based methods return two independent lists of images with different weights. These two lists must be combined in a meaningful way to give the user a combined image list. During the combining process, the user's preferred weighting for text and color should be incorporated. The default weighting is 50% each for both methods, but the user can choose other weighting.

The major difficulty in combining the two weighted lists is that they are obtained using two totally different weighting schemes (one based on term weights and the other on color distribution). So we cannot simply add the weights of each image in the two lists to obtain a combined weight.

A normalization scheme was developed so that the combined list is not biased toward any method unless the user chooses so by changing the preference weightings.

Experimental results show that the integrated method combining text and color produced higher retrieval performance than that of text-based retrieval alone or color-based retrieval alone [27].

A demonstration is available at *http://www-mugc.cc.monash.edu.au/~guojunl/search.cgi*. Figure 8.3 shows an example display from the demonstration. The user normally starts a search using free text search by entering a number of terms. When the initial search results based on free text are returned, the user forms a subsequent query by combining the free text and colors of the selected image. Weights for free text and color are adjustable.

Figure 8.3 The main user interface of IWISE.

8.5.3 Metasearch Engines

Many WWW search engines are available. They index and retrieve multimedia information based on different features and each has its own strengths and weaknesses. Some of these search engines are designed for indexing and retrieving specific types of information. A single system normally cannot access all information available on the WWW. Therefore, if a system can combine all these search engines and select the best ones for different types of queries, both retrieval effectiveness and efficiency are improved. Metasearch engines have developed based on this idea [28].

Metasearch engines serve as common gateways, which automatically link users to multiple or competitive search engines. They accept requests from users, sometimes with user-specified query plans, to select target search engines. The metasearch engines may also keep track of the past performance of each search engine and use it in selecting target search engines for future queries.

A metasearch engine consists of three main components (Figure 8.4). The query converter converts the user query into the formats of the target search engines. The dispatching component decides to which search engines the query should be sent. The display component accepts the user queries, merges the results, and ranks them for display.

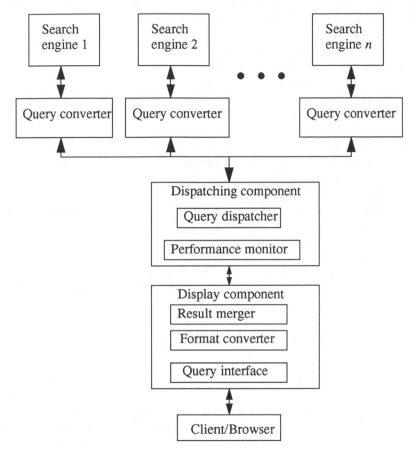

Figure 8.4 Basic components of a metasearch engine. (after [28])

Different metasearch engines use different strategies to implement the above three components. We describe MetaSEEk as an example. MetaSEEk is available at *http://www.ctr.columbia.edu/MetaSEEk*.

The query interface

The MetaSEEk query interface is shown in Figure 8.5. The supported functions are as follows:

- **Get Random**: Retrieves and displays a set of random images from different systems.
- **Number of Images**: Sets the number of images to be displayed. The default is set to eight images.
- **Image URL or Keyword**: If the input starts with "http://," then it is assumed that the search is based on a URL address of an image. The search is then based on the similarity measures explained below. If the input starts with characters other than "http://," then it is assumed that the search is based on text. In this case, only one word can be entered and any other characters after a space are ignored. The text search cannot be used in combination with the similarity measures explained below.
- **Similarity Measures**: When **Color** is selected, if the user clicks on an image or gives the URL address of an image, other images similar in color are retrieved and displayed. Color is computed by calculating the color histogram of an image. When **Texture** is selected, if the user clicks on an image or gives the URL address of an image, other images with similar textures are retrieved and displayed. Texture is computed by measuring the coarseness, contrast, and presence/absence of directionality of an image. The color and texture options are each selected separately or in combination. If none is selected, then the default is the combination of color and texture.
- **Category**: When a category other than "All" is selected, the user is supposed to use query images that belong to the specified category. The system uses this information to recommend appropriate search engines for the search.
- **Number of Searches**: Sets the number of search methods to be queried in parallel by the metasearch engine. The default is set to four searches.
- **Max. Waiting Time**: Sets the maximum waiting time to receive a reply from any of the remote search engines. The default is set to 25 seconds.
- **The "prev" Button**: Displays the previous set of images.
- **The "next" Button**: Displays the next set of images .

The query dispatching component

MetaSEEk currently supports the following target search engines: Visual SEEk, Web-SEEk [24-26], QBIC [18-20], and Virage [22, 23]. MetaSEEk decides which search engines to use for a query based on the following two criteria. First, the search engine should support the method of the query selected by the user (i.e., color and/or texture). Second, the search engine should have a high past performance score for the same or similar queries. Performance scores are calculated for each query image based on the user's feedback. When the query is an image not previously used as a query (by the same user or different users), the performance score of the most similar image used as a query is used. Note that a search engine may have different performance scores for different search options. A search option is a combination of a feature and a search engine. For example, a search engine that supports both color and text features will have two search options.

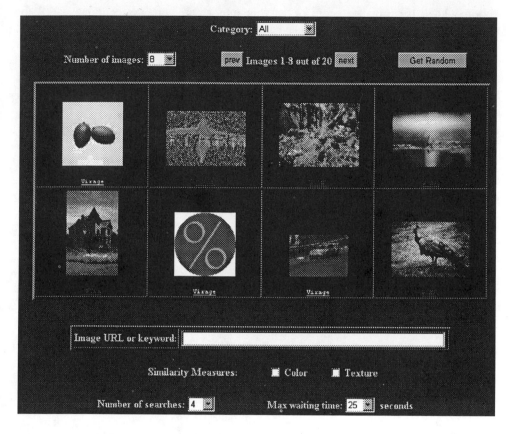

Figure 8.5 The Query interface of MetaSEEk.

The result merger

Once the results are received from each individual search engine, they need to be merged and displayed to the user. Although results obtained from each search engine are ranked, they are ranked based on different features and different distance measurements. An ideal method of merging should calculate similarities or distances between the query, and each of the returned images, based on the same features and same distance measurement and then rank them accordingly. But this approach is too time-consuming. Thus MetaSEEk merges results based on the query image's performance scores. The result images returned by each query option are interleaved before displaying them to the user. The performance scores determine the order of the displayed images and the number of images in each interleaved group. For example, if the images are returned by two query options that have performance scores 2 and 1, MetaSEEk displays two images from the query option with a performance score of 2 first, and then one image from the query option with a performance score of 1. This interleaving process continues until the required number of images are displayed. Any duplicates in the returned results from individual search options are eliminated. Duplication is detected based on image/video file names. If different names are used for the same file by different search engines, duplication will not be detected and multiple copies of the same image or video may be presented to the user.

8.6 SUMMARY

We stressed the advantages and summarized the techniques for integrating multiple features and approaches to multimedia information indexing and retrieval. A general architecture of multimedia information management was also described. It is now possible to implement some useful multimedia information management systems, although many aspects such as portability, scalability, and retrieval effectiveness are yet to be studied and improved.

PROBLEMS

Problem 8.1

What are the main approaches to multimedia information indexing and retrieval? Discuss the strengths and weaknesses of each of these approaches.

Problem 8.2

There are two levels of integration of multimedia retrieval techniques. The first level combines multiple features within a given approach (such as color and texture in content-based image retrieval). The second level combines a number of approaches. Discuss these two levels of integration for video retrieval.

Problem 8.3

Describe a concrete example of a multimedia object.

Problem 8.4

When a retrieval is based on multiple features and approaches, a retrieval list for each feature and approach is produced. These lists must be merged to obtain a final ranked list for presentation to the user. Explain why proper merging is important but difficult to obtain.

Problem 8.5

(1) What is media translation?
(2) Describe two applications of media translation.

Problem 8.6

(1) Describe the general architecture of multimedia information management systems.
(2) Discuss how integration of multiple features and approaches is achieved in this architecture.

Problem 8.7

Describe the main functions of the user interface for the general architecture shown in Figure 8.1.

Problem 8.8

Compare the user interfaces of QBIC, IWISE, and MetaSEEk.

Problem 8.9

Read reference [28] on MetaSEEk. Describe how the performance score of each search option for each query is determined.

Problem 8.10

Try to use MetaSEEk at http://www.ctr.columbia.edu/MetaSEEk to retrieve images/videos by formulating your own queries. Discuss your observations in terms of user friendliness and retrieval effectiveness.

REFERENCES

[1] Yap, K., B. Simpsom-Young, and U. Srinivasan, "Enhancing Video Navigation with Existing Alternate Representations," *Proceedings of Workshop on Image Database and Multimedia Search*, 1997, Amsterdam, pp. 119-126.

[2] Jiang, H., D. Montesi, and A. Elmagarmid, "VideoText Database Systems," *Proceedings of International Conference on Multimedia Computing and Systems*, June 3-6, 1997, Ottawa, Canada, pp. 344-352.

[3] Hjelsvold, R., R. Midtstraum, and O. Sandsta, "Searching and Browsing a Shared Video Database," Chapter 4 in *Multimedia Database and Systems - Design and Implementation Strategies* (K. C. Nwosu, B. Thuraisingham and P. B. Berra, Eds.), Kluwer Academic Publishers, 1996.

[4] Hibino, S., and E. A. Rundensteiner, "A Visual Multimedia Query language for Temporal Analysis of Video Data," Chapter 5 in *Multimedia Database and Systems - Design and Implementation Strategies* (K. C. Nwosu, B. Thuraisingham and P. B. Berra, Eds.), Kluwer Academic Publishers, 1996.

[5] Minami, K., et al., "Enhanced Video Handling Based on Audio Analysis," *Proceedings of International Conference on Multimedia Computing and Systems*, June 3-6, 1997, Ottawa, Canada, pp. 219-226.

[6] Minami, K., et al., "Video Handling with Music and Speech Detection," *IEEE Multimedia Magazine*, July-Sept. 1998, pp. 17-25.

[7] Patel, N. V., and I. K. Wayne, "Audio Characterization for Video Indexing," *Proceedings of the Conference on Storage and Retrieval for Image and Video Databases IV*, San Jose, CA, Feb. 1–2 1996, SPIE Proceedings Series, Vol. 2670, pp. 373-384.

[8] Patel, N. V., and I. K. Sethi, "Video Classification Using Speaker Identification," *Proceedings of the Conference on Storage and Retrieval for Image and Video Databases V*, San Jose, CA, Feb. 13–14, 1997, SPIE Proceedings Series, Vol. 3022, pp.218-237.

[9] Faudemay, P., et al., "Indexing and Retrieval of Multimedia Objects at Different Levels of Granularity," *Proceedings of SPIE Conference on Multimedia Storage and Archiving Systems III*, Nov. 2-4, 1998, Boston, Massachusetts, SPIE Vol. 3527, pp. 112-121.

[10] Yoshitaka, A., et al., "Knowledge-Assisted Content-Based Retrieval for Multimedia Databases", *IEEE Multimedia Magazine*, Winter 1994, pp.12-21.

[11] JCC Consulting, Inc., "SQL Multimedia," http://www.jcc.com/sql_mm.html

[12] Chunyan, M., and M. J. Hu, "Querying and Navigating of Multimedia Objects," *Proceedings of SPIE Conference on Multimedia Storage and Archiving Systems III*, Nov. 2-4, 1998, Boston, Massachusetts, SPIE Vol. 3527, pp. 386-398.

[13] Lewis, H., et al., "Towards Multimedia Thesaurus Support for Media-based Navigation," *Proceedings of Workshop on Image Database and Multimedia Search*, 1997, Amsterdam, pp. 111-118.

[14] Rui, Y., T. S. Huang, and S. Mehrotra, "Relevance Feedback Techniques in Interactive Content-based Image Retrieval," *Proceedings of the Conference on Storage and Retrieval for Image and Video Databases VI*, San Jose, CA, Jan. 28-30, 1998, SPIE Proceedings Series, Vol. 3312, pp. 25-36.

[15] Delanoy, R. L., "Supervised Learning of Tools for Content-based Search of Image Databases," *Proceedings of the Conference on Storage and Retrieval for Image and Video Databases IV*, San Jose, CA, Feb. 1–2 1996, SPIE Proceedings Series, Vol. 2670, pp.194-205.

[16] Kim, Y. H., et al., "Personalized Image Retrieval with User's Preference Model," *Proceedings of SPIE Conference on Multimedia Storage and Archiving Systems III*, Nov. 2-4, 1998, Boston, Massachusetts, SPIE Vol. 3527, pp. 47-56.

[17] Ashley, J., et al., "Automatic and Semiautomatic Methods for Image Annotation and Retrieval in QBIC," *Proceedings of the Conference on Storage and Retrieval for Image and Video Databases III*, San Jose, CA, Feb. 9–10, 1995, SPIE Proceedings Series, Vol. 2420, pp. 24–35.

[18] Flickner, M., et al., "Query by Image and Video Content: The QBIC System," *Computer*, Sept. 1995, pp. 23-32.

[19] Niblack,W., et al., "QBIC Project: Querying Images by Content, using Color, Texture and Shape," *Proceedings of Conference on Storage and Retrieval for Image and Video Databases* (SPIE Proceedings Vol. 1908), Feb. 2-3, 1993, San Jose, California, pp. 173-187.

[20] Niblack, W., et al., "Update to the QBIC System," *Proceedings of the Conference on Storage and Retrieval for Image and Video Databases VI*, San Jose, CA, Jan. 28-30, 1998, SPIE Proceedings Series, Vol. 3312, pp.150-161.

[21] Zhang, H., "SWIM: A prototype Environment for Image/Video Retrieval," *Proceedings of Second Asian Conference on Computer Vision*, Dec. 5-8, 1995, Singapore, pp. II-519 - 523.

[22] Bach, J. R., et al., "The Virage Image Search Engine: An Open Framework for Image Management," *Proceedings of Conference on Storage and Retrieval for Image and Video Databases IV* (SPIE Proceedings Vol. 2670), Feb. 1-2, 1996, San Jose, California, pp. 76-87.

[23] A. Hampapur, A., et al., "Virage Video Engine," *Proceedings of the Conference on Storage and Retrieval for Image and Video Databases V*, San Jose, CA, Feb. 13–14 1997, SPIE Proceedings Series, Vol. 3022, pp.188-198.

[24] Smith, J. R,. and S.-F. Chang, "Visually Searching the Web for Content," *IEEE Multimedia Magazine*, July-Sept. 1997, pp. 12-19.

[25] Smith, J. R., and S.-F. Chang, "Tools and Techniques for Color Image Retrieval," *Proceedings of Conference on Storage and Retrieval for Image and Video Databases IV* (SPIE Proceedings Vol. 2670), Feb. 1-2, 1996, San Jose, California, pp. 426-437.

[26] Chang, S.-F., and John R. Smith, "Finding Images/Video in Large Archives," *D-Lib Magazine*, Feb. 1997, Available at: http://www.dlib/org/dlib/february97/columbia/02chang.html.

[27] Williams, B., "Indexing and Retrieval Of Images on the World-Wide Web Using Text and Color," Honors thesis, Gippsland School of Computing and Information Technology, Monash University, 1998.

[28] Beigi, M., A. B. Benitez, and S.-F. Chang, "MetaSeek: A Content-based Meta-search Engine for Images," *Proceedings of the Conference on Storage and Retrieval for Image and Video Databases VI*, San Jose, CA, Jan. 28-30, 1998, SPIE Proceedings Series, Vol. 3312, pp. 118-128.

[29] Zhang, A., et al., "NetView: Integrating Large-Scale Distributed Visual Databases," *IEEE Multimedia Magazine*, July-Sept. 1998, pp. 47-59.

[30] Lu, G., and J. Phillips, "Using Perceptually Weighted Histograms for Color-Based Image Retrieval," *Proceedings of International Conference on Signal Processing*, Oct. 12-16, 1998, Beijing, China, pp. 1150-1153.

[31] Djeraba, C., et al., "Content Based Image Retrieval Model in an Object Oriented Database," *Proceedings of Workshop on Image Database and Multimedia Search*, 1997, Amsterdam, pp. 263-276.

[32] Huang, L., et al., "Experimental Video Database Management System Based on Advanced Object-Oriented Techniques," *Proceedings of the Conference on Storage and Retrieval for Image and Video Databases IV*, San Jose, CA, Feb. 1–2 1996, SPIE Proceedings Series, Vol. 2670, pp.158-169.

[33] Li, W., et al., "IFQ: A Visual Query Interface and Query Generator for Object-based Media Retrieval," *Proceedings of International Conference on Multimedia Computing and Systems*, June 3-6, 1997, Ottawa, Canada, pp. 353-361.

[34] Narasimhalu, A. D., "Multimedia Databases," *Multimedia Systems*, No.4, 1996, pp.226-249.

[35] Gibbs, S. J., and Dionysios C. Tsichritzis, *Multimedia Programming - Objects, Environments and Frameworks*, Addison-Wesley, 1995.

[36] Amato, G., G. Mainetto, and P. Savino, "An Approach to a Content-Based Retrieval of Multimedia Data," *Multimedia Tools and Applications*, Vol. 7, No. 1/2,, July 1998, pp. 9-36.

[37] Baral, C., G. Gonzalez, and T. Son, "Conceptual Modeling and Querying in Multimedia Databases," *Multimedia Tools and Applications*, Vol. 7, No. 1/2,, July 1998, pp.37-66.

Chapter 9

Techniques and Data Structures for Efficient Multimedia Similarity Search

9.1 INTRODUCTION

Our focus so far has been on how to find feature vectors for text documents, audio, images, and videos, and how to compute the similarity or distance between multimedia objects based on the extracted feature vectors. Feature vectors are usually multidimensional. For example, in the vector space model for text document retrieval, the number of dimensions of feature or document vectors is equal to the number of terms (usually hundreds to thousands) used in the document collection. For audio classification, the number of dimensions of feature vectors is equal to the number of features used (such as brightness, variance of zero crossing rate, and silence ratio). The number of dimensions of a color histogram is equal to the number of color bins used (usually at least 32). Similarly, texture and shape are also represented by multidimensional vectors. The number of dimensions depends on the method chosen. During retrieval, the query is also represented by a multidimensional vector. The retrieval is based on the similarity or distance between the query vector and the feature vectors of the stored objects. When the number of stored objects and/or the number of dimensions of the feature vectors are large, it will be too slow to linearly search all stored feature vectors to find those that satisfy the query criteria. Techniques and data structures are thus required to organize feature vectors and manage the search process so that feature vectors (objects) relevant to the query can be located quickly. This chapter is devoted to a discussion of some of these techniques and data structures.

The main aim of these techniques and data structures is to divide the multidimensional feature space into many subspaces so that only one or a few subspaces need to be searched for each query. Different techniques and data structures differ in how subspaces are formed and how relevant subspaces are chosen for each query.

There are three common query types: point query, range query, and k nearest-neighbor query. In the point query, a user's query is represented as a vector, and those objects whose feature vectors exactly match the query vector are retrieved.

In the range query, the user's query is represented by a feature vector and a distance range. All objects whose distances from the query vector are smaller than or equal to the specified distance range are retrieved. There are many different distance metrics. The ones most commonly used are the L_1 and L_2 norms (Euclidean distance). An alternative range query is specified by a value range for each of the feature vector's dimensions.

In the k nearest-neighbor query, the user's query is specified by a vector and an integer k. The k objects whose distances from the query vector are the smallest are retrieved.

A useful technique or data structure should support all three query types. Data structures can also be optimized for a certain type of query if it is known that only one type query will be commonly used for a particular application.

The basic operations carried out on a data structure are search, insertion, and deletion. Search efficiency is considered the most important criterion for selecting data structures because search is normally carried out on-line (and thus needs quick response), and will be carried out many times (the purpose of building the multimedia database is for quick searching). Ease of dynamic insertion and deletion of objects is helpful but not critical as these operations are carried out off-line and by system administrators only. Furthermore, insertion and deletion can be carried out in batches: objects to be inserted or deleted are accumulated in insertion and deletion lists, and insertion and deletion are only carried out when a sufficient number of objects need to be inserted or deleted. When sufficient changes (insertions and deletions) occur, the data set is reorganized completely to achieve efficient storage and search.

The rest of the chapter is organized as follows. Section 9.2 describes a number of filtering techniques to reduce the search space. Some of these techniques are application or feature dependent; others can be applied to most applications.

Section 9.3 discusses the main concepts of B^+ and B trees. These trees are for organizing objects with single valued keys (i.e., one-dimensional feature vectors). But their concepts are important and are used in multidimensional data structures. Indeed, many multidimensional data structures are considered multidimensional extensions of B^+ and B trees.

Section 9.4 describes clustering techniques for efficient search. The main idea is to put similar objects or feature vectors in the same groups or clusters and only search relevant clusters during retrieval. Clustering can be considered a general approach to data organization, and other multidimensional data structures are applications of the clustering approach. Different data structures differ in how clusters are formed and represented.

Section 9.5 presents the multidimensional B^+ tree (MB^+ tree) which is a direct extension of the B^+ tree. Section 9.6 discusses the k-dimensional tree (k-d tree) which is a multidimensional extension of the binary tree. Section 9.7 describes grid files.

Section 9.8 describes one of the most common and successful multidimensional data structures called the R tree and a number of its variants.

Section 9.9 discusses the telescopic-vector tree (TV tree) which tries to reduce the number of effective dimensions used for indexing and building the tree.

Section 9.10 summarizes the chapter with a brief discussion of the search performance of multidimensional data structures.

9.2 FILTERING PROCESSES FOR REDUCING SEARCH SPACE

It is usually possible to reduce the search space using filtering processes based on certain criteria. Some of these criteria and filtering processes are application or feature dependent, others are not and can be used in most retrieval processes. The basic idea is as follows. The filtering processes, such as those based on attributes, is carried out very efficiently to select items satisfying certain criteria (e.g., containing the attribute). The search based on complicated features (represented by multidimensional vectors) is then carried out on the selected items only. As the number of selected items is significantly smaller than the total number of items in the database, the overall retrieval process is completed quickly. In this section we describe the following filtering methods: filtering with classification and structured attributes, methods based on the triangle inequality, methods specific to color histogram-based retrieval, and latent semantic indexing for vector space-based text retrieval.

9.2.1 Filtering with Classification, Structured Attributes, and Keywords

Structured attributes, such as the date, are associated with most multimedia objects. If the user is only interested in items satisfying certain attributes, we use these attributes to do a preliminary selection and then carry out the search based on the more complicated features of the selected items.

When subject classification is available, the user selects the subjects of interest and searches the items within these subjects only.

The above two approaches are applied generally, without restrictions on the features used. For some specific features, some special attributes are used to reduce the search space. For example, in the region-based shape indexing and retrieval method discussed in Chapter 6, we use shape eccentricity as the filtering criterion – only shapes within the specified eccentricity range need to be searched [1, 2].

9.2.2 Methods Based on the Triangle Inequality

Most feature distance measures, such as Euclidean distance, are metrics. Metrics have a property called the triangle inequality. We use this property to reduce the number of direct feature comparison in a database search [3]. The triangle inequality states that the distance between two objects cannot be less than the difference in their distances to any other object (third object). Mathematically, the triangle inequality is written as

$$d(i, q) \geq |d(i, k) - d(q, k)|$$

where d is a distance metric, i, q, and k represent feature vectors.

The above inequality is true for any k. So when multiple features are used as the comparison objects, we have the following

$$d(i, q) \geq max_{1 \leq j \leq m} |d(i, k_j) - d(q, k_j)|$$

where m is the number of features used as the comparison objects.

We apply the triangle inequality to multimedia information retrieval as follows:

- We select m feature vectors as a comparison base. Normally, m is much smaller than the total number of items in the database.
- For each item i in the database and each comparison vector k_j, we calculate $d(i, k_j)$ off-line and store it in the database.

- During retrieval, we calculate the distance $d(q, k_j)$ between the query q and each of the comparison vectors k_i.

- Find $l(i) = max_{1 \leq j \leq m}|d(i, k_j) - d(q, k_j)|$ for each database item i.

- Only items with $l(i)$ less than a preselected threshold T are selected for calculating the distance from q (being $d(q, i)$). The distances between q and other database items are not calculated as they are guaranteed to be larger than the threshold T, which is selected according to the feature used and the user's requirement.

Note that the unselected items based on $l(i)$ definitely have distances from q larger than T, but not all selected items will have distances from q less than T. We use an example to show the above process. Suppose an image database has eight items represented by feature vectors i_1 to i_8. Two comparison vectors are k_1 and k_2. The distances between each database item and the comparison vectors are calculated off-line as shown in Table 9.1. Suppose we want to find database items whose distance to a query q is less than 3, and the distances between q and each of the two comparison vectors are 3 and 4. The fourth column of Table 9.1 shows $|d(i, k_1)-d(q, k_1)|$ and the fifth column shows $|d(i, k_2)-d(q, k_2)|$, for all database items.

The last column of Table 9.1 shows $l(i)$. Based on the values of this column, only items i_1 and i_7 may have distances to q less than 3 and thus need to be directly compared with q. In this example, only four distances between multidimensional vectors are calculated on-line instead of the eight distances required if the filtering process based on the triangle inequality is not used.

Table 1: An Example Showing the Filtering Process with Triangle Inequality

Database items	$d(i, k_1)$	$d(i, k_2)$	$|d(i, k_1)-d(q, k_1)|$	$|d(i, k_2)-d(q, k_2)|$	$l(i)$
i_1	2	5	1	1	1
i_2	4	9	1	5	5
i_3	7	2	4	2	4
i_4	9	3	6	1	6
i_5	3	8	0	4	4
i_6	2	9	1	5	5
i_7	1	4	2	2	2
i_8	4	10	1	6	6

The filtering process based on the triangle inequality is used in all retrieval techniques whose distance measures are metrics.

9.2.3 Methods Specific to Color-Histogram-Based Retrieval

This section describes a number of search space reduction methods that are applicable to color-histogram-based image retrieval. Recall that the basic color-histogram-based image retrieval technique represents images in the database and query images using histograms with n bins each. The distance between the query and each of the images in the database is calculated as their corresponding histogram distance. So there are two options to reduce the required amount of computation. The first is to reduce the number of bins n. But a smaller n causes lower retrieval accuracy as quite different colors will be classified into the same bin when the number of bins is too small. The second option is to select only a subset of database images for calculating the distances from the query. The number of images in the subset can be much smaller than the total number of images in the database. The question is how to determine this subset.

The solution is to combine the above two options. We first use histograms with very few bins to select potential retrieval candidates, and then use the full histograms to calculate accurate distances between the query and the potential candidates. Striker and Dimai [4] and Ng and Tam [5] described the details of how to chose the initial bins to achieve optimal results.

A special case of the above idea is to carry out filtering based on the average color of the images [6, 7]. Suppose RGB color space is used for image representation (the scheme is equally applicable to other color spaces). We find the average color of an image $\bar{x} = (R_{avg}, G_{avg}, B_{avg})^T$ as follows

$$R_{avg} = \frac{\sum\limits_{p=1}^{P} R(p)}{P}$$

$$G_{avg} = \frac{\sum\limits_{p=1}^{P} G(p)}{P}$$

$$B_{avg} = \frac{\sum\limits_{p=1}^{P} B(p)}{P}$$

where P is the number of pixels in the image, and $R(p)$, $G(p)$ and $B(p)$ are the red, green, and blue components of pixel p. Given the average color vectors $\bar{x}$ and $\bar{y}$ of two images, we define $d_{avg}()$ as the Euclidean distance between these two vectors as follows

$$d_{avg}(\bar{x}, \bar{y}) = \sqrt{\sum_{i=1}^{3} (x_i - y_i)^2}$$

It has been shown that $d_{avg}()$ is a lower bound for the actual distance calculated using the full histogram. That is, the full histogram distance will be no less than $d_{avg}()$. With this result, we can select potential candidates based on $d_{avg}()$ for full histogram distance calculation.

9.2.4 Latent Semantic Indexing for Vector-Space-Based IR

Recall from Chapter 4 (Section 4.4) that in the vector space model, each document is represented by an N-dimensional term weight vector, each element of the vector being the weight of each of N terms in that document. If a document collection has M documents, then the collection is represented as a matrix A of dimension M x N. During retrieval, the query is also represented in an N-dimensional term weight vector. The similarity between the query and each of the stored documents is calculated as either the dot product or the cosine coefficient between the query vector and the document vector.

The above straightforward approach has two main weaknesses. First, a large document collection (such as a library) contains millions of documents with many thousands of terms (i.e., M and N are both very large). So a very large amount of storage is required. For example, if a library has 1 million documents with 10,000 terms, we need 10 GB of storage if each element is stored as 1 byte. A few years ago, this was a huge amount of storage. Second, at least M multiplications of N-dimensional vectors are required during retrieval if the dot product similarity measurement is used, and more are required if the cosine coefficient similarity measure is used. When M and N are large, the required time to complete these calculations is not acceptable for on-line retrieval.

Latent semantic indexing (LSI) was developed to partially solve the above problems [7, 8, 22]. (We say "partially" because other techniques such clustering and multi-dimensional data structures to be discussed later should be combined with LSI for more efficient searching.) The basic idea of LSI is try to group similar terms together to form concepts or topics and the documents are then represented by these concepts. As the number of concepts is much smaller than the number of terms, less storage and computation are required. In addition, because of the LSI's ability to automatically group co-occurring and similar terms to create a thesaurus, retrieval effectiveness has also been reported to be improved [8].

LSI is based on the concept of singular value decomposition (SVD). The theorem of SVD is as follows:

Any $M \times N$ real matrix A can be expressed as

$$A = U \times S \times V^t$$

where U is a column-orthonormal $M \times r$ matrix, r is the rank of the matrix A,
S is a diagonal $r \times r$ matrix and V is a column-orthonormal $N \times r$ matrix.

That U is column-orthonormal means $U^t \times U = I$, where I is the identity matrix. When S is nondecreasing (i.e., its elements are sorted in descending order), the above decomposition is unique.

In the context of text document retrieval, the rank r of A is equal to the number of concepts. U can be thought of as the document-to-concept similarity matrix, while V is the term-to-concept similarity matrix. For example, $u_{2,3} = 0.6$ means that concept 3 has weight 0.6 in document 2, and $v_{1,2} = 0.4$ means that the similarity between term 1 and concept 2 is 0.4.

Based on the SVD, we store matrices U, S, and V instead of A, reducing the storage requirement significantly. For example, assume $M = 1000,000$, $N = 10,000$ and $r = 500$. The total amount of the required storage space is equal to 505.25 MB (1000,000 x 500 + 500 x 500 + 10, 000 x 500), significantly less than the storage requirement of 10 GB for A.

During retrieval, the query document similarity is calculated as follows. The query vector q in term-space is translated into q_c in concept-space by multiplying by V^t as follows

$$q_c = V^t \times q$$

The similarity between the query and each of the documents is calculated as the dot product or the cosine coefficient between q_c and each of the rows of U. So using LSI, we manipulate r-dimensional vectors instead of N-dimensional vectors during the similarity calculation. As r is many times smaller than N, the calculation using LSI is many times faster than using the straightforward method. The search or retrieval efficiency is further improved by clustering the rows of U based on their similarity (to be discussed later).

9.3 B⁺ AND B TREES

So far we have assumed that the similarity or distance calculation is done between the query, and each of stored items within the search space sequentially one by one. This approach is slow even after search space reduction using the techniques discussed in the previous section. The retrieval efficiency can be significantly improved by organizing the feature vectors into certain data structures. We introduce B⁺ and B trees in this section. These trees are for organizing one-dimensional feature vectors or single valued keys of stored items. But many important properties are used in these trees and many multidimensional data structures are developed based on the ideas of B⁺ and B trees.

9.3.1 B⁺ Trees

A B⁺ tree is a hierarchical structure with a number of nodes [9]. Each node (including the root and leaves) in a B+ tree contains n pointers and $n-1$ keys, as shown in Figure 9.1. We call n the degree or order of the tree (being the maximum number of children any node has). Pointer 1 is used to access all records whose key values are less than key 1. Pointer 2 is used to access all records whose key values are greater than or equal to key 1 but less than key 2, and so forth. The last pointer, pointer n, is used to access all records whose key values are larger than or equal to key $n-1$.

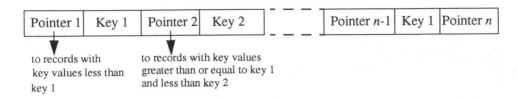

Figure 9.1 The node structure of the B$^+$ tree.

Figure 9.2 shows a B$^+$ tree with an order of 4. Each node has room for four pointers and three key values. Some key value and pointer fields are blank as these nodes have less than three key values (i.e., they are not full). When the rightmost pointer is not used, a 0 is used to indicate the end of the node. The leftmost pointer of the root points to records whose key values are less than 200. The leftmost pointer of the first level 1 node is used to access all records whose key values are less than 50, while the second pointer is used to access records whose key values are greater than or equal to 50 and less than 100. The first three pointers of each of leaf node, if present, point to actual data records. For example, the first pointer of the first leaf node points to the data record identified by key value 10. The fourth pointer of of each of the leaf nodes except for the last leaf node points to the next leaf node. These pointers provide sequential access to data records. That is, data records can be sequentially accessed by following the leaf nodes.

Direct access to data records is easy. Suppose we want to access the record with key value 70. The search starts from the root node. As 70 is less than 200, so the record is pointed to by the first pointer, leading to the first level 1 leaf node. Checking this node, we know that the record must be pointed to by the second pointer, as 70 is between 50 and 100, leading us to the second leaf node. The second pointer of this leaf node will lead us to the correct data record.

When building a B$^+$ tree, we must follow the following rules:
- The tree must be balanced. That is, every path from the root to a leaf node must have the same length.
- The root node must have at least two children, unless only one record is present in the tree.
- If the tree has order n, each node, except for the root and leaf nodes, must have between $n/2$ and n pointers. If $n/2$ is not an integer, round up to determine the minimum number of pointers. That is, each nonroot and nonleaf node should be at least half full.
- If the tree has order n, the number of key values in a leaf node must be between $(n-1)/2$ and $n-1$. If $(n-1)/2$ is not an integer, round up to determine the minimum number of key values.
- The number of key values contained in a nonleaf node is 1 less than the number of pointers.

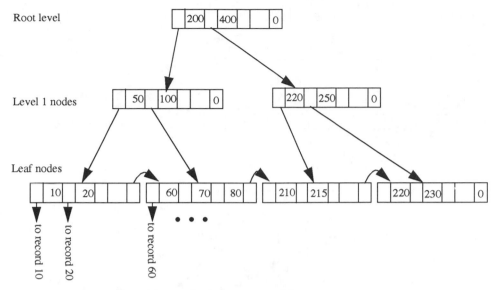

Figure 9.2 An example B$^+$ tree

Direct access in B$^+$ trees is very efficient. If the order of the tree is n and number of record is N, the required number of key value comparison and memory (or disk) access is in the order of $O(\log_n N)$. For example, we can find any record in a B$^+$ tree with an order of 10 and 100,000 records using 5 key value comparisons and memory accesses.

Now we consider insertion and deletion of records in a B$^+$ tree. The basic principle is that the above five rules should not be violated after record insertion and deletion. The insertion and deletion processes can be complicated if the nodes are full before insertion or if the nodes are too empty after deletion. We use examples to show the insertion and deletion processes.

Consider the B$^+$ tree in Figure 9.2. Suppose that we want to insert a record with key value of 30. With a similar process to a search, we identify that the record should be inserted in the first leaf node. As the leaf node is not full, we can directly insert the key value and pointer into the fifth and sixth fields of the node. The resulting B$^+$ tree is shown in Figure 9.3 (a). Now suppose we want to insert a record with key value of 90. It should be inserted into the second leaf node. But this is full, so we have to split the leaf node and readjust the first level 1 node. We put the key values 60 and 70 in the new second leaf node and 80 and 90 in the new third leaf node, and insert a new entry 80 in the first level 1 node. The resulting B$^+$ tree is shown in Figure 9.3(b). This case is not the most complicated. If the first level 1 node was full before insertion, we would have to readjust the root node. And if the root node was full before readjustment, we have to split the root node and add a new root node.

232

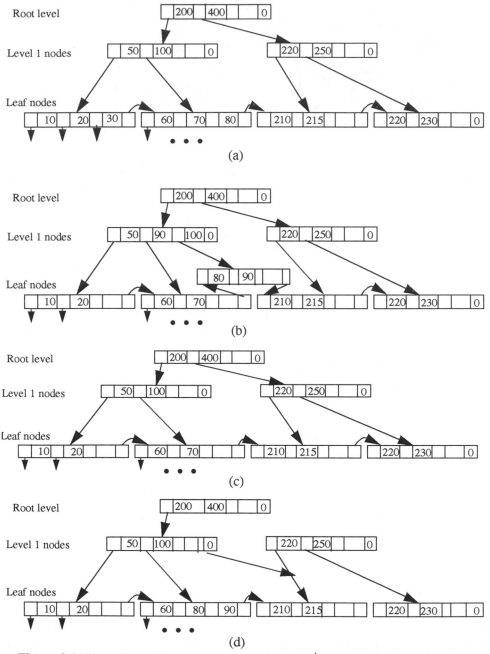

Figure 9.3 Illustrations of insertion and deletion in B$^+$ tree: (a) after inserting the record with key value 30 into Fig.9.2; (b) after inserting the record with key value 90; (c) after deleting record with key value 80 from the tree in Fig.9.2; (d) after deleting record with key value 70 from (c).

Now let us look at the deletion process. Suppose we want to delete the record with key value 80 in the B$^+$ tree of Figure 9.2. We can delete it directly from the second leaf node as the B$^+$ tree rules will not be violated after deletion. The resulting tree is shown in Figure 9.3(c). But if we want to delete the record with key value 70 from the tree in Figure 9.3(b), we have to do some reorganization, as the second leaf node would be too empty after deletion. So we have to combine the second and third leaf nodes, and delete the entry 90 from the first level 1 node. The resulting tree is shown in Figure 9.3(d).

9.3.2 B Trees

In B$^+$ trees, some key values are repeated in many nodes. For example in the tree of Figure 9.2, the key value 220 is repeated in the second level 1 node and the last leaf node. A B tree structure is similar to B$^+$ tree, but it does not have this type of key value repetition. It achieves this by using two pointers preceding each key value in nonleaf nodes (see Figure 9.4 for the general node structure of B trees). One pointer points to the record with key values greater than the previous key value and less than the key value, and the other pointer points to the record with the key value.

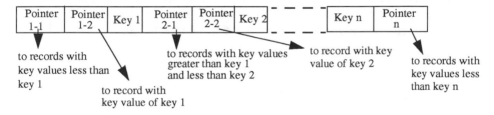

Figure 9.4 The nonleaf node structure of a B tree.

9.4 CLUSTERING

In Chapter 5 we discussed using the cluster-based model for text document retrieval. The same principle can be applied to any feature with any similarity measurement [10, 23].

The basic idea of using clustering for efficient retrieval is as follows. Similar information items are grouped together to form clusters based on a certain similarity measurement. Each cluster is represented by the centroid of the feature vectors of that cluster. During retrieval, we calculate the similarity between the query vector and each of the clusters (represented by their centroids). Clusters whose similarities to the query vector are greater than a certain threshold are selected. Then the similarity between the query vector and each of the feature vectors in these clusters is calculated and the k nearest items are ranked and returned.

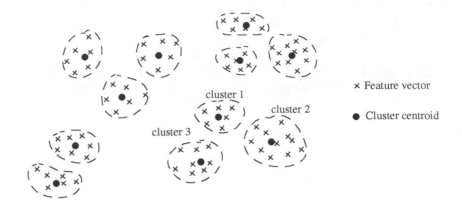

Figure 9.5 A clustering example.

As an example, feature vectors in Figure 9.5 are grouped into 11 clusters. During retrieval, the query vector is compared with each of the 11 cluster centroids. If we find that the centroid of cluster 2 is most similar to the query vector, we then calculate the distance between the query vector and each of the feature vectors in cluster 2. The number of required distance calculations is much smaller than the total number feature vectors in the database.

In the above clustering-based retrieval method, the similarity is calculated between the query and each of the centroids and each of feature vectors within selected clusters. When the number of clusters is large, multiple levels of clusters are used to reduce the number of similarity calculations between the query and centroids. Similar clusters are grouped to form superclusters. During retrieval, the query vector is first compared with supercluster centroids, and then with cluster centroids within selected superclusters, and finally with feature vectors within selected clusters. Considering the feature space in Figure 9.5, we can form four superclusters as shown in Figure 9.6. During retrieval, the query vector is compared with each of the four supercluster centroids. If we find that the centroid of supercluster 1 is closest to the query vector, we compare the query vector with the three cluster centroids within the supercluster 1. If we find that the centroid of cluster 2 is closest to the query vector, we calculate the distances between the query vector and each of the feature vectors in cluster 2. In this example of two-level clustering, the number of required distance calculations between the query vector and centroids (of superclusters and clusters) is 7 (4+3), smaller than the 11 calculations required in the one level clustering.

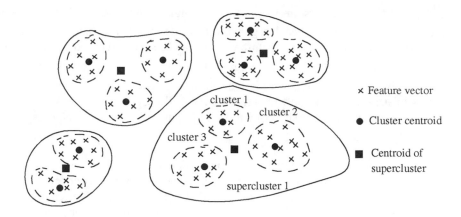

Figure 9.6 An example of two-level clustering.

Clustering not only makes retrieval efficient, but also facilitates browsing and navigation. For browsing and navigation, one representative item whose feature vector is closest to the centroid of its cluster is displayed for each cluster. If the user is interested in a representative item, he or she can view other items in the cluster. This mechanism is similar to the video browsing and storyboard technique we described in Chapter 7, if we consider a cluster as a video shot.

Clustering techniques can be used together with other data structures for higher search efficiency. Similar items are grouped into clusters. Centroids of clusters and/or items within each cluster are organized using a certain data structure for efficient search.

9.5 MULTIDIMENSIONAL B⁺ TREE

The multidimensional B^+ tree (MB^+ tree) is an extension the standard B^+ tree from one dimension to multiple dimensions [11]. The structure and the insertion and deletion algorithms of MB^+ trees are very similar to those of B^+ trees. However, the search methods are different as MB^+ trees support similarity queries (i.e., range and k nearest neighbor queries).

For ease of visualization and explanation, we describe the MB+ tree in a two-dimensional space. Extension to higher dimensions is explained later.

9.5.1 Overview of MB⁺ Trees in Two-Dimensional Space

In two-dimensional space, each feature vector has two dimensions and is considered as a point in a two-dimensional (feature) space. The entire feature space is considered as a large rectangle identified by its lower left corner (x_{min}, y_{min}) and top right corner (x_{max},

y_{max}). All feature vectors are within this rectangle. If we divide this feature space into rectangular regions so that each region has a similar number of feature vectors and these regions are somehow ordered, feature vectors can be accessed based on their corresponding region numbers. MB$^+$ trees are built based on this idea. Therefore, the MB$^+$ tree is obtained by extending the B$^+$ tree in the following ways:

- Replace each key value with a rectangular region.;
- The pointers of leaf nodes point to lists of feature vectors within corresponding rectangular regions.

We use an example to illustrate the basic idea. Figure 9.7 shows a feature space that is divided into eight regions. Each region is identified by its lower left corner and top right corner. These eight regions don't overlap but cover the entire feature space. They are ordered in ascending order as follows (we discuss how the feature space is divided into regions and how regions are ordered later):

$$D_{0,0}, D_{0,1}, D_{1,0}, D_{1,1}, D_{1,2}, D_{2,0}, D_{2,0}, D_{2,1}, D_{3,0}$$

Figure 9.8 shows a possible two-dimensional MB$^+$ tree for the above regions (The MB$^+$ tree shown in [11] does not seem to be correct).

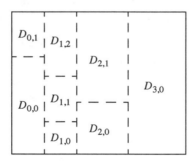

Figure 9.7 Rectangle regions of a feature space. (Based on [11]).

Each pointer (except for the last one) in each leaf node points to a list $L_{m,n}$ containing the following information:

- All feature vectors belonging to the corresponding region;
- A pointer associated with each feature vector linking to the actual multimedia object.

In the following we describe the details of building an MB$^+$ tree and search processes for different types of queries.

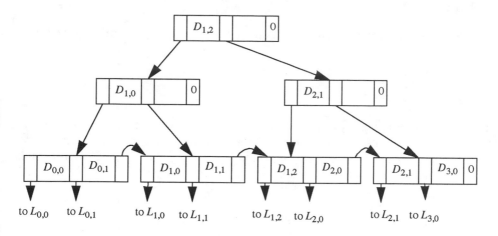

Figure 9.8 A possible MB$^+$ tree of the regions in Figure 9.5.

9.5.2 Building a Two-Dimensional MB$^+$ tree

We first decide the order of the tree and the maximum number of feature vectors in each region (the maximum size of $L_{m,n}$). An MB$^+$ tree is built up by inserting one feature vector at a time. Initially, the two-dimensional MB$^+$ tree has only one leaf node that is also the root of the tree. The node has only one region corresponding to the entire feature space, and there is only one list. Each feature vector inserted is simply added to the unique list until it is full. The splitting operation is required for the next insertion, and the space is divided into two vertical strips with a similar number of feature vectors in each strip. The process continues and the space is divided into smaller strips. When the width of a vertical strip reaches a preset value, horizontal dividing is used within the vertical strip. For a region obtained from horizontal dividing, only horizontal dividing is applied.

Regions are ordered in the following way. The vertical strips are ordered from left to right in the horizontal dimension. The regions within the same vertical strip are ordered from bottom to top in the vertical dimension.

When a list $L_{m,n}$ becomes too small because of the deletion of feature vectors, it is merged with another list. Two neighboring regions within the same vertical strip are merged, and a vertical strip not divided by a horizontal line is merged only with another such vertical strip. After two lists merge together, one leaf entry is deleted from the tree and parent nodes may need to be rearranged.

In summary, the insertion and deletion operations are similar to those of B$^+$ trees. The only difference is that the tree is organized based on the ordering of the regions instead of key values, and each region corresponds to a list of feature vectors instead of a data record.

9.5.3 Search in MB⁺ trees

All three types of queries – point, range and k nearest-neighbor – are supported by an MB⁺ tree.

Point query

In this type of query, a query feature vector (x, y) is given. Starting from the root, we find the region that contains the query vector. Then we scan the feature vector list to determine if the region contains the required vector. We use the point query search to implement a k nearest-neighbor query search.

Range query

A range query is converted into a rectangle query, specified by its lower left and top right corners. Starting from the root, we find all regions that overlap with the query rectangle. We then scan each of the lists associated with these regions to find all feature vectors that are within the query rectangle.

k Nearest-neighbor query

Given a point (x, y) and a positive integer k, the k nearest-neighbor query tries to find the k nearest feature vectors with respect to the chosen distance measure. The common distance measure is the weighted Euclidean distance.

We implement the k nearest-neighbor query in two approaches. First, we estimate the query rectangle entered at (x, y) based on the k nearest-neighbor query and use the range query search method to find candidate feature vectors. Then we calculate the distance between (x, y) and each of these candidate feature vectors to find the k nearest feature vectors. The estimated query rectangle can be too small or too large, so a few iterations may be required. Second, we use the point query search to find the region containing (x, y). We then calculate the distance between (x, y) and each of the feature vectors in the region to find the k nearest feature vectors. But there are cases where feature vectors in other regions may have shorter distances to (x, y) and should be included in the k nearest feature vectors. We detect these cases by checking whether the distance to the k-th feature vector (after ordering in ascending order of distances) is larger than the distance from (x, y) to any of the boundaries of the region. If so, we have to search for the feature vectors in the neighboring region sharing that boundary. Alternatively, we draw a small circle centered at (x, y) (suppose Euclidean distance measure is used), and increase the radius until either k feature vectors are contained in the circle or the circle intersects with another region. If the circle containing the k feature vectors is within the region, we are done. Otherwise, we have to search the region intersecting with the circle.

9.5.4 Higher Dimensional MB⁺ trees

The idea of two-dimensional MB⁺ trees is easily generalized into a k-dimensional space for $k>2$. We order the k dimensions in a desired manner and name them the first dimension, the second dimension, and so on. During insertion, we divide the space along the first dimension first until the edge of a region reaches a certain preset value on that dimension. We then divide each hypercube on the second dimension independently, and so on.

9.6 k-d TREES

The k-d tree is an extension of the binary tree [12]. So let's quickly review the principle of the binary tree. A node in the binary tree has three elements: a key value x, a left pointer pointing to the records having key values less than x, and a right pointer pointing to records with key values equal to or greater than x (Figure 9.9). Each key value in the tree is commonly associated with a data record. When building a binary tree, the first record inserted is the root. The second record goes left or right, depending on whether its key value is less than the root key value. This process applies for each insertion. The binary tree is unbalanced and its structure depends on the order in which records are inserted into the tree.

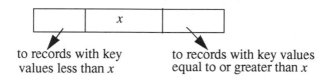

to records with key   to records with key values
values less than x equal to or greater than x

Figure 9.9 Node structure of the binary tree.

In a k-d tree, each key is a k-dimensional vector instead of a single-valued number. Therefore, to extend the binary tree to a k-d tree, we have to decide how to branch at each level. If we name the k-dimensions as dimension 1, dimension 2, and so on to dimension k, and name the root of a k-d tree as level 1, its child as level 2, and so on, the k-d tree is constructed as follows. At level 1, the tree is branched based on the value of the first dimension of the k-dimensional vector; at level 2 the tree is branched based on the value of the second dimension of the k-dimensional vector, and so on. This process continues until all dimensions have a turn and we then start from the first dimension again. Figure 9.10 shows a three-dimensional tree built from the following three-dimensional vectors:

$(10, 13, 7), (9, 14, 8), (20, 9, 17), (7, 13, 6), (8, 12, 7), (6, 10, 9), (11, 8, 14),$
$(15, 13, 11), (10, 6, 17), (16, 12, 21), (17, 3, 15)$

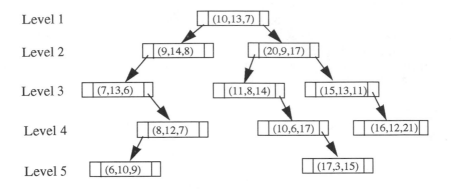

Level 1   (10,13,7)

Level 2   (9,14,8)   (20,9,17)

Level 3   (7,13,6)   (11,8,14)   (15,13,11)

Level 4   (8,12,7)   (10,6,17)   (16,12,21)

Level 5   (6,10,9)   (17,3,15)

Figure 9.10 An example three-dimensional tree.

Note that the tree depends on the order in which the vectors are inserted. The first vector (10, 13, 7) is the root. When inserting the second vector (9, 14, 8), the branch is based on the value of the first dimension. Since 9 is smaller than 10, (9, 14, 8) is inserted to the left of the root. When inserting the third vector (20, 9, 17), since 20 is larger than 10, it is inserted to the right of the root. When inserting the fourth vector (7, 13, 6), we first compare 7 with 10, and decide it should go left as 7 is smaller than 10. We then compare the second elements and find that 13 is smaller than 14, so (7, 13, 6) is inserted to the left of (9, 14, 8). Other vectors are inserted similarly.

The search process in a k-d tree is similar to the insertion process. For example, suppose we want to find the vector (17, 3, 15) in the three-dimensional tree of Figure 9.10. Starting from the root, we go right as 17 is larger than 10. We then go left as 3 is smaller than 9 at level 2. At level 3, we go right as 15 is greater than 14. At level 4, we go right again as 17 is greater than 10 and we find the vector (17, 3, 15). We discuss search for range queries later.

Deletion in a k-d tree can be complicated. We must find the node to be deleted first using the above search process. If the node is the leaf, we simply delete it and set the pointer originally pointing to it to nil. We are then done. However, the deletion process is more complicated when the node is not a leaf node. We do not discuss it further here. An alternative approach is to mark the nodes to be deleted and leave the tree unchanged. When a sufficient number of nodes have been marked, we rebuild the tree for the unmarked nodes.

Range queries can be implemented relatively easily in a k-d tree. Basically, we need to find all feature vectors with each dimension within a certain range. For example, in a three-dimensional tree, we may need to find all feature vectors (x, y, z) meeting the following conditions:

$$x_1 \leq x \leq x_2$$

$$y_1 \leq y \leq y_2$$

$$z_1 \leq z \leq z_2$$

Only a small part of the tree is searched to answer the range query. This is because key values decrease on a left branch and increase on a right branch. So only nodes in a part of the tree will meet the requirement.

The main problem with k-d trees is that the tree is not balanced and depends on the order of object insertion. The search complexity is the same as linear search in the worst case.

9.7 GRID FILES

The grid file is an extension of the fixed-grid (FG) access structure [13]. In the FG structure, an n-dimensional space is divided into equal-sized hypercubes. Each hypercube contains zero or more feature vectors. They are accessed by a pointer associated with the hypercube. Each hypercube is indexed based on its location within the n-dimensional space. We use a two-dimensional space in Figure 9.11 to explain the FG structure. The feature space is divided into 16 fixed equal-sized grids. Feature vectors are scattered in these grids. Feature vectors in each grid are accessed via a pointer associated with it. The pointers of these 16 grids are arranged in a two-dimensional array as shown in Figure 9.11(b). The indices of each pointer are determined by the value ranges of its grid and the value-range to index mapping on a linear scale. In the figure, the value range 0 to 49 is mapped to index number 0, and 50 to 99 is mapped to 1, and so on.

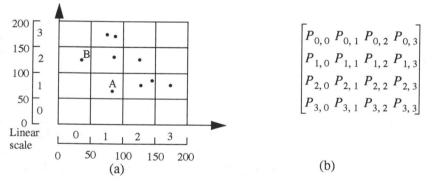

$$
\begin{bmatrix}
P_{0,0} & P_{0,1} & P_{0,2} & P_{0,3} \\
P_{1,0} & P_{1,1} & P_{1,2} & P_{1,3} \\
P_{2,0} & P_{2,1} & P_{2,2} & P_{2,3} \\
P_{3,0} & P_{3,1} & P_{3,2} & P_{3,3}
\end{bmatrix}
$$

(a)　　　　　　　　　　　　　　　　　(b)

Figure 9.11 An example of the fixed grid structure.

Insertion and search in a fixed grid structure are easy. For example, if we want to insert a feature vector (80, 70) into the fixed grid in Figure 9.11, we easily determine that the vector belongs to the grid with indices (1, 1). We then add the feature vector into the list pointed to by $P_{1,1}$. A search for point query is done similarly. For example, if we want to find feature vector B (40, 125), we determine that it belongs to the grid with indices (0, 2). We then scan through the list of feature vectors pointed to by $P_{0,2}$ and find the matching vector. For range queries, we need to retrieve all lists of feature vectors pointed to by grids intersecting with the query range rectangle. We then select those vectors within the specified range. For k nearest-neighbor queries, we need to find the grid to which the query vector belongs, and possibly some neighboring grids, depending on the location of the query vector. We then calculate the distances between the query and each of feature vectors in the grid(s) and select the k nearest ones.

The fixed grid structure is simple and very effective when feature vectors are evenly distributed in the feature space. However, when feature vectors are unevenly distributed in the feature space, some grids will be empty or almost empty while others will be too full, leading to lower search efficiency. The grid file is introduced to overcome the problem of the FG structure. The grid file method divides the feature space based on distribution of feature vectors instead of using fixed-size grids. That is, smaller grid sizes are used for densely populated areas and larger grid sizes for sparsely populated areas. Other concepts are the same as those of the fixed grid structure.

9.8 R TREE FAMILY

The R tree structure and its variants, such as R*- and R$^+$ trees, are commonly used for multidimensional data organization [14–16]. In this section, we first describe the basic R tree concepts and then briefly describe a number of its variants. In the following discussion, we use two-dimensional space as an example. The concept is easily extended to multidimensional spaces.

9.8.1 An Overview of the R tree Structure

The R tree is a multidimensional generalization of the B$^+$ tree, and hence the tree is height balanced [14]. In a nonleaf node, an entry contains a pointer pointing to a lower level node in the tree and a bounding rectangle covering all the rectangles in the lower nodes in the subtree. The R tree is used for either region objects (such as a town boundary in a map), or point data (such as feature vectors in a feature space). When the tree is used for region objects, an entry in a leaf node consists of an object-identifier and a bounding rectangle that bounds the region object. When the tree is used for point data, an entry in a leaf node consists of a pointer pointing to a list of feature vectors and a bounding rectangle that bounds all feature vectors of the list. Each bounding rectangle (of leaf and nonleaf nodes) is represented by the coordinates of its lower left and top right corners. As in the B$^+$ tree, each nonleaf node in the R tree, with the exception of the root, must be at least half full. Figure 9.12 shows a two-dimensional feature space with bounding rectangles and the corresponding R tree.

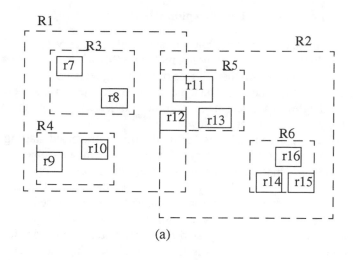

(a)

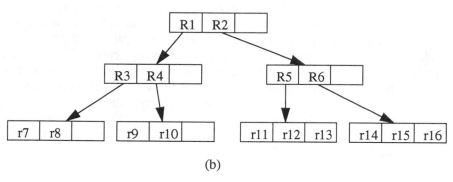

(b)

Figure 9.12 The structure of an R tree. (a) A two-dimensional feature space with bounding rectangles. (b) The R tree corresponding to (a)

The R tree was originally developed for spatial databases such as graphical information systems that deal with region objects. Each bounding rectangle only bounds one region object. Most of the literature on R trees does not mention how to handle point data. It may be assumed that point data is a special case of region object: a region being shrunk into a point. However, this approach to point data handling is not efficient as each point data or feature vector requires an entry in the leaf nodes. For this reason, we take a different approach to handling point data. Region objects are handled as usual: one bounding rectangle at the leaf nodes bounds only one region object. For point data, one bounding rectangle bounds a list of points or feature vectors. In the following, we describe search, insertion, and deletion in an R tree of region objects and point data.

9.8.2 Search, Insertion, and Deletion of Region Objects

A common query is to find all objects that intersect with the query object. The query object is represented by its minimum bounding rectangle (MBR). Starting from the root, the search algorithm traverses down the subtrees of bounding rectangles that intersect the query rectangle. When a leaf node is reached, the query MBR is tested against each of the object-bounding rectangles of the leaf node, and those objects whose bounding rectangles intersect with the query MBR are retrieved.

To insert an object represented by its MBR, the tree is traversed starting from the root. The rectangle that needs the least enlargement to enclose the new object is selected. If more than one rectangle meets the least enlargement criterion, the one with smallest area is selected. The subtree pointed to by the pointer of the selected rectangle is traversed recursively based on the same criteria until a leaf node is reached. A straightforward insertion is made if the leaf node is not full. For each node that is traversed, the bounding rectangle in the parent is readjusted to tightly bound the entries in the node. However, the leaf node needs splitting if it is already full before insertion. A new entry is added to the parent node of the leaf node, and existing entries are adjusted to tightly cover all entries in its leaf nodes if the parent is not full before adding the new entry. Otherwise, the parent node needs to be split and the process may propagate to the root.

The object deletion algorithm uses a similar tree traversal process to that of search: nonleaf nodes whose bounding rectangles intersect with the MBR of the object to be deleted are traversed. When a leaf node is reached, the MBR to be deleted is compared with each of the entries of the leaf node and the matching entry is deleted. If the deletion of the object causes the leaf node to underflow, the node is deleted and all the remaining entries of that node are reinserted using the insertion algorithm. The deletion of a leaf node may cause further deletion of nodes in the upper levels.

9.8.3 Search, Insertion, and Deletion of Point Data

We can have point, range, and k nearest-neighbor queries for point data. Point and range queries are implemented in a similar way to region object search. The only difference is that each entry of the leaf nodes contains a list of points or feature vectors instead of just one object. A k nearest-neighbor query is implemented as a range query by appropriately estimating ranges on each dimension.

For a point data R tree, insertion and deletion is done for each point or feature vector instead of each rectangle. So for point insertion, after reaching an appropriate leaf node, an entry that needs least enlargement and least area is found. The point is then inserted into the list pointed to by the pointer of the entry, and the bounding rectangle is adjusted accordingly to bound the new point and existing points if the list is not full. If the list is full, it is split into two lists (and two bounding rectangles) and a new rectangle is inserted. The insertion of a point then becomes the insertion of a region object (an MBR) as discussed in the previous section.

For point deletion, we delete the point from the selected list directly if the list does not underflow after deletion. Otherwise, the entry is deleted and the remaining points of the entry reinserted.

9.8.4 Search Efficiency in the R Tree

It has been demonstrated that the search efficiency of an R tree is largely determined by coverage and overlap [16]. Coverage of a level of an R tree is the total area of all the rectangles associated with the nodes of that level. Overlap of a level of an R tree is the total area contained within two or more nodes. Efficient R tree search demands that both coverage and overlap be minimized. Minimal coverage reduces the amount of empty space covered by the nodes. Minimal overlap is more critical than minimal coverage because node overlap leads to requiring traverse multiple-paths, slowing down the search. For example, to find r12 in Figure 9.12, we have to traverse all nonleaf nodes R1, R2, R3, R4, R5, and R6 because R1 and R2 overlap.

Minimization of both coverage and overlap is crucial to the performance of the R tree. However, it is impossible to minimize both at the same time. A balanced criterion must be used to achieve the best result.

Another factor affecting the R tree performance is the order of the insertion of data. Different trees may be constructed from the same data set with different insertion orders. Therefore, node reorganization after some insertions and deletions may improve the R tree performance.

9.8.5 R* tree, R$^+$ tree and VAMSplit R tree

The R* tree is an R tree improved by minimizing coverage [15]. Based on the fact that the clustering of rectangles with low variance in the lengths of the edges tends to reduce the area of the cluster's covering rectangle, the R* tree ensures that quadratic covering rectangles are used in the insertion and splitting algorithms.

The R$^+$ tree was proposed to overcome the overlap problem of internal nodes of the R tree [16]. The R$^+$ tree differs from the R tree in the following ways:

- Nodes of an R$^+$ tree are not guaranteed to be at least half full;
- The entries of any internal (nonleaf) node do not overlap;
- Entries of leaf nodes may be repeated.

The repetition of leaf node entries leads to the nonoverlapping of internal nodes. An R$^+$ tree of the feature space in Figure 9.12 is shown in Figure 9.13. The main difference from the R tree in Figure 9.12 is that R1 and R2 now do not overlap, R7 is added to bound r11 (partially) and r12, and r11 is repeated in the leaf nodes pointed to by R5 and R7. The use of disjoint covering rectangles avoids the multiple search paths of the R tree for point queries and reduces the number of search paths for rectangle search. For example, when searching for r12 we don't need to search the subtree pointed to by R2.

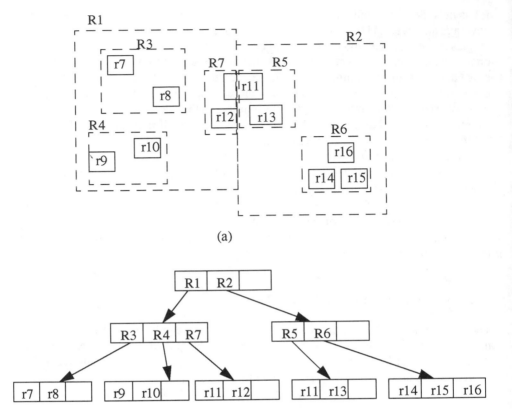

Figure 9.13 The Structure of an R$^+$ tree. (a) A planar representation
of an R$^+$ tree. (b) The corresponding R$^+$ tree of (a).

Another improved R tree is called the VAMSplit R tree [17]. The basic idea is that given a set of multidimensional feature vectors, we split the feature space into rectangles by recursively choosing *splits* of the data set using the dimension of the maximum variance and choosing a split that is approximately the median.

9.8.6 SS tree and SS$^+$ tree

Many recently proposed multi dimensional data structures, including the above mentioned R*, R$^+$, and VAMSplit R trees, are variants of the R tree. They differ from the R tree and from each other mainly in the criteria used for node splitting and branching. Similarity Search trees (SS trees) [18] and SS$^+$ trees [19, 20] are two relatively new variants of the R tree.

The minimum bounding region used in an SS tree is a sphere. The SS tree split algorithm finds the dimension with highest variance in feature vector values, and chooses the split location to minimize the sum of the variance on each side of the split. To insert a new feature vector, the branch or subtree whose centroid is closest to the new feature vector is chosen.

The SS^+ tree is similar to the SS tree. The main difference is that the SS^+ tree uses a tighter bounding sphere for each node, which is an approximation to the smallest enclosing sphere, and a different split algorithm. For details about SS- and SS^+ trees, readers are referred to [18-20].

9.9 THE TV TREE

The TV tree can also be considered a variant of the R tree [21]. It organizes the data into a hierarchical structure. Objects (feature vectors) are clustered into the leaf nodes of the tree, and the description of their minimum bounding regions is stored in their parent nodes. Parent nodes are recursively grouped too, until the root is formed. The minimum bounding region can be any shape, depending on the application. It may be a hyper-rectangle, cube, or sphere.

The name "TV tree" came from the concept that the feature vectors can "contract" and "extend" dynamically, resembling a telescope. Thus it was named the telescopic-vector tree, or TV tree. The basic assumption made is that a set of multidimensional feature vectors tends to have same values on some dimensions. Since dimensions with the same values are not useful for discriminating among feature vectors, we need only use dimensions that have different values (called active dimensions) to build a tree. The number of active dimensions adapts to the number of objects to be indexed, and to the level of the tree that we are at. This approach effectively reduces the number of dimensions used to organize (index) feature vectors, thus leading to a shallower tree requiring fewer disk accesses.

The main problem with the TV tree is that it can only be applied to some very specific applications where its assumption holds. In many general multimedia information retrieval applications, the value of each dimension of feature vectors is a real number and the number of different possible feature vectors is enormous. Thus the assumption that feature vectors will share the same values on many dimensions is not true. For example, in the modest case that each feature vector has 10 dimensions and the value on each dimension is an integer ranging from 0 to 255, the total number of possible feature vectors is 256^{10}. The chance that a set of feature vectors will have the same values on many dimensions is extremely low.

9.10 SUMMARY

In this chapter we described a number of application-specific filtering techniques and some general multidimensional data structures for efficient multimedia information search and retrieval. In practice, a number of filtering techniques and data structures should be used in combination. Filtering techniques are used to narrow the search space, and data structures are used to organize feature vectors within the narrowed feature space.

The search computation complexity of almost all data structures increases exponentially with the number of feature vector dimensions. Thus the number of dimensions of the feature vectors should be chosen to be as low as possible. So far no comprehensive performance comparison has been made among different data structures. Reported performance of different data structures has been obtained on different (usually small) sets of test data. The performance criterion used was usually the number of disk access instead of a combination of a number of criteria. As more and more main memory becomes available on computers, the whole data structure may be brought into the main memory and the number of disk accesses will not be a valid criterion. The number of required operations becomes more important. Nevertheless, we can get some indication of the performance of different data structures from reported work [17-19, 21]. White and Jain [17] concluded that the VAMSplit R tree provides better overall performance than the R* tree, SS tree, and optimized k-d tree variants.

Problems

Problem 9.1

Based on the techniques of indexing and retrieval of text, audio, images, and video described in Chapters 4-8, what is the range of the number of feature vector dimensions required for representing text, audio, images, and video?

Problem 9.2

Discuss common query types for multimedia information retrieval.

Problem 9.3

A collection of multimedia objects can be considered as a set of feature vectors (points) spread in a multidimensional feature space. Intuitively, how can we organize feature vectors so that we can locate feature vectors relevant to queries without linearly searching the entire feature space?

Problem 9.4

Describe the filtering method based on the triangle inequality. Use an example to illustrate its usefulness or otherwise.

Problem 9.5

Obtain and read [5]. Discuss how the efficiency of color histogram search is improved.

Problem 9.6

Describe the principle of the LSI for efficient text document retrieval. Discuss the feasibility of applying the concept of LSI to the indexing and retrieval of other media such as audio and images.

Problem 9.7

Construct a B^+ tree of order 3 for the 14 records with the following key values: 10, 20, 30, 40, 50, 60, 70, 80, 90, 100, 110, 120, 130, 140.

Problem 9.8

Suppose we want to insert a record with key value 45 and delete a record with key value 90 from the B^+ tree constructed in Problem 9.7. Show the tree after the insertion and deletion.

Problem 9.9

Construct an MB^+ tree for the two-dimensional feature space partitioned as below. You should label each of the regions.

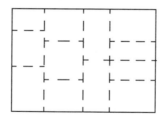

Problem 9.10

Discuss the advantages and disadvantages (if any) of using clustering-based retrieval techniques.

Problem 9.11

Construct a three-dimensional tree for the following three-dimensional vectors (they should be inserted in the order given): (30, 40, 50), (20, 45, 60), (40, 20, 70), (25, 35, 45), (28, 33, 47), (50, 5, 80), (60, 30, 100), (5, 20, 10), (45, 10, 35).

250

Problem 9.12

Describe the basic structure of an R tree. Discuss the search algorithm in an R tree for range queries.

Problem 9.13

Obtain and read reference [18] on the SS tree. Describe the basic structure of the SS tree and the main principles of search, insertion and deletion in an SS tree.

Problem 9.14

Obtain and read reference [21] on the TV tree. Discuss the strengths and weaknesses of the TV tree.

REFERENCES

[1] Sajjanhar, A,. and G. Lu, "Indexing 2D Non-occluded Shape for Similarity Retrieval," *SPIE Conference on Applications of Digital Image Processing XX*, Proceedings Vol. 3164, July 30 - August 1, 1997, San Diego, USA, pp. 188-197.

[2] Sajjanhar, A., and G. Lu, "A Grid Based Shape Indexing and Retrieval Method," *Australian Computer Journal*, Special Issue on Multimedia Storage and Archiving Systems, Vol. 29, No.4, November 1997, pp. 131-140.

[3] Berman, A., and L. G. Shapiro, "Efficient Retrieval with Multiple Distance Measures," *Proceedings of the Conference on Storage and Retrieval for Image and Video Databases V*, San Jose, CA, Feb. 13–14, 1997, SPIE Proceedings Series, Vol. 3022, pp.12-21.

[4] Stricker, M., and A. Dimai, "Color Indexing with Weak Spatial Constraints," *Proceedings of the Conference on Storage and Retrieval for Image and Video Databases IV*, San Jose, CA, Feb. 1–2 1996, SPIE Proceedings Series, Vol. 2670, pp.29-40.

[5] Ng, R. T,. and D. Tam, "Analysis of Multilevel Color Histograms," *Proceedings of the Conference on Storage and Retrieval for Image and Video Databases V*, San Jose, CA, Feb. 13–14, 1997, SPIE Proceedings Series, Vol. 3022, pp.22-34.

[6] Faloutsos, C., *Searching Multimedia Databases by Content*, Kluwer Academic Publishers, 1996.

[7] Faloutsos, C., et al., "Efficient and Effective Querying by Image Content," *Journal of Intelligent Information Systems*, Vol. 3, 1994, pp. 231-262.

[8] Foltz, P. W., and S. T. Dumais, "Personalized Information Delivery: an Analysis of Information Filtering Methods," *Comm. of ACM*, Vol. 35, No. 12, December 1992, pp.51-60.

[9] Elmasri, R., and A. B. Navathe, *Fundamentals of Database Systems, 2nd Ed*. The Benjamin/Cummings Publishing Company, Inc., 1994.

[10] Vellaikal, A., and C.-C. J. Kuo, "Hierarchical Clustering Techniques for Image Database Organization and Summarization," *Proceedings of SPIE Conference on Multimedia Storage and Archiving System III*, Nov. 2-4, 1998, Boston, Massachusetts, SPIE Vol. 3527, pp. 68-79.

[11] Dao, S., Q. Yang, and A. Vellaikal, "MB$^+$-Tree: An Index Structure for Content-Based Retrieval," Chapter 11 of *Multimedia Database Systems: Design and Implementation Strategies* (K. C. Nwosu, B. Thuraisingham, and P. B. Berra, Eds.), Kluwer Academic Publishers, 1996.

[12] Bentley, J. L., "Multidimensional Binary Search Trees in Database Applications," *IEEE Transactions on Software Engineering*, Vol. SE-5, Vol. 4, July 1979, pp. 333-340.

[13] Nievergelt, J., H. Hinterberger, and K. C. Sevcik, *"The Grid File: An Adaptive, Symmetric Multikey File Structure"*, *ACM Transactions on Database Systems*, Vol. 9, no. 1, March 1984.

[14] Guttman, O., "R-tree: A Dynamic Index Structure for Spatial Searching," *Proceedings of ACM SIG-MOD International Conference on Management of Data*, Boston, MA, 1984, pp. 47-57.

[15] Beckmann, N., et al., "The R*-Tree: An Efficient and Robust Access Method for Points and Rectangles," *Proceedings of ACM SIGMOD International Conference on Management of Data*, Atlantic City, 1990, pp.322-331.

[16] Sellis, T., N. Roussopoulos, and C. Faloutsos, "The R⁺-Tree: A Dynamic Index for Multi-Dimensional Objects," *Proceedings of the 13th Conference on Very Large Databases*, Brighton, England, Sept. 1987, pp. 507-518.

[17] White, D. A., and R. Jain, "Similarity Indexing: Algorithms and Performance," *Proceedings of the Conference on Storage and Retrieval for Image and Video Databases IV*, San Jose, CA, Feb. 1–2 1996, SPIE Proceedings Series, Vol. 2670, pp. 62-75.

[18] White, D. A., and R. Jain, "Similarity Indexing with the SS-Tree," *Proc. 12th IEEE International Conference on Data Engineering*, New Orleans, Louisiana, Feb. 1996.

[19] Kurniawati, R., J. S. Jin, and J. A. Shepard, "SS⁺ Tree: An Improved Index Structure for Similarity Searches in a High-Dimensional Feature Space," *Proceedings of the Conference on Storage and Retrieval for Image and Video Databases V*, San Jose, CA, Feb. 13–14, 1997, SPIE Proceedings Series, Vol. 3022, pp.110-120.

[20] Jin, J. S., et al., "Using Browsing to Improve Content-based Image Retrieval," *Proceedings of SPIE Conference on Multimedia Storage and Archiving System III*, Nov. 2-4, 1998, Boston, Massachusetts, SPIE Vol. 3527, pp. 101-109.

[21] Lin, K. I., H. V. Jagadish, and C. Faloutsos, "The TV-Tree: An Index Structure for High-Dimensional Data," *VLDB Journal*, Vol.3, No.4, Oct. 1994, pp.517-549.

[22] Subrahmanian, V. S., *Principles of Multimedia Database Systems*, Morgan Kaufmann Publishers, Inc., 1997.

[23] Prabhakar, S., D. Agrawal, and A. E. Abbadi, "Data Clustering for Efficient Range and Similarity Searching," *Proceedings of SPIE Conference on Multimedia Storage and Archiving System III*, Nov. 2-4, 1998, Boston, Massachusetts, SPIE Vol. 3527, pp. 419-430.

Chapter 10

System Support for Distributed Multimedia Databases

10.1 INTRODUCTION

The previous chapters focused on multimedia information indexing and retrieval. In this chapter, we assume that the relevant multimedia items have been identified, and discuss system support to retrieve and present them in a smooth and timely fashion to the user. Note that it is not possible to describe every aspect of system support in detail within the scope of this book. We only highlight important issues and techniques for supporting multimedia communication. The chapter is still very long because a distributed multimedia system encompasses many subsystems, including storage devices, computer hardware, operating systems, networks, and transport protocols.

The common scenario for accessing a remote multimedia database is as follows (Figure 10.1). The user issues a query through the user interface of a client. The client sends the query through a network connection to the server, which searches the database stored in the storage devices to find the relevant items. The list of relevant items is sent back to the client for display. The user then selects one or more items for viewing. The data for the selected items is retrieved from storage devices through the storage manager, goes through the transport stack on the server, passes through the network to the transport stack at the client end, and is processed and decoded by the decoders before being presented to the user. When information items include audio and video, stringent requirements, in terms of throughput, delay and delay jitter, are placed on all components or subsystems used in the above retrieval process. This is because audio and video have very high data storage and transmission requirements and strict temporal requirements, as discussed in Chapter 2.

To achieve smooth and effective multimedia retrieval and presentation, each subsystem of a distributed multimedia management system (DMDBMS) must meet certain requirements in terms of throughput (bit rate), delay, and delay jitter. The major subsystems and the requirements imposed on them in a DMDBMS are as follows.

Server Storage Devices and Managers

Feature vectors for text, audio, image, and video are organized and stored in chosen data structures, and actual objects (media data) are stored separately, as we discussed in previous chapters. The responsibility of the server storage devices is to efficiently store these media data and retrieve and deliver requested objects smoothly and in a timely

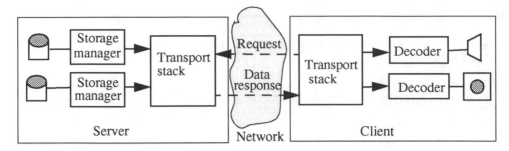

Figure 10.1 End-to-end communication process for retrieval applications.

way. The access time and transfer rate of storage devices are normally not fixed in a shared environment. A storage device may serve multiple applications at the same time. To provide performance guarantees, special storage device managers have to be designed and developed. We discuss server storage devices and managers in Section 10.3.

Server and Client Transport Stacks

Data is moved from the storage device to the server transport stack and from the client transport stack to the decoder under the control of software. Most transport stacks are implemented in software. Due to the time-sharing nature of client and server hosts (called end systems), the execution time of this software varies, depending on the load on the system if a conventional computer architecture and operating system are used. It is likely that the end system executing this software will be a bandwidth bottleneck and cause significant delay and delay jitter to the data. We look at the design of computer architectures and operating systems suitable for multimedia applications in Sections 10.5 and 10.6. We also look at protocol design to minimize data copying and reduce delay and delay jitter in Section 10.8.

Network Access

Different networks have different network access control protocols. Some networks guarantee that a packet will be able to access the transmission medium within a certain time; in other networks, network access time cannot be determined. Obviously, the latter access control protocol is not suitable for multimedia applications. We examine this issue in Section 10.7.

Network Transmission

Once data is on the network, it may go through many intermediate nodes before reaching its destination. These intermediate nodes may have insufficient resources to forward the data; some data may be discarded, some may be delayed. This also depends on the transport protocols and network management used. We discuss network support for digital audio and video in Section 10.7, and transport protocol support in Section 10.8.

Decoder

Decoders can be implemented in hardware or software. Hardware decoders normally have little effect on bit rate, delay, and delay jitter. But hardware decoders are not flexible. For a software decoder to provide performance guarantees, new approaches to the design of computer architectures and operating systems are required, as we discuss in Sections 10.5 and 10.6.

In the above discussion, we focused on the data path from the server to the client. The path from the client to the server is for transmitting user queries and feedback. It is less critical in terms of bit rate and delay jitter, provided the delay is acceptable.

Note that performance guarantees must be provided end-to-end, from issuing a query to displaying data. The arrival bit rate is determined by the slowest subsystem in the communications system. Thus the slowest device should be able to support an average bit rate at least equal to the data consumption rate required for smooth presentation. The end-to-end delay is the sum of the delays of all subsystems of the communications system, so the delay of each subsystem should be bounded. Similarly, the worst delay jitter is the sum of the delay jitter of all subsystems. Thus delay jitter for each subsystem must be bounded. In theory, delay jitter is also bounded when the delay is bounded: it is given by the difference between the maximum packet delay and minimum packet delay. But an acceptable overall delay may not guarantee an acceptable delay jitter. For example, in information retrieval applications, a 2-second maximum delay may be acceptable. But a delay jitter of 1.9 seconds is not acceptable (assuming that the minimum delay is 100 ms), because to buffer 1.9 seconds of a video stream may require a buffer requirement of several MB. In this case, a delay jitter bound must also be specified and guaranteed.

Another important parameter is error rate. There are two types of errors: bit error and packet loss. Bit error is normally caused by noise and interference. It is very low in modern networks. Packet loss is mainly caused at network switches when there is insufficient buffer space.

Throughput, delay, and error rate are related. When a system (or network) has insufficient throughput, packets are delayed or discarded. Therefore, if a network meets both delay and error rate requirements, the throughput requirement is automatically met. But in practice, the throughput requirement is still explicitly specified together with delay, and error rate to facilitate resource management when a connection is requested and established.

Multimedia systems are often described as real-time systems because of the delay and delay jitter requirements. But these should be differentiated from another type of real-time system, called a *critical real-time system*, in which a system is completely programmed to provide a single service, such as air-traffic control or rocket guidance. Critical real-time systems have very tight time constraints, and disaster can occur if such a system fails to meet those constraints. In contrast, failing to meet a multimedia application's constraint is annoying but hardly disastrous.

Extensive research has been carried out into critical real-time systems and these systems exist and are in use today. Their design principles, however, are not directly applicable to multimedia system design due to the different ways in which they operate. A critical real-time application is run on a dedicated system: all system resources are devoted to this application. When enough resources are available, the application constraints can always be met. However, in multimedia systems it is assumed that system resources (memory, CPU cycles, disk access, network, etc.) are shared among many applications. It is hard to predict the availability of the resources. This makes it challenging to design a multimedia system.

Although failing to guarantee multimedia application performance is not disastrous, the guarantee should be provided at a very high percentage level to attain a consistently good presentation quality. Studies suggest that human users tend to remember the failings of a system more than its successes. A multimedia application that has occasional lapses in audio and video quality will be remembered as giving poor quality even if the audio and video quality is quite good most of the time.

There are two ways to achieve good presentation quality. The first is to fully meet the application performance requirements. The second is that in case of failure to meet the application's performance requirements, less important data is sacrificed to keep more important data, and error concealment techniques are used to make the perceived presentation quality high. The second approach is called *graceful quality degradation* or *media scaling*. For example, in the situation of buffer space shortage where data has to be discarded in an MPEG-coded video stream, data is discarded in the following order: B-picture data, P-picture data, and I-picture data. If an audio packet is delayed, it may be better to discard it to minimize the effect on the audio play quality.

Some researchers propose a scheme in which a client retrieves and stores a complete multimedia file before it displays the file. This scheme has its appeal because it does not impose strict timeliness requirements on the server and the network. It, however, imposes high storage requirements on the client. The system response time may also be very long when the file is large. In addition, the user may find that the retrieved and stored file is not interesting or useful when it is displayed, thus the time and bandwidth used to transmit the file are wasted. Because of these limitations, we do not discuss this type of system further. In this chapter, we are interested in "streaming" systems in which data streams are displayed continuously while they are being received from the server.

The rest of the chapter is organized as follows. Section 10.2 presents a general framework for communication QoS management. In Section 10.3, we discuss the design goals of multimedia systems. Section 10.4 deals with multimedia storage devices and management. Sections 10.5 and 10.6 discuss multimedia computer architectures and operating systems. In Sections 10.7 and 10.8 we discuss multimedia networks and transport protocols. Section 10.9 discusses multimedia synchronization issues.

10.2 QoS MANAGEMENT

10.2.1 Definition

Multimedia communications need end-to-end performance guarantees. The concept of QoS was introduced to provide a uniform framework for different applications to specify required performance guarantees, and for systems to provide the required guarantees [1-

3]. There is no universally accepted definition for QoS at the moment. Intuitively, however, QoS defines characteristics that influence the perceived quality of an application. We use the following definition in this book: QoS is a quantitative and qualitative specification of an application's requirement, which a multimedia system should satisfy in order to achieve desired application quality [7].

Based on this definition, there are two aspects to QoS: applications specify QoS requirements and systems provide QoS guarantees. QoS is normally specified by a set of parameters—notably bit rate, error rate, delay bound, and delay jitter bound. One or more values are associated with each QoS parameter. They specify a desired value or a value range for the parameter. Different QoS parameters are used at the different layers or subsystems of a multimedia system.

10.2.2 General QoS Framework

A simplified QoS operation model of a multimedia communications system is as follows. An application specifies its QoS requirements, which are submitted to the system. The system determines whether it has sufficient resources to meet the requirements. If yes, it accepts the request and allocates the necessary resources to serve the application so that its requirements are satisfied. If it has insufficient resources to meet the application's requirements, it may either reject the application's request or suggest a lower QoS requirement that it can satisfy. In the latter case, if the application accepts the new set of QoS parameters, the it is accepted and executed at the lower QoS. Failing this, the application's request is rejected, and may try later in the hope that some resources have been released by other applications. Based on this operating model, the following elements are needed to provide QoS guarantees:

- A QoS specification mechanism for applications to specify their requirements;
- Admission control to determine whether the new application should be admitted without affecting the QoS of other ongoing applications;
- A QoS negotiation process so that as many applications as possible can be served;
- Resource allocation and scheduling to meet the QoS requirement of accepted applications;
- Traffic policing to make sure that applications generate the correct amount of data within the agreed specification.

In addition to the above basic elements, other elements are needed to meet the diverse requirements of multimedia applications. First, a QoS renegotiation mechanism is required so that applications can request changes in their initial QoS specifications. Second, the actual QoS provided to the ongoing sessions should be monitored so that appropriate action can be taken in case of any problem in meeting the specified QoS guarantees. Third, media scalability and graceful quality degradation techniques should be used together with the above mechanisms to provide satisfactory services to multimedia applications.

All subsystems must provide the above mechanisms and cooperate to provide end-to-end QoS guarantees. In the following we describe important elements and issues of QoS management.

10.2.3 QoS Specification

To provide QoS specification and guarantees, a connection-oriented session should be used. Before the session is established, QoS parameters are specified and negotiated among all subsystems concerned. Since in most cases the end receivers of multimedia information are human users, the result of QoS is the quality perceived by the user. The end user is also normally the initiator of QoS. At the user level, the quality is normally measured qualitatively, such as excellent, good, acceptable, unacceptable, or very poor. This quality perception also depends on how much the user is paying for the service and his or her expectations. For example, for a user expecting a color presentation, to receive a high-quality black-and-white presentation is not acceptable. Ideally, the system should guarantee the quality presented to the user at least at an acceptable level. To achieve this, the user must tell applications and the system what is acceptable; that is, the user must specify QoS requirements.

Different system layers (*levels*) handle different *data objects*. For example, at the video application layer, the logical data object is a picture or a frame. At the network layer, the data object is a packet, and at the physical layer, the data object is a bit. Consequently, different QoS parameters are used at different system levels. Higher layer requirements are mapped onto lower layer requirements.

10.2.4 Admission Control, QoS Negotiation, and Renegotiation

When a connection with specified QoS is established, QoS parameters are translated and negotiated among all relevant subsystems. Only when all subsystems agree with and guarantee the specified QoS parameters can the end-to-end QoS requirements be met. During the QoS negotiation process, a number of steps take place. First, QoS parameters are mapped or translated from one layer (or one subsystem) to another. Second, each layer or subsystem must determine whether it can support the required service; if so, certain resources are reserved for this session. Only when all subsystems accept the QoS parameters is the session established. Otherwise, the session is rejected. A sophisticated system may indicate to the user what level of QoS it can support. If the user is happy with the suggested quality level, the session is established. To cope with the complexity of QoS specifications and negotiations, a technique called a *QoS broker* has been proposed by Nahrstedt and Smith [4].

Multimedia communications are normally not static. During an active communication session, changes in QoS may be necessary for various reasons. Therefore, it is necessary to provide QoS renegotiation mechanisms to meet the changing requirements of multimedia communications. It is sometimes not possible to meet the requirement to increase the QoS because the required resources may not be available.

10.2.5 Different Levels of Guarantee

In the above discussion, we generally stated that QoS should be *guaranteed*. In practice, the user can specify the degree (or level) of guarantee. In general, there are three levels of guarantees:

1. *Hard* or *deterministic guarantee*: the user-specified QoS should be 100% met. This guarantee is most expensive in terms of system resources. Resources are normally reserved for the application on a worst-case basis. Even when some reserved resources are not being used, they are not allowed to be used by other applications, resulting in low resource utilization. For example, a variable bit-rate-encoded video has an output bit rate ranging from 200 kbits/s to 4 Mbits/s. To satisfy the videostream to 100%, resources should be reserved based on 4 Mbits/s. When the videostream is not at the peak rate, some reserved but unused resources are wasted. It is easy to achieve hard guarantees when resources are reserved statically, but the resource utilization is very low. More recently, Knightly and Zhang [5, 6] proposed a traffic model called D-BIND, which allows hard guarantees without reserving resources on a worst-case basis. Lu and Kang proposed to use the average bit rate instead of the peak bit rate to reserve resources for hard performance guarantees by studying the stream characteristics in advance [7].

2. *Soft* or *statistical guarantee*: the user-specified QoS should be met to a certain specified percentage. This is the most appropriate type of guarantee for continuous media, because continuous media normally do not need 100% accuracy in playback. In addition, this type of guarantee uses system resources more efficiently. Resource usage is based on statistical multiplexing: resources unused by one application can be used by other applications. This is the desired mode of operation for multimedia communication, but it is difficult to implement because of the dynamic nature of traffic and resource usage.

3. *Best effort*: no guarantee is provided and the application is executed with whatever resources are available. The traditional computer system operates in this mode.

Note that the above three different types of guarantees may all be required in a multimedia communication session. Different levels of guarantee are used for different types of traffic. It is up to the user to determine which type of guarantee to use. Again, the charging policy is related to the level of guarantee. The hard guarantee is the most expensive and the best effort is the cheapest. In some cases, one connection may use different levels of guarantee for different QoS parameters. For example, the user may request that the specified bit-error rate should be 100% met (hard guarantee) but the specified delay jitter value should be 90% met (soft guarantee).

10.2.6 Providing QoS Guarantees

QoS is guaranteed only when sufficient resources are available and proper scheduling of processes is implemented. Preventing overload requires admission control, and preventing applications using more resources than has been allocated requires policing mechanisms. Since end-to-end QoS is required, each subsystem of a multimedia communications system plays an important role. The entire communications system, from source to sink, is like a pipeline. When one segment of the pipe is blocked, the required QoS is not achieved. Therefore, each subsystem should have QoS management functions including the five elements listed above: QoS specification, admission control, negotiation and renegotiation, resource allocation, and traffic policing. The five important subsystems of a DMDBMS are multimedia storage, computer architectures, operating systems, networks, and transport protocols. We discuss these five subsystems in Sections 10.4 to 10.8. Synchronization is related to overall perceptual quality and requires coordination among all processes and streams. We briefly discuss synchronization in Section 10.9.

10.2.7 An Example of QoS Handling

The following example illustrates how the QoS concepts are used in a practical system. Suppose a client wants to retrieve and play back an audio piece of telephone quality from a remote server. The following steps establish the session for the user:

1. The user selects the audio file name and telephone audio quality (possibly after a search process) by way of the user interface.
2. The retrieval application translates the user requirement into the following parameters: sample rate = 8 kHz (i.e., one sample must be played every 125 µs), bits per sample = 8.
3. The application passes the request to the client operating system, which determines whether it can process one byte every 125 µs with the current load on the client. If not, the session request is rejected.
4. The operating system passes the request to the transport system, including transport protocol and all lower layers, and the transport system determines whether it can support a bit rate of about 64 kbits/s. If not, the session request is rejected.
5. The transport system passes the request to the server operating system, which determines whether it can process one byte every 125 µs. If not, the session request is rejected.
6. The server passes the request to the disk controller to determine whether it can support a transfer rate of 64 kbits/s without affecting the QoS of existing sessions. If not, the session request is rejected.
7. The session is successfully established and the user hears the requested audio piece.

The above example shows the basic conceptual steps. Details, such as delay and delay jitter parameters, how admission tests are done, and what scheduling and queuing algorithms are used, are not discussed.

10.3 DESIGN GOALS OF MULTIMEDIA SYSTEMS

Each subsystem of a DMDBMS must meet certain requirements. To meet these requirements, the implementation details of different subsystems may differ, but they share some common design goals. The important common goals are:

1. The system should have sufficient resources to support multimedia applications;
2. The system should be able to use available resources efficiently;
3. The system should be able to provide QoS guarantees;
4. The systems should be scalable.

Each subsystem should have sufficient types and amounts of resources to support multiple applications simultaneously. An end system should be able to process multiple applications. Networks, servers, and storage devices should be able to support a number of sessions or streams simultaneously. This number must be high enough to make the operation of the system economical. It does not make sense if only one user can access the video server of a video-on-demand service at a time.

Because the resources of a multimedia system are shared among many applications, they must be shared in an efficient way so that the maximum number of applications can be supported, given a certain amount of resources. This is achieved by exploiting the fact that multimedia information needs only a statistical or soft guarantee and compressed multimedia data are bursty. So we use statistical multiplexing to make efficient use of network bandwidth, and use different traffic priorities to achieve the best presentation quality by transmitting the minimum amount of data.

It is undesirable if the available resources are shared by many applications, but no application gets the required service quality. So the important challenge is to use resources efficiently and at the same time to guarantee QoS for each application.

Finally, a multimedia system should be scalable and extensible to meet growth in user requirements and demands. Scalability refers to the system ability to adapt to changes in the number of users to be supported, the amount of information to be stored and processed, and the geographical area of to be covered by the network.

In the following sections, we discuss issues and techniques to satisfy the above requirements by different subsystems. Note that some discussions on different subsystems are similar in terms of general principles. Multimedia storage devices, end systems, networking, and OS are different levels or subsystems of a multimedia communications system. Their common goal is to provide QoS guarantees while using system resources efficiently. The only difference is that at different levels or subsystems, QoS requirements and resource types are different, leading to different handling techniques. In general, the easier the QoS specification, the easier the QoS guarantees can be provided.

10.4 MULTIMEDIA DATA STORAGE DEVICES AND MANAGEMENT

Data storage devices and their management systems are very critical components of a DMDBMS, as they have to efficiently store large amounts of data and serve many requests at the same time. For brevity, we use the term storage server to refer to storage devices and the management in the following discussion. Note that this section only deals with functions and issues related to storage. We deal with computer architectures and operating systems in Sections 10.5 and 10.6. Our focus is on handling continuous media (audio and video) data, as it is the most demanding in terms of amount of data and timely delivery. The organization and efficient search of indexing data (feature vectors) was discussed in the previous chapter.

This section is organized as follows. Section 10.4.1 discusses the requirements imposed on the storage server to provide end-to-end performance guarantees to the retrieval applications. Section 10.4.2 describes various types of storage devices and their roles in a multimedia server. An important type of magnetic disk array known as a redundant array of inexpensive disks (RAID) is discussed in detail. The way data is placed on storage devices determines effectiveness of resource (storage and throughput) use and types of user interactions supported by the server. We discuss data placement in Section 10.4.3. Section 10.4.4 deals with disk scheduling and admission control required to support QoS guarantees to multimedia streams. Section 10.4.5 describes how user interactions such as pause and fast forward are supported by a multimedia server. Section 10.4.6 discusses interconnection among storage devices and between the server and the network. The interconnection should not become a bandwidth bottleneck to the entire distributed multimedia system and should be scalable. Finally, Section 10.4.7 summarizes the section.

10.4.1 Multimedia Storage Server Requirements

The characteristics of multimedia data—being data intensive and time critical—impose a number of requirements on multimedia storage servers. First, the storage capacity and data transfer rate should be high enough to support many clients simultaneously to make the system economical. Digital audio and video data are normally compressed to reduce the data storage requirements and transfer bandwidth. But even after compression, digital audio and video still require large amounts of data to represent them, as discussed in Chapter 2.

Second, a multimedia server should provide QoS guarantees to streams requested by clients. To accomplish this, the server should implement admission control and real-time scheduling. For constant-bit-rate-coded streams, QoS requirements are relatively easy to specify, and thus admission control and scheduling can be implemented relatively easily to meet the requirements. When streams are variable-bit-rate coded, the peak bit rate can be used to reserve server resources to achieve hard guarantees. This leads to low server resource use, however. With proper characterization of VBR streams, hard guarantees can be achieved without reserving storage resources based on the peak bit rates. To further improve resource use, soft guarantees should be used and clients should permit graceful quality degradation. The problem with soft guarantees by graceful quality degradation is that QoS specification, resource management, and application design become complicated.

Third, the architecture and techniques used in the server should be scalable and able to potentially support a large user population.

Fourth, many multimedia applications require user interaction, so the server should be able to support various user interactions such as pause, fast forward, and rewind.

Figure 10.2 illustrates a model of storage servers. The main components are storage devices, a scheduler, and smoothing buffers. The scheduler determines which stream is serviced next. As data reading is bursty for individual streams, smoothing buffers are used to deliver continuous media streams to applications or to a transport system. The aim of the server is to simultaneously serve as many streams as possible while meeting the continuity requirements of streams and keeping the buffer requirements to a minimum. To achieve this, appropriate storage devices, data placement on these devices, and scheduling techniques must be used.

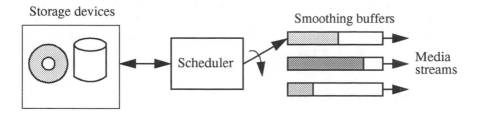

Figure 10.2 A multimedia server model.

10.4.2 Storage Devices

In this subsection, we first describe storage capacity and transfer bandwidth requirements for a general-purpose multimedia server. We then briefly compare various types of storage devices in terms of their strengths and weaknesses. We finally look at techniques to improve storage capacity and transfer bandwidth by using multiple disks and forming a storage hierarchy using different types of storage devices.

10.4.2.1 Storage Capacity and Transfer Bandwidth Requirements

Assume that the server stores 2,000 movies of 100 minutes each. These movies are MPEG-2-compressed at 8 Mbps with digital television quality, and the server serves 1,000 clients simultaneously. Then the required storage capacity is 12 TB and transfer bandwidth is 8 Gbps. These numbers roughly indicate what a storage device or a combination of storage devices of a typical server should provide for storage capacity and data transfer bandwidth. Note that the transfer bandwidth is the perceived bandwidth by the users and not the peak bandwidth of the storage devices. The actual bandwidth can approach the peak bandwidth only when the seek time is minimized. Minimizing seek time is achieved by appropriate data placement and disk scheduling, as discussed later.

10.4.2.2 Comparison of Different Types of Storage Devices

Common storage devices are magnetic disks, optical disks, and tapes. Magnetic disks have desirable features to support multimedia applications: they allow fast random access and have high data-transfer rates. However, they are relatively expensive compared to other types of storage devices. Optical disks have relatively high capacity and allow random access, but the access time is long and the transfer rate is low. Tapes have the highest storage capacity and are cheapest per gigabyte. However, they cannot be accessed randomly and the transfer rate is low. Therefore, it is not possible for a single device to economically meet the storage capacity and transfer bandwidth requirements described in Section 10.4.2.1. The solution is to use multiple storage devices in a server or across multiple servers over the network. We describe two approaches in the following. The first uses multiple disks to form disk arrays to improve storage capacity and transfer bandwidth. The second takes advantage of the strengths of various storage devices to form a cost-effective storage hierarchy for a large multimedia server. Note that in this book the term *disk* refers to magnetic disk when it is used alone.

10.4.2.3 Disk Arrays and RAID

Magnetic disks are the most suitable storage devices for multimedia applications because of their short access time, high transfer rate, and random access capability. But a single disk is not able to store many multimedia files and support many users simultaneously. A natural solution is to use multiple disks to form an *array*. Forming disk arrays improves both storage capacity and transfer rate.

Arrays of inexpensive disks (AID) were developed to improve data transfer throughput. AIDs can be interleaved for large transfers or be independent for many small transfers. But these inexpensive disks are not reliable. To overcome the reliability problem, extra disks are used to contain redundant information to recover the original information when a disk fails. The AID with redundancy is called a redundant array of inexpensive disks or RAID. Because RAIDs provide improvement of an order of magnitude compared with single, large expensive disks in performance, reliability, power consumption, and scalability, they are used in many computer systems and as multimedia data storage. In the following, we briefly describe five different organizations (levels) of RAID [8]. A basic understanding of these levels is needed to determine a suitable level of RAID for a particular application.

First-Level RAID: Mirrored Disks

In the first-level RAID, each data disk has a mirror disk called a *check disk*. Every write to a data disk is also a write to a check disk. During data reading, data in both the data disks and check disks is read, and errors are detected when data in these two types of disks is different. In this organization, data disks are read or written either individually or as a group.

However, duplicating all disks means doubling the cost of the storage or using only 50% of the disk storage capacity. To overcome this limitation, other levels of RAID have been designed.

Second-Level RAID: Hamming Code for Error Correction

In the second-level RAID, a number of disks or all disks of a RAID form a group for error-correction purposes. Data is bit-interleaved across the disks in a group and then enough disks are added to detect and correct a single bit error. Error detection and correction are achieved by using Hamming code: in a codeword (data bits plus check bits), bits are numbered consecutively, starting from bit 1 at the left end. A single bit error can be corrected if the bits that are powers of 2 (1, 2, 4, 8, 16, etc.) are check bits, and the remaining bits (3, 5, 6, 7, 9, etc.) are filled with data bits. Therefore, for example, if the number of data disks in a group is 10, 4 check disks are required. If the number of data disks in a group is 25, 5 check disks are required.

This arrangement is good for group reads or writes. However, reads of less than the group size require reading the whole group to be sure the information is correct, and writes to a portion of the group need three steps:

1. A read step to obtain the rest of the data;
2. A modify step to merge the new and old data;
3. A write step to write the full group, including check information.

Therefore, a level 2 RAID is suitable for large reads or writes but inappropriate for small, individual reads and writes.

Third-Level RAID: Single Check Disk Per Group

In level 2 RAID, most check disks are used to determine which disk failed. For error detection only one redundant parity disk is needed. The extra disks for locating a failed disk are not necessary in practice since most disk controllers can already detect if a disk has failed, either through special signals provided in the disk interface, or via the extra checking information at the end of a sector used to detect and correct soft errors. Therefore, it is important to reconstruct the information on the failed disk. This is achieved by calculating the parity of the remaining good disks, and then comparing it with the original parity of the full group stored on the parity disk. If these two parities are the same, the data on the failed disk was 0, otherwise it was 1. If the parity disk fails, just read all the data disks and replace the parity disk. Note that the chance that two disks fail at the same time is very low.

Level 3 RAID uses the above principle. The read and write performance of level 3 RAID is the same as level 2 RAID, but the storage overhead is reduced by using only one parity disk. Actually the overhead of RAID 3 is at the lowest: only one bit for one group read or write. The next two levels improve the performance of small individual accesses without changing storage overhead or reliability.

Fourth-Level RAID: Independent Reads

The fourth-level RAID improves the performance of small transfers through parallelism—the ability to do more than one I/O per group at a time. The individual transfer information is no longer spread across several disks but kept in a single disk, that is, the primary difference between a level 4 RAID and level 3 RAID is that data are interleaved between disks at the sector level rather than at the bit level. By storing a whole transfer unit in a sector, reads can be independent and operate at the maximum rate of a disk, and error detection relies on the disk controller. The parity disk and other disks are only involved when an error is detected. Parities are still calculated across all disks of the group to facilitate group access.

Therefore, level 4 RAID improves small read performance. Writes are still limited to one per group, since every write must read and write the check disk.

Fifth-Level RAID: No Dedicated Check Disk

Fifth-level RAID improves the performance of small writes over the level 4 RAID. In level 5 RAID, no single disk is dedicated to storing parity information. Data and parity information are distributed across all disks (there is no dedicated check disk). In this organization, the parity information for different sectors is stored on different disks. Hence it is possible, for example, to write to sector 1 of disk 1 with parity in sector 1 of disk 5, and to sector 2 of disk 3 with parity in sector 2 of disk 4 at the same time as these two writes use different disks.

Therefore, a level 5 RAID is nearly the best of both worlds: small read-modify-writes perform close to the speed per disk of a level 1 RAID, while keeping the large transfer performance and useful storage capacity percentage of levels 3 and 5 RAIDs. Level 5 RAID is attractive for applications requiring both small and large transfers. The only disadvantage is that it is the most complicated in data organization.

10.4.2.4 Storage Hierarchies

Magnetic disks are most suitable as multimedia storage but they are relatively expensive. To use the high capacity of optical disks and tapes, a storage hierarchy comprising various types of storage devices is used to develop cost-effective, large-scale servers [9-11].

There are several approaches to building such a storage hierarchy. One approach is to use tapes and optical storage as archival storage, and use magnetic disks only as storage for the beginning segments of the multimedia files. These segments can reduce the start-up latency and ensure smooth transitions in the playback. However, this approach cannot support many streams at the same time due to the relatively low transfer rates of optical disks and tapes. When tapes are used, random access is not possible.

In the second approach, an entire file is moved from tapes to disks when requested. The drawback of this approach is that the startup delays associated with loading the entire file are very high for large files such as a movie. In most multimedia applications, this problem is solved by exploiting the following two factors. First, there are not many different files or movies popular at the same time, so we load the most popular files onto the disks before they are requested or when they are first requested. The disks are used as a cache for the most popular files. Second, user patterns are predictable in many applications. For example, a user who retrieves episode one of a series is likely to retrieve episode two when he finishes episode one. Thus we can load the predicted files onto the disks before they are requested.

In many applications, the information previously retrieved from a remote server will be required again by the same user and/or different users closely located. To save network bandwidth and transmission time, the information is cached in local main memory or disks for future use. Information caching has been used extensively in information retrieval on the WWW [12, 13].

Since tapes and optical disks are used as archival storage in most large-scale servers, in most cases users retrieve data directly from magnetic disks. So in the following discussion we focus on management (data placement and scheduling) of magnetic disks.

10.4.3 Data Placement on Disks

The aim of multimedia servers is to meet the time constraints of multimedia streams and to simultaneously serve as many streams as possible. To achieve this aim, appropriate data placement on disks, disk scheduling, and admission control are essential. This section discusses the data placement issue. The other two issues are discussed in the next section. In most cases, these three issues are directly related and dependent on each other: a certain disk scheduling discipline requires a particular type of data placement and relies on a particular admission control algorithm.

A file is normally broken into a number of storage blocks for reading and writing. There are two general methods to place these blocks: they are either placed contiguously on a disk or scattered around a disk. To improve performance, variations on these two methods have been proposed. When disk arrays are used, there are different ways to place blocks of a file onto these disks. In the following, we discuss these data placement methods.

10.4.3.1 Contiguous Data Placement

In contiguous placement, data blocks of a file are stored on a disk contiguously. There is no gap within a file. Contiguous files are simple to implement. When reading from a contiguous file, only one seek is required to position the disk head at the start of the file if a disk head is dedicated to reading one file. But contiguous placement has two limitations for data editing. First, large data copying overheads during insertions and deletions are required to maintain contiguity: when a block of data needs to be inserted at a point in the file, all data blocks behind this point must be moved backward for one block of space. When a block is deleted, all blocks of this file behind this block must be moved one block forward to remove the gap. Second, contiguous placement may cause disk fragmentation. When a file is deleted, the place left can only be used to store another file with the same or smaller size. The chance of finding a file of the same size is low, so frequently a smaller file takes the place and a gap is left behind it, wasting disk space.

Therefore, contiguous files are only appropriate for applications where data is written once and read many times. Information retrieval belongs to this type of application.

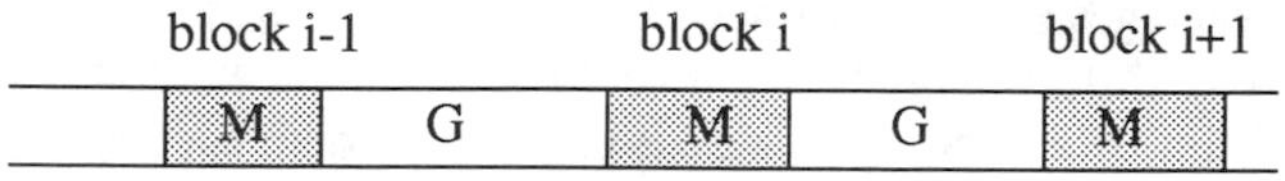

Figure 10.3 Constrained data placement.

A variation on contiguous data placement is called constrained placement, in which a constrained gap is placed between consecutive blocks, as shown in Figure 10.3 [14, 15]. This placement uses the fact that the reading rate by a disk head is higher than the playout rate of one stream. Assume that M is the amount of data within each block and the gap corresponds to G amount of data. The transfer rate for each disk head is r and it takes T seconds to play out M bytes of data. Then, the file can be played out continuously if the following condition is met:

$$T \geq (M + G)/r$$

Blocks of other files can be placed in the gaps and the continuity of these files can also be met by adjusting the block sizes. The above condition is actually the admission condition when a round-robin-service discipline is used (see Section 10.4.4).

10.4.3.2 Scattered Data Placement

Scattered placement scatters the data blocks of a file around the disks and does not have the limitations of the contiguous placement. It does have its own limitations, however. First, some mechanisms are needed to track the blocks of a file. Second, when reading several blocks in a scattered file, a seek could be incurred for each block read. Even when reading a small amount of data, it is possible that half of the data might be stored in one block and the other half in the next block, thereby incurring intrafile seeks.

To implement a file system with scattered placement, we have to keep a map of how to travel from one block to the next in a file. There are several ways to achieve this file mapping, each with its own merits and limitations. A simple method for tracking blocks is a linked list, where each block contains a pointer to the next block in the file. The file descriptor only needs to contain a pointer to the first block of the file. A serious limitation of this approach is that random access is very inefficient, as accessing a random block requires accessing all previous blocks to find the location of the required block.

The second approach to mapping blocks is to use a *file allocation table* (*FAT*) as used in some conventional file systems such as DOS. In a FAT, there is a table entry containing a pointer to the location for each block on the disk. If the FAT is kept in main memory, random access is very fast. However, in large multimedia servers, it may not be possible to keep the entire FAT in the main memory.

The third approach is to use an index for each file. This is used in UNIX, where the index is called an *I-node*. In this approach, the index contains pointers to each block of the file. This creates a similar problem to that of the FAT when many large files are opened: these indexes may be too large to be stored in the main memory.

To use the advantages of both the linked list and index approaches, a hybrid solution has been proposed. In this solution, both a linked list and an index are stored. The linked list is used for real-time playback. The index is used for random access. The drawback of this solution is that extra storage is required to store both the linked lists and indices.

A simple solution for avoiding intrafile seeks in scattered files is to keep the amount of data for each read corresponding to a block, so there is no seek within each read. This is easy to achieve for constant-bit-rate-coded streams, but difficult for variable-bit-rate-coded streams.

10.4.3.3 Data Placement in Disk Arrays

When disk arrays are used, there are several options for storing a file. A simple method is to store an entire multimedia file on one disk. However, the number of concurrent accesses to that file is limited by the throughput of the single disk. For example, if the disk throughput is 4 Mbps and playout rate of a stream is 1 Mbps, then the maximum number of concurrent accesses is 4. This is not high enough for popular files. To overcome this limitation, the popular files are copied to multiple disks, but this requires additional disk space. A more cost-effective method is to scatter the blocks of a file across multiple disks. In this way more users can access the file simultaneously without requiring multiple copies of each file.

There are two techniques for scattering blocks across multiple disks. The first technique is called *data striping* in which blocks are organized for group access; that is, all disks are spindle synchronized and the same sectors on all disks are accessed at the same time. The second technique is called *data interleaving*, in which disks are not spindle synchronized and blocks on different disks are accessed independently. To facilitate disk scheduling, data blocks are placed on disks in a cyclic pattern. Buddhikot and Parulkar presented a distributed cyclic layout (DCL) scheme in which file blocks are placed on disks sequentially to form a logical ring [16].

It is preferable that a storage block corresponds to a logical media unit. For video, a block can correspond to a frame or a group of pictures when MPEG compression is used. For audio, the logical data unit is a sample or group of samples. It is commonly required to synchronize audio with video, so it is convenient to make the audio block size correspond to the number of samples in an interval of a videoframe. Note that in some designs, all disks of a RAID are treated as a single storage device.

So far in our discussion we have assumed that the streams are constant-bit-rate coded. When they are variable-bit-rate coded, data placement, scheduling, and admission control becomes more complicated if we want to make efficient use of resources.

10.4.4 Disk Scheduling and Admission Control

Storage devices must deliver data to the network at the same rate as the playout rate at the client. Since disk operation is nondeterministic due to random access time and sharing with other applications, some special disk scheduling disciplines are needed to maintain the continuity of continuous media. Performance guarantees can only be achieved when the system is not overloaded. Thus admission control is required to prevent system overload.

To prevent data starvation, data retrieval from disks should get ahead of data transmission at the server (assuming that the transmission rate is the same as the playout rate at the receiver). The data ahead of the transmission are buffered. However, this buffer should not be too big, because a large buffer means that the system is expensive and data will suffer long delays. Therefore, the server's task is to prevent data starvation while minimizing the buffer requirement and delay. As throughput of a disk head is higher than the playout rate of most of individual streams, to efficiently use resources a disk head should serve as many streams as possible. This is achieved by special disk scheduling and admission control techniques. We discuss a number of common disk scheduling disciplines in this section. Admission control techniques are normally associated with disk scheduling disciplines. Admission control at the storage server is based on the following criterion:

The total bandwidths (TB) of all requested streams should be lower than the transfer rate (R) of the disk.

In practice, *TB* should be much lower than *R* because there is nonzero seek time when the disk head finishes serving one request and moves to another place to serve the next request. For scheduling disciplines with distinctive service round, the sum of service time to all streams plus seek time in a round should not be larger than the round time.

10.4.4.1 Traditional Disk-Scheduling Algorithms

Even in traditional file systems, disk-scheduling algorithms are used, but their purpose is to reduce seek time and rotational latency, achieve high throughput, or provide fair access to each application. The common traditional disk-scheduling algorithms are first-come-first-served (FCFS), shortest seek time first (SSTF), and scan. We briefly describe these algorithms.

In FCFS, requests are served according to their incoming order. Disk head location and movement are ignored, so average seek time is high.

SSTF tries to minimize seek time by serving the request whose data is closest to the current disk head location. SSTF favors the requests in the middle of a disk. When the server is heavily loaded, data transfer requests from the innermost and outermost tracks may not get served at all.

Scan also tries to minimize seek time by serving requests in the order of disk head movement. It first serves all requests in one direction until all requests are served in this direction. The head movement is then reversed and requests are served once in that direction. Scan minimizes seek time and serves all requests in a single trip of the head movement.

These disk-scheduling algorithms do not take into account the timeliness of each stream. Therefore, they cannot be directly used for multimedia server scheduling. However, if we limit the number of simultaneous requests and service time for each request, the scan algorithm provides service guarantees to each request.

10.4.4.2 Earliest Deadline First

The earliest deadline first (EDF) is the most common algorithm for real-time scheduling of tasks with deadlines. EDF schedules the media block with the earliest deadline for retrieval. The limitation of EDF applied to disk scheduling is that it ignores the disk head position, leading to long seek times and rotational latency. Since a lot of time is wasted in moving the disk head around the disk without actually reading useful data, the disk throughput is not fully used.

Suppose that the server is serving n-1 requests with hard performance guarantees. The sufficient condition for accepting a new request n for hard performance guarantees is

$$(b_1 + b_2 + \ldots + b_i + \ldots + b_n) + (n-1) \times S \times r \leq r$$

where b_i is the maximum data rate of stream i, S is the maximum seek time of the disk, and r is the throughput of the disk.

Because EDF does not impose any specific data placement, and seek time can vary from 0 to the maximum seek time between serving two requests, it is difficult to develop an admission-control algorithm that uses resources efficiently while meeting all streams' continuity requirements.

10.4.4.3 Scan-Earliest Deadline First

Scan-earliest deadline first (scan-EDF) combines scan with EDF to reduce the average seek time of EDF [17]. Scan-EDF serves the request with earliest deadline first, just like EDF. But when several requests have the same deadline, their respective blocks are accessed with the scan algorithm. Clearly, the more the requests with the same deadline, the more effective is the scan-EDF. When all requests have the same deadline, scan-EDF is reduced to Scan only. On the other hand, if all requests have a different deadline, scan-EDF is reduced to EDF only. To improve the effectiveness of scan-EDF, techniques have been proposed to increase the number of requests with the same deadline. For example, one can enforce that all requests have deadlines that are multiples of a period of p. In this case, deadlines are batched.

The admission control of scan-EDF is similar to that of EDF. But instead of using the maximum seek time for each service switching, the maximum seek time is used only when switching from a request with one deadline to another request with different deadline. Thus the scan-EDF simultaneously serves more requests than (or at least the same number of requests as) EDF.

10.4.4.4 Round-Robin

In scan, requests are served in rounds. But requests are served in a different order in different rounds depending on the data placement. The maximum time interval between two successive services for a stream is equal to the time of two rounds, as a stream can be served first in one round (one disk head movement direction) and last in the next round (another disk head movement direction). In EDF, there is no distinct round. Streams with frequent requests may be served several times while others are just served once.

In a round-robin scheduling scheme, streams are served in distinct rounds and service order for each stream is fixed in all rounds. Thus the time interval between two successive services for a stream is bounded by the round duration. If the round duration is constant, then the interval is also constant. Since service order for streams is fixed, data placement is important in determining the seek time.

When round-robin is used with constrained data placement, the seek time is minimized and the continuity of each stream is maintained [14, 15]. For example, in Figure 10.4, three streams are retrieved continuously.

Figure 10.4 Round-robin scheduling with constrained placement.

To meet the continuity requirement of streams, data placement must meet inequity (1) for each stream. Comparing Figures 10.3 and 10.4, the gap G for stream 1 is ($M2+M3$). During implementation, M and G are adjusted to meet the continuity requirement. For example, if an HDTV-quality videostream is compressed at 0.5 Mbits/frame and recorded at 60 frames/s on a disk with data transfer rate of 25,600 sectors/s (each sector equals 512 bytes, yielding a transfer rate of 100 Mbps), then choosing each stream block to contain one videoframe yields a storage pattern (M, G) to be (128, 298) sectors. So a block of 128 sectors of data is separated by a 298 sector gap (or data of other streams).

The time interval between successive retrievals of a stream of data has several implications for playback startup delay and buffer requirements. For round-robin, playback of a stream is started after the first block of the stream has been retrieved (assuming playback is at the same machine as the server). With Scan, however, playback must wait until the end of the first round. To prevent output device starvation, round-robin needs enough buffer space to satisfy data consumption for one round, while scan needs enough to satisfy consumption for nearly two rounds. But generally speaking, the round length for scan is shorter than that of round-robin as the seek time is normally shorter for scan (except in the case of constrained placement). The buffer requirement is equal to the maximum interval times the data rate of the stream.

10.4.4.5 Group Sweeping Scheduling

In group sweeping scheduling (GSS), each round is partitioned into groups. Each stream is assigned to a group, and the groups are serviced in a fixed order in each round, as in round-robin. Within each group, scan is used to serve streams of the group. Scan reduces the round length and round-robin reduces the interval between successive services. Thus GSS is a tradeoff between the round length and the successive service interval. Figure 10.5 compares the round lengths and the maximum successive service intervals for scan, round-robin, and GSS. Round length is shortest for scan but the maximum service interval is almost double the round length. The round length of round-robin is longest but the maximum service interval is equal to the round length. The round length of GSS is between the round lengths of scan and round-robin. Its maximum service interval is slightly larger than its round length. So in most cases, the service interval of GSS is shortest.

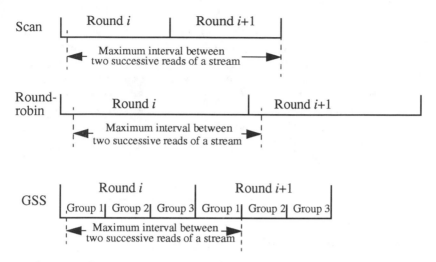

Figure 10.5 Comparison of round lengths and the maximum intervals between two successive reads of a stream for scan, round-robin, and GSS.

10.4.5 Provision of User Interaction

A multimedia information retrieval system should support user interactions such as pause, resume, and fast forward.

A server can provide two types of file access interface to the client: file-system-oriented or stream-oriented. In a file-system-oriented interface, multimedia documents are treated as normal files. The client uses typical file operations such as open, close, and read to access multimedia documents. The server uses the open operation to enforce admission control. Certain amounts of data are read for each read operation. Prefetch can also be implemented to minimize delay. Using this interface, the client can easily implement the pause and resume operations by simply ceasing to issue read commands and the resume operation by continuing to issue read commands. But it is difficult to implement fast forward and fast backward. Further, it may be difficult to maintain stream continuity using this type of interface because the read command may be randomly delayed by the network.

In a stream-oriented file interface, the client issues a start command and the server periodically sends data to the user at the predefined rate without further read requests from the client. This is the preferred operating mode as it is easy to maintain stream continuity. In the following we describe how to implement VCR-like operations—pause, resume, fast forward, and fast backward.

10.4.5.1 Pause and Resume

If a user is accessing a stream independently from other viewers (users), it is relatively easy to implement pause and resume operations by simply sending the respective commands to the server, as his or her action does not affect other viewers. However, even in this simple case, care must be taken to deal with the extra data sent to the client after issuing the pause command. This is because the pause command takes some time to arrive at the server, and during this time the server may have sent a few Mbytes data to the client. As shown in Figure 10.6 , the user issues pause command at point P, but before the server receives the command it has sent data up to the point Q of the stream. So what should we do with the data between points P and Q?

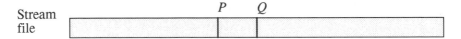

Stream
file

Figure 10.6 The pause command is issued at point P but the server
stops sending data at point Q.

There are three options for dealing with this "extra" data:

- In the first option, the client does not stop playing back the stream immediately after the user issues the pause command. Instead, it continues to play back until point Q, and stops when it receives a pause confirmation from the server. When the user issues a resume command, the stream resumes at point Q.
- In the second option, the client stops playing back immediately at the point P and buffers the data between points P and Q. When the user issues the resume command, the playback starts from point P using the buffered data and the server sends data from point Q.
- In the third option, the client stops playing back at point P and data between points P and Q is discarded. When the user issues the resume command, the client requests the server to retrieve and transmit data starting from point P. After some initial delay, the client starts playing at point P.

It seems that options 1 and 2 are more efficient as they use the data between points P and Q without the server sending them twice. However, it is difficult to achieve intermedia and intramedia synchronization using the first two options. This is because the time intervals between P and Q are different for different streams, due to different network delays experienced by the pause command transmission from the client to different servers. In addition, it is difficult in the second option to make sure the display is smooth at point Q due to variation of network delays. Therefore, the third option is preferred after the overall considerations.

When viewers are batched and the server reads data once and then broadcasts this data to several viewers at the same time, implementation of the pause and resume operations is complicated because many viewers are sharing a stream, and it is necessary that one user's interaction should not interfere with the viewing of others [18, 19]. There are two solutions to this problem. In the first solution, the system imposes that the user can only pause for certain intervals. For example, if the server is broadcasting a movie with a phase difference of 5 min (i.e., the second batch of viewers will start 5 min after the first batch has started, the third batch starts 5 min after the second batch, and so on), then the viewer can only pause for an interval that is a multiple of 5 min. In the second solution, a large buffer and complicated buffer management are required to provide independent interaction to individual viewers [19].

10.4.5.2 Fast Forward and Backward

There are two ways to implement fast forward. The first is to play back media at a higher rate than the original normal rate. The second is to play at the normal rate while skipping some frames. For example, if alternative frames are skipped, the video advances at double speed. The first option seems easy to implement, but it requires higher bandwidth and processing power. The network and the client may not be able to cope with the bandwidth and computational requirements. The requirements can be reduced by using scalable video-coding techniques. When the video is compressed with subband (scalable) techniques, only the first band with low-quality video can be transmitted for fast operations.

The fast backward can be implemented in similar ways to those for fast forward, except that data is read backwards. To support backward reading, video-frames or media blocks must be indexed properly. FAT or I-node approaches are most appropriate. A linked-list normally support forward reading, so it cannot be directly used.

The implementation of fast forward and backward is complicated by two compression features: variable bit rate and interframe coding. When video is variable bit rate coded, different frames have different amounts of data. A storage block may contain a different number of frames. Therefore to implement fast forward and backward, each frame should be indexed individually. When video is interframe coded, decoding of some frames depends on the availability of data from other frames. For example, in MPEG-coded video, there are three types of pictures: I-, P-, and B-pictures. Decoding of I-pictures does not depend on any other frames. Decoding of a P-picture depends on an I- or another P-picture. Decoding of a B-picture depends on two reference pictures (I- and/ or P-pictures). So only I-pictures are suitable for fast operations. The first option in this case is to tag frames suitable for fast operations, and during fast forward or backward only these frames are used. The problem with this method is that the data rate for fast operations is significantly higher than the data rate of the normal play, because I-pictures contain much more data than P- and B- pictures. An alternative is to store a highly compressed stream (in addition to the normal compressed stream), which is used for fast forward and backward. In MPEG, there is a type of picture called D-pictures, which are intraframe coded with a very high compression ratio but with low quality. So a stream consisting of D-pictures can be used for video browsing (fast forward and backward operations). There are other proposals to implement fast operations. Most depend on the compression schemes used and rely on specific data-placement methods to achieve fast operations.

10.4.5.3 QoS Issue Related to User Interactions

There is a difficult QoS issue caused by the above interactions. This issue is important but has not attracted much attention so far. The issue is that when the user changes play-back from normal mode to other modes (pause, fast forward, and fast backward), QoS requirements for that session also change.

During a pause, the session is not active for an unspecified duration. If the resources originally reserved for the session are switched to serve other sessions, the user may find that there are insufficient resources when he or she issues a resume command and play-back cannot be resumed. But if the resources are kept for the session during the pause, the user may have to pay for the reserved resources even though he or she is not using them.

QoS requirements are normally increased during fast forward and fast backward as explained above. Therefore, when a user issues a fast-forward or fast -backward command, he or she may find that there are insufficient resources to carry out the operation if a sufficient amount of resources is reserved only for normal operation. This is not desirable. But if each session has to reserve extra resources in case it wants to do fast operations, these resources are wasted most of the time and the user may incur a high charge. This is not desirable either. Overall, the first solution is preferred in the expectation that some extra resources are usually available when fast operations are carried out. But the best solution is to compress the video and place the compressed data in such a way that no extra QoS requirements are needed during fast operation.

10.4.6 Server Configuration and Network Connection

We have so far concentrated on data placement and scheduling for the storage devices. Now we turn to the issue of how to interconnect storage devices in a server, and how to connect a multimedia server to the network so that the server can deliver as many streams as possible to the users at the same time. The issues in building a server are similar to those of building a general end-system discussed in the next section, but multimedia servers should be more powerful as they must support many simultaneous streams.

There are many methods for interconnecting storage devices and connecting these devices to the network. The most common one uses an asynchronous transfer mode (ATM) network to perform the interconnection [20, 21], similar to the desk-area network discussed in the next section. Figure 10.7 shows the common architecture for a multimedia server.

There is a central processor that has access to metadata (feature vectors) of streams stored on other storage devices. Storage devices are grouped into storage nodes. Some nodes contain magnetic disks, others may contain optical disks and tapes. These nodes can be independent or related by using data stripping. Each node is network capable to send data directly to the network. Depending on the need for bandwidth, more than one access link to the network may be needed for a server. The central processor's function is to receive requests from clients, find the relevant items, carry out admission tests, and set up connections for accepted requests on the storage nodes' behalf.

The above server architecture is scalable to some extent. More storage devices can be added when required. But the network interface may become the performance bottleneck. A partial solution is to use multiple network interfaces and network access links.

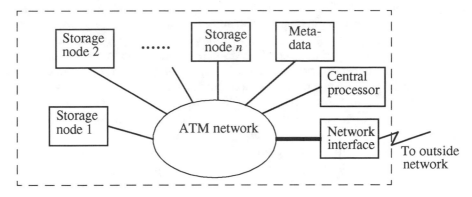

Figure 10.7 Architecture of a multimedia server.

10.4.7 Summary

Multimedia storage servers are very critical components in a distributed multimedia information system. They must store large amounts of multimedia data, simultaneously serve many streams (users), and provide QoS guarantees.

Common storage devices are magnetic disks, optical disks, and magnetic tapes. Magnetic disks are most suitable as multimedia storage devices because they have low random access time and high transfer rate. A single disk will not meet the requirements of a multimedia server, so disk arrays are used. For cost-effective implementation, a storage hierarchy consisting of magnetic disks, optical disks, and/or tapes is used for a large-scale multimedia server.

To use server resources efficiently and provide QoS guarantees, appropriate data placement, disk scheduling, and admission control should be performed.

Provision of user interactions is also an important requirement for a multimedia server. Implementation of user interactions is complicated by shared-viewing of a stream by many viewers, variable-bit-rate coding, and data dependencies.

The architecture of a multimedia server should provide high-access bandwidth to the network and should be scalable. A server based on an ATM network can meet these requirements.

10.5 MULTIMEDIA COMPUTER ARCHITECTURES

We refer to the hosts of clients and servers as end systems. An end system includes two major components; hardware architecture and an operating system. The hardware provides raw resources, such as processing power, memory, and data transfer bandwidth. The operating system manages these resources so that they can be fully used, and the end system as a whole can meet the application's requirements. We describe hardware architectures in this section and operating systems in the next. Note that it is sometimes difficult to separate hardware elements from operating system elements. For example, a data-copying problem is both a hardware issue and operating system issue. Cooperation between hardware architecture and the operating system is necessary to provide required services to applications.

The end-system support for a DMDBMS is required for the following reasons. First, part of the communications protocol stack is implemented in software and executed by the end system. The implementation of a communications protocol may have a few hundred or a few thousand instructions. If the end system cannot guarantee the execution time for these instructions, there will be no real-time communications system no matter how well networking support is provided. Second, if the media data needs to be processed (including decompression) before presentation, the processing time should be predictable. Otherwise, a meaningful presentation is not achieved.

Multimedia applications impose the following requirements on the hardware architecture:

1. The hardware should have high processing power, and high data transfer throughput, as digital audio and video are very data intensive;
2. Many multimedia applications need to access several input/output devices at the same time, so some sort of parallel architecture is preferred;
3. The hardware architecture should be scalable to accommodate new input/output devices and applications;
4. The hardware architecture should be versatile and flexible (programmable) to support different types of data and applications.

There are two levels of hardware architecture. The first level is processor architecture (within a processor chip), and the second the computer architecture (at the board level). We discuss processor architectures that make use of the characteristics of and are suitable for multimedia processing in Section 10.5.1. Issues related to computer architectures are discussed in Section 10.5.2.

10.5.1 Processor Architectures for Multimedia

There are two general types of processors for multimedia processing: dedicated multimedia processors and general-purpose processors [22]. Both these types of processors increase processing power by using two architectural schemes to take advantage of the characteristics of multimedia processing. The two architectural schemes are single instruction multiple data (SIMD) and very long instruction word (VLIW). In the following, we first describe the concepts of SIMD and VLIW, and then discuss the two types of processors for multimedia processing.

10.5.1.1 SIMD and VLIW

Multimedia processing (e.g., image compression and decompression) requires a lot computing power. But it is usually the case that a common computation process is carried out repetitively on different data. For example, most compression techniques carry out the same computation on different image blocks. SIMD and VLIW are used in multimedia processors to take advantage of this characteristic of multimedia processing.

SIMD is a parallel processing model in which a single instruction is used to process multiple data. It is particularly suited for multimedia processing where a common operation is required to be carried out on different data. For example, if a SIMD processor operates on 8 bytes of data at the same time, 8 image pixels are accessed and processed using one instruction (assuming each pixel is represented by 1 byte). This significantly improves the multimedia processing performance.

While SIMD performs the same operation on multiple data, VLIW performs multiple operations on the same data. A typical VLIW architecture uses long instruction words with a few hundreds of bits in length. Each instruction word contains multiple independent functional units, each of which performs the different functions on the same data. This is again very suitable for multimedia processing, as it is usual that each set of multimedia data has to go through multiple processing stages. The VLIW architecture reduces the number of cycles required to process a set of data. For example, in most image compression algorithms, one VLIW instruction can read a block of pixels into a register, process the data using a transform operation (consisting of a number of multiplications and additions), and then write the processed data into memory. This is possible because one VLIW can contain all of these operation functions (read, multiplication, addition, and write). This is in contrast to normal short instruction word architecture where each operation requires a read and a write cycle.

The SIMD and VLIW are normally combined in multimedia processor design.

10.5.1.2 Dedicated Multimedia Processors

Dedicated multimedia processors are typically custom designed to perform specific multimedia functions. These functions usually include compression and decompression of audio, images, and video, and some two-dimensional and three-dimensional graphics operations. Designs of dedicated multimedia processors ranges from fully custom architectures, called function-specific architecture, to fully programmable architecture.

Function-specific dedicated multimedia architectures provide limited, if any, programmability, because most operations are "hard-wired" in the processors. The advantage of the function-specific architecture is that it is more efficient and faster than programmable architectures.

In contrast to the function-specific approach, programmable architectures enable the processing of different tasks under software control. The main advantage of programmable architectures is increased flexibility. Different algorithms and standards performing similar functions are implemented by software. However, the programmable architectures are more expensive to produce and slower than function-specific architectures.

10.5.1.3 General-Purpose Processors

While dedicated multimedia processors are being used for real-time multimedia processing, advanced general-purpose processors are now capable of providing some general multimedia processing. The common approach is to incorporate the SIMD architecture into general-purpose processors by introducing some new instructions and data types useful for multimedia processing. A typical example of general-purpose processors with multimedia enhancement is Intels' MMX technology. The MMX processor uses SIMD architecture to process 64 bits of data at the same time. The 64 data bits can be organized into 8x8 bits, 4x16 bits, or 2x32 bits, depending on the application. So, for example, an MMX can process 8 pixels at the same time using the 8x8 organization, assuming each pixel is represented by 8 bits.

10.5.2 Multimedia Computer Architectures

The previous section discussed processor architectures for multimedia processing. But a processor alone cannot make up a computer. A processor requires the support of memories, input devices, and output devices to function effectively and efficiently. The interconnection between the processor and these devices significantly affects the overall computer performance. This section discusses issues and approaches to improving multimedia computer performance. We first present the basic organization of computers based on a common system bus. We discuss bus limitations in supporting data-intensive multimedia applications. To overcome the limitations of the bus organization, researchers have proposed and developed special audio and video devices directly attached to the network, relegating the normal computer's function to providing a control interface only. We discuss the basic ideas of this approach.

One innovative design of multimedia workstations is to use an ATM switch instead of a common bus to interconnect all workstation components. The main advantage of this organization is that these components have their dedicated bandwidth, the architecture is scalable, and the workstation's internal communication uses the same format as the inter-workstation communication, assuming that ATM is used for communication among workstations, thus removing the network interface bottleneck. We describe an example of such a workstation.

10.5.2.1 The Basic Architecture

A basic computer organization is shown in Figure 10.8. It has a system bus with various functional components attached to it.

All communications between functional components must be through the common system bus. The bus is a multiplexed and shared resource for all other workstation components. Normally, each block of data has to pass through the bus at least twice. For instance, when a block of video data is received, it is passed from the network interface to the main memory, where the data is processed and then passed to the display or video I/O for display. When multiple continuous media are involved in an application, the bandwidth of the bus reaches its limit, causing data delay.

Another problem with a bus shared by several devices is the low scalability of the system, because the fixed capability of the bus limits the number of attached devices and processing elements.

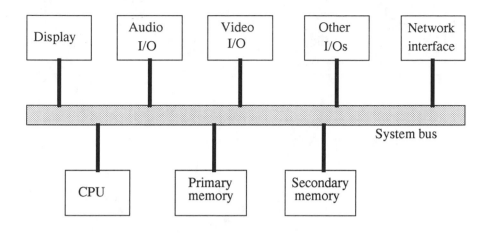

Figure 10.8 Basic organization of a multimedia end system.

10.5.2.2 The Use of Local Buses

To overcome the limitations of using a common system bus, some designers have designed and developed special local buses to connect workstation components, as shown in Figure 10.9. The use of local buses eases the system bus bottleneck problem to some extent, as some data is passed directly between workstation components without going through the common system bus.

However, the use of local buses has a number of limitations. First, such an arrangement using special buses imposes significant constraints because the dedicated communication paths do not allow a flexible, open architecture. If, for example, the video codec delivers a decoded high-volume data stream directly to the graphics output only, there is no possibility of editing the decoded stream, and the workstation remains dedicated to playback purpose.

Second, local buses are normally proprietary. They are ad hoc solutions to specific problems of specific applications. This creates an incompatibility problem between system components from different manufacturers, adding confusion to the already confused situation of many types of system buses.

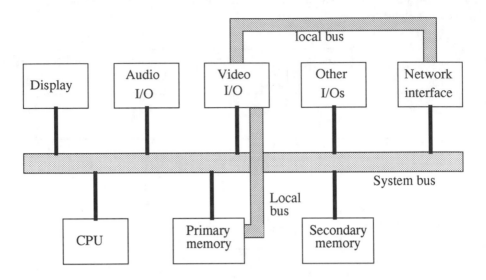

Figure 10.9 A multimedia end system with local buses.

10.5.2.3 The Use of Dedicated Multimedia Devices

To overcome the common bus limitations, some researchers have proposed to build dedicated audio and video devices directly attached to the network. The role of normal workstations is reduced to just providing control to these devices. The principle of this approach is similar to that of using dedicated local buses: to let multimedia data bypass the workstation's system bus. Two notable projects adopting this approach are Olivetti Research's Pandora's box [23] and Lancaster University's multimedia network interface (MNI) [24].

Figure 10.10 shows a general system configuration using this approach. Dedicated multimedia devices are directly connected to the network and are responsible for handling multimedia data. Multimedia data does not pass through the host computer. The main function of the host computer is to provide the user interface for users to interact with the system (e.g., to issue queries).

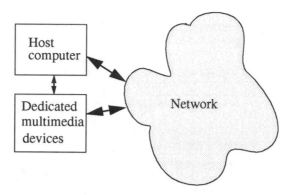

Figure 10.10 The use of dedicated multimedia devices.

The major limitation of Pandora's box and MNI is a lack of flexibility in terms of building services. The set of services available on Pandora's box and the MNI unit is static, and it is impossible to dynamically add new services (e.g., compression modules) to the system without reassigning processes to transputers and reconfiguring the software. They are thus dedicated to one or a limited set of applications. Another limitation is a lack of integration between multimedia devices and host computers. They are almost independent, and access and manipulation of multimedia data by the host computers is limited.

10.5.2.4 Network-Based Multimedia Computer Architecture

To achieve the goal of workstations being fast, flexible, and scalable, a number of research groups have proposed to build multimedia workstations based on a small network, commonly an ATM network (we will discuss ATM networks in Section 10.7) . As an example, we describe the architecture based on a small ATM network called a desk area network (DAN) [25].

As discussed in Section 10.7, ATM has many features suitable for supporting multimedia communications. Researchers at Cambridge University proposed and developed a multimedia workstation based on an ATM switch (Figure 10.11). All modules of an end system are interconnected by a small ATM network. Each module is ATM capable (i.e., it is able to transmit and receive cells) and is directly connected to the small ATM network. As these modules and the small ATM network are normally situated on a desk, this system is called a desk area network (DAN). The DAN is connected to a LAN or WAN through a network interface. It is assumed that the LAN or WAN is also ATM based.

As mentioned earlier, traditional computer systems are based on some buses; incoming data is demultiplexed based on information within the received packets, and then routed over the bus to the memory or peripheral for which it is destined. Similarly, outgoing data is transferred over the bus to the network interface for transmission. Basically the network interface is required to translate between the multiplexing mechanism used on the bus and that used on the network.

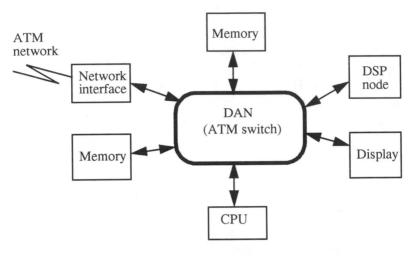

Figure 10.11 An example DAN system.

The DAN does away with this translation step in the data path by using the same multiplexing mechanism within the machine as is used in the network; multiplexing and protocol techniques used in an ATM network are extended to the links between devices and processors within a machine. The use of ATM within the end system preserves the advantages of using ATM all the way to the real endpoints of the communication. When moving data, the network interface is now a straightforward cell router, while from a control and security point of view, it is the point at which the different protocols and policies used in the DAN and the outside network meet.

A workstation based on a DAN is flexible and scalable, as components can be added and/or removed easily and the communication bandwidth between the components is dedicated.

10.6 MULTIMEDIA OPERATING SYSTEMS

This section deals with operating system support for distributed multimedia applications. Specifically, Section 10.6.1 describes multimedia operating system requirements. Section 10.6.2 describes design issues in meeting the multimedia application requirements. Section 10.6.3 discusses the limitations of conventional time-sharing operating systems and describes real-time features contained in the current workstation operating systems. A common problem for the most conventional operating systems is the overhead caused by multiple data copying within the end systems. Section 10.6.4 explains this problem and describes solutions to reduce this overhead. Another costly overhead is caused by context switching (among different processes) and domain switching (between user space and kernel space). Section 10.6.5 explains these problems and describes common techniques used to solve them.

Apart from efficiency, another important requirement of multimedia operating systems is QoS support. Section 10.6.6 deals with issues related to operating system QoS support, including QoS specification, admission control, resource reservation and scheduling, and policing.

10.6.1 Multimedia Operating System Requirements

Hardware is just raw system resources and it alone cannot provide the required services to applications. These resources must be managed properly to meet the application's requirements. Resource management is one of the main functions of an operating system. Multimedia operating systems should meet the following requirements:

1. They should use the hardware resources efficiently so that use of these resources is maximized.
2. QoS requirements of multimedia applications should be guaranteed by using appropriate resource management and process scheduling. One of the major QoS requirements at the operating system level is the guaranteed processing time for each task.
3. It is preferred that the operating system run multimedia applications and traditional computer applications simultaneously. This has two implications. First, the traditional application programming interface (API) should be maintained. Second, the traditional applications should not be starved of resources while QoS requirements of multimedia applications are guaranteed.

10.6.2 Design Issues of Multimedia Operating Systems

There are currently three approaches to developing multimedia operating systems. The first one is to modify and improve a current operating system, such as UNIX, to meet multimedia application requirements. The advantage of this approach is that existing applications can still be run, but the disadvantage is that a small modification may not be good enough to meet multimedia application requirements. The second approach is to modify and extend certain microkernels to support real-time applications while providing a "personality" to run existing applications. The third approach is to design a multimedia operating system from scratch to meet multimedia application requirements. Existing applications may or may not be supported.

For efficiency reasons, many multimedia operating systems use the microkernel architecture. A microkernel is an operating system kernel that is only responsible for manipulating low-level system resources, and is independent of any specific user-level computational paradigm.

To meet the multimedia operating system requirements, the following issues have to be addressed:

- It has been identified that data copying, switching from one process to another (called *context switching*) and switching from user space to kernel space or from kernel space to user space (called *domain switching*) are very expensive in terms of processing time. So these operations should be eliminated or reduced, or their cost should be reduced to achieve high efficiency.
- To provide QoS support, mechanisms for QoS specification, admission control,

resource management and scheduling, and policing are required. In addition, adaptive QoS graceful degradation should be supported.

- To support both real-time and nonreal-time applications requires a compatible API and special scheduling considerations. It is easy to understand why a compatible API is needed to run traditional applications. Special scheduling considerations are required because if resource scheduling is based purely on priority and urgency, then traditional applications may not be able to get processing time at all, because most workstations would not have spare resources after running even some simple multimedia applications. Special consideration should be given to ensuring that the traditional applications (nonreal-time applications) have a chance to run. This issue is addressed in the next section where we discuss real-time features in current commercial operating systems.

10.6.3 Conventional Time-Sharing Operating Systems and Incorporation of Real-time Features

A fundamental task of any operating system is the effective and efficient management of the system's resources. Resources that must be properly managed include processor cycles, memory, and I/O bandwidth. Conventional operating systems, such as UNIX, do not provide the necessary resource management and scheduling. Resource scheduling and allocation are based on fairness among processes and applications, instead of their priorities or urgency. Thus they cannot provide timely services to time-critical tasks.

In addition, conventional time-sharing operating systems implement heavyweight processes only, leading to a high context switch overhead. Data-copying overheads in data transmission and reception are also heavy, as discussed in the next section.

New versions of workstation operating systems incorporate some real-time features. Implementing real-time features requires careful design of the scheduler and related aspects of the operating system. First, the system must have priority scheduling, and real-time processes must have the highest priority. Second, the dispatch latency must be small. The smaller the latency, the faster a real-time process can start executing once it is runable.

It is relatively simple to ensure that the former property holds. However, ensuring the latter property is much more involved. The problem is that many operating systems, including most versions of UNIX, are forced to wait for either a system call to complete, or for an I/O block to take place before doing a context switch. The dispatch latency in such systems can be long, since some system calls are complex and some I/O devices are slow.

To keep dispatch latency low, system calls should be preemptible. There are several ways to achieve this goal. One is to insert preemption points in long-duration systems calls, which check to see whether a high-priority process needs to be run. If so, a context switch takes place and, when the high-priority process terminates, the interrupted process continues with the system call. Preemption points can be placed only at "safe" locations in the kernel – only where kernel data structures are not being modified. Even with preemption points dispatch latency can be large, because only a few preemption points can be practically added to a kernel.

Another method for dealing with preemption is to make the entire kernel preemptible. To ensure correct operation, all kernel data structures must be protected. With this method, the kernel can always be preemptible, because any kernel data being updated is protected from modification by the high-priority process.

What happens if the higher priority process needs to read or modify kernel data that are currently being accessed by another, lower priority process? The high-priority process would be waiting for a lower priority one to finish. This situation is known as *priority inversion*. In fact, there could be a chain of processes, all accessing resources that the high-priority process needs. This problem is solved with the *priority-inheritance* protocol, in which all these processes (the processes that are accessing resources that the high-priority process needs) inherit the high priority until they are done with the resource in question. When they are finished, their priority reverts to its natural value.

Full preemption reduces the dispatch latency significantly. For example, in Solaris 2 (SunOS 5.0), the dispatch latency with preemption disabled is normally over 100 ms. However, the dispatch latency with preemption enabled is usually reduced to 2 ms [26].

Process scheduling purely based on priorities, however, may not meet the application's requirements satisfactorily. UNIX System V release 4 (SVR4) provides a real-time static priority scheduler, in addition to a standard UNIX time-sharing scheduler. By scheduling real-time tasks at a higher priority than other classes of tasks, SVR4 UNIX allows real-time tasks to obtain processor resources when needed to meet their timeliness requirements. This solution claims to provide robust system support for multimedia applications by allowing applications such as those that manipulate audio and video to be placed in the real-time class. However, Nieh et al. [27] found experimentally that the SVR4 UNIX scheduler manages system resources poorly for both so-called real-time and time-sharing activities, resulting in unacceptable system performance for multimedia applications. Not only are the application latencies much worse than desired, but lockup occurs with the scheduler such that the system no longer accepts user input. There are two main reasons for these problems. First, the amount of resources are not adequate. A video application running at a high priority uses all the resources, and thus lower priority activities, such as mouse movement and keyboard input, do not have any chance to be executed, leading to the system lockup. Second, the static priority scheduler is too rigid, especially when the resources are not abundant. Graceful degradation of real-time application quality should allow other activities to run. Alternatively, some small-percentage resources should be reserved for nonreal-time tasks. Solaris 2 is based on SVR4 with a static fixed priority scheduler, but it incorporates a mechanism to prevent low-priority processes from being starved of system resources.

To summarize, new versions of commercial workstation operating systems have some real-time features, but they are still not suitable for multimedia applications for the following reasons:

- Although continuous media can be assigned high priority, their deadlines may not be met. Audio samples and videoframes have their fixed deadlines. The OS must provide a mechanism for applications to specify QoS (including deadline) requirements, which should be guaranteed if the applications are accepted.
- These operating systems do not exercise admission control. Without admission control, the system can be overloaded. An overloaded system is not able to provide any performance guarantees.

- Multimedia applications require many input and output transactions. However, current operating systems, such as Solaris 2, do not schedule I/O based on real-time requirements.

10.6.4 Solutions to Data-Copying Problem

Data copying within an end system is very expensive. This section looks at this data-copying problem and its solutions.

10.6.4.1 Data-Copying Problem

Data copying within end systems reduces system performance and may become a serious performance bottleneck for the following reasons. First, memory speed is normally much slower than CPU speed. Second, data is moved more than once in a typical application. At the client, a block of data is read from secondary storage into the main application memory. Then the block of data is moved from the application's memory to a transport processing buffer (normally in the kernel, thus called *kernel memory*) to add header and/or trailer information. Finally, the data is moved from the kernel memory into a network interface buffer, to be transmitted onto the network. At the client side, the reverse process happens. The data is moved from the network to the network interface, to the transport processing buffer to remove the header and/or trailer, to the application's memory, and finally, to the display device's memory. Therefore, a block of data is normally moved three times at each end. When the transport system is implemented in a layered fashion, as is commonly the case, data may be moved several times within the transport stack from one layer to another.

To summarize, data copying is a slow and expensive process, and yet data is copied many times in current communications end systems, limiting the data throughput of these end systems. Therefore, the obvious approach to improving the throughput is to reduce the amount of data copying needed in the end systems.

10.6.4.2 Two Data Movement Methods

The techniques most commonly used for moving data are direct memory access (DMA) and programmed input/output (PIO). In DMA, the I/O adaptor transfers data directly to or from main memory, without involving the CPU. PIO requires the CPU to transfer every word between main memory and the I/O adaptor in a programmed loop.

With DMA, the data transfer proceeds concurrently with other CPU activities, allowing parallelism. Moreover, it is generally possible to transfer large blocks of data in a single bus transaction, thereby achieving transfer rates close to the limits of the main memory and the I/O bus. DMA is the preferred method when data movement is unavoidable.

10.6.4.3 Single-Copy and Zero-Copy Architecture

The amount of data movement can be reduced, using a technique in which the kernel and application share the memory space using a technique called virtual memory mapping. At the client side, data is moved from the network interface to the kernel space, where the headers and/or trailers are removed. Then the operating system informs the application of the data availability by passing a pointer to the data without actually copying it. At the server side, the application informs the kernel if there is data to be transmitted. The kernel adds headers/trailers to the data, before it is passed to the network interface. This method saves one data copy operation at each end. An alternative is to share the kernel memory and network interface memory, removing the data copying between the network interface and the kernel. Using virtual memory mapping, only one copy is needed at each side (assuming that there is no separate memory for data processing and no data copying within the transport stack). So these virtual memory mapping techniques are called *single-copy architectures*.

The amount of data copying can be reduced further. The basic idea is to treat the interface memory as regular pages in the application memory space, which is shared by the kernel as well. The application would preallocate some interface pages to use as its sending data buffers. Thus by placing data in its buffers, the application is automatically placing data in the interface memory, ready to be transmitted after the headers and/or trailers are added by the kernel. Similarly, at the receiver side, data packets would not have to be copied; they would already be in pages that could be remapped into the receiving application's space. This type of memory organization is called *zero-copy architecture*, as reported by Kitamura et al. [28].

10.6.5 Solutions to Reduce Context and Domain Switch Overhead

When there are tasks waiting in queues, to achieve high resource use the processor should not be idle. When the processor is servicing a task, the execution time is determined by the CPU speed and other hardware. It is fixed for a particular machine. But the time required to switching from serving one task to another varies. When a processor stops executing code for one task and starts executing code for another task, it has to save the state of the old task, and then load the state and code for the new task from memory. This changing of state and code is called a *context switch*. During the context switch, the processor is not doing useful work for applications. Therefore, to improve CPU efficiency, this time should be made as short as possible.

Context switches are typically very expensive because they require both new code and new data to be loaded into the processor cache, as the new code typically wants to reference data not in the cache. Researchers found that a context switch could take hundreds of instruction cycles to complete and it affects cache hit rate for many more cycles. Therefore, the number of context switches should be kept low in multimedia operating systems. To reduce context switch overhead, a type of lightweight process, called a *thread*, has been introduced. The overhead to switch between threads is much lower than that to switch between normal processes. A thread is a basic unit of CPU use, and consists of a program counter, a register set, and a stack space. It shares with peer threads its code section, data section, and operating system resources such as open files and signals.

In contrast, a process has all these things for itself. A process is equal to a task with one thread. The extensive sharing among threads makes CPU switching among peer threads and the creation of threads inexpensive, compared with context switches among processes. Although a thread context switch still requires a register set switch, no memory-management related work need be done. In multimedia applications, we can take advantage of threads by creating different threads for different media types (i.e., one for audio and one for video) instead of using processes.

Another overhead during program execution is caused by a *domain switch*, which refers to the switch between kernel space and user space. To minimize this overhead, it is necessary to place as much as possible of the required system functions in the same address space as the application itself. The drawback of this arrangement is that the kernel loses control of resource usage and scheduling power. To solve this problem, Govindan and Anderson proposed split-level scheduling [29], which was later used by Coulson and Blair in their SUMO project [30]. In split-level scheduling, there are two schedulers, a user-level scheduler (ULS) and a kernel-level scheduler (KLS). These two schedulers cooperate to achieve high performance.

10.6.6 QoS SUPPORT

For the OS to provide QoS guarantees to an application, the application must specify its resource requirements and what to guarantee. Based on this specification, the OS determines whether the application can be admitted without affecting the QoS promises granted to ongoing applications. If not, the application is not started. If yes, the OS reserves appropriate amounts of resources for the application, and schedules all accepted applications so that their QoS requirements are guaranteed. To prevent applications from using more resources than they have been allocated, the OS has to implement certain policing mechanisms. In the following, we discuss QoS specification, admission control, resource reservation and policing, and process scheduling disciplines.

10.6.6.1 QoS Specification

Among the four QoS management elements, the first one, QoS specification, is the most fundamental. Only when QoS requirements are specified properly can we design and implement the other three elements. But surprisingly, there has been little work carried out in QoS specification. This is mainly due to the difficulty in quantitatively specifying computer resource requirements for general applications. It is relatively easy to specify memory requirements for an application, but it is difficult to specify CPU time and bus bandwidth requirements for a general application, partly because they are CPU-speed and hardware-architecture dependent.

The common way to specify QoS requirements is by a processor (usage) percentage, which is the processor time required by the application during an interval divided by the duration of the interval. This specification is called a *processor capacity specification*. For example, a video application may require 10 ms of processor time every 30 ms. This specification can be made easily for periodic applications, assuming the computation time is fairly constant in each interval or period. When the computation time is not constant, a conservative worst-case estimate reserves the necessary processor capacity, and the unused time is used for background processing. For nonperiodic applications, capacity specification is difficult.

In real-time Mach [31, 32], applications can specify the minimum, maximum, and most desirable levels of the computation time, and the minimum, maximum, and most desirable levels of the period. In other words, if an application chooses a range of acceptable computation times or periods, the operating system is free to pick a legal value in this range. The QoS server tries to provide to each application the maximum quality value in this range but does not go below the minimum requested value once an application is admitted. The QoS specification can be changed by the application dynamically subject to an admission control test.

10.6.6.2 Admission Control

In operating systems, admission control is tightly coupled with the process scheduling discipline used and is called a *schedulability test*. When the system meets deadlines of all tasks, we say these tasks are *schedulable*. When a new task arrives, the scheduler determines whether existing tasks plus the new task are schedulable. The new task is accepted or admitted when the scheduler can produce a feasible schedule for all tasks. If the QoS requirements are specified using a processor percentage, then it is relatively easy to perform the schedulability test: when the sum of the processor percentages of all tasks is less than or equal to 1, these tasks are schedulable.

10.6.6.3 Resource Reservation and Policing

CPU time is implicitly reserved for each admitted task after the schedulability test. This is true only when each task does not use more processor time than it initially requested. A policing mechanism is required to make sure that tasks do not use more processor time than their reserves. In practice, implementation of the policing mechanism is complicated due to the difficulty of measuring the execution time of each task, as explained below.

Carrying out reservation enforcement requires precise performance-monitoring software. Typical operating systems do not provide this software. Operating systems usually accumulate usage statistics for each process by sampling during regular clock interrupts, but this information is imprecise over short intervals. Further, the execution behavior of the monitored program must be independent of the sampling period. A more precise mechanism measures durations between context switches and accounts for interrupt processing time and other system overheads.

Even if the system can accurately measure capacity consumption on a per-process basis, other problems arise. Usage statistics in traditional operating systems consist of system-level usage time and user-level time for each process. For monolithic operating systems, measuring the system-level usage time and user-level time is sufficient. But for a microkernel system where operating system services are offered by different user-level servers, the usage statistics of an activity cannot be found in a single process. An activity may invoke separate operating system servers to perform file-system access, networking naming, and so forth. To maintain an accurate picture of an activity's processor usage, the cost of these services must be charged to the activity itself rather than to the individual servers. Thus, capacity reserves must be maintained independently of any particular thread of execution, so that work done by any process or thread on behalf of the reserved activity can be charged to that activity. This is done by creating an independent reserve abstraction, which may be bound dynamically to different threads of execution [31].

With accurate usage measurements, and a mechanism to generate a scheduling event when a program attempts to overrun its capacity reservation, the scheduler can control the execution of programs and prevent them from interfering with other reservations.

10.6.6.4 Process Scheduling Disciplines

During run time, the main function of an OS is to allocate resources to active tasks. For the CPU resource, run-time allocation is performed by a dispatcher. A run-time resource allocation model is shown in Figure 10.12. The dispatcher sees application resource requests as a series of task arrivals t_i, which are placed in individual queues waiting to be allocated the required resource. Whenever the CPU finishes servicing a request, the dispatcher selects a task from the head of one of the queues based on a certain scheduling discipline. The selected task is allocated the processor resource for some amount of time.

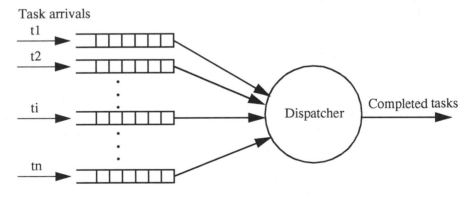

Figure 10.12 Resource allocation model.

Therefore, one of the most important factors determining whether an OS can provide QoS guarantees is the process scheduling discipline used. This section describes a number of common scheduling disciplines. Some were developed for traditional real-time systems, but may be modified to suit multimedia applications.

Rate Monotonic

In rate monotonic (RM) scheduling [33], tasks are assigned with static priorities such that tasks with higher arrival rates have higher priorities. The tasks are executed preemptively in a system with a dispatcher that always runs the runable task with the highest priority.

It is assumed that tasks meet the following constraints:

- Processes are periodic and their deadline in each period is the same as the end of the current period.
- Processes are independent of each other and their execution time is fixed.

With these assumptions it has been shown that when the sum of processor use of all processes is less than $ln2$, then there is a feasible schedule for these processes (i.e., the deadlines of these processes can be met). This result is conservative. It is a sufficient but not a necessary condition for determining whether a set of periodic tasks is schedulable using the RM assignment of fixed priorities.

Earliest Deadline First

The earliest-deadline-first (EDF) algorithm schedules processes or threads based on the following principle: Every time a process becomes runable, or a periodic process invocation completes, the runable process with the earliest deadline is selected to run next [33].

EDF is an optimal and dynamic algorithm, since it is guaranteed to find a valid schedule (i.e., one that meets the deadlines of all threads) if such a schedule exists. CPU resources are fully used when there are runable processes. For periodic processes with a deadline equal to the end of the current period, the admission test is simple: we need only make sure that the sum of processor use of all processes is less than 100%.

Mauthe and Colson [34] extended the basic EDF to schedule processes whose deadlines are earlier than the current period. Giving a process a tight deadline is useful for reducing delay jitter. For example, if the period of a process is 40 ms and the deadlines are the same as the end of each period, then the maximum delay jitter is 40 ms. But when the deadlines are set to be 10 ms before the end of each period, the maximum jitter is reduced to 30 ms.

Time-Driven Resource Management

In the time-driven resource management (TDRM) scheme [35], all resource management decisions are made on the basis of the timeliness and importance of the applications requesting the resources. Timeliness and importance are taken into account when making decisions concerning processor allocation, memory allocation, synchronization operations, interprocess communication, I/O operations, and so forth. Resource management involves making decisions based on the requester's deadlines, importance, and expected resource requirements. A system's effectiveness may be reduced if it permits computations to consume resources when they can no longer provide value to the user (e.g., after they miss their deadlines). Rather than strictly using deadlines that fail in overload cases, or priorities that are too static, a time and value evaluation is made to choose among all the requests for system resources. The system's architecture directly implements and encourages graceful degradation strategies.

10.6.6.5 QoS Graceful Degradation and Media Scaling

Multimedia data can tolerate some data loss or delay to some extent. By using an appropriate encoding technique, the quality of playback can be degraded gracefully while allowing high use of resources.

The key to graceful degradation is the encoding method. If the encoding method does not allow media scaling, a resource shortage may reduce the QoS to an unacceptable level. For example, if an image is coded using a nonscalable method, then data loss or incomplete compression of the image due to a resource shortage may result in the entire image being undecodable and undisplayable. But on the other hand, if the image is coded with a progressive multiscan method, loss of some data or an entire low-priority scan may not affect the decoding and displaying of the image, as an image of reasonable quality can be reconstructed from the high-priority scans.

QoS graceful degradation and media scaling are especially important in operating systems. Questions to be answered are: What action should be taken if the operating system does not have sufficient resources to complete the encoding or decoding of an image in the specified interval? How does the application use this partially processed data? How can QoS requirements be specified so that resources are used efficiently while the quality is acceptable to applications?

A number of experimental multimedia operating systems have been developed. They meet the requirements listed in Section 10.6.1 to some extent. We briefly mention four examples here. Interested readers should refer to the following references. YARTOS (yet another real-time operating system) found in [36, 37] provides hard guarantees with strict admission control. The work of Hyden [38] advocates soft QoS guarantees with graceful quality degradation. The SUMO project emphasizes operating system efficiency [30]. Real-time Mach provides many features suitable for distributed multimedia applications [31, 32].

10.7 MULTIMEDIA NETWORKS

This section deals with network support for multimedia communications. We discuss what network technologies are suitable for multimedia communications.

In this book, we use the term *network support* to encompass all layers below the transport layer in the OSI Reference Model (OSIRM). Figure 10.13 shows the relationship between our discussion model and the OSIRM. The transport support, discussed in the next section, corresponds to the OSI transport layer. We also discuss some network-layer protocols when we discuss transport support for multimedia communications, as the transport layer relies on some network-layer functions to perform certain operations. A communications system consists of both a transport protocol and a network protocol (collectively called a transport *suite* or transport *system*). We generally refer to all layers above the transport layer as the *application-oriented layers*.

This section is organized as follows. Section 10.7.1 examines the characteristics of networks suitable for multimedia communications. Based on these characteristics, we obtain a list of network technologies potentially suitable for multimedia communications. They include fiber distributed data interface (FDDI), distributed queue dual bus (DQDB), and ATM networks. Section 10.7.2 describes ATM which is one of the most important networking technologies. Section 10.7.3 briefly describes the elements required for providing QoS guarantees at the network level.

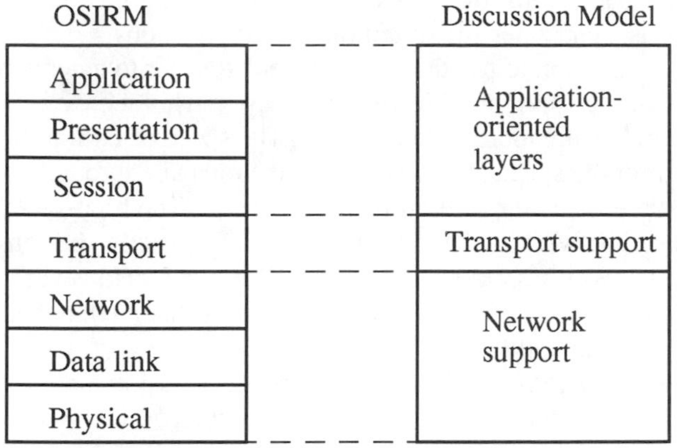

OSIRM   Discussion Model

Application		Application-oriented layers
Presentation		
Session		
Transport		Transport support
Network		Network support
Data link		
Physical		

Figure 10.13 Relationship between our discussion model and the OSIRM.

10.7.1 NETWORK CHARACTERISTICS SUITABLE FOR MULTIMEDIA COMMUNICATIONS

We examine the suitability of network technologies for multimedia communications using the four general design goals of multimedia systems described in Section 10.3. When these four design goals are used in the context of networks, they become the criteria to determine the suitability of a particular network technology for multimedia communications. These four criteria are:

(1) The network bandwidth should be high enough to support many applications at the same time;
(2) Network resources should be shared efficiently among applications so that as many applications as possible are supported;
(3) The network should provide performance guarantees to applications, if required;
(4) The network should be scalable.

In the following, we discuss these four criteria or features. From the discussion, it is clear which network technologies are obviously unsuitable and which network technologies are (potentially) suitable for multimedia communications.

10.7.1.1 Network Speed or Bandwidth

High bandwidth is the basic requirement for supporting multimedia communications. Without sufficient bandwidth, the network is definitely unsuitable as high bandwidth requirement is a basic characteristic of multimedia applications.

Although it is common to use the word "speed" to refer to a network's transmission capability, note that the speed at which data bits are transmitted over different networks and transmission media are more or less similar. The speed of light in fiber is not significantly different from the speed at which electrons propagate through copper. The actual difference is the time interval representing each data bit. The high-speed network differs from the slow-speed network in that bits are smaller. So strictly speaking, we should say "high-bandwidth network" instead of "high-speed network." However, the term *speed* is so more commonly used, so we use speed and bandwidth interchangeably to describe network transmission capability.

Network speed is determined by the physical transmission medium used, protocols, distance between intermediate nodes, and switching speed of intermediate nodes. Among twisted pair, coaxial cable, and optic fiber, optical fiber offers the highest transmission bandwidth. In theory, a single optical fiber can support a few terabits/s [39].

We should distinguish speed at two different points of a network. One point is the *user access point*. The bandwidth at this point is called *user access bandwidth*. With compression, each user needs a few Mbps to support multimedia applications. Note that for information-retrieval-type applications, the bandwidth required for the channel from the client to the server is very small, perhaps a few kbits/s is sufficient.

Another important network bandwidth is between network exchanges[1] over a long distance. This bandwidth is often called *aggregate bandwidth* and should be at least a few hundred Mbits/s to support a reasonable number of users and applications at the same time. At this speed over a long distance, optical fiber is a better choice.

10.7.1.2 Efficient Sharing of Network Resources

Because each user requires a large amount of bandwidth, network bandwidth is very valuable. Multimedia data is bursty, especially after compression. Therefore, if each user reserves bandwidth equal to its peak bit rate, some bandwidth is wasted when the output bit rate is not at its highest. The best approach is to use the principle of *bandwidth on demand* or *statistical multiplexing*: an application uses as much bandwidth as it needs subject to a maximum value. When the application is not using some or all its maximum bandwidth, other applications can use it.

It is clear that circuit-switching technology is not suitable, because it sets up a circuit of fixed bandwidth between the source and destination even though the bandwidth may not be used fully. Likewise, synchronous time division multiplexing (STDM) packet switching is not suitable because the bandwidth for each channel is fixed regardless of its usage. (We discuss STDM further in Section 10.7.2.) Therefore a form of packet-switching network is more suitable for efficient use of network resources.

Both circuit switching and STDM are capable of providing hard performance guar-

1. The terms "exchange," "switch," and "intermediate node" are used interchangeably in this book.

antees. But for many multimedia applications, a statistical guarantee is sufficient. Statistical multiplexing, sharing bandwidth based on the bandwidth-on-demand principle, can support more applications given the same amount of bandwidth [40]. Statistical multiplexing is a technique that multiplexes many independent datastreams onto a high-bandwidth channel. Assuming these streams are bursty and independent, some streams are at low bit rates while some streams are at high bit rates. The total aggregate bandwidth at any time is smaller than the sum of the peak bit rates of these streams. Thus statistical multiplexing can use bandwidth efficiently. The formal statement of this observation is the *strong law of large numbers*: given a large number of uncorrelated datastreams, the total amount of bandwidth required to satisfy all the streams stays nearly constant, even though the individual streams may substantially vary the amount of data they send. The constant depends on the statistical characteristics of each stream. For example, assume that we have 50 variable bit-rate-coded independent videostreams. The peak bit rate and average bit rate of each stream are 8 Mbps and 2 Mbps respectively, using STDM we need a link bandwidth of 400 Mbps to transmit these 50 videostreams. However, using statistical multiplexing requires a link bandwidth of about 100 Mbps. Note that for simplicity, we used the average bit rate to calculate the aggregate bandwidth. In practice, the calculation is based on the statistical distribution of each videostream, and the total aggregate bandwidth also depends on the allowed packet loss rate and delay. This is because in statistical multiplexing, packets may be delayed or discarded when insufficient network resources are reserved. There is a tradeoff between network resources required and packet loss rate and delay.

Packet size also affects the efficiency of bandwidth usage. When packet size is too big, many packets are not full, especially the last packet of a message, wasting bandwidth. When packet size is too small, too much bandwidth is wasted on carrying packet overhead information. We consider these and other factors in choosing packet size later.

Another issue concerning efficient network resource use is whether retransmission of lost data should be carried out. For live playout of digital audio and video, retransmission is not desirable. First, retransmission causes extra delay to succeeding packets so that they may be too late for playout. Second, we can tolerate some loss and error in multimedia presentation. In general, retransmission wastes bandwidth and causes extra delay to subsequent packets. Automatic retransmission should not be used in the low-level network architecture. If some applications need error-free transmission, it should be implemented in the application-dependent higher layers. In addition, the simple network protocol allows the development of fast switches.

A better approach to reduce the effect of lost packets on playback quality is to use traffic priorities. Physical transmission media, especially optical fiber, are very reliable. The most likely source of data loss is buffer shortage in network exchanges. If traffic priorities are assigned to data according to their importance, the exchange will discard the lower priority data first in the case of a buffer shortage. Since lower priority data is less important to a multimedia presentation, its loss will not affect the presentation much. For example, with subband coding, the most important data is coded in the first band and less important data in other bands. Loss of data in less important bands will not affect the presentation quality much or may not be perceived at all.

10.7.1.3 Performance Guarantees

We are interested in performance guarantees in the statistical multiplexing environment. To guarantee performance, the network should guarantee that a packet can access the network within a specified time, and that when the packet is on the network, it is delivered within a fixed amount of time. There are two possibilities when performance is not guaranteed. The first is with the transmission medium access control (MAC) protocols. Some MACs do not guarantee network access time. A packet can take a very long time to get onto the network. For example, CSMA/CD used in ethernet lets stations wait until the network is not busy before transmission. After transmission, collision is still possible. If collision does occur, that same packet competes with other data for network access and may take an undefined amount of time before it can again access to the network. Another undesirable feature of CSMA/CD is that the minimum packet size is determined by the transmission speed and cable length. In a 10-Mbps Ethernet, the minimum packet size is 64 bytes for a 5-km cable. But if a 1-Gbps network used CSMA/CD, the minimum packet size would be about 6,400 bytes, which is too big for efficient bandwidth use (many packets will be unfilled) and for continuous media communications (the time taken to assemble a packet is too long).

The second possibility of failing performance guarantees is at the network switches. Once a packet is on the network, the transmission medium conveys the packet at the fixed electron or light speed from the source to the destination directly, or to a network intermediate node or switch. If the source and destination are directly connected without going through any interchange, the packet is delivered without additional delay or jitter problems. If the packet has to go through one or more switches, extra packet delay or loss may occur. Because the packet must be buffered at each exchange, the outbound channel for the packet is determined, and only when the channel is available does the packet transmit[1]. This store-and-forward process is nondeterministic. The buffer in the switch may be full, causing the packet to be discarded. The processor may be busy, delaying the switching decision. The outbound channel may be busy, causing extra delay.

The second problem is solved by proper admission control and proper management of network resources, especially queues in switches. If a channel's performance cannot be guaranteed, or its acceptance affects other existing channels, this channel should not be admitted.

10.7.1.4 Network Scalability

There are three types of scalability: distance, bandwidth, and the number of users. In terms of distance, the same network architecture and protocol should be able to operate on LANs as well as WANs, so the interconnection between these networks is easy. In terms of bandwidth, the network bandwidth should be able to grow with the growth of user's bandwidth demands without the changing of network protocols. The network should be able to support a large number of users, and the available bandwidth to each should not be affected by the number of active stations connected to the network. Most LANs use a shared medium: all stations are attached to a common transmission medium

---

1. This type of switch is called *store-and-forward switch*.

and share the fixed amount of total bandwidth. The bandwidth share for each station decreases when the number of active stations increases. This is not desirable.

10.7.1.5 Networks Suitable for Multimedia Communications

From the above discussion, we conclude that network technologies suitable for multimedia communication should meet the following requirements:

- The individual access bandwidth should be at least a few Mbps. The aggregate bandwidth should at least be in the order of 100 Mbps at the local area, and higher for WANs.
- The network should be based on packet-switched statistical multiplexing instead of dedicated circuits for efficient sharing of network resources.
- The network should provide throughput, error rate, delay, and delay jitter guarantees to applications.
- The network should be scalable in terms of bandwidth, the number of users, and distance covered.
- The network should have multicasting capability. It is easier to implement multicasting in packet-switched networks than in circuit-switched networks.

We use these requirements to determine which networks are (potentially) suitable for multimedia communications. Let us first list existing or proposed network technologies. There are three network categories: local area networks (LAN), metropolitan area networks (MAN), and wide area networks (WAN). In the LAN category, the common networks are:

- 10-Mbps Ethernet based on CSMA/CD (IEEE 802.3);
- 10-Mbps token bus (IEEE 802.4);
- 4- or 16-Mbps token ring (IEEE 802.5);
- 100-Mbps FDDI;
- ATM LAN.

The common MAN is 100-Mbps DQDB. The FDDI is sometimes also classified as a MAN. The following networks provide wide area digital services:

- Circuit-switching ISDN;
- X.25;
- Frame relay;
- Switched Multimegabit Data Service (SMDS);
- ATM networks.

We do not deal with each of these networks in detail. Readers should see references [41-46] for details of these networks. What we do here is eliminate networks that are not suitable for multimedia communications from the above list, based on the five requirements. We then obtain a list of networks that are potentially suitable for multimedia communications.

The bandwidth of common LANs, except FDDI and ATM LAN, is too low to support general-purpose multimedia communications. Note that we are interested in general-purpose multimedia applications instead of cases where an entire network is dedicated to one or two carefully tuned applications. So common LANs, except FDDI and ATM LAN, are not suitable for multimedia communications, even without considering the other requirements. Currently, there are two trends in developing LANs. The first is to use a cheap transmission medium to support high-speed data transmission. One example is 100-Mbps Ethernet based on twisted pair. (In terms of speed, the fast Ethernet is reasonably fast, but it is still not entirely suitable for multimedia communications because of its CSMA/CD MAC protocol.) The second development is a LAN switch to which all network stations are directly connected. A packet entering the switch is forwarded to one output connection only. In this way, an application can use the entire link bandwidth. When the switch is fast and an appropriate switching algorithm is used, LANs based on switches are suitable for multimedia communications to some extent in local areas. A new development in this direction is isochronous Ethernet (isoENET), which has an additional isochronous channel on top of the 10 Mbps of the conventional Ethernet. The isochronous channel has a bandwidth of 6.144 Mbps composed of 96 independent 64-kbps subchannels. These subchannels are used in a similar way as ISDN channels: separately or as aggregate channels, depending on the bandwidth requirement of applications.

FDDI and DQDB are reasonably fast and have features suitable for supporting real-time communications, so they can be used as multimedia LANs or MANs. But since both FDDI and DQDB use shared media, the available bandwidth to each station decreases as the number of active stations increases. So they do not scale well.

Circuit-switching networks (including ISDN) can provide performance guarantees within the bandwidth supported. But they cannot use resources efficiently and cannot support multicasting and multiple connections over one access point. Thus they are not good candidates for general-purpose multimedia applications, although they are being used for videophony and videoconferencing.

X.25, frame relay, and SMDS are designed for carrying nonreal-time data and cannot provide performance guarantees, so they are not suitable for multimedia communications.

ATM promises to meet all five requirements and is potentially suitable for multimedia communications. It has been adopted by ITU-TS as the multiplexing and switching mechanism for broadband integrated services digital network (BISDN). BISDN promises to support all types of applications. Although ATM was originally designed for WANs, it can be used in LANs to overcome the scalability problem other LANs have as a result of shared media.

In addition to the above networking technologies, there is another class of networking technology specifically for the home. The basic characteristic of this class of technology is the use of existing telephone lines and TV cables to provide digital services, such as video on demand, by using advanced modulation techniques [47].

To summarize, FDDI and DQDB are good candidates for multimedia LANs and MANs. ATM is potentially suitable for multimedia communication in both local and wide areas. We use the word "potentially" because ATM technology for general purpose multimedia applications is not mature yet. Most current installations are for conventional data communications. We discuss ATM in the following section.

10.7.2 ATM

10.7.2.1 What Is ATM?

Transfer mode refers to the multiplexing and switching mechanism of a network. The key word in ATM is *asynchronous*. Asynchronous highlights the difference between ATM and traditional STDM. As shown in Figure 10.14, in STDM, time on a transmission link is divided into fixed-length frames, which are further divided into fixed-length timeslots. Each timeslot is numbered. A connection between a given source and destination pair can only use the same timeslot of each frame, and therefore data transmission occurs synchronously with time. STDM multiplexing is done by reservation. If the source does not have data to send during the timeslot assigned to its connection, that timeslot is wasted and cannot be used by any other connection. A timeslot can only be used by the channel that reserved it during the call setup. If the source has more data to send, it has to wait for the timeslot in the next frame, or it must reserve more than one timeslot in each frame. If each timeslot corresponds to 64 kbps (ISDN standard), then a connection can only have bandwidth that is a multiple of 64 kbps. If a connection just needs 16 kbps, one timeslot must be reserved and 48 kbps are wasted. If a connection needs 70 kbps, two timeslots (128 kbps) in each frame must be reserved and 58 kbps are wasted.

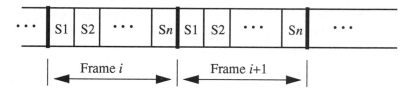

Figure 10.14 STDM: time is divided into fixed-length frames, which in turn are divided into fixed-length timeslots. Each timeslot can only be used by the channel that reserved it.

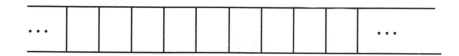

Figure 10.15 ATM: time is divided into fixed-length slots. Slots can be used by any channel based on availability and demand.

In ATM, time on a transmission link is divided into small fixed-length time-slots (Figure 10.15). But in contrast to STDM, timeslots are not reserved for any connection. A connection can use any available timeslot to transmit data. Thus the data transmission of each channel is asynchronous. ATM is a time-division multiplexing scheme in which timeslots are not assigned to any particular connection. For this reason, ATM is also called asynchronous time-division multiplexing (ATDM). Note that cell slots are fixed and synchronous with time; "asynchronous" means that these slots can be used independently by any channel. The main advantage of ATM is bandwidth on demand: each connection can use as much bandwidth as it needs subject to a maximum bandwidth. Unused timeslots can be used by any other channel. In this way, the network bandwidth is shared efficiently among applications.

In ATM, all data presented by the users is sent to the network by access links in small packets fitting into the timeslots. These fixed-length small packets are called *cells*. The user equipment is responsible for transforming the data generated by application devices into this common format. In such an approach, large datablocks or continuous bit-rate datastreams are segmented and delivered to the network as a sequence of fixed-length cells; the larger datablocks are then reassembled from the cells arriving at the receiver. The only feature that distinguishes a low-bandwidth application from a high-bandwidth application is the frequency of cell generation, and users access bandwidth on demand at any effective datarate up to the maximum speed permitted by the access link. Within the network, all cells are handled autonomously. The network operates only on the cell header that contains the information needed by the network to deliver the cell to its intended receiver. The network disregards the nature or contents of the cell payload, which may contain voice, data, image, or video information (though different priorities for different types of traffic may be used).

ATM cell size chosen for BISDN by ITU-TS (formerly CCITT) is 53 bytes, out of which 5 bytes is header and 48 bytes is user data called *payload*, as shown in Figure 10.16. The cell size was determined by compromising between bandwidth efficiency and network transmission delay. All types of traffic presented by end users are formatted into cells and delivered to the appropriate destination based on the header information. Thus it is very flexible—one user needs just one access point and can transmit and receive all types of information through this point.

5 bytes header	48 bytes payload

Figure 10.16 ATM cell format.

10.7.2.2 B-ISDN Protocol Reference Model

B-ISDN is a layered architecture allowing multiple services and applications, such as voice, data, and video, to be mixed over the network. It has four layers. The application layer or user layer produces and displays the various types of data. Three lower layers have been defined to implement the features of ATM as shown in Table 10.1.

The physical layer defines the electrical characteristics and network interfaces. This layer "puts the bits on the wire," and actually determines transmission bit rate. Bit rates of 155 and 622 Mbps were initially proposed for optical transmission, but other transmission bit rates have also been defined for other transmission media. ATM is not tied to a specific type of physical transport, but the common medium considered for long distance is optic fiber using the synchronous optical network (SONET) protocol.

The ATM layer takes the data to be sent and adds the 5-byte header information that assures the cell is sent on the right connection. It is a switching and multiplexing layer independent of the physical layer.

The ATM adaptation layer (AAL) assures the appropriate service characteristics to applications and divides all types of data into the 48-byte payload that makes up the ATM cell.

Table 10.1
ATM Layers and Functions

Layers	*Functions*
ATM adaptation layer (AAL)	Segmentation Reassembly Application dependent functions (e.g., error control)
ATM layer	Generic flow control Cell header generation/extraction Cell VPI/VCI translation Cell multiplex and demultiplex
Physical layer	Bit transmission over a transmis- sion medium

Different AALs may be used for different types of traffic or applications. ITU-TS determined the following four types of applications:

1. Time-sensitive, constant-bit-rate applications. These applications send and receive data at constant bit rates. They also require that the delay from the source to destination be bounded. This type of application includes constant-bit-rate-coded audio and video communications.
2. Time-sensitive, variable-bit-rate applications. These applications send data at variable-bit-rates, but still require delay bounds. Examples include variable-bit-rate coded audio and video communications.
3. Connection-oriented data applications. This class was intended to support applications that historically used a network service like X.25.
4. Connectionless data applications. Applications in this class send and receive data using connectionless datagrams.

To support these different classes of services, the ITU-T proposed three different adaptation layers: AAL 1, AAL 2, and AAL 3/4. The ATM Forum[1] proposed a new layer AAL 5 and is investigating AAL 6.

- AAL 1 is for class A service and employs packetization/depacketization functions

---

1. The ATM Forum consists of over 600 members, including almost all major providers of data and telecommunication equipment. Its main function is to define and promote ATM technology.

to convert constant bit-rate streams into cells at the sender, and to assemble cells into the constant-bit-rate streams at the receiver. A fully synchronized bitstream has to be delivered at the receiver, requiring a tight delay and jitter control within the network.

- AAL 2 provides class B service. Due to its variable bit rate, it is difficult to reserve resources for this kind of traffic and thus difficult to implement AAL 2. We will discuss traffic characterization for bursty traffic in Section 5.8. The details of AAL 2 have not been defined.
- AAL 3/4 implements class C and D services. The main function of AAL 3/4 is segmentation and reassembly for large messages.
- AAL 5 also provides class C and D services (as proposed by computer manufacturers in the ATM Forum). It is simpler and more efficient than AAL 3/4, and thus was initially called the simple and efficient adaptation layer (SEAL).
- AAL 6 is in the discussion stage. The ATM Forum is investigating an AAL suitable for packetized multimedia streams, in particular for MPEG and MPEG-II video. Issues under discussion include the use of forward error-correction (FEC) techniques to increase the communication reliability to a level where no extra error recovery is needed, and for the support of MPEG synchronization requirements.

Note that AALs do more than segmenting and reassembling data—they actually implement transport protocols suitable for different types of applications.

10.7.2.3 Why is ATM Suitable for Multimedia Communications?

ATM is established as the basis for broadband networks. We examine a number of reasons for this choice and explain why ATM is potentially suitable for multimedia communications. The following list is largely based on the five multimedia networking requirements discussed at the beginning of this section. Note that some features are promised but have not been specified or realized.

1. Bandwidth: ATM promises high-speed access for each end system. Two access speeds of 155 Mbps and 622 Mbps have been standardized, though lower and higher speeds are possible. These access speeds are sufficient for any type of multimedia application with current compression technology.
2. Flexibility and QoS guarantees: ATM networks can support applications with very diverse traffic characteristics and communication requirements, which include bandwidth, delay constraints, and error sensitivity. ATDM allows dynamic bandwidth allocation for each application, while the connection-oriented service provided by ATM can reserve resources to guarantee the QoS of each application.
3. Scalability: Since the ATM protocol is not bandwidth dependent, and allows any application of arbitrary communication requirements (especially bandwidth) to share the same access point, ATM provides a very scalable architecture for customer premise equipment (CPE). Access bandwidth for each access point is not affected by the number of active users connected to the network.
4. Integration: The ATM protocol can simultaneously support multiple applications with diverse characteristics and requirements through the same access point. This is

crucial to the support of multimedia applications, because multiple virtual circuits may need to be set up concurrently. This also means that a single link to the B-ISDN is sufficient to support different applications (assuming this link has enough bandwidth) to distinct locations. This implies a tremendous simplification and cost savings over today's separate networking solutions for different applications.

5. Architecture: The point-to-point mesh physical topology employed by B-ISDN provides a much higher dedicated bandwidth for each user compared with networks such as FDDI and DQDB using shared media. Moreover, it allows the same architecture to be deployed as both a public and private networking solution, both running essentially the same protocol.

6. Efficiency: Since ATM employs statistical multiplexing for sharing transmission bandwidth, the statistical gain is significant when applications with high peak to average bandwidth ratio (i.e., bursty traffic) are multiplexed. Since a lot of the multimedia and collaborative applications tend to be very bursty, the resulting statistical gain implies very efficient sharing of transmission cost.

7. Standardization: ATM has grown out of the need for a worldwide standard to allow interoperability of information, regardless of the end system or type of information. With ATM, the goal is one international standard. There is an unprecedented level of acceptance throughout the industry of both the technology and the standardization process. With ATM, we are seeing an emerging technology being driven by international consensus, not by a single vendor's view or strategy. This ensures the growth of ATM and compatibility.

10.7.3 Network Performance Guarantees

The five elements of QoS guarantees described in Section 10.2 are all required to achieve performance guarantees at the network level. But at the network level, the requirements and resources are stated more specifically, as follows:

- QoS specification: we need to characterize the traffic to be delivered over the network and the functions and performance to be guaranteed. To facilitate QoS specification, traffic can be modified or shaped into a certain model.
- QoS negotiation: to determine a set of QoS parameters acceptable for both the application and the system with the aim of supporting as many applications as possible.
- Admission control: the network determines whether the requested traffic can be supported without affecting the performance of other traffic based on available resources.
- QoS guarantees and resource reservation: the network should reserve an appropriate amount of resources for each admitted connection to provide agreed QoS guarantees. The resources at the network level are link bandwidth and buffer or queue space in switches. Queues should be managed and scheduled properly so that the performance of accepted traffic can be guaranteed.
- Traffic policing: the network must monitor each individual connection of traffic to ensure that the data transmitted is within the agreed traffic specification.

Although we have so far focused on ATM-based networks, much work is underway to extend the widely deployed Internet to support multimedia applications. It is likely that ATM-based networks will use some Internet techniques, such as routing and multicast, and the Internet will use some ATM ideas to manage QoS. It may be possible that ATM networks and the Internet will merge into one network that can support all applications. We discuss Internet-based protocols in the next section.

10.8 MULTIMEDIA TRANSPORT PROTOCOLS

We discussed issues of network support for multimedia communication in the last section. These network technologies are necessary for supporting multimedia communications, but they alone are insufficient. Applications use the network through a transport protocol. It is no good if the network is capable of supporting multimedia communications but the transport protocol does not provide appropriate functions and performance to the applications. This section discusses design issues of multimedia transport protocols and reviews a number of proposed multimedia transport protocols. Since transport protocols rely on lower level protocols to perform certain functions, network layer protocols are also described. In a multimedia transport system, the network layer protocol is particularly important, as it performs resource reservation as well as routing and other functions. When we use the terms transport system, transport protocol stack, or communications system, we refer to the collection of transport protocol, lower level protocols, and the underlying network.

The discussion in this section is based on packet networks. For cell-based ATM networks, most transport functions should be incorporated into the AALs.

In Section 10.8.1, we discuss some of the main requirements of multimedia transport protocols. In Section 10.8.2, we explain why the traditional transport protocols TCP, TP4, and XTP are not suitable for multimedia communications.

Resource reservation protocols are required at the network layer to reserve necessary resources to meet the QoS requirements of applications. In Section 10.8.3, we describe two resource reservation protocols, ST-II and RSVP.

Protocols at the transport layer provide required services to applications by making use of network layer resource reservation protocols. In Section 10.8.4, we describe a real-time transport protocol (RTP). Section 10.8.5 briefly describes two multimedia communication protocols, HeiTP and the Tenet communication suite.

10.8.1 Requirements of Multimedia Transport Protocols

The basic function of any transport protocol is to provide the functions and services required by the application by using the lower level protocols and the underlying network. Readers who are unfamiliar with the functions and design issues of conventional transport protocols are referred to some good textbooks [48, 49]. This section looks at what is expected from transport protocols if they are to support multimedia communications.

A multimedia transport protocol differs from a conventional data transport protocol in that it should support QoS guarantees to multimedia applications. The transport protocol's function is to establish and maintain a connection[1] with QoS guarantees over the network and provide an interface to applications. Two main requirements are that the throughput of the protocol is high, and the interface provides a QoS specification guaranteed by low-layer protocols.

10.8.1.1 High Throughput

Multimedia data, especially video, requires sustained high-transmission bandwidth. For example, a compressed high-quality video requires a bandwidth of about 5 Mbps. The bandwidth requirement of uncompressed video is 50 to 100 times higher than this. All data goes through the transport stack, and thus the transport protocol should be fast enough to support the bandwidth requirements of the application. As an application may involve a number of datastreams, the transport protocol speed should be higher than the aggregate bandwidth requirement of these streams.

Another way to look at the throughput requirement of a transport protocol is in terms of the overall communications system. The throughput of a transport protocol should be higher than the network access speed. Otherwise, the bandwidth provided by the network access points cannot be fully used, and the transport protocol becomes the bottleneck of the overall communications system.

Protocols optimized for high speed but not supporting QoS guarantees are called lightweight or high-speed transport protocols. Good surveys of these protocols are found in [50, 51].

10.8.1.2 QoS Specification and Guarantee

Multimedia datastreams require end-to-end QoS guarantees in terms of bandwidth, delay, and delay jitter. To meet these requirements, a transport system must provide a mechanism for applications to specify and negotiate QoS requirements.

The QoS requirements specified to the transport protocol are passed to the network-layer protocol. The network-layer protocol, called the *reservation protocol*, propagates these requirements and reserves necessary resources along a network connection.

Part of the transport stack (including the transport protocol, network protocol, and other lower layer protocols) is implemented in software in *hosts*. The execution of this software is controlled by the *host operating system*. To guarantee the performance of the execution of the transport stack, an operating system (OS) that can provide QoS guarantees to multimedia applications is required, as discussed in Section 10.6.

10.8.2 Why Traditional Transport Protocols are not Suitable for Multimedia Communications

The most common transport protocols are TCP of the Internet protocol suite and TP4 of the OSI protocol suite [48, 49]. These protocols are designed for reliable data communications on low-bandwidth and high-error-rate networks. As a result, they are not optimized for high-speed operation. In addition, they lack QoS support. Thus they are unsuitable for multimedia communications [52]. In the following, we describe some

---

1. To provide QoS guarantee, a connection-oriented service is preferred.

aspects of these protocols that make them unsuitable for high-speed multimedia applications. Experience and lessons learned from these protocols help us in designing multimedia transport protocols.

10.8.2.1 Data Copying

The two major objectives of the OSI-RM and TCP/IP suites have been to break the problem of networking into simple manageable layers of functions, and to allow interoperability at the different levels of functionality of network protocols. High performance was clearly not among the objectives of layering protocols.

The nature of layered protocols presents an inherent bottleneck to communication. The raw data moves from one layer to another, where in each layer the data is processed again; typically, it is copied to a new address space in memory, and a new header or trailer or both are added. The dataframe is stored and forwarded by each layer. Such unnecessary copying contributes to network latency [53]. Data copying is time consuming because memory access is a relatively slow process compared with CPU speed, and every data byte must be moved for each instance of data copying.

The solution to this problem is to reduce the amount of data copying and to pass pointers between layers instead of actually copying data.

10.8.2.2 Flow Control

The common flow control mechanism is the sliding window flow control, which allows a fixed number of bytes (a *window* of bytes) to be transmitted, without needing confirmation or acknowledgment from the receiver. After this fixed number of bytes is transmitted, the transmitter transmits more data, only when the receiver permits it to do so, by sending an acknowledgment. The window size used by TCP is 64 kbytes. For a slow network, this window size is considered to be very large. For example, if the transmission speed is 64 kbps, it takes 8 sec to transmit 64 kbytes of data. The normal roundtrip delay is much shorter than 8 sec, so before the transmitter finishes transmitting the data of the current window, it receives an acknowledgment if the receiver buffer is not full, so that the transmitter can transmit data continuously.

For high-speed transmission, however, the sliding window flow control is not suitable. First, the window size is too small and the transmitter will be waiting for the transmission permission from the receiver most of the time. Thus the transmission bandwidth would not be fully used. For example, a transmitter will send 64 kbytes in 50 ms at a speed of 10 Mbps. For a WAN, the roundtrip delay is normally much larger than 50 ms. The partial solution to this problem is to use a larger window size [54, 55].

Second, with high-transmission speed, the bandwidth-delay product is very large. For example, for a transmission speed of 10 Mbps and roundtrip delay of 300 ms, the bandwidth-delay product is 3 Mbits. The slide window flow control is not effective any more with such a high bandwidth-delay product, because by the time the receiver detects a congestion condition and sends a warning to the transmitter, it is too late. Before the transmitter receives the warning, another few Mbits of data have been transmitted, causing congestion in the network and/or at the receiver. In other words, with a large bandwidth-delay product, the message received by the transmitter does not reflect the current status of the network and the receiver.

Finally and most importantly, this type of flow control mechanism itself is not suitable for multimedia data. Sliding window flow control assumes that the transmission bit rate is able to adapt to the network and receiver conditions. This is not possible for continuous media, which should be sent at their intrinsic data rate. For example, if an audio signal is sampled at 8,000 samples per second with 8 bits per sample, 8,000 sample values (perhaps with an acceptable small variation) must be transmitted and received every second for the receiver to have a smooth audio playback as discussed in Chapter 4. The network either supports this traffic fully or does not transmit at all. Intermittent data transmission and arrival of audio and video data are useless to real-time multimedia applications.

The more appropriate flow control mechanism for high-speed continuous data transmission is rate-based control. The transmitter, network, and receiver agree on a transmission bit rate in terms of average, peak rate, and so forth before data transmission. This bit rate is normally determined by the nature of the application. When the rate is accepted by all parties, the transmitter sends at this rate, the network provides certain guarantees to this traffic, and the receiver allocates sufficient resources to receive and present the data at the specified rate.

10.8.2.3 Error Control

The TCP and TP4 provide reliable data communication. When a packet is lost or corrupted, that packet is retransmitted. This strategy is not suitable for multimedia communications. First, multimedia data can tolerate some error or loss. Second, retransmission causes delay to the following data, resulting in more useless data at the receiver (late data is as useless as lost data for continuous media). Third, the implementation of the retransmission strategy requires a number of timers and large buffers, making the transport protocol complicated and slow.

For multimedia communications, error detection should be provided, and it should be up to the application to decide whether retransmission is needed. When retransmission is required, selective retransmission is better than the go-back-N strategy. In the selective retransmission, only lost packets or packets with errors are retransmitted. In the go-back-N technique, all packets from the last error or loss are retransmitted although most packets have been received correctly. For example, if the transmitter has sequentially sent packets 1 to 100 and the receiver detects that packet 30 is corrupted, then the transmitter must transmit all packets from 30 to 100 again. Go-back-N retransmission wastes bandwidth and introduces more delay to the following packets.

Another solution is to use forward error correction (FEC) code, in which extra information is sent to allow error correction at the receiver without the need for retransmission [56]. The drawback of this is that it consumes additional bandwidth.

10.8.2.4 Positioning and Handling of Control Information

All protocols operate by exchanging protocol state information, either by physically attaching that information to a packet with headers and/or trailers, or by sending specialized, nondata protocol control packets, or both. In either case, the protocol-state machine must parse the protocol control information to decode its contents.

Several factors affect the implementation complexity and protocol throughput. The first factor is whether the position of control information is fixed within every packet. Fixed position allows simpler implementation and higher throughput. The second factor is whether the control information is aligned to machine byte or word boundaries. Byte or word alignment allows faster implementation. The third factor is whether the packet structure is suitable for hardware implementation. In traditional transport protocols, most control information, including checksums, is attached to the packet header. If implemented in software, it makes little difference where the individual control information is placed. For example, if it is assumed that the checksum is calculated in software, then placing the transport data checksum in the header (as is done with TCP and TP4) is no more or less efficient than placing it anywhere else. Once the protocol has the full packet, the checksum is calculated by some algorithm and the resulting checksum is placed in the appropriate field. But what if the checksum is to be calculated in hardware rather than software? Then the position of the checksum field does affect the efficiency. If the data checksum is located in the trailer, then the packet can pass through a hardware checksum unit and the checksum can be attached to the trailer on the fly.

10.8.2.5 Lack of QoS Support

The above issues are mainly concerned with the efficiency and throughput of transport protocols. These issues can be addressed to some extent and high-speed transport protocols can be achieved by optimization, parallelism, and hardware implementation. Indeed, it is reported that a speed close to gigabits per second is achievable by optimizing the implementation of TCP [53, 55].

As previously noted, high speed is necessary, but other features such as QoS guarantees and multicast are required for multimedia communications. In TCP, there is no notion of QoS. TP4 allows QoS parameter negotiation, but the parameters are data-communication oriented and not sufficient or suitable for multimedia communications.

10.8.2.6 Suitability of eXpress Transport Protocol

The eXpress Transport Protocol (XTP) [57, 58] is a lightweight protocol. It has many features, such as high throughput, multicast, and selectable error control, flow control, and retransmission, which are suitable for multimedia communications. The major feature that the XTP lacks is QoS management. There is no mechanism in XTP to provide QoS specifications (except the maximum rate and burst specification) and QoS guarantees. Therefore XTP is not entirely suitable for multimedia communications.

10.8.3 Resource Reservation Protocols

To provide QoS guarantees, resource management techniques must be used. Without resource management in end systems, networks, and switches, multimedia systems cannot provide reliable quality of service to users. Transmission of multimedia data over unreserved resources (CPU processing cycles, network bandwidth, buffer space in switches and receivers) leads to delayed and dropped packets due to the unavailability of the required resources. Thus resource management plays an important role in multimedia communications systems. For this reason, a very important part of a multimedia communications system is the resource reservation protocol at the network layer. Note that, a resource reservation protocol performs no reservation of the required resources itself, it is only a vehicle to transfer information about resource requirements, and to negotiate the QoS values users desire for their end-to-end applications. Reservation protocols rely on resource administration functions in each subsystem to enforce and schedule resource accesses during the data transmission phase.

Although media scaling, which adjusts the amount of multimedia data according to the currently available system resources, is used in some systems, some sort of guarantee is still expected from the system. Media can be scaled only to some extent; they cannot be scaled arbitrarily. Multimedia communications systems should combine resource management and media scaling techniques to achieve the best service quality with a fixed amount of resources.

In this section, we describe the general principles and concepts of two resource reservation protocols, ST-II and RSVP, and provide a comparison of these two protocols.

10.8.3.1 ST-II

ST-II is an experimental Internet protocol designed in 1990 to transmit real-time data [59]. It is a successor of the ST protocol that was specified in 1979. ST-II has been implemented for audio and video communications in different networks [60, 61]. ST-II provides a connection-oriented service and supports multicast and QoS negotiation. Data can only be sent after a stream (a one-to-many connection, equivalent to a flow) has been established successfully. In the following, we discuss the connection setup procedure and flow specification.

ST-II Connection Setup

ST-II models connection setup and resource reservation as simplex datastreams rooted at the sources and extending to all receivers. Stream setup is initiated when a source ST agent generates a *Connect* packet listing the flow specification and an initial set of participants. Each intermediate ST agent processes the *Connect* packet to determine the set of next hop subnets required to reach all downstream receivers, installs multicast forwarding state, and reserves network-level resources along each next-hop subnet. Multiple targets are reached using the IP multicast algorithm [62]. If the actual resource allocation obtained along a subnet is less than the amount requested, this is noted in the *Connect* packet by updating the flow specification. Upon receiving a *Connect* indication, a receiver must determine whether it wishes to join the group, and return either an *Accept* or a *Refuse* message to the stream source. In the case of an *Accept*, the receiver may further reduce the resource request by updating the returned flow specification.

The stream source must wait for an *Accept* or *Refuse* reply from each initial receiver before beginning data transmission. ST-II treats the entire stream as a homogeneous distribution path. Whenever the source receives an *Accept* with a reduced flow specification, it must either adapt to the lower QoS for the entire stream, or reject group participation for the specific receiver by sending it a *Disconnect* message. All participants receive data with the same flow specification, although the display capabilities may differ from one receiver to another.

In the normal transmission case, where no router failure occurs, streams that were established using ST-II are served with a guaranteed QoS. However, ST-II just provides the mechanism to pass and negotiate QoS. The actual resource reservation and scheduling is not specified within ST-II. These have to be implemented in each ST-II agent.

As a connection-oriented protocol, ST-II performs routing decisions during connection setup. Data is not protected by checksums. Hence, the data transmission process is simple, leading to high throughput.

Flow Specification

The first step to achieve QoS guarantees is to specify the flow. The specification largely determines the final achievable QoS and system resource use. Figure 10.17 shows the flow specification used in ST-II. For a real-time connection, we are mainly interested in guaranteed bandwidth, delay and delay jitter upper bounds, and data error rate. In the ST-II flow specification, the minimum bandwidth is specified by the product of *LimitOnP-DUBytes* and *LimitOnPDURate*. The delay upper bound is specified by the parameter *LimitOnDelay*. There is no explicit parameter to specify the delay jitter upper bound. Theoretically, the jitter upper bound is equal to the delay upper bound. In practice, the parameter *AccDelayVariance* indicates the expected delay jitter. The upper layers determine whether this value is acceptable. Applications allocate delay-jitter-smoothing-buffer size based on this value. The maximum bit error rate is specified by the parameter *ErrorRate* and packet loss rate is indicated by the parameter *Reliability*. For a VBR application using ST-II, the most challenging task is to determine the minimum bandwidth required to support its QoS requirements without reserving excessive network resources.

bits: 0   16   31

PCode	PBytes	Version = 3	0
DutyFactor	ErrorRate	Precedence	Reliability
Tradeoffs		RecoveryTimeout	
LimitOnCost		LimitOnDelay	
LimitOnPDUBytes		LimitOnPDURate	
MinBytesXRate			
AccdMeanDelay			
AccdDelayVariance			
DesPDUBytes		DesPDURate	

Figure 10.17 ST-II flow specification.

10.8.3.2 RSVP

Reservation Protocol (RSVP) is at the network layer level but is not a complete network-layer protocol [60, 63, 64]. It reserves resources along the data path, but it is not responsible for data transfer. A companion protocol such as IP may be used for data transfer.

RSVP is similar to ST-II in that a datastream is modeled as a simplex distribution tree rooted at the source and extending to all receivers. However, the mechanisms of resource reservation and the reservation styles supported differ substantially from the ST-II model.

In RSVP, a source application begins participation in a group by sending a *Path* message containing a flow specification to the destination multicast address. The *Path* message serves two purposes: to distribute the flow specification to the receivers, and to establish the *Path* state in intermediate RSVP agents to be used in propagating reservation requests toward a specific source. RSVP does not restrict a source from transmitting data even when no receiver has installed a reservation for it; however, data service guarantees are not enforced.

Before establishing a reservation, each receiver must first join the associated multicast group to begin receiving *Path* messages. This multicast group-joining operation is a function of the multicast routing protocol and is outside the scope of RSVP. Each receiver may use information from *Path* messages and any local knowledge (computing resources available, application requirements, cost constraints) to determine its QoS requirements; it is then responsible for initiating its own *Reservation* request message.

Intermediate RSVP agents reserve network resources along the subnet leading toward the receiver and use the established *Path* state to propagate the *Reservation* request toward the group sender(s). *Reservation* message propagation ends as soon as the reservation "splices" into an existing distribution tree with sufficient resources allocated to meet the requested QoS requirements. When receivers' QoS requirements differ from (normally by being lower than) the source flow specification, traffic filters are used to reduce the QoS requirements at appropriate RSVP agents. For example, if a receiver is only capable of displaying black-and-white pictures, and the source is delivering data for color pictures, a filter is used to remove the color components. The filter may also combine several datastreams into one before sending to the receiver. The purpose of filtering is to save network bandwidth. This receiver-initiated reservation style enables RSVP to accommodate heterogeneous receiver requirements.

Since RSVP does not transfer data itself, a mechanism to associate the reserved route with data transmission is needed. It is not very clear how this can be done effectively to guarantee QoS of data transmission [60].

10.8.3.3 Comparison of ST-II and RSVP

Although both ST-II and RSVP have a common goal of providing multiparty communication with QoS guarantees, they have many differences.

Their first major difference is in their approaches to reservation initiation. In ST-II, the reservation is initiated by the sender transmitting a flow specification to the receivers. During the propagation of the flow specification from the sender to the receivers, some flow specification parameters are modified based on the available resources on the path. The final flow specification to be used by the sender for data transmission has the minimum resource requirements that are agreed on by all receivers and the network agents. After a flow is established, all receivers receive the data with the same flow specification regardless of their capabilities.

In RSVP, the reservation is initiated by the receivers. Each receiver determines the required QoS parameters based on the types of information to be received (obtained from the *Path* messages) and its available resources.

The implication of this difference is that RSVP is more efficient in network resource use for the following reasons. First, in RSVP, each receiver just receives the amount of data it needs, so there are no resources wasted. Second, the flow in ST-II is a one-to-many connection starting from a particular sender. If more than one sender needs to transmit data, each sender has to establish a one-to-many connection. So each receiver may have multiple connections, one for each sender. These connections reserve resources but may not be active all the times, wasting resources. In RSVP, a flow is a many-to-many connection. Each receiver just needs one connection to receive data from multiple senders. This connection can be used by different senders in turn or in combination. For applications such as a videoconferencing where not all senders are active at the same time, RSVP allows very efficient use of network resources, especially when the multicast group is large.

The efficiency gained by RSVP is based on the assumption that filters performing media scaling and mixing are installed in the network nodes. The implementation of these filters may not be easy. First, unless there are a very small number of media standards commonly accepted by all users, many different types of filters are required in the network nodes. There are suggestions that filters can be provided by senders or receivers during the resource reservation phase, but the exact mechanism to achieve this is not clear. Second, for real-time applications, filters must perform their functions in real time. This may be difficult as some filtering functions are computationally very intensive, and network switches are already normally heavily loaded. To some extent, we can argue that RSVP reduces network bandwidth requirements by requiring more processing power from the network nodes. Nevertheless, the efficiency argument is important, especially in the resource-scarce Internet. For this reason, RSVP now seems more prominent.

The second difference between ST-II and RSVP is in their positions or roles in the protocol stack. ST-II is a full internetwork protocol that contains data-handling as well as resource reservation functions. It replaces IP at the internetwork layer. RSVP, on the other hand, is a companion protocol to IP that controls routing and data transmission. The advantage of the RSVP approach is that RSVP can work with different routing and data transmission protocols. But the problem is how to ensure that other protocols, such as IP, can use the resources reserved by RSVP. As IP is connectionless, different packets may be routed through different paths. If this is the case, QoS for these IP packets may not be guaranteed.

The third difference is in the way connection state information is managed. ST-II is a connection-oriented protocol that requires corresponding state information for connections to be held by each participating node. Similar to ST-II, RSVP stores on each participating node information about existing streams. However, this information is "soft-state," which means that state information is kept on a timeout basis and needs periodic refreshing.

To summarize, ST-II and RSVP take different approaches to resource reservation. RSVP may use network resources more efficiently, especially when the multicast group is large. However, many issues related to RSVP implementation, such as flow specification by receivers, filtering, and integration with other protocols remain to be solved. These issues are being actively investigated by a group within the Internet Engineering Task Force (IETF) and other researchers [72].

10.8.4 Real-time Transport Protocol (RTP)

RTP is being developed by the Audio/Video Transport group within the IETF [65]. Its aim is to provide end-to-end, real-time communication over the Internet. Note that it provides a data transport function and is called a *transport protocol*, but it is currently often used on top of UDP, which is a connectionless transport protocol. To provide QoS guarantees, RTP should operate on top of a resource reservation protocol such as ST-II. The relationships among these protocols are shown in Figure 10.18.

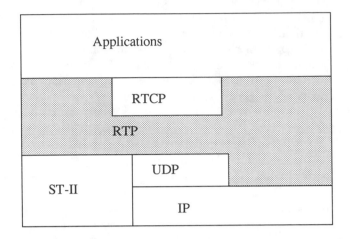

Figure 10.18 Relationship among RTP and other protocols.

There is no notion of a connection in RTP. It can work on both connection-oriented and connectionless lower-layer protocols. RTP consists of two parts: a data part and a control part. Application data is carried in RTP data packets. The RTP control (RTCP) packets provide some control and identification functions.

RTP offers no reliability mechanisms, as they are likely to be inappropriate for real-time applications. Data packet order is not maintained; the receiver must reorder data packets based on the sequence number. If an application needs reliability, the receiver can detect packet loss based on sequence number and ask for retransmission if required. In addition, a data checksum can be included in the application-dependent header extension to check data integrity. Features of RTP suitable for multimedia applications are:

1. It is a lightweight protocol, thus high throughput can be achieved. There is no error control and flow control mechanism, though the sender can adjust the transmission rate based on the feedback information provided by the control packets.
2. Time stamp and SSRC (synchronization source identifier) information can be used to realize intramedia and intermedia synchronization for multimedia applications.
3. Multicast is possible if lower layers provide multicast routers.
4. RTP specifies connection QoS through a traffic profile. It assumes that there are a number of predefined traffic profiles that define QoS requirements for typical applications. For example, if the profile specified is "telephone audio," the parameters stored in the profile may look like this: bit rate = 64 kbps, maximum delay = 100 ms, and maximum error rate = 0.01.

10.8.5 Other Multimedia Transport Protocols: HeiTP and Tenet

The Heidelberg transport protocol (HeiTP) is designed to run on top of ST-II for multimedia communications over the Internet [61, 66]. It is a connection-oriented protocol;

connections may be one-to-one full-duplex or one-to-many simplex. Although one-to-many full-duplex connections are not provided, the flow of the HeiTP control message is always bidirectional, so that targets are allowed to send control information back to the origin. Transport connections and ST-II network connections have a one-to-one relationship (i.e., only one transport datastream is allowed to use a network connection). This is suitable for multimedia communications because different streams may have different QoS requirements and should thus use different network connections with different QoS guarantees. HeiTP relies on ST-II to achieve one-to-many multicast functionality.

The Tenet Group in the Computer Science Division of the University of California at Berkeley and the International Computer Science Institute have developed a real-time communications protocol suite [67-70]. It consists of a number of data delivery protocols and control protocols. The protocol suite provides packet-based data delivery services with guaranteed delay and jitter bounds, bandwidth, and bounded packet loss.

The original Tenet protocol suite, called Tenet Suite 1, supports one-to-one communication only [67]. The Tenet Suite 1 has been extended to support multicast services [71]. The extended suite is called Tenet Suite 2.

10.9 Achieving Overall Synchronous Presentation

Synchronization is defined as the correct or desired temporal appearance (presentation) of the media items. Thus the ultimate goal of multimedia communications is to achieve synchronization. A synchronization scheme defines mechanisms used to achieve the required synchronization.

The correct or desired temporal appearance of the media items in a multimedia application has three meanings when used in different situations. When used for a single time-continuous stream, it means that audio samples or videoframes must be played out at fixed intervals, as this is required to achieve the desired effect. When used to describe temporal relationships among multiple mediastreams, it means that desired temporal relationships between media must be maintained. In some multimedia applications, interactivity is an important feature. When used in this type of application, it means that the right response should be provided in a relatively short time to achieve reasonably good interaction. Therefore, there are three types of synchronization in multimedia applications:

- Intramedia synchronization—to ensure continuous media are played at their fixed rate. It is sometimes called *intrastream synchronization* or *serial synchronization*. It can be thought of as the synchronization between data consumption rate at the receiver, and the rate at which data is recorded or generated at the transmitter.
- Intermedia synchronization—to maintain temporal relationships between media involved in an application. In the literature, it is sometimes called *interstream synchronization* or *parallel synchronization*.
- Interaction synchronization—to ensure that the right event (response) happens in a reasonably short time. This is also called *event synchronization*.

The main work in multimedia synchronization is divided into two categories. Work in the first category has focused on methods for specifying temporal relationships between media. Work in the second category has attempted to find mechanisms to meet the specified temporal relationships by overcoming variable processing and transmission delays, and handling anomalous situations.

Achieving multimedia synchronization is the ultimate goal of multimedia communications, so synchronization requirements are the overall QoS requirements of applications. Mechanisms of multimedia support discussed in previous sections are needed to meet the QoS requirements. When the QoS paradigm is used and all subsystems or components provide QoS guarantees, synchronization is achieved easily, as described in Section 10.9.4.

However, not all proposed synchronization schemes are based on the QoS paradigm. Many are ad hoc schemes addressing a particular synchronization problem. There are two major reasons for this situation. First, subsystems including end systems and transport systems that guarantee QoS are not yet widely available. Second, there are some issues, such as synchronization of clocks in the distributed end systems, that need to be addressed specifically for achieving synchronization.

In Section 10.9.1, we briefly review principles and methods for specifying temporal relationships. The purpose of this review is to provide pointers to the rich literature in this area.

Section 10.9.2 analyzes the main causes of losing synchronization. In Section 10.9.3, we look at mechanisms used to counter the causes of losing synchronization.

The general synchronization scheme is based on the QoS paradigm and relies on the support of all subsystems as discussed in the previous chapters. In Section 10.9.4 we describe a multimedia synchronization solution assuming that QoS requirements are guaranteed by all subsystems.

10.9.1 Synchronization Specification

The aim of the synchronization specification is to effectively represent temporal and spatial relationships between multimedia objects. We only focus on temporal relationships in this section. Many temporal specification methods have been proposed [73-75]. In the following we briefly describe three specification techniques: scripts, time-line-based, and petri nets.

10.9.1.1 Scripts

A script uses a structured language to specify temporal relationships among related media. (In addition to temporal relationships, spatial relationships can also be specified using a script, but we will not consider spatial synchronization in this book.) Scripts are powerful and can be used to specify all types of relationships and user interactions. The weakness of scripts is that the specification may be complicated and difficult for nonprogrammers to use. The following is an example of a simple script specifying a slide show:

```
Script slide-show
{
Parallel
```

319

```
      Display picture1.jpg For 5 Seconds
      Display audio1.au For 5 Seconds
Parallel
      Display picture2.jpg For 6 Seconds
      Display audio2.au For 7 Seconds
Parallel
      Display picture3.jpg For 10 Seconds
      Display audio3.au For 10 Seconds
}
```

The first line in the example specifies the name of the script. Parallel, Display, For and Seconds are keywords of the script. *Parallel* specifies that the following statements are executed in parallel. *Display* and *For* are self-explanatory. A parallel structure completes when all statements within it complete. So in the second parallel structure of the example, the audio continues to play for 1 sec after the display of picture 2 has ended. The third parallel structure starts when audio 2 completes.

10.9.1.2 Time-Line-Based Temporal Specification

In a time-line-based (also called track-based) temporal specification, the presentation time of each stream is specified relative to a common clock. Streams are treated as independent. Removal of one or more streams does not affect the synchronization of the other streams. Synchronization is achieved by ensuring that each stream is presented at its specified time relative to the common clock. An example of time-line-based specification is shown in Figure 10.19, which specifies that stream 1 should be presented at time $t1$ and end at time $t4$, stream 2 starts at time $t2$ and ends at time $t3$, and stream 3 starts at time $t2$ and ends at time $t4$. Note that the term *stream* is used generally to refer to both continuous and static media.

The advantage of the time-line-based specification is that it is simple and easy to use. It is also easy to implement, because streams are treated independently during execution. The weakness of the time-line-based specification is that it cannot specify user interactions or streams with unpredictable duration.

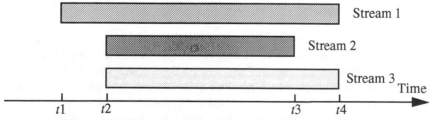

Figure 10.19 An example of time-line-based specification.

320

10.9.1.3 Petri Nets

Petri nets are directed graphs and are commonly used to model concurrent systems. Little and Ghafoor extended petri nets into object composition petri nets (OCPNs) to specify temporal relationships [76]. There are three basic types of elements in an OCPN (Figure 10.20): a set of transitions (bars), a set of places (circles), and a set of directed arcs (arrows). A place normally contains a logical data unit (LDU) with a specific active duration. When all input places of a transition complete their durations, the transition fires and all output places are activated. Figure 9.3 shows the OCPN specification of the slide show example of Section 10.9.1.1.

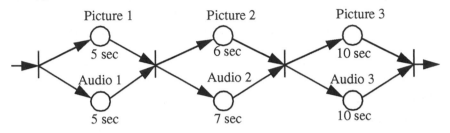

Figure 10.20 An example of an OCPN specification.

The strength of the OCPN is that it can specify all kinds of temporal relationships and user interactions. The drawback of the OCPN is the complexity of the specification.

10.9.2 Analysis of Causes of Losing Multimedia Synchronization

We examine causes of losing multimedia synchronization and reasons why synchronization is difficult to achieve. After we understand these causes, it is easy for us to discuss corrective or preventive measures to synchronize multimedia presentations. We examine these causes by looking at each component or subsystem of an entire multimedia communications system. Note that the following discussion is very similar to the discussion of end-to-end QoS guarantee requirements in Section 10.1. The causes of losing synchronization again highlight the need for QoS guarantees at all system components. In Section 10.9.4, we outline a synchronization scheme when systemwide QoS guarantees are provided.

In a retrieval application, the receiver (client) sends information requests to the respective information sources (servers). The requested information is retrieved from the secondary storage under the control of the storage device manager. This information is normally in compressed form. At the receiver's side, this data is passed to the transport stack for depacketization before it is decoded for presentation. Now let us look for all possible causes of losing synchronization in each stage of the communication process.

For retrieval applications, the information request packets may experience different amounts of delay on the paths from the client to the servers, especially when information sources (servers) are at different locations. This causes difficulty in coordinating transmission time for different mediastreams. Usually, the secondary storage is shared among many processes. Some scheduling mechanisms are needed to retrieve the required amount of data within the fixed time intervals, as discussed in Section 10.4.

The next stage is the transport stack, including packetization and protocol processing. Both packetization and protocol processing take varying amounts of time, causing delay jitter and intermedia skew.

Next we consider network transmission. This stage consists of network access time, packet transmission time, and buffering time at switches or gateways. All these times vary from packet to packet and from time to time, causing delay jitter within a stream and skew between streams.

At the receiver (client) side, depacketization time and protocol processing times vary for different packets. The decoding times for different media are different. If a software decoder is used, decoding time varies from time to time even for the same stream. All these factors will cause delay jitter within a stream and skew between streams.

So far we have considered individual subsystems causing asynchrony. There are other possible causes of losing synchronization:

1. The clock rates at the transmitter and the receiver might be different. If the clock rate is faster at the transmitter than at the receiver, the transmitter sends more data than the receiver can consume, causing data overflow at the receiver. On the other hand, if the clock rate is slower at the transmitter than at the receiver, the receiver has a data-starvation problem. Both situations are undesirable, because they will affect the smooth playout of continuous media. In addition, in many-to-one applications, if clock rates at the different sources are different, data transmission rates at these sources is difficult to coordinate, causing intermedia synchronization problems at the sink.
2. When a connectionless transport protocol is used or when an aggregate of bandwidth larger than a single channel bandwidth is required, packets belonging to a stream may arrive at the receiver out of order.
3. When multiple sources are involved, it may be difficult to coordinate the stream transmission times at different locations.
4. Interaction is an important feature of multimedia systems. So it is important to maintain synchronization during and after interactions. For example, when a presentation is resumed after pausing for some time, the presentation should be resumed synchronously. Synchronization is complicated by user interactions.
5. In addition to the above causes, there may be other anomalies, such as data starvation due to momentary network congestion.

Based on above discussion, the possible causes of losing synchronization are summarized as follows:

1. Information-requesting packets may experience different amounts of delay;
2. Secondary storage devices may not meet the bandwidth and delay requirements of continuous media;
3. Packetization and protocol processing times may vary for different packets;
4. Network transmission times may vary for different packets;
5. Depacketization and protocol processing times may vary;
6. Decoding times for different streams may vary;

7. If a software decoder is used, decoding time may vary from time to time within a stream;
8. The clocks used in transmitters and receivers may have different rates;
9. Packets may arrive at the receiver out of order when transmitted over packet-switched networks;
10. It may be difficult to coordinate packet transmission times when multiple sources are involved;
11. User interaction may cause problems for synchronization;
12. Some other anomalies, such as data starvation and overflow, may still happen after measures are taken against the above causes.

Some of the above causes can be combined into more general ones. Causes 3, 5, and 7 are due to host software processing. We group them together and call this group *variation of host processing time*. We discuss countermeasures to these causes under the heading "Workstation Support." Cause 6 is due to different amounts of processing time determined by the nature of the medium and coding method employed. We call it *media specific processing skew*. This skew is fixed for a pair of media when coding methods to be used are decided. Cause 1, *delay variation of information requesting packets*, consists of protocol processing and network transmission delay variations. Thus it is a combination of other causes. It is implicitly considered when other causes are considered.

In the next section, we discuss corrective and preventive measures used to counter causes listed above.

10.9.3 Mechanisms to Achieve Multimedia Synchronization

10.9.3.1 Measures to Counter Network Delay Variations

The network delay variation or jitter, if not smoothed out, affects both intramedia and intermedia synchronization; that is, it causes intermedia skew and jitter in the playout of continuous media. Delay jitter is a fundamental characteristic of a packet-switched network. Measures to counter delay jitter are divided into two groups: *corrective* and *preventive*. Corrective measures do nothing to the transport protocol and underlying network. They try to smooth out the jitter at the destination before media data is presented to the user. Preventive measures try to minimize delay and delay jitter by improving the transport protocol and underlying networks, as discussed in Sections 10.7 and 10.8.

Corrective Measures

Delay jitter is caused by many factors, such as packet processing time differences, network access time differences, and queuing delay differences. Delay jitter can be removed with a first-in first-out (FIFO) buffer at the destination before playing. Arriving packets are placed in this buffer at a variable rate; the display device removes samples in the buffer at fixed intervals determined by the nature of the medium. The principle of this buffering technique is to add a variable amount of delay to each packet so that overall delay for each packet from source to sink is the same (Figure 10.21). For this reason, it is often called a *delay-equalizing buffer*. In the figure, the processing blocks include all operations carried out at the end systems. Suppose a packet experiences delay (excluding delay-equalizing buffer time) ranging from the minimum $d$min to the maximum $d$max. If a packet experiencing a delay d is buffered for a time ($d$max - d), each packet has the same total delay of $d$max. In other words, if the client starts displaying data $d$max seconds after it is sent, each packet will be played on time, assuming the playout rate is the same as the data generation rate. This buffering strategy is very important and is used in almost all systems that attempt to smooth delay variations.

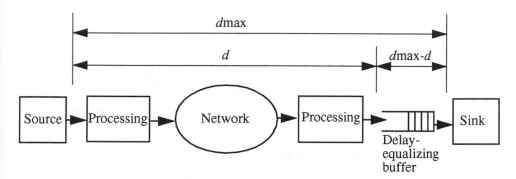

Figure 10.21 A conceptual multimedia system with a delay-equalizing buffer.

In this buffering scheme, the maximum required buffering time for a packet is ($d$max - $d$min), which is the maximum delay jitter. The larger the delay jitter, the larger the buffer requirement. The appropriate values for $d$max, $d$min and actual packet delay d are determined using a number of heuristic methods [77].

When multiple streams are used in an application, to achieve intermedia synchronization in spite of the existence of delay jitter, a multimedia virtual circuit (MVC) [78] and synchronization marker (SM) [79] are used. In the MVC scheme, all related datastreams are multiplexed and share the same channel. In this way, data transmitted at the same time arrives at the receiver at the same time for presentation, thus achieving intermedia synchronization. In the SM scheme, different streams use different connections. Data packets of different streams transmitted at the same time are stamped using the same time mark. At the receiver, earlier arrivals are buffered before they are presented, until all packets with the same time mark arrive. The limitation of these two schemes is that they cannot be applied to cases where more than one information source is involved.

To synchronize streams from multiple sources, their transmission times have to be coordinated. This requires a common time base. One solution is to have a network synchronous clock [80], discussed in Section 10.9.3.3. The other solution is to base all packet transmission and presentation times on the common sink's clock [74].

Preventive Measures: Network and Transport Support for Continuous Media

The above schemes use buffers to smooth network delay jitter without considering the transport protocol or underlying network. When delay jitter is too large, corrective measures are not very useful, because they require a large buffer and long buffering time, which is not appropriate for many applications. A general solution is to use the network and transport protocol support mechanisms as discussed in Sections 10.7 and 10.8. With these mechanisms, delay and delay jitter are bounded. The delay jitter within the bound is smoothed out simply by providing a small buffer, so that the total end-to-end delay of each packet is equal to the delay upper bound. A scheme based on this idea is discussed in Section 10.9.4.

10.9.3.2 Measures to Counter Media-Specific Processing Skew

Media processing skew is fixed for a pair of mediastreams when coding methods are decided. Therefore, this skew can be overcome by buffering the mediastream with less processing time for a period equal to the processing time difference before presentation.

10.9.3.3 Measures to Counter Clock Rate Difference

A synchronized network clock is required for the following reasons:

1. Data transmission and consumption rates are normally based on the local clock rates. A clock rate difference between the transmitter and receiver causes either data overflow or data starvation at the receiver, if the clock rate difference is significant. Of course, this also depends on the length of the mediastream because the effect is cumulative. When the length is relatively short, the effect of a clock rate difference is not significant. For example, if the rate difference is 50 parts per million (ppm), then for a communication of 5 min, the accumulated drift is 15 ms, which may not affect the smooth playback. However, if the duration is 2 hours, the length of a typical movie, then the accumulated drift is 360 ms (the equivalent in time of about 10 videoframes), which will very likely cause either data overflow or starvation, depending on which clock is faster.
2. In a many-to-one applications, if the clock rates of sources are significantly different, the receiver has problems synchronizing streams from these sources. At least one of the streams has data overflow or starvation problems as explained in 1.
3. In a many-to-one application, to synchronize streams from multiple sources, it is normally necessary to coordinate the transmission times of these streams. The coordination requires a common time base.
4. Time stamps are commonly used to measure transmission delay, as used in the techniques to smooth network delay jitter discussed earlier. To compare the packet transmission time and arrival time, a common time base is required.

To solve problems 1 and 2, we require that the clock rates of sources and sinks be the same or very close. However, to solve problems 3 and 4, we require that the clock readings as well as clock rates be the same between sources and sinks.

Problem 1 has been encountered since packet voice and video were introduced. The common solution is to adapt the receiver clock frequency to the transmitter's by a digital phase lock loop (DPLL) [81, 82]. But this only works for constant-bit-rate-coded streams. For variable-bit-rate-coded streams, it is difficult to synchronize the clock rates based on packet arrival rate. To minimize the effect of this clock discrepancy, the receiver may have to intelligently skip or repeat some packets. This is mentioned later. For problem 2, the receiver can lock onto one of the transmitter's clock rates. This is normally the transmitter that handles the most time-sensitive stream, such as audio. The data from the other streams are either skipped or repeated to keep intermedia synchronization with the most time sensitive stream.

For problems 3 and 4, a synchronized network clock is required. The most well-known network time synchronization protocol is the network time protocol (NTP) [83]. In NTP, there are two types of time servers: the primary time server and the secondary time server. The time in the primary servers is directly synchronized to external reference sources such as timecode receivers, which receive standard time information from radio or satellite broadcast stations. The secondary servers synchronize to the primary servers by exchanging messages. Special algorithms are used to minimize the effect of delay jitter. It is now possible to synchronize clocks to within a few milliseconds.

10.9.3.4 Measures to Counter Packet-Out-of-Order Problems

It is desirable to use a connection-oriented service so that required QoS parameters are negotiated before the transmission starts. However, due to the lack of availability of this kind of transport protocol, many current research projects [74, 84] use connectionless services (such as UDP). The reasons why UDPs are chosen rather than TCP are as follows: TCP reliability and flow control mechanisms are not appropriate for continuous media communications. Occasional packet loss causes only a small and acceptable reduction in presentation quality, while allowing time for retransmission would cause a longer playback delay and delay jitter, making interactive conversation and smooth play-out more difficult. Flow control is not required because packets are generated at a regular rate and must be communicated and consumed at that rate. Another reason for choosing UDP is that it works well with IP multicast to reach many destinations, while TCP is limited (so far at least) to point-to-point connections.

When an unreliable connectionless service is used, packets may arrive at the receiver out of order or duplicated. The common approach to this problem is to attach a sequence number to each packet when it is transmitted. At the receiver side, packets are reordered according to the sequence number and duplicated packets are discarded.

10.9.3.5 Measures to Coordinate Multiple Sources for Synchronous Transmission

When applications need to retrieve information from distributed multiple sources for presentation to one user, media retrieval and transmission times must be coordinated. There are two approaches. The first approach relies on a network synchronous clock. One station acts as the coordinator to control retrieval and transmission times.

In the second approach, no network synchronous clock is required. The client initiates the retrieval and transmission of different media based on the playout schedule [74]. All retrieval times and transmission times are relative to the common client clock. The roundtrip delay jitter is compensated for by the use of the control time.

10.9.3.6 Workstation and Server Support for Continuous Media

Workstation support considers aspects of the hardware architecture of the workstation, the operating system, and storage management. The main issues are to specify QoS or synchronization requirements at this level, and the workstation or server should meet the requirements. We have discussed these issues in previous sections. With this support, delay and delay jitter within end systems are bounded.

10.9.3.7 Measures to Provide User Interaction Synchronization

To provide user interaction, the main concerns are response time, interactivity, and maintenance of synchronization after an interaction (e.g., how to resume synchronous playout after a pause).

System response time is the sum of the delays of all subsystems. This total delay should be specified at the start of the application and met collaboratively among all subsystems.

Interactivity depends on synchronization specification models. To maintain synchronization after interaction, a proper retrieval and playout strategy is needed. In Section 10.4, we discuss how to resume video playing synchronously after a pause. A similar strategy should be used for other media and other interactions.

10.9.3.8 Playout Techniques to Achieve Optimal Presentation Effects

After taking all of the above measures, there is still a chance that the receiver will have data starvation or overflow problems, or difficulty in maintaining intermedia synchronization for reasons such as wrong estimation of control time. The common solution to this problem is to skip or repeat some data units as appropriate so that the quality of the presentation is degraded gracefully. Since human perception is more sensitive to audio jitter, the common practice is to play out audio as smoothly as possible while skipping or repeating videoframes to keep intermedia synchronization. Also note that which frame to skip depends on the compression technique used. For example, the reference frames I and P are more important than nonreference frames B in MPEG streams, so I- and P-frames are normally not skipped, because their absence will affect the decoding of many frames.

As the case may allow, the other solution is to modify QoS requirements to change the pace of data delivery so that synchronization is maintained, or QoS is degraded gracefully.

10.9.4 An Ultimate Solution Based on QoS Framework

We have examined synchronization requirements, causes of losing synchronization, and mechanisms to counter these causes to achieve synchronization. Most of these mechanisms are ad hoc and application specific. The general approach to achieving networked multimedia synchronization should be based on a QoS paradigm and relies on the mechanisms of multimedia support discussed in the previous sections. The integration of these mechanisms provides end-to-end QoS guarantees required for multimedia communication. With this support, it is also easier to achieve a network synchronous clock as delay and delay jitter are bounded.

In the following, we summarize a synchronization scheme when end-to-end QoS guarantees are provided:

1. No matter how synchronization is specified, the specification is transformed into a timeline presentation, in which each medium and its logical units have a specified presentation time relative to the common timeline with certain skew tolerance. The presentation schedule is a series of *{data unit, presentation time ±tolerance}* pairs.
2. For each stream, a connection is negotiated with the file server, operating system, and transport system, and is set up with agreed QoS.
3. With these QoS guarantees, each stream starts transmitting T seconds before its presentation time; T being the upper delay bound for that stream connection. Each packet is time-stamped and buffered for a period equal to T minus the actual packet delay before being presented. The transmitter sends at the fixed presentation rate requested by the receiver. Transmission rate and presentation rate are matched easily when a network synchronous clock is present. In this case, both intermedia and intramedia synchronization are achieved.
4. Event (interaction) synchronization is achieved in a similar way to that above. The only difference is that the presentation starts at some specified position rather than at the beginning of the multimedia document or object.
5. Each stream is treated independently for a simple implementation. When abnormalities such as data starvation and overflow happen to a stream, certain corrective actions such as skipping and repeat are taken, to keep to the presentation schedule.

PROBLEMS

Problem 10.1

In a distributed multimedia system, audio samples and video frames should be played out at their fixed rate. This property is called isochrony. But data arriving at the client suffers different transmission delay jitter. Explain what the receiver can do to remove the delay variation to maintain isochrony of audio and video.

Problem 10.2

Explain why an end-to-end throughput guarantee is required for multimedia applications.

Problem 10.3

Describe the major differences between multimedia systems and critical real-time systems.

Problem 10.4

List the performance-critical subsystems in a multimedia information retrieval system and explain why they are critical.

Problem 10.5

What is QoS? Why is the concept of QoS important in distributed multimedia systems? What are the main elements required to provide QoS guarantees?

Problem 10.6

Among the five levels of RAID, discuss which level is most suitable for multimedia information retrieval applications.

Problem 10.7

Compare the disk-scheduling schemes Scan, EDF, Scan-EDF, round-robin, and GSS in terms of their seek time, startup delay, and buffer requirements.

Problem 10.8

Discuss how pause and resume operations are implemented.

Problem 10.9

Data copying exacerbates the bus bottleneck problem and reduces effective operating speed. Discuss the data-copying problem and solutions to this problem.

Problem 10.10

Discuss the advantages and disadvantages of the dedicated MNI approach to multimedia workstation development.

Problem 10.11

Among the RM, EDF, and TDRM scheduling disciplines for operating systems, discuss which is the most suitable for multimedia application scheduling.

Problem 10.12

Explain why CSMA/CD is not suitable for high-speed multimedia communications where QoS guarantees are required.

Problem 10.13

Discuss the main network characteristics suitable for multimedia communications.

Problem 10.14

Describe the operating principle of ATM. Discuss why it is potentially suitable for multimedia communications.

Problem 10.15

What is flow control? What is sliding window flow control? Why is sliding window flow control not suitable for high-speed multimedia communications?

Problem 10.16

QoS guarantees are needed for multimedia communications. What network and protocol components are needed to provide these guarantees?

Problem 10.17

Are the flow specification parameters used in ST-II adequate for most traffic types? If they are not adequate, what else is needed? Use examples to support your argument.

Problem 10.18

What is multimedia synchronization? Describe the three most important causes of losing synchronization.

Problem 10.19

The most common method to remove packet-delay variations is to use a *buffer*. Elaborate on this method and discuss how to determine the buffering time of each packet and buffer size.

Problem 10.20

Assuming QoS can be guaranteed by the network, transport protocols, end systems and storage server, design a synchronization scheme for distributed multimedia information systems.

REFERENCES

[1] Vogel, A. et al., "Distributed Multimedia and QoS: A Survey," *IEEE Multimedia*, Vol. 2, No.2, pp.10–18, 1995.

[2] Nahrstedt, K., and R. Steinmetz, "Resource Management in Networked Multimedia Systems," *Computer*, pp. 52–63, May 1995.

[3] Campbell, A., et al., "A Quality of Service Architecture," *Computer Communication Review*, Vol. 24, no.2, pp. 6–27, 1994.

[4] Nahrstedt, K., and J. M. Smith, "The QoS Broker," *IEEE Multimedia*, Vol. 2, No. 1, pp. 53–67, Spring 1995.

[5] Knightly, E., and H. Zhang, "Traffic Characterization and Switch Utilization Using Deterministic Bounding Interval Dependent Traffic Models," *Proceedings of IEEE INFOCOM '95*, Boston, MA, April 1995, pp. 1,137–1,145.

[6] Knightly, E., "H-BIND: A New Approach to Providing Statistical Performance Guarantees to VBR Traffic," *Proceedings of IEEE INFOCOM '96*, San Francisco, CA, Mar. 1996. Also available at URL: <ftp://tenet-berkeley.edu/pub/telenet/Papers/Knightly96.ps>

[7] Lu, G., and C. Kang, "An Efficient Communication Scheme for Media On-Demand Services with Hard QoS Guarantees," *Journal of Network and Computer Applications*, Vol.21, No. 1, Jan. 1998, pp. 1 -15

[8] Patterson, D., G. Gibson, and R. Katz, "A Case for Redundant Arrays of Inexpensive Disks (RAID)," *Proceedings of the ACM SIGMOD Conference*, June 1988, pp. 109–116.

[9] Gemmell, D. J., et al., "Multimedia Storage Servers, A Tutorial," *IEEE Computer*, May 1995, pp. 40–49.

[10] Federighi, C. and L. A. Rowe, "A Distributed Hierarchical Storage Manager for a Video-on-Demand System," *Proceedings of the Conference on Storage and Retrieval for Image and Video Databases II*, San Jose, CA, SPIE Proceeding Vol. 2185, Feb. 1994, pp. 185–197.

[11] Doganata, Y. N., and A. N. Tantawi, "Making a Cost-Effective Video Server," *IEEE Multimedia*, Vol. 1, No. 4, pp. 22–30, Winter 1994.

[12] Liu, Z., P. Nain, and N. Niclause, "Static Caching of Web Servers", *Proceedings of SPIE International Conference on Multimedia Computing and Networking*, Jan. 26-28 1998, San Jose, California, pp. 179-190.

[13] Tewari, R., et al., "Resource-based Caching for Web Servers," *Proceedings of SPIE International Conference on Multimedia Computing and Networking*, Jan. 26-28 1998, San Jose, California, pp. 191-204.

[14] Vin, H. M., and P. V. Rangan, "Designing a Multi-User HDTV Storage Server," *IEEE Journal on Selected Areas in Communication*, Special Issue on High-Definition Television and Digital Video Communication, Vol. 11, No. 1, Jan. 1993.

[15] Ragan, P. V., H. M. Vin, and S. Ramanathan, "Designing an On-Demand Multimedia Service," *IEEE Communications Magazine*, Vol. 30, No. 7, pp. 56–64, July 1992.

[16] Buddhikot, M. M., and G. Parulkar, "Efficient Data Layout, Scheduling and Playout Control in MARS," *Proc. 5th Intl. Workshop on Network and Operating System Support for Digital Audio and*

Video, Durham, NH, April 18–21, 1995, pp. 339–350.

[17] Reddy, A. L. N., and J. C. Wyllie, "I/O Issues in a Multimedia System," *Computer*, Vol. 7, No. 3, Mar. 1994, pp. 69–74.

[18] Dan, A., D. Sitaram, and P. Shahabuddin, "Dynamic Batching Policies for an On-Demand Video Server," *Proc. ACM Multimedia '94*, New York, pp. 15–24, Oct. 1994.

[19] Wong, J. W. T. and K. K. Pang, "Random Access Support for Large Scale VoD," *Proc. Australian Telecommunication Networks and Applications Conference*, Dec. 11–13, 1995, Sydney, Australia, pp. 225–230.

[20] Buddhikot, M. M., G. M. Parulkar, and J. R. Cox, "Design of a Large Scale Multimedia Storage Server," *Computer Networks and ISDN Systems*, Vol. 27, 1994, pp. 503–517.

[21] Rooholamini, R., and V. Cherkassky, "ATM-Based Multimedia Servers," *IEEE Multimedia*, Vol. 2, No. 1, pp. 39–52, 1995.

[22] Furht, B., "Processor Architectures for Multimedia: A Survey," *Proceedings of International Conferences on Multimedia Modeling*, Singapore, Nov. 17-20, 1997, pp.89-109

[23] Hopper, A., "Pandora—An Experimental System for Multimedia Applications," *ACM Operating Systems Review*, Vol. 24, No. 2, pp. 19–34, April 1990.

[24] Blair, G., et al., "A Network Interface Unit to Support Continuous Media," *Journal of Selected Area in Communications*, Vol. 11, No. 2, pp. 264–275, Feb. 1993.

[25] Hayter, M. D,. and D.R. McAuley, "The Desk Area Network," *ACM Operating Systems Review*, Vol. 25, No. 4, Oct. 1991.

[26] Silberschatz, A., and P. Galvin, *Operating System Concepts* (4th ed.), Addison-Wesley, Nov. 1994.

[27] Nieh, J., et al., "SVR4 UNIX Scheduler Unacceptable for Multimedia Applications," *Proceedings of 4th International Workshop on Network and Operating System Support for Digital Audio and Video*, Lancaster House, Lancaster, UK, pp. 35–47, Nov. 1993.

[28] Kitamura, H., et al., "A New OS Architecture for High Performance Communication Over ATM Networks - Zero-Copy Architecture," *Proc. of 5th International Workshop on Network and Operating System Support for Digital Audio and Video*, Durham, NH, April 18–21, 1995, pp. 87–90.

[29] Govindan, R., and D. P. Anderson, "Scheduling and IPC Mechanisms for Continuous Media," *13th ACM Symposium on Operating Systems Principles*, Pacific Grove, CA, *SIGOPS*, vol. 25, pp. 68–80, 1991.

[30] Coulson, G. and G. Blair, "Architectural Principles and Techniques for Distributed Multimedia Application Support in Operating Systems," *ACM Operating System Review*, Vol. 29, No. 4, Oct. 1995, pp. 17–24. Also available at URL: <http://www.comp.lanc.ac.uk/pub/mpg/MPG-95-09.ps.Z>.

[31] Mercer, C. W., S. Savage, and H. Tokuda, "Processor Capacity Reserves: Operating System Support for Multimedia Applications," *Proceedings of the IEEE International Conference on Multimedia Computing and Systems*, May 1994.

[32] Real-Time Mach home page (containing many papers on the real-time Mach) at URL: <http://www.cs.cmu.edu/afs/cs/project/rtmach/public/papers/>.

[33] Liu, C. L., and J. W. Layland, "Scheduling Algorithms for Multiprogramming in a Hard Real-Time Environment," *Journal of the Association for Computing Machinery*, vol. 20, no. 1, pp. 46-61, Feb. 1973.

[34] Mauthe, A. and G. Coulson, "Scheduling and Admission Testing for Jitter Constrained Periodic Threads," *Proc. of 5th International Workshop on Network and Operating System Support for Digital Audio and Video*, Durham, NH, pp. 219–222, April 1995.

[35] Hanko, J. G., et al., "Workstation Support for Time-Critical Applications," *Proceedings of Second International Workshop on network and Operating System Support for Digital Audio and Video*, Heidelberg, Germany, Nov. 18-19, 1991, pp. 4-9.

[36] Jeffay, K., et al., "Kernel Support for Live Digital Audio and Video," *Proceedings of Second International Workshop on Network and Operating System Support for Digital Audio and Video*, Heidelberg, Germany, Nov. 18–19, 1991, pp. 10–21.

[37] Jeffay, K., D. L. Stone, and F. D. Smith, "Kernel Support for Live Digital Audio and Video," *Computer Communications*, Vol. 15, No. 6, pp. 388–395, July/Aug. 1992.

[38] Hyden, E. A., *Operating System Support for Quality of Service*, PhD Dissertation, University of Cambridge, 1994.

[39] Partridge, C., *Gigabit Networking*, Addison-Wesley Publishing Company, 1994.

[40] Cuthbert, L. G., and J. C. Sapanel, *ATM: The Broadband Telecommunications Solution*, the Institute of Electrical Engineers, 1993

[41] Acampora, A. S., *An Introduction to Broadband Networks: LANs, WANS, ATM, B-ISDN, and Optical Networks for Integrated Multimedia Telecommunications*, Plenum Press, 1994.

[42] Ross, F. E., "An Overview of FDDI: The Fiber Distributed Data Interface," *IEEE Journal on Selected Areas in Communications*, Vol. 7, No. 7, pp. 1,043–1,051, Sept. 1989.

[43] Martini, P., and T. Meuser, "Real-Time Traffic in FDDI-II Packet Switching vs. Circuit Switching," *Proceedings of IEEE Infocom '91*, pp. 1,413–1,420.

[44] Watson, R. M. and S. Ward, "Prioritization in FDDI Networks," *Computer Communications*, Vol. 17, No. 1, pp. 35–45, Jan. 1994.

[45] Cooper, C. S., "High-Speed Networks: the Emergence of Technologies for Multiservice Support," *Computer Communications*, Vol. 14, No.1, pp. 27–43, 1991.

[46] Stallings, W., *Local and Metropolitan Area Networks*, 4th ed., MacMillan Publishing Company.

[47] Sutherland, J., and L. Litteal, "Residential Video Services," *IEEE Comm.* Vol.30, No.7, July 1992, pp.36-41.

[48] Tanenbaum, A. S., *Computer Networks*, 2nd ed., Prentice-Hall, 1989.

[49] Stallings, W., *Data and Computer Communications*, 4th ed., MacMillan Publishing Co., 1994.

[50] Doeringer, W. A., et al., "A Survey of Light-Weight Transport Protocols for High-Speed Networks," *IEEE Transactions on Communications*, Vol. 38, No. 11, Nov.1990, pp. 2,025–2,039.

[51] Dupuy, S., W. Tawbi, and E. Horlait, "Protocols for High-Speed Multimedia Communications Networks," *Computer Communications*, Vol. 15, No. 6, July/Aug. 1992, pp. 349–358.

[52] Field, B., and T. Znati, "Experimental Evaluation of Transport Layer Protocols for Real-Time Applications," *Proceedings of 16th Conference on Local Computer Networks*, Minneapolis, MN, Oct. 14–17, 1991, pp. 521–534.

[53] Clarck, D., et al., "An Analysis of TCP Processing Overhead," *IEEE Communications Magazine*, Vol. 27. No. 6, July 1988, pp. 23–29.

[54] Jacobson, R. Braden, and D. Borman, "TCP Extension for High Performance," Internet RFC 1323, May 1992.

[55] Partridge, C., *Gigabit Networking*, Addison-Wesley Publishing Co., 1994.

[56] Biersack, E. W., "A Performance Study of Forward Error Correction in ATM Networks," *Proceedings of Second International Workshop on Network and Operating System Support for Digital Audio and Video*, Heidelberg, Germany, Nov. 18–19, 1991, pp. 391–402.

[57] Weaver, A. C., "Making Transport Protocols Fast," *Proceedings of 16th Conference on Local Computer Networks*, Minneapolis, MN, Oct. 14–17, 1991, pp. 295–309.

[58] Weaver, A. C., "The Xpress Transport Protocol," *Computer Communications*, Vol. 17, No.1, pp. 46–52, Jan. 1994.

[59] Topolcic, C., "Experimental Internet Stream Protocol, Version 2 (ST-II)," Request for Comments RFC 1190, Internet Engineering Task Force, Oct. 1990.

[60] Delgrossi, L., et al., "Reservation Protocols for Internetworks: A Comparison of ST-II and RSVP," *Proceedings of 4th International Workshop on Network and Operating System Support for Digital Audio and Video*, Lancaster, UK, Nov. 3–5 1993, pp. 195–203.

[61] Delgrossi, L., et al., "HeiTP - A Transport Protocol for ST-II," *Globecom '92*, pp. 1,369–1,373.

[62] Deering, S., "Host Extensions for IP Multicasting," RFC 1112, Stanford University, Aug. 1989.

[63] Zhang, L., et al., "ReSource ReserVation Protocol (RSVP) - Functional Specification," Internet Draft, Mar. 1994.

[64] Mitzel, D. J., et al., "An Architectural Comparison of ST-II and RSVP," *Proceedings of Infocom '94*, Toronto, Canada, June 1994.

[65] Schulzrinne, H., et al., "RTP: A Transport Protocol for Real-Time Applications," Internet Draft (work-in-progress) draft-ietf-avt-rtp-07.txt, Nov. 1994

[66] Herrtwich, R. G., and L. Delgrossi, "Beyond ST-II: Fulfilling the Requirements of Multimedia Communication," *Proceedings of Third International Workshop on Network and Operating System Sup-*

port for Digital Audio and Video, La Jolla, CA, Nov. 12–13, 1992, pp. 25–31.

[67] Banerjea, A., et al., "The Tenet Real-Time Protocol Suite: Design, Implementation, and Experiences," Technical Report TR-94-059, International Computer Science Institute, Berkeley, CA, Nov. 1994.

[68] Ferrari, D., and D. C. Verma, "A Scheme for Real-Time Channel Establishment in Wide-Area Networks," *IEEE J. Selected Areas in Commun.* Vol. 8, pp. 368–379, April 1990.

[69] Wolfinger, B., and M. Moran, "A Continuous Media Data Transport Service and Protocol for Real-Time Communication in High Speed Network," *Proceedings of Second International Workshop on Network and Operating System Support for Digital Audio and Video*, Heidelberg, Germany, Nov. 18–19, 1991, pp. 171–182.

[70] Zhang, H., and T. Fisher, "Preliminary Measurement of RMTP/RTIP," *Proceedings of Third International Workshop on Network and Operating System Support for Digital Audio and Video*, La Jolla, CA, Nov. 12–13, 1992, pp. 185–196.

[71] Bettati, R., et al., "Connection Establishment for Multi-Party Real-Time Communication," *Proceedings of Fifth International Workshop on Network and Operating System Support for Digital Audio and Video*, Durham, NH, April 18–21, 1995, pp. 255–266.

[72] IETF, Resource Reservation Setup Protocol (RSVP) Charter, URL: <http://www.ietf.cnri.reston.va.us/html.charters/rsvp-charter.html>

[73] Stefani, J., L. Hazard, and F. Horn, "Computational Model for Distributed Multimedia Applications Based on a Synchronous Programming Language," *Compt. Comm*, Vol. 15, No.2, Mar. 1992, pp. 114–128.

[74] Lu, G., et al., "Temporal Synchronization Support for Distributed Multimedia Information Systems," *Computer Communications*, Vol. 17, No. 12, Dec. 1994, pp. 852–862.

[75] Qazi, N. U., M. Woo, and A. Ghafoor, "A Synchronization and Communication Model for Distributed Multimedia Objects," *Proceedings of ACM Multimedia'93*, Anaheim, CA, August 1–6, 1993, pp. 147–155

[76] Little, T. D. C., and A. Ghafoor, "Scheduling of Bandwidth-Constrained Multimedia Traffic," *Computer Communications*, Vol. 15, No. 6, July/Aug. 1992, pp. 381–387.

[77] Barberis, G., and D. Pazzaglia, "Analysis and Optimal Design of a Packet-Voice Receiver," *IEEE Transactions on Communications*, Vol. Com-28, No. 2, Feb. 1980, pp. 217–227.

[78] Leung, W. H. F., et al., "A Software Architecture for Workstations Supporting Multimedia Conferencing in Packet Switching Networks," *IEEE Journal on Selected Areas in Communications*, Vol. 8 No. 3, April 1990, pp. 380–390.

[79] Shepherd, D. and M. Salmony, "Extending OSI to Support Synchronization Required by Multimedia Applications," *Computer Communications*, Vol. 13, No. 7, pp. 399–406.

[80] Escobar, J., D. Deutsch, and C. Patridge, "Flow Synchronization Protocol," *Proceedings of IEEE Globecom Conference*, Orlando, Florida, Dec. 1992.

[81] Dannenberg, R. B., "Tactus: Toolkit-level Support for Synchronized Interactive Multimedia," *Multimedia Systems*, Vol. 1, No. 2, Sept. 1993, pp. 77–86.

[82] Bastian, F., and P. Lenders, "Media Synchronization on Distributed Multimedia Systems," *Proceedings of the IEEE International Conference on Multimedia Computing and Systems*, Boston, MA, May 14–19, 1994, pp. 526–531.

[83] Mills, D. L., "Precision Synchronization of Computer Network Clocks," *ACM Computer Communication Review*, Vol. 24, No. 2, April 1994, pp. 28–43.

[84] Rowe, A. L., and B. C. Smith, "A Continuous Media Player," *Proc. 3rd International Workshop on Network and OS Support for Digital Audio and Video*, San Diego, CA, Nov. 1992.

Chapter 11

Measurement of Multimedia Information Retrieval Effectiveness

11.1 INTRODUCTION

We dealt with multimedia indexing and retrieval techniques in the previous chapters. The indexing and retrieval process is summarized as follows. Information items in the database are preprocessed to extract features and they are indexed based on these features. During information retrieval, a user's query is processed and its main features are extracted. The query's main features are then compared with the features or index of each information item in the database. Information items whose features are deemed similar to those of the query are retrieved and presented to the user.

There are three ways for the system to present the search results. In the first one, a fixed number of items, regardless of the query, are presented to the user in decreasing order of similarity. In the second method, all items with similarity higher than a predefined threshold are returned. In the final method, all items are ranked according to their similarity and are available for the user to browse.

This chapter deals with how to measure the performance of a multimedia retrieval system. There are two main parameters used to measure the performance of a retrieval system: efficiency and effectiveness. Efficiency is mainly concerned with the response time of the system. It is determined by the data structures used for organizing feature vectors as discussed in Chapter 9, and by the support systems as discussed in Chapter 10. There are two aspects of system effectiveness. The first aspect is concerned with the presentation quality, which is part of the QoS discussed Chapter 10. The second aspect is concerned with the system's ability to retrieve relevant items and discard irrelevant items, and is the focus of this chapter. The term "effectiveness" is used to refer to the system's ability to retrieve relevant items and discard irrelevant items. Without losing generality, we use image retrieval as an example of content-based multimedia information retrieval in the following discussion.

There is no need to measure effectiveness in traditional DBMSs, because DBMSs retrieve items based on exact match, and all retrieved items are relevant to the query. In contrast, multimedia information retrieval is based on the similarity between the query and items in the image database, based on a similarity metric, instead of an exact match techniques. Since it is difficult to design a similarity metric that exactly conforms to human perception, it is likely that some items determined to be relevant or similar to the query by the system are actually judged not relevant to the query by the user. Therefore, we need an objective method to measure the effectiveness of multimedia indexing and retrieval techniques so that we can compare the performance of different techniques and systems.

A good effectiveness measurement is difficult to achieve for a number of reasons. First, there are different levels of similarity or relevance between information items. The question is how to determine these relevance levels and use them in an effectiveness calculation. Second, multimedia items are information rich, so it is hard to judge relevance between them. Third, the effectiveness is measured against human judgment, which is subjective.

In the current multimedia information retrieval literature, retrieval effectiveness is either not reported or is measured using different measurements by different researchers, causing difficulty in comparing the retrieval performance of different techniques. In Sections 11.3 to 11.5 we describe three common effectiveness measurements. These three methods are recall and precision pair [1-3], percentage of weighted hits [4] , and percentage of similarity ranking [5]. As the effectiveness is measured against human relevance judgment, we first describe common methods of collecting human judgment data in Section 11.2. In Section 11.6 we discusses the strengths, weaknesses, and suitability of the three common effectiveness measurements. Section 11.7 briefly describes a new measurement that overcomes the identified weaknesses. Different retrieval techniques and systems have different retrieval effectiveness. In Section 11.8, we briefly discuss factors that affect the retrieval effectiveness of different techniques and systems. Section 11.9 summarizes the chapter.

11.2 COLLECTION OF HUMAN JUDGMENT DATA

In order to compute retrieval effectiveness, we must determine relevant items (judged by humans) in the database for each query used in testing. As perceptual relevance varies from person to person, relevance data must be collected from a large subject group. In this section, we first describe three common methods for collecting the relevance data. We then discuss how to select a suitable data collection method and the need for standard test databases.

Method 1

In the first method, each subject is asked to select items from the database relevant to each test query. Items selected for each query by more than a predefined number of subjects are considered relevant to that query. The final result of the subject testing is that items are divided into relevant and irrelevant groups for each query.

Method 2

In the second method, each subject is again asked to select items from the database relevant to each test query. But instead of making an overall decision on whether the item is relevant to the query, the number of subjects who selected the item is recorded. Initially, all items start with zero weight for each test query. Each time a subject selects an item, the weight of that item for that particular test query is increased by one. Thus the weight of an item (w_i) with respect to a query is equal to the number of persons who selected it. In this way, the final result of the subject test is that each item has a relevance weight to each testing query.

Method 3

In the third method, each subject selects a similarity ranking of each item in the database for each testing query, instead of judging whether an item is either relevant or not. The most relevant item has the rank of one and next one has the rank of two, and so forth. In this way, the final result of the subject test is a matrix $Q_j(i, k)$ for each query j, where $Q_j(i, k)$ indicates the number of subjects who ranked item i at the kth position for query j.

Selection of data collection methods

Which data collection method to use is determined by the effectiveness measurement method to be used. Although data may be converted from one form to another, the conversion may not be accurate. For example, we can convert $Q(i, k)$ to w_i by making the assumption that item i is relevant when k is small and Q is larger than a certain threshold. The problem is that the threshold varies from query to query and is difficult to determine. This is because an item may not be relevant although k is small and Q is very large, because there are not many items in the database that are actually relevant to the query. On the other hand, an item may be actually relevant although k is large and Q is very small, because there are many items in the database that are relevant to the query. Therefore, the appropriate data collection method to be used depends on what data is used in the calculation of retrieval effectiveness.

Need for standard test databases

At the moment, different researchers use different test multimedia databases (as well as different effectiveness measurements) to evaluate their retrieval techniques or systems. This situation should be changed and a set of common standard test databases used by all researchers, as in the case of text document retrieval, where a set of standard test document collections were created for evaluating IR techniques. It is envisaged that a number of standard databases will be used to evaluate different aspects of a retrieval system. For example, when evaluating image retrieval, we may need one database for evaluating the color-based technique, one for the shape-based techniques, one for the texture-based techniques, and another for the integrated techniques.

Standard test databases are essential for the following two reasons. First, they facilitate performance comparison among different techniques. It is meaningless to compare performance results obtained from different test databases. Second, building a test database is a very expensive process. No matter which method of collecting human judgment data is used, many subjects must go through the database many times to collect relevance data. This is a tedious and time-consuming process when a database of useful size (tens of thousands of items) is used. When common standard databases are used, once human judgment data is obtained, it is available for all researchers. Using common standard databases not only saves time and money, but also removes many irregularities (such as subjectiveness and bias in the selection of databases) in obtaining human judgment data.

11.3 RECALL AND PRECISION PAIR (RPP)

This retrieval effectiveness measurement method uses the results of subjective test method 1. For each query, the system returns a ranked list. Each item in the list is determined as either relevant or not, according to the subject test results. Then the effectiveness is measured by recall and precision. This is the most common effectiveness measurement method used in IR and multimedia information retrieval [1-3].

We discussed definitions of recall and precision, and their calculations in Section 4.8. The important point to note is that recall and precision must be used together to measure the performance of a system or technique. Recall measures the ability to retrieve relevant items, and precision measures the ability to reject irrelevant items. To use only one parameter (either recall or precision) to measure the effectiveness of a system is not meaningful, because a system can have very high recall but very low precision, or have very high precision but very low recall. A good system should have both high recall and precision values.

11.4 PERCENTAGE OF WEIGHTED HITS (PWH)

This retrieval effectiveness measurement method uses the results of subjective test method 2 [4]. For each query, a fixed number of items are returned. Then the percentage of weighted hits P is defined as follows

$$P = \frac{\sum\limits_{i=1}^{n} w_i}{\sum\limits_{j=1}^{N} w_j}$$

where n is the number of items returned, w_i is the number of subjects selecting the returned item i as relevant to the query, N is the total number of items in the database, w_j is the number of subjects selecting item j as relevant to the query

We see that the percentage of weighted hits P is similar to recall, except that it takes into account of the different number of subjects selecting the item as relevant. To indicate the average performance of a system, many queries should be performed, and the average percentage of weighted hits over these queries is used to measure the retrieval effectiveness of the system.

11.5 PERCENTAGE OF SIMILARITY RANKINGS (PSR)

This retrieval effectiveness measurement method uses the results of subjective test method 3 [5]. Each image i has a value $Q_j(i, k)$, representing the percentage of people that ranked the ith image in the kth position in relation to query j. From $Q_j(i, k)$, we calculate the mean value $\bar{p}_j(i)$ and standard deviation $\delta_j(i)$, representing the average ranking of the ith image for a given query j and degree of disagreement of the ranking among subjects, respectively. For example, if all subjects ranked image 10 in 5th position in relation to query 2, then $Q_2(10, 5) = 100\%$, $\bar{p}_2(10)=5$, $\delta_2(10)= 0$.

To measure the system performance and take into account the variability of human judgment, the percentage of people who ranked an image in the position $\bar{p}_j(i)$ or in a very close neighborhood of $\bar{p}_j(i)$ is considered. The system returns a ranking position $P_j(i)$ of item i for query j. The system effectiveness in ranking item i in relation to query j is represented by the sum of the percentage of people who ranked the item in positions between $P_j(i) - \left\lceil \dfrac{\delta_j(i)}{2} \right\rceil$ and $P_j(i) + \left\lceil \dfrac{\delta_j(i)}{2} \right\rceil$. Therefore, the percentage of similarity rankings $S_j(i)$ is defined as

$$S_j(i) = \sum_{k = P_j(i) - \left\lceil \frac{\delta_j(i)}{2} \right\rceil}^{P_j(i) + \left\lceil \frac{\delta_j(i)}{2} \right\rceil} Q_j(i, k)$$

$S_j(i)$ represents the degree of agreement between $P_j(i)$ and $\bar{p}_j(i)$. When $P_j(i)=\bar{p}_j(i)$, $S_j(i)$ will be close to 1 (or 100%). When the difference between $P_j(i)$ and $\bar{p}_j(i)$ is larger than $\delta_j(i)$, $S_j(i)$ will be close to 0 (or 0%).

In practice, we are only interested in a number of highest ranked (by the system) items. So for each query, we usually start with the highest ranked item, we determine its item number, and find its percentage of similarity rankings. Percentages of similarity ranking for items ranked at second, third, and so forth are calculated similarly. Finally, plots of $S_j(i)$ as a function of rankings $P_j(i)$ (being 1, 2,, 3, ...) are presented. They show the degree of agreement between the subjects and the system in ranking the ith item in the $P_j(i)$ position, for each query.

To measure the average performance, many queries should be performed and their similarity rankings averaged.

11.6 SUITABILITY OF THE COMMON EFFECTIVENESS MEASUREMENTS

We have so far described three common retrieval effectiveness measurement methods. We now present an example using the three effectiveness measurements to compare two image retrieval techniques. Based on this example, we discuss the strengths and weaknesses of these three measurements.

11.6.1 A Numerical Example

The example is taken from [6]. We use the three effectiveness measures to compare the performance of two retrieval techniques: QBIC [7, 8] and a method based on moment invariants [4, 9, 10]. We only present the results, for details on how the results are obtained, refer to [6].

Figure 11.1 shows the retrieval performance of individual queries and the average performance calculated using the percentage of similarity ranking method.

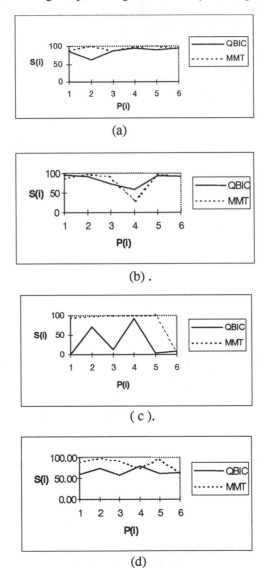

(a)

(b) .

(c).

(d)

Figure 11.1 Performance measured using the percentage of similarity ranking.
(a) Performance for query 1. (b) Performance for query 2.
(c)Performance for query 3. (d) Average retrieval performance.

Figure 11.2 shows the retrieval performance of individual queries and the average performance calculated using recall and precision pairs.

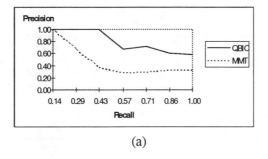

(a)

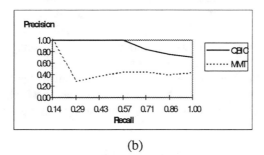

(b)

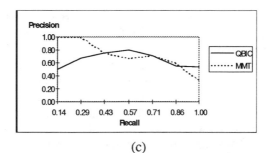

(c)

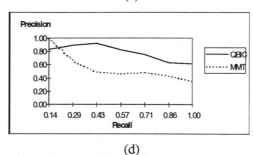

(d)

Figure 11.2 Performance measure using the recall and precision curves.
(a) Performance for query 1. (b) Performance for query 2.
(c)Performance for query 3. (d) Average retrieval performance.

Table 11.1 shows the retrieval performance of QBIC and MMT measured using the percentage of weighted hits method.

Table 11.1

Retrieval Performance Measured Using the Percentage of Weighted Hits

	QBIC (%)	MMT (%)
Query 1	69.5	35
Query 2	56.3	32.8
Query 3	58.3	58.8
Average	61.4	42.2

We see that different calculation methods result in different performance measures using the same subjective relevance and system ranking data. Based on the percentage of similarity ranking, MMT has higher performance. However, based on recall and precision curves and percentage of weighted hits, QBIC has the higher performance. This example shows that the different effectiveness measurements are not equally reliable.

11.6.2 Strengths and Weaknesses of PSR, PWH, and RPP

The objective of information retrieval systems is to retrieve as many relevant items as possible, and meanwhile to reject as many irrelevant items as possible. A good effectiveness measurement should indicate the system's ability to meet this objective.

The percentage of similarity ranking measures how well the system's ranking matches the human ranking. This one-to-one ranking match may not be a necessary requirement. In most cases, the user will be happy if the system returns an item at the position close to the human ranking (instead of exactly the same position). PSR takes into account all $Q(i, k)$ around $P(i)$ within the standard deviation. But the standard deviation used is the standard deviation around the subjective mean ranking. If the percentage of subjects giving a particular item a particular ranking is high, then the standard deviation for the item would be small. This would result in poor PSR if the system ranking differs from the subjective mean ranking. But on the other hand, if the standard deviation is large, then the measured performance would be high, even if the ranking by the system ranking differs substantially from the subjective mean ranking. This is why MMT performs better than QBIC according to PSR, although the MMT ranking is not as good as the QBIC ranking according to the subjective test results in the above example. Another major problem with PSR is that it requires each subject to rank each item in terms of its similarity to each test query. When the test database is large and there are a large number of items similar to queries, it is difficult if not impossible for subjects to provide an accurate ranking.

In calculating PWH, it is assumed that a fixed number of items are returned. This may not be desirable as different queries may have different numbers of relevant items. Also, PWH does not measure the ability to reject irrelevant items. PWH can be high but there are many irrelevant items in the returned list. One good thing about PWH is that items that more people think are relevant have a higher weight.

RPP measures both the ability to retrieve relevant items and to reject irrelevant items. But it does not consider the different degrees of relevance and thus may not reflect human judgment accurately. For example, a system's recall may be very high, but some most relevant items may not actually be retrieved. This is because regardless of the different degrees of relevance, all relevant items have the same weight. In the next section we briefly describe a modified RPP measurement that combines the strengths of PWH and RPP.

11.7 Modified RPP

In the modified RPP, each item has a weight for each query, as in PWH [6]. The weight is equal to the number of people selecting the item as relevant. The modified recall is equal to the ratio of the sum of the weights of retrieved items and the sum of the weights of all items in the database. The calculation of precision is the same as in RPP: precision is equal to the ratio of the number of relevant items retrieved and the total number of items retrieved. Irrelevant items are those for which the number of people who select them as relevant is below a certain threshold.

The modified RPP measures retrieval effectiveness more accurately because it takes into account the different degrees of relevance in calculating the ability to retrieve relevant items. The precision measures the ability to reject irrelevant items. The modified recall value is equal to the PWH value when the number of returned items is the same.

11.8 FACTORS AFFECTING RETRIEVAL EFFECTIVENESS

We described common retrieval effectiveness measurement methods and indicated that the modified RPP may be the best measurement method. In this section, we briefly describe the factors that affect the retrieval effectiveness of a system.

There are three main factors that determine the retrieval effectiveness of a system. The first factor is the feature(s) chosen to represent multimedia information items. For example, we can use color, shape, texture, or a combination of these features to represent color images. Different features represent different aspects of image content and will result in the retrieval of different images. The second factor is how to represent or describe the chosen feature(s). For example, once we choose color as the representative feature, we have to decide how to represent color and color distribution, as there are many different color spaces and histogram representations. These different feature representations will lead to different retrieval results. The final factor affecting retrieval effectiveness is the distance or similarity metric used to measure distance or similarity between feature vectors. The two common metrics used are the L_1 and L_2 norm. But they may not be the best metrics [11]. Research is needed to understand human similarity judgment and to use this knowledge to develop new similarity metrics.

The above three factors are critical to the retrieval effectiveness of a system and should be addressed to develop effective multimedia retrieval systems.

11.9 SUMMARY

A good retrieval effectiveness measurement method is important in order to compare different retrieval techniques. We described three common measurement methods and evaluated their strengths and weaknesses. The discussion demonstrated that a good measurement method should be able to indicate the capability of retrieving relevant items and rejecting irrelevant items, and also take into account different degrees of relevance based on subjective tests. In view of this, we described the modified RPP. It is expected that the modified RPP would provide a better measurement for content-based multimedia retrieval effectiveness, as it combines the strengths of RPP and PWH.

Another important issue is that performance evaluations should be carried out using a set of common standard test databases. Currently they are nonexistent.

Problems

Problem 11.1

Discuss the differences between the performance evaluation of a traditional DBMS and a content-based multimedia information retrieval system.

Problem 11.2

Discuss the strengths and weaknesses of the three methods of collecting human relevance data described in Section 10.2. When the test database used is large (containing many thousands of items), what are the main problems of each method? How can these problems be overcome?

Problem 11.3

Why are both recall and precision used in RPP to measure retrieval effectiveness? Suppose a database has 2,000 items in total, out which 30 are relevant to a particular query. The system returned the following list in response to the query: R, R, R, I, R, I, R, R, I, I, R, R, I, R, I, where the Rs denote items actually relevant to the query, and the Is denote items irrelevant to the query as judged by the subjects. Draw the recall-precision graph for that query.

Problem 11.4

Discuss the suitability of the modified RPP for measuring the effectiveness of multimedia information retrieval. Is there any problem with this measurement method?

Problem 11.5

Discuss the main issues or problems in achieving a good multimedia information retrieval effectiveness measurement.

References

[1] Salton, G., *Introduction to Modern Information Retrieval*, McGraw-Hill Book Company, 1983.

[2] Sajjanhar, A., and G. Lu, "A Grid Based Shape Indexing and Retrieval Method," *Australian Computer Journal*, Special Issue on Multimedia Storage and Archiving Systems, Vol. 29, No.4, November 1997, pp. 131-140.

[3] Chua, T. S., K-L. Tan, and B. C. Ooi, "Fast Signature-based Color-Spatial Image Retrieval," *Proceedings of the IEEE International Conference on Multimedia Computing and Systems*, June 3-6, 1997, Ottawa, Canada, pp. 362-369.

[4] Scassellati, B., S. Alexopoulos, and M. Flickner. "Retrieving Images By 2d Shape: A Comparison Of Computation Methods With Human Perceptual Judgments," *Storage and Retrieval for Image and Video Databases II, SPIE Proceedings*, Vol. 2185, pages 2-14, 1994.

[5] Bimbo, A. D., and P. Pala, "Visual Image Retrieval by Elastic Matching of User Sketches," *IEEE Transactions on Pattern Analysis and Machine Intelligence*, Vol.19, No.2, Feb. 1997, pp.121-132.

[6] Lu, G., and A. Sajjanhar, "On Performance Measurement of Multimedia Information Retrieval Systems," *International Conference on Computational Intelligence and Multimedia Applications*, Feb. 9-11, 1998, Monash University, Gippsland Campus, Australia, pp. 781-787.

[7] Flickner, M., et al., "Query by Image and Video Content: The QBIC System," *Computer*, Sept. 1995, pp. 23–32.

[8] Niblack, W., et al., "Update to the QBIC System," *Proceedings of the Conference on Storage and Retrieval for Image and Video Databases VI*, San Jose, CA, Jan. 28-30, 1998, SPIE Proceedings Series, Vol. 3312, pp.150-161.

[9] Hu, M. K., "Visual Pattern Recognition by Moment Invariants," *IRE Trans. Info. Theory*, Vol. IT-8, Feb. 1962, pp. 179–187.

[10] Sajjanhar, A., G. Lu, and J. Wright, "An Experimental Study of Moment Invariants and Fourier Descriptors for Shape Based Image Retrieval," *Proceedings of the Second Australian Document Computing Symposium*, April 5, 1997, Melbourne, Australia.

[11] Santini, S., and R. Jain, "Similarity Matching," *Technical Report of Visual Computing Laboratory*, University of California, San Diego, CA, 1995.

Chapter 12

Products, Applications, and New Developments

12.1 INTRODUCTION

We have so far discussed the main concepts, issues, and techniques in developing distributed multimedia information indexing and retrieval systems. In this chapter, we summarize the content of Chapters 1 to 11 and describe some of the main products, applications, and new developments in the area of multimedia information indexing and retrieval.

In Chapter 1, we gave an overview of multimedia database management systems (MMDBMSs) and examined the roles of traditional database management systems and text information retrieval techniques in developing MMDBMSs.

As the main difference between MDBMS and DBMS stems from the differences in the characteristics of alphanumeric data and multimedia data, we discussed the characteristics and requirements of text, audio, images, and video in Chapter 2. Based on these characteristics and requirements, we discussed the main design issues in developing MMDBMSs in Chapter 3.

In Chapters 4 to 7, we dealt with indexing and retrieval of text, audio, images, and video. Chapter 8 then discussed how to integrate these techniques to index and retrieve multimedia documents.

Chapters 4 to 8 focused mainly on how to index multimedia items and then find relevant items, without considering search speed or efficiency. In Chapter 9, we discussed techniques and data structures for efficient search of multimedia items in large databases.

After finding the relevant items in the database, the next step is to retrieve and display them to the user effectively. Chapter 10 discussed supporting systems required to achieve effective and efficient multimedia retrieval, transmission, processing, and presentation.

Content-based multimedia information retrieval is based on similarity between items instead of exact match. Some items considered relevant by the system may not be judged relevant by the user. Different retrieval techniques and systems may have different retrieval effectiveness. Thus it is important to know how to measure the retrieval effectiveness. Chapter 11 described the strengths and weaknesses of three common effectiveness measurements, and proposed a promising measurement by combining the strengths of two common measurements.

In this concluding chapter, we look briefly at the main products, applications, and new developments in MMDBMSs. Section 12.2 briefly describes the products that are currently available. Many types of applications can be developed based on the techniques discussed in the previous chapters. Section 12.3 briefly discusses three main applications of multimedia indexing and retrieval techniques: WWW multimedia search engines, digital libraries, and video-on-demand systems.

Section 12.4 looks at an issue not discussed in previous chapters but which will, to some extent, determine if an application will be successful. This issue is security, including privacy, authentication, and copyright protection.

Finally in Section 12.5, we conclude with a note on a forthcoming international standard, MPEG-7, which will play a central role in the development of multimedia database management systems.

12.2 PRODUCTS OF MULTIMEDIA DATABASE MANAGEMENT SYSTEMS

A number of software products that have multimedia indexing and retrieval capabilities are or soon will be available. There are two general types of products. The first type provides a development kit that contains a set of tools such as feature extraction and similarity calculation. Developers use these tools to build applications. In the second type of product, multimedia indexing and retrieval capabilities are incorporated into traditional database management systems. In this section, we briefly describe products developed by IBM and Virage.

In Chapters 6 and 7, we described a number of technologies used in IBM's QBIC system, which allows content-based indexing, retrieval, and presentation of images and video. The software kit for QBIC can be purchased from IBM (http://wwwqbic.almaden.ibm.com/).

Many of QBIC's multimedia capabilities have been incorporated into IBM's DB2 Universal Database Version 5 as DB2 extenders (http://www.software.ibm.com/data/db2/extenders/about.html). The extenders that are relevant to multimedia information indexing and retrieval are text extender, audio extender, image extender, and video extender.

Virage (http://www.virage.com) offers a suite of software solutions critical to organizations that create, manage, and distribute media on an enterprise scale. Virage's products include turnkey applications for scalable, automated indexing of media content. From any analog or digital video source, Virage's VideoLogger and AudioLogger products watch, read, and listen to the video in real-time, creating a textual and visual index that allows users to query on and retrieve a specific clip of video. Virage also offers a suite of developer tools that facilitate rapid integration of Virage's video and audio indexing applications into a wide variety of environments.

For indexing and searching of still images, Virage's Visual Information Retrieval (VIR) Image Engine automatically indexes thousands or even millions of digital images by content. With the VIR engine, developers build visual search applications allowing users to search for visually similar image content.

The Virage database plug-in products help system integrators build sophisticated video management solutions with VideoLogger and Oracle8.

12.3 APPLICATIONS OF MULTIMEDIA INDEXING AND RETRIEVAL

In this section, we briefly describe three common applications of multimedia indexing and retrieval. They are WWW multimedia search engines, digital libraries, and video-on-demand services. These applications share many common technologies, but have different emphases.

12.3.1 WWW Multimedia Search Engines

One of the most important applications of multimedia indexing and retrieval is to develop WWW multimedia search engines. There are many WWW search engines now available. But most commercial search engines are text based, that is, they index and retrieve WWW documents based on text. There are a number of research prototype multimedia search engines such as WebSEEk and IWISE as discussed in Chapter 8.

With the advancement of technologies, many commercial search engines incorporate multimedia search capabilities. For example, Compaq's AltaVista already has content-based image search capabilities by incorporating the Virage image search engine (http://www.altavista.com). One of the main issues in developing multimedia search engines is how to design a user interface so that the user can issue multimedia queries easily. One approach is to start a search with text and then use the retrieved images as new queries, as described in Chapter 8. AltaVista uses this approach.

12.3.2 Digital Libraries

The main reason for the initial development of digital libraries was to preserve some rare documents and serve wider and remote communities. Thus the main focuses of developing a digital library were how to scan in documents, how to compress and store them, and how to display them at very high quality. Search is carried out using traditional library methods, based on fields such as the title and the author. We consider these digital libraries as direct conversion from paper-based documents to a form suitable for electronic delivery.

More recently, some large and sophisticated digital library projects have been initiated. For example, the University of California at Berkeley, University of California at Santa Barbara, University of Michigan, University of Illinois, Standford University, and Carnegie Mellon University (CMU) are working on the 4-year, $24 million Digital Library Initiative, started in 1994 and supported by the NSF, DARPA, and NASA. The project's goal is to develop the technologies for intelligent access to massive, distributed collections of photographs, satellite images, maps, full text documents, and multimedia documents. Each university has its own research focus and has a number of industry partners. Many technologies used in the project are discussed in the previous chapters. But there are others specific to digital libraries. Such issues include interoperability, economic, and legal issues. For details, the reader is referred to the web sites of the project participants listed on the UC Berkeley Digital Library project web page (http://elib.cs.berkeley.edu/).

Another project carried out by CMU is the Informedia Digital Video Library, which uses intelligent and automatic mechanisms to provide full-content search and retrieval from an extremely large (scaling to several thousand hours) on-line digital video library (http://www.informedia.cs.cmu.edu/html/enter.html) [10]. The project is developing tools that can automatically populate the library and support access via desktop computers on local, metropolitan and wide area networks. Its approach uses combined speech, language, and image understanding technology to transcribe, segment, and index the linear video. These same tools will be applied to accomplish intelligent search and selective retrieval. Initially, a highly accurate, speaker-independent speech recognizer is used to automatically transcribe video soundtracks, which are then stored in a (time-track corresponding) full-text information retrieval system. This text database in turn allows for rapid retrieval of individual "video paragraphs" about an arbitrary subject area based on words in the soundtrack. Another innovative concept is the implementation of "video skimming." This enables accelerated viewing of the key video and audio sequences without the perceptual disturbance of simply speeding up the frame rate and audio. A video abstract is thus created that conveys the essence of the content in 5 to 20% of the time.

Initial versions of the video library will use commercial compression and deliver a VHS-quality playback. It is anticipated that the primary media-server file system will require one terabyte (1,000 gigabytes) of storage to archive the 1,000 hours of video. The project will also incorporate pay-per-view accounting, as subsequent commercial versions of the system will require protection of intellectual property. Understanding the real-world economics of digital libraries will also be critical for their successful implementation. The project's modular plan will allow installation of early testbeds in Carnegie Mellon and local area public schools.

The project will also facilitate the establishment of commercial information services to provide metropolitan area network access over new, low-cost, high-bandwidth networks, and to collect and repurpose other video libraries. The work also addresses human factor issues: learning, interaction, motivation, and effective usage modes for secondary, postsecondary, and lifelong learning.

Apart from technological issues, the success of digital libraries and other similar applications depends on solutions to issues such as copyright protection and privacy. In theory, only one digital copy of each book or document is sufficient to serve all users around the world. So the questions are how to implement access control, how to prevent illegal copying, how to reward authors, and how to verify if the document is original or not. We discuss some of these issues in Section 12.4.

12.3.3 Video-on-Demand (VOD) Systems

Conceptually, VOD systems are similar to WWW search engines and digital libraries: the client sends information requests to the server and the server sends the requested information to the client for presentation. However, due to their different applications, markets, and origins, there are the following major differences between these two types of systems:

1. The target application of VOD is real-time audio and video transmission.
2. Currently, VODs use dedicated networks, while the WWW search engines and digital libraries use the existing Internet shared by many applications.

3. Current VOD systems use a dedicated receiver (a set-top-box), while the WWW client is based on general-purpose computers. A set-top-box (STB) sits on top of a normal TV set decoding compressed video (and audio) signals sent from the video server.

4. VOD systems require that multimedia servers provide real-time retrieval, while the WWW servers are based on general-purpose computers, which currently do not provide timely retrieval of requested data.

Despite these differences, when the technologies are further developed, these systems might merge in the future.

Video servers have been described in Chapter 10. In the following we describe networks supporting VOD and STBs.

12.3.3.1 Networking Support for VOD

The major market for VOD is home entertainment. So the challenge is to bring real-time digital audio and video to millions of homes [1, 2]. The network follows a hierarchical structure (Figure 12.1). In WANs and MANs, ATM is or will be used to connect central servers and offices. In the subscriber loop (between subscribers and head end) there are currently four technologies being used for VOD. The first one is asymmetric digital subscriber line (ADSL) technology, which uses the existing telephone lines and an advanced modulation/demodulation technique. The second technology is called hybrid fiber coax (HFC), which is the existing delivery system for cable TV (CATV). The third technology is a high-speed digital subscriber line (HDSL), which uses the existing telephone copper lines. The fourth technology uses optical fiber connections to homes.

Asymmetric Digital Subscriber Line

ADSL technology enables the phone company to offer affordable VOD and interactive services because existing twisted-pair copper lines are used for communications between subscribers and head ends. The term "asymmetric" in ADSL refers to a much higher data rate in the downstream direction (to the subscriber) than in the upstream direction (from the subscriber). This is suitable for VOD because only the downstream needs to carry audio and video data, and the upstream only needs to carry user's command or control data.

With ADSL, a single copper twisted pair can support a channel of up to 6 Mbps in the downstream direction (from server to client), a 16-kbps channel in the upstream direction (from client to server), and a full duplex plain old telephone service (POTS) [3]. So ADSL allows delivery of a high-quality MPEG compressed video (with audio) to the subscriber in addition to the existing telephone service.

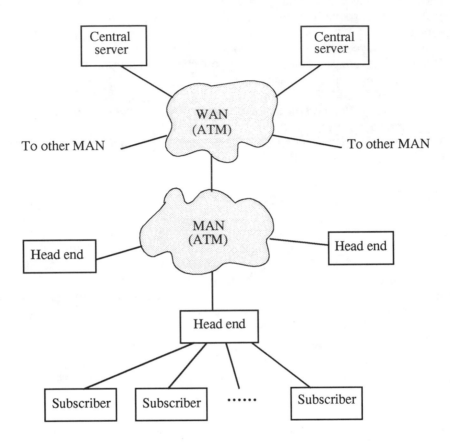

Figure 12.1 Hierarchical configuration of VOD networks.

Hybrid Fiber Coax

HFC is used for CATV. In HFC, optical fiber is used between the cable head end or telephone company's central office and a neighborhood fiber-optical node. From the optical node, coax (coaxial cable) is used to connect to homes.

A typical cable plant has a bandwidth of 450 MHz. Assuming each analog video channel is 6 MHz, more than 70 channels can be supported by each cable for analog CATV broadcasting. Using the quadrature modulation (QAM) technique, a single 6-MHz channel can transmit more that 40 Mbps, which can accommodate more than 10 MPEG-2 compressed digital movies (assuming the compressed data rate is between 3 and 4 Mbps including video, audio, and control data). Therefore, a multiplexing strategy can be devised so that some bandwidth of the cable is used for normal analog CATV broadcasting, some bandwidth for digital movie broadcasting, and some bandwidth for VOD applications.

It is also possible to upgrade the cable plant to 750 MHz. With this amount of bandwidth, hundreds of homes in a neighborhood can be supported using HFC. Note that for VOD, each home needs a virtual channel over the same cable. So if 300 MHz is used for VOD purposes, each head end can support 500 ((300/6) x 10) homes.

As the original HFC is for one-way transmission only, some adaptation is needed to run VOD to send control data upstream. From homes to the fiber-optic node, all homes can share a reverse-channel via a multiple access technology. A separate fiber is needed to carry the control data from the fiber-optical node to the central office.

High-Speed Digital Subscriber Line

A HDSL supports ISDN rates of 1.544 or 2.048 Mbps for full-duplex communication on existing telephone copper lines. Thus HDSL can be used to carry a VOD service or videoconferencing.

Direct Optical Fiber Connection

This approach requires that optical fibers be connected to each home. Then many VOD channels share the bandwidth of the optical fiber using a certain multiplexing technique. It is an expensive approach, but represents a long-term investment. The fibers installed can be used for future broadband applications.

12.3.3.2 Set-Top-Boxes

To interact with personalized, on-demand, multimedia services, subscribers need a device for sending their control signals and decoding received data. The most likely device is an STB. The STB is the bridge between the subscriber's display device (TV set), an input device, and the communication channel. This channel connects the STB and the information infrastructure of service providers. In addition, the STB gives software developers a means to develop a user-friendly application interface.

The basic function of the STB is to decode audio and video in real-time and to accept and send a user's control signal to the server. Since the expected audio and video quality is high—audio at CD-quality and video at HDTV quality—the required processing power (for decompression) is very high, considering that a current powerful workstation can barely decompress and display a video of resolution 352 by 240 at full motion rates. To meet this requirement, special integrated circuits for decompression must be developed.

To use the STB, a subscriber must have a simple infrared remote controller with about a dozen buttons. The limited number of buttons and limited functionality of a remote controller (compared with keyboards) impose several challenges on designers of software-based navigation systems. The users want minimal complexity while selecting services from an extensive menu.

In addition to these basic functions, other peripherals such as a game controller, CD-ROM and magnetic disks for massive storage, and printers may also be provided by the

STB. To support all these functions, a small real-time operating system is required within the STB.

There have been many VOD trials [2]. At the moment, these systems support a limited number of users and user interactions. VOD success depends on the cost of the service, information content, compatibility (one STB can receive information from multiple providers), and security.

12.3.3.3 Future Developments

The main consideration for current VOD delivery systems is to use existing telephone lines and cables as much as possible, because direct fiber into homes is still expensive. This situation may change, and a flexible network based on fiber or high-bandwidth cables may be used in the future for the following reasons:

1. Fiber is becoming cheaper.
2. The bandwidth of telephone lines is limited and the communication is mainly one way. This limits the possibility of using one network to provide both on-demand applications and conversational applications. It is expected that home videophones will be used in the near future.
3. At the moment, several networks are needed if a home needs diverse applications: a telephone network, cables for CATV, VOD based on one of them. Nevertheless, it is difficult to access the Internet and to have videophone facilities, so it is desirable to have one network capable of providing all these applications. This network is likely to be ATM based on SONET or cables. As discussed in Chapter 5, ATM promises to provide all these functions.

A single bandwidth-on-demand ATM network provides us with all current and expected applications including normal telephone, videophone, VOD, and Internet applications. The complexity of a full-service STB is close to a general workstation and perhaps needs even more processing power. In the near future, it is possible that a general workstation will replace the STB and TV set. Then we would have just one network (possibly ATM) and one workstation for all types of work or leisure applications.

Another development for VOD systems is to provide content-based search capability. At the moment, users select video or movies based on the titles. This is not adequate. Sophisticated users may need to view certain relevant clips only. Technically, this is achievable using the techniques discussed in previous chapters. The issue is how to provide VOD services cost-effectively to compete with other similar services.

12.4 Multimedia Security

We use the term security very generally to include issues of privacy, authentication, and copyright protection. There are many potential security risks in the operation of a distributed multimedia database system. First, it is quite easy for unauthorized persons to find out what information a user is retrieving over an "open network" like the Internet (i.e., the privacy of the user is not maintained). Second, digital audio, images and video can be easily manipulated (i.e., the information may not be authentic). Third, digital audio, images and video can be easily copied without losing quality (i.e., copyright may easily be violated). To overcome these risks, the following security services are required in a distributed multimedia database system.

- **Privacy and confidentiality.** Users of multimedia information may not want others to know what information they have searched for and downloaded for reasons such as commercial confidentiality and personal privacy. The system should provide this confidentiality and privacy.
- **Authentication.** Users may need to know whether the sources and data are authentic (i.e., the data is original, has not been tampered with and is from the alleged sources). The system should provide a mechanism for this verification.
- **Copyright protection.** Authors of multimedia information need a way to protect their rights. To do that they must be able to prove that they are the original authors. The system should provide tools for this purpose.

In the following, we discuss security issues and the techniques to provide these three security services.

12.4.1 Providing Privacy and Confidentiality

Privacy and confidentiality are normally ensured by the use of encryption techniques. Original information (called plain text) is encrypted into cyphertext. Only persons with appropriate key(s) can decrypt the cyphertext and view the information.

The two most common types of encryption are secret-key or symmetric encryption and public-key or asymmetric encryption. In secret-key encryption, the same key is used for encryption and decryption. Thus the privacy of encrypted information depends on the privacy of the key. The advantage of the secret-key encryption is that it is simple and fast to carry out encryption and decryption. The disadvantage is that it is hard to pass the secret key securely to a remote communicating partner. In the context of multimedia information retrieval, the question is how to share a secret key between the client and server without anybody else also obtaining it.

In public-key encryption, two keys are used. One key is used for encryption and the other for decryption. The encryption key is available to the public and thus is also called a public key. The decryption key is kept secret and thus is also called a private key. When a person (say Bob) wants to send a message securely to another person (say Joe), Bob has to find Joe's public key and then use it to encrypt the message before sending it to Joe. When Joe receives the encrypted message, he decrypts the encrypted message using his private key. Other people may be able to get hold the encrypted message, but they cannot decrypt it because only Joe knows his private key. The advantage of public-key encryption is that it is very secure as there is no need to transmit the private key. Another advantage is that because only the owner of the private key knows it, we can use the private key to identify the person. One application of this idea is to provide digital signatures. Those who are interested in details about digital signatures and other security concepts are referred to [4]. The main disadvantage of public-key encryption is that it is computationally complex and it is slow to carry out encryption and decryption, especially when the message to be encrypted is large.

In the context of multimedia information retrieval, we are interested in encrypting digital audio, images, and video that are potentially very large in file size. So we face a dilemma in choosing a suitable encryption technique to use. Secret-key encryption is fast but not very secure, while public-key encryption is secure but very slow. The solution to this problem is to use both types of encryption techniques in the communication process. We use the private-key encryption technique to encrypt the actual information (including audio, images, and video), and use the public-key encryption technique to transmit the private key used in the secret-key encryption. We use an example to illustrate how this works. Suppose a server wants to send an image securely to a client. The server can encrypts the image using the secret-key encryption technique with a secret key Ks. The server then encrypts Ks using public-key encryption with the client's public key. The encrypted image and secret key Ks are sent to the client. When the client receives them, it decrypts the encrypted Ks with its private key and then uses Ks to decrypt the message. The encryption and decryption are very efficient, as Ks is normally much smaller than the image.

12.4.2 Authentication Verification

Authentication means determining that a message is from its alleged sender and that it has not been altered. Authentication is achieved by both secret-key encryption and public-key encryption.

We use a secret-key technique to encrypt the entire message. As the secret key is only supposed to be known between the communicating parties, the message and the sender are proven authentic if the receiver can decode the message with the secret key. But the remaining problem of this approach is how the secret key is shared among communicating parties.

In the case of public-key encryption, the sender encrypts the message with his or her private key. The encrypted message is then encrypted again using the public key of the receiver. By doing so, both privacy and authentication are achieved. When the message is large, this method of authentication is not efficient, as discussed in Section 12.4.1.

We can introduce a hash function to solve the above inefficiency problem. A hash function converts a variable length message into a smaller fixed-length message digest. Different messages result in different digests. A hash function is one-way process, meaning that we can convert a message into a digest but not vice versa. Thus to achieve authentication, the sender obtains the digest of the message to be sent. The digest is sent to the receiver together with the message. The receiver calculates the digest from the received message using the same hash function used by the sender. If the newly calculated digest is the same as the received digest, the message is deemed authentic.

Using a hash function alone for authentication is not secure. When an attacker modifies the digest as well as the message, the receiver will not be able to detect the change. In addition, without encryption of the message, there is no privacy and confidentiality. An efficient and effective privacy and authentication system can be achieved by a combining secret-key encryption, public-key encryption, and a hash function. It works like this. When Bob wants to send a message, requiring both privacy and authentication to Joe, Bob calculates the digest of the message, encrypts the message with the secret-key encryption technique using secret key Ks, and then encrypts the message digest and Ks with the public-key encryption technique using Joe's public key. The encrypted message, digest, and *Ks* are sent to Joe. When they arrive, Joe decrypts the encrypted digest and *Ks* using his private key. He then decrypts the encrypted message with *Ks* and calculates the digest of the decrypted message. If the newly calculated digest is the same as the received digest, the message is authentic. The above process is secure and efficient.

12.4.3 Copyright Protection

One of the advantages of digital media (e.g., digital audio and video) is that they can be easily copied without losing quality. But this advantage is also a problem for information providers: people can copy their works without obeying the copyright rules. Copyright protection is a complicated issue in the digital world. One aspect of the issue is how to prove the ownership of a particular work, say an image. We briefly discuss this aspect of copyright protection in this section.

The common approach to prove ownership is to use a process called watermarking, which embeds an invisible a label, mark, or signature (called a watermark) into an image or video. When conflict arises, the embedded signature is extracted to prove the rightful ownership. To be useful, the watermark should be recoverable despite intentional or unintentional modification of the image. That is, the watermark should be robust against normal image processing operations such as filtering, scaling, cropping, and compression. It must also be invulnerable to deliberate attempts at forgery and removal.

For detailed discussions of watermarking techniques, refer to [5-8].

12.5 MPEG-7

As discussed in previous chapters, many features can be extracted from multimedia information items using different methods, and many similarity measures can be used to calculate the similarities between extracted features. Without a standard to describe the extracted features, it is not possible for one system to use features extracted by another system (i.e., information exchange is not possible). The international standard MPEG-7 is being developed to address this issue. We described the main objectives of MPEG-7 in Section 2.6.3.2. We now highlight the role of MPEG-7 in developing multimedia databases or multimedia information indexing and retrieval systems.

Figure 12.2 shows an abstract diagram of a multimedia information retrieval system based on MPEG-7. Multiple features can be extracted in any way and feature extraction mechanisms will not be specified by MPEG-7. The main reason is that their standardization is not required to allow interoperability, while leaving space for industry innovation and competition. The scope of MPEG-7 is to standardize the description of extracted features so that different search engines can search for multimedia items based on extracted features in the standard description.

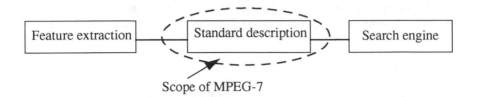

Scope of MPEG-7

Figure 12.2 Role of MPEG-7 in multimedia information retrieval.

MPEG-7 will not define a monolithic system for content description but a set of methods and tools to support a wide variety of applications. The way MPEG data will be used to answer user queries (to develop applications) is outside the scope of the standard. In principle, any type of multimedia material may be retrieved by means of any type of query material (medium type). This means, for example, that video material may be queried using video, music, speech, or combination of these media. It is up to the search engine to match the query data and the MPEG-7 multimedia information description. The following query examples shows the types of applications that can be developed based on MPEG-7 content descriptions [9].

- **Music**: The user plays a few notes on a keyboard and gets in return a list of musical pieces containing (or close to) the required tune or images, somehow matching the notes (e.g., in terms of emotions).
- **Graphics**: The user draws a few lines on a screen and gets in return a set of images containing similar graphics, logos, ideograms, and so forth.
- **Image**: The user defines objects, including color patches or textures and gets in return images and video clips relevant to the defined objects.
- **Movement**: On a given set of objects, the user describes movements and relations between objects and gets in return a list of animations fulfilling the described temporal and spatial relationships.
- **Scenario**: On a given content, the user describes some actions and gets a list of scenarios where similar actions happen.
- **Voice**: The user plays an excerpt of Pavarotti's voice, and gets a list of Pavarotti's records, video clips where Pavarotti is singing, or video clips where Pavarotti is present.

MPEG-7 will also enable inclusion of copyright, licensing, and authentication information related to content and its description. Detailed information on MPEG-7 context, objectives, applications, and the MPEG-7 development process can be obtained from the MPEG Home Page at http://drogo.cselt.stet.it/mpeg/.

MPEG-7 is scheduled to become an international standard in September 2001. It is expected to play a central role in developing multimedia databases and multimedia information retrieval systems.

Problems

Problem 12.1

Discuss the similarities and differences between WWW multimedia search engines, digital libraries and video-on-demand systems.

Problem 12.2

What are the common core technologies required to develop effective and efficient WWW multimedia search engines, digital libraries, and video-on-demand systems?

Problem 12.3

Discuss security issues or problems in distributed multimedia database systems. Describe how to overcome these security problems.

Problem 12.4

Why is MPEG-7 being developed? How will it meet its proposed objectives?

References

[1] Furht, B., D. Kalra, F. L. Kitson, A. A. Rodriguez, and W. E Wall, "Design Issues for Interactive Television Systems," *IEEE Computer*, May 1994, pp. 25–38.

[2] Little, T. D. C., and D. Venkatesh, "Prospects for Interactive Video-on-Demand," *IEEE Multimedia Magazine*, vol. 1, no. 3 1994, pp. 14–24.

[3] Sutherland, J., and L. Litteral, "Residential Video Services," *IEEE Comm.* Vol. 30, No. 7, July 1992, pp. 36–41.

[4] Stallings, W., *Network and Internetwork Security*, Prentice Hall, Inc., 1995

[5] Goffin, F., et al., "Low Cost Perceptive Digital Picture Watermarking Method," *Proceedings of SPIE International Conference on Storage and Retrieval for Image and Video Databases V*, Feb. 13-14, 1997, San Jose, California, pp. 264-277.

[6] Langelaar, G. C., et al., "Robust Labeling Methods for Copy Protection of Images," *Proceedings of SPIE International Conference on Storage and Retrieval for Image and Video Databases V*, Feb. 13-14, 1997, San Jose, California, pp.298-309.

[7] Nikolaidis, N., and I. Pitas, "Copyright Protection of Images using Robust Digital Signatures," *Proceedings of IEEE International Conference on Acoustic, Speech, and Signal Processing*, 1996.

[8] Boland, F. M., J. J. K. O'Ruandaidh, and C. Dautzenberg, "Watermarking Digital Images for Copyright Protection," *Proceedings of IEE Image Processing and Its Application Conference*, 1995, pp. 326-330.

[9] MPEG Requirements Group, "MPEG-7: Context and Objectives," DOC. ISO?MPEG N2460, MPEG Atlantic City Meeting, October 1998. Available at http://drogo.cselt.stet.it/mpeg/

[10] Wactlar, H. D., et al., "Lessons Learned from Building a Terabyte Digital Video Library," *Computer*, Vol.32, No. 2, Feb. 1999, pp. 66-73.

List of Acronyms

AAL	Asynchronous transfer mode (ATM) adaptation layer
AC	Alternate current
ADC	Analog-to-digital converter
ADPCM	Adaptive differential pulse-code modulation
ADSL	Asymmetric digital subscriber line
ANN	Artificial neural network
ANSI	American National Standards Institute
API	Application programming interface
ASCII	American Standard Code for Information Interchange
ASR	Automatic speech recognition
ATDM	Synchronous time-division multiplexing
ATM	Asynchronous transfer mode
AV	Audio-visual
B-ISDN	Broadband integrated services digital network
BLOB	Binary large object
CBR	Constant bit rate
CCIR	Consultative Committee on International Radio
CCITT	Consultative Committee on International Telephony and Telegraphy
CD	Compact disc
CD-ROM	Compact disc-read only memory
CGI	Common gateway interface
CHI	Chromaticity histogram image
CIE	International Commission on Illumination
CIF	Common intermediate format
CLP	Cell loss priority
CM	Continuous media
CPE	Customer premise equipment
CPU	Central processing unit
CRT	Cathode ray tube
CSCW	Computer-supported cooperative work
CSMA/CD	Carrier sense multiple access with collision detection
DAC	Digital-to-analog converter
DAN	Desk area network
DAT	Digital audio tape
dB	Decibel
DBMS	Database management system
DC	Direct current

DCT	Discrete cosine transform
DFT	Discrete fourier transform
DM	Delta modulation
DMA	Direct memory access
DNS	Domain name server
DPCM	Differential pulse-coded modulation
dpi	Dots per inch
DPX	Digital moving picture exchange
DQDB	Distributed queue dual bus
DSM	Digital storage medium
DSP	Digital signal processing
DTD	Document type definition
DVD	Digital video broadcasting
EBCDIC	Extended binary coded decimal interchange code
EDD	Earliest-due-date
EDF	Earliest-deadline-first
ETM	Elastic template matching
FAT	File allocation table
FC	Fiber channel
FCFS	First-come, first-serve
FD	Fourier descriptors
FDCT	Forward discrete cosine transform
FDDI	Fiber distributed data interface
FEC	Forward error correction
FFT	Fast fourier transforms
FG	Fixed-grid
FIFO	First-in first-out
FQ	Fair queuing
FTP	File transfer protocol
GB	Gigabyte
GFC	Generic flow control
GIF	Graphic interchange format
GIS	Geographic information system
GOP	Group of pictures
GSS	Group sweeping scheduling
HDSL	High-speed digital subscriber line
HDTV	High-definition television
HeiTS	Heidelberg high-speed transport system
HFC	Hybrid fiber coax
HMM	Hidden Markov model
HTML	Hypertext Markup Language
HTTP	Hypertext Transport Protocol
HVC	Hue, value and chroma
IDCT	Inverse discrete cosine transform
IDFT	Inverse discrete fourier transform
I/O	Input/output
IETF	Internet Engineering Task Force

IFS	Iterated function system
IOD	Information on demand
IP	Internet protocol
IR	Information retrieval
ISDN	Integrated services digital network
ISO	International Standardization Organization
ITU-TS	International Telecommunication Union-Telecommunication Sector (formerly CCITT)
IWISE	Integrated WWW image search engine
JBIG	Joint Bilevel Image Expert Group
JPEG	Joint Photographic Expert Group
JTC	Joint ISO/IEC Technical Committee
KLT	Karhunen-Loeve transform
LAN	Local area network
LSI	Latent semantic indexing
LTS	Logical time system
LZW	Lempel-Ziv-Welch
MAC	Medium access control
MAN	Metropolitan area network
MB	Megabyte
MBone	Multicast backbone
Mbps	Mega bits per second
MBR	Minimum bounding rectangle
MFCC	Mel-frequency cepstral coefficient
MHEG	Multimedia and Hypermedia Information-Encoding Expert Group
MIDI	Music instrument digital interface
MIME	Multipurpose internet mail extension
MIRS	Multimedia indexing and retrieval system
MMDBMS	Multimedia database management system
MMO	Multimedia object
MNI	Multimedia network interface
MPEG	Motion Picture Expert Group
MSC	Media synchronization controller
MVC	Multimedia virtual circuit
NLP	Natural language processing
NMW	Networked multimedia workstation
NNI	Network-Network Interface
NSP	Network synchronization protocol
NTP	Network Time Protocol
NTSC	National Television Standards Committee
OCPN	Object composition petri net
ODA	Office document architecture
OO	Object-oriented
OODBMS	Object-oriented database management system
OS	Operating system
OSI	Open Systems Interconnection
OSIRM	Open Systems Interconnection Reference Model

PAL	Phase alternating line
PC	Personal computer
PCM	Pulse-coded modulation
PDF	Probability density function or portable document format
PDU	Protocol data unit
PHY	Physical
PIO	Programmed input/output
PSR	Percentage of similarity rankings
PTS	Presentation time stamp
PU	Presentation unit
PWH	Perceptually weighted histogram or percentage of weighted hits
QBIC	Query by image content
QCIF	Quarter CIF (common intermediate format)
QOS	Quality of service
RAID	Redundant array of inexpensive discs
RAM	Random access memory
RDBMS	Relational database management system
RGB	Red, green, and blue
RISC	Reduced instruction set computer
RM	Rate monotonic
RMTP	Real-Time Message Transport Protocol
RPC	Remote procedure call
RPP	Recall-precision pair
RSVP	Resource Reservation Protocol
RTCP	Real-Time Control Protocol
RTIP	Real-Time Internet Protocol
RTP	Real-Time Transport Protocol
SC	Synchronization channel
SCAM	Scalable multimedia server
SEAL	Simple and efficient adaptation layer
SECAM	Sequential color and memory
SGML	Standard Generalized Markup Language
SIF	Source input format
SM	Synchronization mark
SMPTE	Society of Motion Picture and Television Engineers
SNR	Signal-to-noise ratio
SONET	Synchronous optical network
SPD	Spectral power distribution
SQL	Structured Query Language
SSTF	Shortest seek time first
ST-II	Stream Transport Protocol Version Two
STB	Set-top box
STC	System time clock
STDM	Synchronous time-division multiplexing
STFT	Short time fourier transform
STG	Scene transition graph
TB	Terabyte

TCP/IP	Transmission Control Protocol/Internet Protocol
TDM	Time-division multiplexing
TDRM	Time-driven resource management
THT	Token holding timer
TIFF	Tagged image file format
TRT	Token rotation timer
TTRT	Target token rotation time
TV-tree	Telescopic-vector-tree
UDP	User datagram protocol
ULC	User-level scheduler
UNI	User-network interface
URL	Uniform resource locator
VBR	Variable bit rate
VC	Virtual channel, Virtual clock
VCI	Virtual channel identifier
VCR	Videocassette recorder
VIMSYS	Visual information management system
VLC	Variable-length code
VO	Video object
VOL	Video object layer
VOD	Video-on-demand
VP	Virtual path
VPI	Virtual path identifier
VQ	Vector quantization
WAN	Wide area network
WBC	Wideband channel
WFQ	Weighted fair queuing
WG	Working Group
WHT	Walsh-Hadamard transform
WWW	World Wide Web
XTP	Xpress transfer protocol
YARTOS	Yet Another Real Time Operating System
ZC	Zero crossing
ZCR	Zero crossing rate

About the Author

Guojun Lu is currently a senior lecturer at Gippsland School of Computing and Information Technology, Monash University. He has held positions in Loughborough University of Technology, National University of Singapore, and Deakin University.

Dr. Lu's main research interests are in multimedia information indexing and retrieval, multimedia data compression, quality of service management, and multimedia compression. He has published over 50 technical papers in these areas and authored the book *Communication and Computing for Distributed Multimedia Systems* (Artech House, 1996). He has over 10 years of research experience in multimedia computing and communications. Projects that he has worked on include the U.K. Alvey project UNISON (on multimedia networking), European RACE project MultiMed (on multimedia applications in telemedicine), fractal image compression, networked multimedia synchronization, and integrated image retrieval systems.

Dr. Lu obtained his PhD in 1990 from Loughborough University of Technology, and a BEng in 1984 from Nanjing Institute of Technology (now South East University).

Dr. Lu can be contacted at his e-mail address: guojun.lu@infotech.monash.edu.au. His WWW home page is at URL: <http://www-gscit.fcit.monash.edu.au/~guojunl/>.

Index

Recent Titles in the Artech House Computing Library

Practical Process Simulation Using Object-Oriented Techniques and C++,
José Garrido

Risk Management Processes for Software Engineering Models,
Marian Myerson

Secure Electronic Transactions: Introduction and Technical Reference,
Larry Loeb

Software Process Improvement With CMM, Joseph Raynus

Software Verification and Validation: A Practitioner's Guide,
Steven R. Rakitin

Solving the Year 2000 Crisis, Patrick McDermott

User-Centered Information Design for Improved Software Usability,
Pradeep Henry

For further information on these and other Artech House titles,
including previously considered out-of-print books now available through
our In-Print-Forever® (IPF®) program, contact:

Artech House	Artech House
685 Canton Street	46 Gillingham Street
Norwood, MA 02062	London SW1V 1AH UK
Phone: 781-769-9750	Phone: +44 (0)20 7596-8750
Fax: 781-769-6334	Fax: +44 (0)20 7630-0166
e-mail: artech@artechhouse.com	e-mail: artech-uk@artechhouse.com

Find us on the World Wide Web at:
www.artechhouse.com